CHILTON BOOK COMPANY

REPAIR & TUNE-UP GUIDE

VOLKSWAGEN FRONT WHEEL DRIVE 1974-87

All U.S. and Canadian models of Dasher • Fox • GTI • Golf • Jetta • Quantum • Rabbit • Rabbit Pick-Up • Scirocco

President LAWRENCE A. FORNASIERI
Vice President and General Manager JOHN P. KUSHNERICK
Editor-in Chief KERRY A. FREEMAN, S.A.E.
Senior Editor RICHARD J. RIVELE, S.A.E.
Editor MICHAEL A. NEWSOME

CHILTON BOOK COMPANY
Radnor, Pennsylvania
19089

SAFETY NOTICE

Proper service and repair procedures are vital to the safe, reliable operation of all motor vehicles, as well as the personal safety of those performing repairs. This book outlines procedures for servicing and repairing vehicles using safe, effective methods. The procedures contain many NOTES, CAUTIONS and WARNINGS which should be followed along with standard safety procedures to eliminate the possibility of personal injury or improper service which could damage the vehicle or compromise its safety.

It is important to note that repair procedures and techniques, tools and parts for servicing motor vehicles, as well as the skill and experience of the individual performing the work vary widely. It is not possible to anticipate all of the conceivable ways or conditions under which vehicles may be serviced, or to provide cautions as to all of the possible hazards that may result. Standard and accepted safety precautions and equipment should be used during cutting, grinding, chiseling, prying, or any other process that can cause material removal or projectiles.

Some procedures require the use of tools specially designed for a specific purpose. Before substituting another tool or procedure, you must be completely satisfied that neither your personal safety, nor the performance of the vehicle will be endangered.

Although the information in this guide is based on industry sources and is as complete as possible at the time of publication, the possibility exists that the manufacturer made later changes which could not be included here. While striving for total accuracy, Chilton Book Company cannot assume responsibility for any errors, changes, or omissions that may occur in the compilation of this data.

PART NUMBERS

Part numbers listed in this reference are not recommendations by Chilton for any product by brand name. They are references that can be used with interchange manuals and aftermarket supplier catalogs to locate each brand supplier's discrete part number.

SPECIAL TOOLS

Special tools are occasionally necessary to perform a specific job or are recommended to make a job easier. Their use has been kept to a minimum. When a special tool is indicated, it will be referred to by a manufacturer's part number and where possible, an illustration of the tool will be provided so that an equivalent tool may be used. These tools are available from Zelenda Tool and Machine Company, 66-02 Austin Street, Forrest Hills, New York 11374 or an equivalent tool can be purchased locally from a tool supplier or parts outlet. Before substituting any tool for the one recommended, read the SAFETY NOTICE at the top of this page.

ACKNOWLEDGMENTS

The Chilton Book Company expresses its appreciation to Volkswagen of America, Inc., Detroit, Michigan for their generous assistance.

Copyright © 1987 by Chilton Book Company
All Rights Reserved
Published in Radnor, Pennsylvania 19089 by Chilton Book Company

Manufactured in the United States of America
    34567890   654321098

Chilton's Repair & Tune-Up Guide: Volkswagen Front Wheel Drive 1974–87
ISBN 0-8019-7754-1 pbk.
Library of Congress Catalog Card No. 86-47776

CONTENTS

Quick Reference Specifications For Your Vehicle

Fill in this chart with the most commonly used specifications for your vehicle. Specifications can be found in Chapters 1 through 3 or on the tune-up decal under the hood of the vehicle.

 ## Tune-Up

Firing Order_____

Spark Plugs:

    Type_____

    Gap (in.)_____

Torque (ft. lbs.)_____

Idle Speed (rpm)_____

Ignition Timing (°)_____

    Vacuum or Electronic Advance (Connected/Disconnected)_____

Valve Clearance (in.)

    Intake_____   Exhaust_____

Capacities

Engine Oil Type (API Rating)_____

    With Filter Change (qts)_____

    Without Filter Change (qts)_____

Cooling System (qts)_____

Manual Transmission (pts)_____

    Type_____

Automatic Transmission (pts)_____

    Type_____

Front Differential (pts)_____

    Type_____

Rear Differential (pts)_____

    Type_____

Transfer Case (pts)_____

    Type_____

FREQUENTLY REPLACED PARTS

Use these spaces to record the part numbers of frequently replaced parts.

PCV VALVE	OIL FILTER	AIR FILTER	FUEL FILTER
Type_____	Type_____	Type_____	Type_____
Part No._____	Part No._____	Part No._____	Part No._____

General Information and Maintenance

HOW TO USE THIS BOOK

Chilton's Repair and tune-Up Guide for the Volkswagen Front Wheel Drive covers repair and maintenance procedures for both gasoline and diesel model vehicles. Unlike many workshop manuals available to the public, this guide does not automatically assume that you have years of experience in dealing with mechanical eccentricities and the tricks of the trade that are second nature to the professional mechanic. Instead, procedures are laid out for you in easy to follow chapters, highlighted with scores of illustrations. Everything from testing your coil to changing your oil filter.

The first two chapters will be the most used, since they contain maintenance and tune-up information procedures. The following chapters concern themselves with the more complex systems of your Volkswagen. This Chilton manual won't explain transaxle overhaul because of the special tools and experience needed. This guide does cover just about every other practical mechanical operation possible on you car.

Before diving under your car's hood, take the time to read through the entire procedure. This will give you the overall view of what tools and supplies that will be required. Each section begins with a brief discussion of the system and what it involves, followed by adjustments, maintenance, and removal and installation procedures. When the repair is considered too complicated or special test equipment is required, we tell you how to remove the part and then how to install the new or rebuilt replacement.

Two basic mechanic's rules should be mentioned here. First, whenever the left side of the car is referred to, it is meant to specify the driver's side of the car. Conversely, the right side of the car means the passenger's side of the car. Second, most screws and bolts are removed by turning counterclockwise and tightened by turning clockwise. Safety is always the most important rule, and common sense is your best defense against injury.

TOOLS AND EQUIPMENT

It would be impossible to catalog each and every tool that you might need to perform all the operations included in this book. It would also not be wise for the amateur to rush out and buy an expensive set of tools on the theory that he may need one of them at some time. Therefore, the best approach is to proceed slowly, gathering together a quality set of those tools that are used most frequently. Don't be misled by the low cost of bargain tools, it is a better investment to spend a little more money and get a lot more quality. Always look for tools with a lifetime guarantee. As any good mechanic can tell you, there are few experiences worse than trying to work on a car or truck with bad tools. Begin accumulating those tools that are used most frequently; those associated with routine maintenance and tune-up. Your Volkswagen uses metric nuts, bolts and screws. In addition to the normal assortment of screwdrivers and pliers, you should have the following tools for routine maintenance jobs:

1. Metric wrenches, sockets and combination open-end/box wrenches to at least 19mm; note that many parts of the car also use allen head bolts. Make sure your set includes a deep socket spark plug wrench
2. Jackstands for support
3. Band wrench for oil filters
4. Oil filler spout for pouring oil
5. Grease gun for chassis lubrication
6. Hydrometer for checking the battery
7. A container for draining oil
8. Many rags for wiping up the inevitable mess

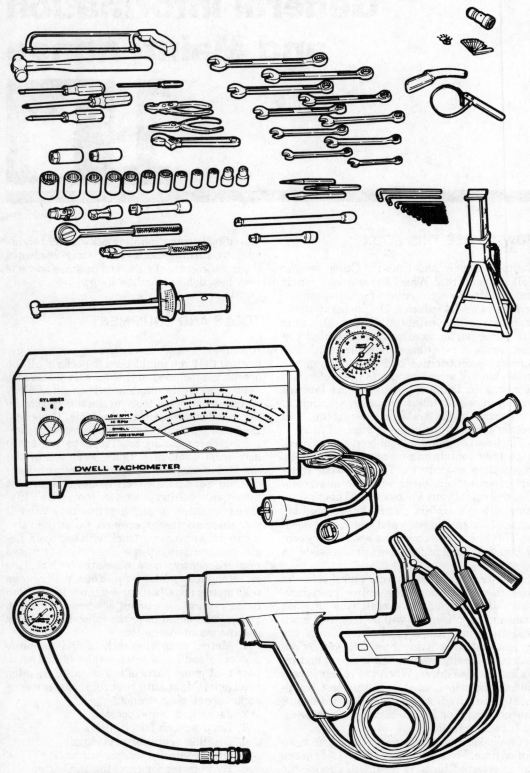

You need only a basic assortment of hand tools for most maintenance and repair jobs

In addition to the above items, there are several others that are not absolutely necessary, but handy to have around. These include oil dry, a transmission funnel and the usual supply of lubricants, antifreeze and fluids, although these can be purchased as needed. This is a basic list for routine maintenance, but only your personal needs and desire can accurately determine your list of tools.

The second list of tools is for tune-ups. While the tools involved here are slightly more sophisticated, they need not be outrageously expensive. There are several inexpensive tach/dwell meters on the market that are every bit as good for the average mechanic as the $100 professional model. Just be sure that it goes to at least 1,200–1,500 rpm on the tach scale and that it works on 4, 6 and 8 cylinder engines. A basic list of tune up equipment could include:

1. Tach-dwell meter
2. Spark plug gap adjuster and wire feeler gauge
3. Timing light (a DC light that works from the car's battery is best, although an AC light that plugs into 110v house current will suffice at some sacrifice in brightness
4. A flat-bladed feeler gauge set
5. Valve adjusting tools (VW 10–208 and 10-209 or Tool 2078 if you are working on a 1.8 liter engine). You'll need these if you plan to adjust the valves. See Special Tools below for where to order them.

Keep your tools clean, and if they sit in your tool box for extended periods without use, make sure you spray them with silicone or oil them to prevent rust.

SPECIAL TOOLS

In addition to the above basic tool kit, there are several other tools and gauges you may find useful. These include:

1. A compression gauge. The screw-in type is slower to use, but eliminates the possibility of a faulty reading due to escaping pressure
2. A manifold vacuum gauge
3. A test light
4. An induction meter. This is used to determine whether or not there is current flowing in a wire, and thus is extremely helpful in electrical troubleshooting.
5. A torque wrench. This is necessary for all but the most basic work. The beam type models are perfectly adequate. The newer click (breakaway) type torque wrenches are more accurate, but are much more expensive, and must be periodically recalibrated.

NOTE: *Special tools are occasionally necessary to perform a specific job or are recom-*

mended to make a job easier. Their use has been kept to a minimum. When a special tool is indicated, it will be refered to by a manufacturer's part number, and, where possible, an illustration of the tool will be provided so that an equvalent tool may be used. These tools are available from Zelenda Tool and Machine Co., 66-02 Austin Street, Forest Hills, NY 11374.

SERVICING YOUR CAR SAFELY

It is virtually impossible to anticipate all of the hazards involved with automotive maintenance and service, but care and common sense will prevent most accidents. The rules of safety for mechanics range from 'don't smoke around gasoline,' to 'use the proper tool for the job.' The trick to avoiding injuries is to develop safe work habits and take every possible precaution.

Do's

• Do keep a fire extinguisher and first aid kit within easy reach.

• Do wear safety glasses or goggles when cutting, drilling, grinding or prying, even if you have 20-20 vision. If you wear glasses for the sake of vision, they should be made of hardened glass that can serve also as safety glasses, or wear safety goggles over your regular glasses.

• Do shield your eyes whenever you work around the battery. Batteries contain sulphuric acid. In case of contact with the eyes or skin, flush the area with water or a mixture of water and baking soda and get medical attention immediately.

• Do use safety stands for any undercar service. Jacks are for raising vehicles; safety stands are for making sure the vehicle stays raised until you want it to come down. Whenever the car is raised, block the wheels remaining on the ground and set the parking brake.

• Do use adequate ventilation when working with any chemicals or hazardous materials. Like carbon monoxide, the asbestos dust re-

Always use jackstands when working under your car

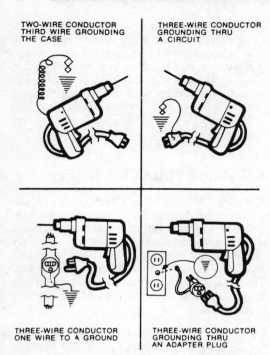

TWO-WIRE CONDUCTOR
THIRD WIRE GROUNDING
THE CASE

THREE-WIRE CONDUCTOR
GROUNDING THRU
A CIRCUIT

THREE-WIRE CONDUCTOR
ONE WIRE TO A GROUND

THREE-WIRE CONDUCTOR
GROUNDING THRU
AN ADAPTER PLUG

Power tools should always be properly grounded

sulting from brake lining wear can be poisonous in sufficient quantities.

• Do disconnect the negative battery cable when working on the electrical system. The secondary ignition system can contain up to 40,000 volts.

• Do follow manufacturer's directions whenever working with potentially hazardous materials. Both brake fluid and antifreeze are poisonous if taken internally.

• Do properly maintain your tools. Loose hammerheads, mushroomed punches and chisels, frayed or poorly grounded electrical cords, excessively worn screwdrivers, spread wrenches (open end), cracked sockets, slipping ratchets, or faulty droplight sockets can cause accidents.

• Do use the proper size and type of tool for the job being done.

• Do, when possible, pull on a wrench handle rather than push on it, and adjust your stance to prevent a fall.

• Do be sure that adjustable wrenches are tightly closed on the nut or bolt and pulled so that the face is on the side of the fixed jaw.

• Do select a wrench or socket that fits the nut or bolt. The wrench or socket should sit straight, not cocked.

• Do strike squarely with a hammer; avoid glancing blows.

• Do set the parking brake and block the drive wheels if the work requires the engine running.

Don'ts

• Don't run an engine in a garage or anywhere else without proper ventilation -- EVER! Carbon monoxide is poisonous; it takes a long time to leave the human body and you can build up a deadly supply of it in your system by simply breathing in a little every day. You may not realize that you are slowly poisoning yourself. Always use power vents, windows, fans or open the garage doors.

• Don't work around moving parts while wearing a necktie or other loose clothing. Short sleeves are much safer than long, loose sleeves; hard-toed shoes with neoprene soles protect your toes and give a better grip on slippery surfaces. Jewelry such as watches, fancy belt buckles, beads or body adornment of any kind is not safe working around a car. Long hair should be hidden under a hat or cap.

• Don't use pockets for toolboxes. A fall or bump can drive a screwdriver deep into your body. Even a wiping cloth hanging from the back pocket can wrap around a spinning shaft or fan.

• Don't smoke when working around gasoline, cleaning solvents or other flammable material.

• Don't use gasoline to wash your hands; there are excellent soaps available. Gasoline may contain lead, and lead can enter the body through a cut, accumulating in the body until you are very ill. Gasoline also removes all the natural oils from the skin so that bone dry hands will suck up oil and grease.

• Don't service the air conditioning system unless you are equipped with the necessary tools and training. The refrigerant, R-12, is extremely cold when compressed, and when released into the air will instantly freeze any surface it contacts, including your eyes. Although the refrigerant is normally non-toxic, R-12 becomes a deadly poisonous gas in the presence of an open flame. One good whiff of the vapors from burning refrigerant can be fatal.

SERIAL NUMBER IDENTIFICATION

Vehicle Identification Plate and Vehicle Compliance Sticker

The Vehicle Identification Plate and Safety Compliance Sticker is located on the crossmember under the hood, just above the grille, or on the left door jamb. It is your assurance that the vehicle complies with all Federal Motor Vehicle Safety Standards (FMVSS) in effect at the time of manufacture. It also shows the month and year of manufacture and the vehicle identification number of your car.

Chassis/VIN Number

The chassis number is located on the driver's side windshield pillar on the Scirocco and Dasher, and on the left front corner of the instrument panel on all Rabbit, Golf, Fox and Jetta models. The Rabbit, Golf, Fox, Jetta and Quantum chassis number is visible through the windshield. The Dasher and Quantum chassis number is also stamped on the firewall over the windshield washer reservoir. The Rabbit, Golf, Fox, Jetta and Scirocco chassis number is also on top of the right suspension strut mounting. It also appears on the vehicle identification plate. 1981 and later models use a seventeen digit code. On seventeen digit codes, the fifth position indicates engine and the tenth, the year. The year code will be a letter. 'B,' 1981, 'C,' 1982, etc.

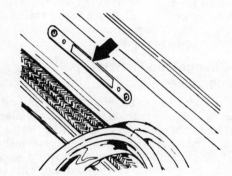

Dasher and Scirocco chassis number

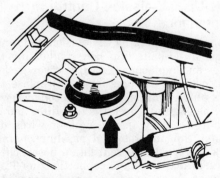

Rabbit, Jetta chassis number

Engine Number

The engine number is stamped on the engine block between the fuel pump and the distributor, on all models except the Fox. The Fox's engine number is located on the left side of the engine bolck just below the cylinder head, and on the vehicle data plate.

Engine Codes

Model	Year	Engine Capacity	Engine Code
Dasher	1974	1.5 liter	XW,XV XZ,XY
	1975	1.5 liter	XS,XR
		1.6 liter	YG,YH
Rabbit, Scirocco	1975–78	1.5 liter	FC,FG CK (diesel)
		1.6 liter	FN,EF EE
Dasher	1976–78	1.6 liter	YK,YH YG
	1979–80	1.6 liter	YK,YH YG
		1.5 liter	CK (diesel)
Rabbit, Scirocco,	1979–80	1.5 liter	EH,CK (diesel) FX
Jetta		1.6 liter	EJ
Rabbit, Scirocco, Jetta, Quantum, Dasher	1981–82	1.6 liter	EJ,EH,FX CR (diesel)
		1.7 liter	WT,EN
Rabbit, Scirocco,	1983	1.6 liter	JK,CY (diesel)
Jetta, Quantum		1.7 liter	EN,JF,WT
		1.8 liter	JH
		2.1 liter	KM
Golf	1984–87	1.8L F.I.	GX
Jetta		1.8L GTI	HT
Scirocco		1.6 Diesel	JP,ME
Quantum		1.6 Turbo Diesel	JR,MF
Fox		1.8L F.I.	UM
Scirocco 16V		1.8L F.I.	—

Manual Transmission

The manual transmission type number is located on a pad above the left hand driveshaft on the Dasher, Fox and Quantum, and stamped either on or below the left hand axle yoke retainer on the Rabbit, Jetta, and the Scirocco.

The code letters and date of manufacture are stamped on the top right-hand side of the bell housing on the 1974–75 Dasher, and on the top of the transmission above the axle yokes on the 1976 and later Dasher and Quantum. The code letters and date of manufacture for the Rabbit, Fox, Jetta and Scirocco are stamped on a pad at the lower center of the bell housing next to the starter.

Automatic Transmission

The automatic transmission type number for the Dasher and Quantum is stamped on the

Transmission Codes

Model	Year	Type	Codes
Dasher	1974	4 Spd	ZS
		Auto	EN
	1975	4 Spd	YZ
		Auto	EO
	1976	4 Spd	YZ,XH
		Auto	ET
	1977–78	4 Spd	XK
		Auto	ET
	1979–80	4 Spd	YZ,XH
		Auto	ET
Rabbit, Scirocco, Jetta	1975–78	4 Spd	GC
		Auto	EQ
	1979–81	4 Spd	GC,GP
		5 Spd	FF
		Auto	EQ,TB
	1982–83	4 Spd	GL,GY
		5 Spd	FK,FN
		Auto	TB,TC,TF, TG,TH
Quantum	1982–83	5 Spd	2M,3M,5M, 9Q
		Auto	KJ,KU, KAC,KAF
Scirocco	1984–87	5 Spd	4K,9A
		Auto	TN,TNA
Jetta	1984	4 Spd	4A
		5 Spd	FN,2H,7A,4K
		Auto	TB,TC,TF,TG TH,TM,TK,TN
Rabbit GTI	1984	4 Spd	GL,GY
		5 Spd	7A,4K,FN,FK,2H
		Auto	TCA,TK,TB,TC,TF, TG,TH,TM
Quantum	1984	5 Spd	2W,QF,3Z,2N, 2M,3M,5M,9Q
		Auto	KU,KJ,KAC,KAF, RR,RBB
Jetta	1985–87	5 Spd	9A,ACH,ACN
		Auto	TJ,TL,TNA
Golf GTI	1985–87	5 Spd	9A,ACH,ACN
		Auto	TJ
Quantum	85–87	5 Spd	9Q,2N,ABV,3Z
		Auto	KAC,KAF
Fox	1987	4 Spd	PW

top of the rear section of the transmission. The automatic transmission type number for the Rabbit, Jetta and the Scirocco is stamped into the center of the case near the dipstick.

The code letter and date of manufacture are stamped on the front of the bell housing near the dipstick on the Dasher and Quantum, and on a pad on the upper center portion of the bell housing on the Rabbit, Jetta and Scirocco.

Drive Axle

The drive axle identification number is stamped onto the axle, on all models.

ROUTINE MAINTENANCE

NOTE: *15, 30, 45, 60, 75, and 90 thousand miles are the main maintenance intervals. On all other intervals, you need only change the oil (not the filter), do routine emission control maintenance (tightening belts, checking air filter), and test the coolant for freezing temperature and replenish if necessary. If you drive under severe operating conditions, such as high speed, extended idling periods, dusty conditions or most driving under 10 miles -- more frequent maintenance (oil and filter changes, etc.) is required.*

Oil Change and General Maintenance

This includes changing the oil filter and oil; checking the transmission fluid level; cleaning or replacement of the air cleaner filler; testing the freezing level of the coolant and replenishing if necessary; topping up the battery electrolyte; and checking the brake fluid. This is also a good time to lubricate the door hinges and door check rods.

Tune-Up & Emission Control Maintenance

This includes checking the tension and condition of all V-belts (fan belts); adjusting the valves and replacing the valve cover gasket. Do a cylinder compression test; replace the spark plugs, ignition points and condenser on gasoline engines; check the fuel filter and replace if necessary; inspect ignition wires, distributor cap and rotor on gasoline engines; check the crankcase ventilation hoses; check the fuel tank, lines and connections for leaks and wear; check the engine for leaks; check the EGR system on fuel injected gasoline engines; check clutch free-play and adjustment.

Vehicle Maintenance

Inspect the brake system for damage and leaks; inspect the brake linings and pads (front and rear), and replace as necessary; check wheels for distortion and cracks, check tires for wear and air pressure; inspect visible boots and dust seals on transaxle for ripping or leaks; check for play in the steering; check the

Maintenance Interval Chart

(See text for a description of required maintenance)

Thousands of Miles or every 6 months	5	7.5	10	15	20	22.5	25	30	35	37.5	40	45	50
Oil Change & General Maintenance	*	*	*	*	*	*	*	*	*	*	*	*	*
Tune Up & Emission Control	—	—	—	*	—	—	—	*	—	—	—	*	—
Vehicle Maintenance	—	—	—	*	—	—	—	*	—	—	—	*	—
Fuel Injected Engine (FI)	—	FI	—	FI	—	FI	—	FI	—	FI	—	FI	—
Carburetor Engine (C)	—	C	—	C	—	C	—	C	—	C	—	C	—
Diesel Engine (D)	—	D	—	D	—	D	—	D	—	D	—	D	—
Turbo Diesel Engine (TD)	TD	—	TD	TD	TD	—	TD	TD	TD	—	TD	TD	TD

operation of all lights and accessories (windshield wipers and blades, windshield washer fluid).

Air Cleaner

The air filter is a key part of the engine. A restrictive, dirty element will cause a reduction in fuel economy and performance and an increase in exhaust emissions. The air filter should be cleaned or replaced according to the maintenance interval chart in this chapter.

Depending on the model, year and type of engine (fuel injected, carburetor or diesel) the air cleaner element is contained in a round metal or oblong plastic container, usually connected by hoses to the intake system.

REMOVAL AND INSTALLATION

1. Unsnap the cover retaining clips and lift off the cover. On models with double sets of clips, unsnap the lower clip(s) first and pull the assembly away from the bracket slightly, then unsnap the other clips and lift off the cover.
2. Lift out the paper element. If the element is very dirty and you cannot see light through the filter, discard.
3. If the element is only slightly dirty, tap on table top to loosen up dirt and blow compressed air through to clean.
4. Wipe out the housing and reinstall the clean, or new element.
5. Replace the cover and secure with clips. If you have a two part cover, secure the lower clip(s) first, check that the two locating pins are fully engaged in their respective mounts, then snap the remaining clips.

NOTE: *Do not run your engine without the air cleaner even for a little while. Dirt and grit will pass into the combustion chambers and cause premature wear.*

Fuel Filter

REMOVAL AND INSTALLATION

GASOLINE ENGINES

Carbureted engines with mechanical fuel pumps have a strainer in the top cover of the fuel pump. Remove the center screw and re-

Large canister type fuel filter used on gasoline fuel injected models

Remove the diesel fuel filter from the mounting studs (arrows)

Smaller inline fuel filter, usually used on carbureted models

Invert the filter and loosen it

move the cover and strainer. Clean the strainer with compressed air and replace, using new gaskets. Be sure to align the notch in the cover with the groove in the body. Various models are equipped with a fuel strainer in the fuel tank attached to the sending unit. This strainer should be trouble-free.

All later models are equipped with in-line fuel filters. On Carbureted models, the filters are small, usually made of plastic and are attached to the fuel line by clamps. On fuel injected models, the fuel filters are large, metal containers with banjo bolt connections. In both cases, arrows point in the direction the filter must be installed. The arrow should be pointing in the direction of fuel travel.

Engines equipped with electric fuel pumps maintain fuel pressure even when the engine has not been run. In this case, have a container ready to catch the fuel that will squirt out when you loosen the clamps or couplings on the fuel filter.

Diesel Engines

Two styles of fuel filters are used with diesel engines, both are canister types. Depending on year and model, the filter canister can be above or below the mounting base.

The filter is mounted on the passenger's side of the car, next to the air cleaner on the Rabbit,

Golf and Jetta, and next to the brake master cylinder on the Dasher and Quantum.

If the canister is mounted above the base, remove the two filter support mounting nuts and remove the filter from the studs. Turn the filter upside down and replace mounting over the studs. Install the nuts temporarily to hold the filter. Use a wrench on the ends of the canister or use a band wrench to loosen the canister from the base. Have a container ready to catch the fuel as it spills out. Turn the filter canister and base over. Unscrew the canister and discard. Apply a thin film of diesel fuel to the new canister gasket and screw onto mounting base, tighten by hand. Reinstall the filter on the mounting studs and secure nuts. Start the engine, accelerate several times until engine is running smoothly. Allow engine to idle and check for fuel leaks.

If the filter canister is mounted below the base, loosen the drain plug at the bottom of the canister and drain the fuel into a container. Reinstall the drain plug. Use a band wrench

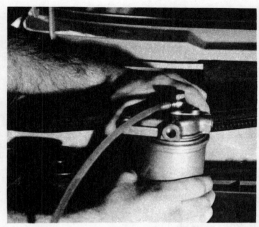

Turn the filter right side up and remove the cartridge

Fuel filter with primer pump and vent screw

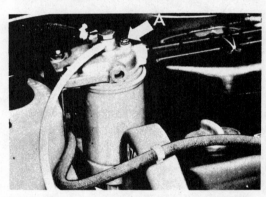

Filter without primer pump, but with vent screw (A)

and loosen the canister from the base. Remove by hand. Discard the old filter canister. Apply a thin film of diesel fuel to the mounting gasket. Install canister and tighten by hand. Start the engine, accelerate several times until the engine is running smoothly. Allow the engine to idle and check for fuel leaks.

BLEEDING THE FUEL SYSTEM

Bleeding the fuel system is not required. After the filter or other fuel system parts have been replaced, simply crank the engine until it starts and accelerate a few times until the engine runs smoothly.

DRAINING WATER FROM THE DIESEL FUEL FILTER

Diesel fuel tends to collect water, which will settle in the bottom of the filter housing. It is very important to drain the water out periodically.

Fuel Filter with Primer Pump and Vent Screw

Loosen the vent screw (A) and the drain plug and drain water out into a container until clean fuel appears. Close the vent screw, and the drain screw. Start the engine and accelerate until the engine runs smoothly.

Fuel Filter Without Primer Pump and With Vent Screw

Loosen the vent screw and drain plug and drain water out into a container until clean fuel appears. Close the drain plug and vent screw. Start the engine and accelerate a few times until the engine runs smoothly.

Fuel Filter Without Vent Screw

Disconnect the fuel return line at the injection pump. Loosen the filter drain plug and drain

water out into a container until clean fuel appears. Reconnect the fuel return line at the injection pump. Start the engine and accelerate a few times until the engine runs smoothly.

Crankcase Ventilation

Blow-by gas, caused by some of the air compressed in the cylinders leaking past the piston rings and valve guides, is routed from the camshaft cover to the air cleaner or carburetor, where it is reburned. Various models and 1975–77 Rabbits and Sciroccos incorporate a PCV valve in the hose between the valve cover and the air cleaner. To check the PCV valve, disconnect the hose from the valve cover end of the valve. Place your finger over the end of the valve. Idle speed should drop when the valve is blocked, if not, the valve is not operating and should be replaced.

Check the hoses at every tune-up for clogging or deterioration and clean or replace them as necessary. A clogged ventilation hose or

Fuel filter without vent screw. On all types of filters, drain water by loosening the drain plug (arrow)

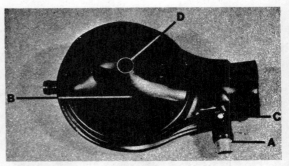

Restrictor valve modification—see PCV valve text

5. Install the elbow on the carburetor with tube end (D) pointing into the carburetor secondary barrel.

6. Remove the crankcase ventilation hose and remove the restrictor which is located inside the bend of the hose where it connects to the valve cover.

7. Cut about $^3/_8$ in. off the valve cover end of the hose, then measure $3^9/_{32}$ in. along the outside curve of the same end of the hose and cut that piece off too.

8. Install a PCV valve (part number 211 129 101) at the place where you cut the $3^9/_{16}$ in. piece off the hose and attach the other end of the hose to the elbow. Use the $3^9/_{16}$ in. piece to attach the PCV valve to the valve cover. Secure the hose ends with clamps.

Evaporative Canister
GASOLINE ENGINES ONLY

This system prevents the escape of raw fuel vapors (unburned hydrocarbons, or HC) into the atmosphere. Along with the activated charcoal filter canister and connector hoses, the system consists of an unvented fuel filler cap, fuel tank expansion chamber, and a sealed carburetor on non-fuel injected gasoline engines. A

PCV valve will cause excessive crankcase pressure and result in oil leaks. Keep the lines clean.

1975–76 carbureted Rabbits and Sciroccos without PCV valves often have a restrictor in the ventilation hose between the valve cover and the air cleaner elbow above the carburetor. This restrictor has been known to cause carburetor top icing. To prevent icing, Volkswagen suggests installing a PCV valve in the hose.

To install the valve, proceed as follows:

1. Disconnect the air intake hose from the air cleaner at the elbow and remove the elbow. The elbow is the round metal cap right on top of the carburetor.

2. Remove the flat, spot welded baffle plate inside the elbow.

3. Insert the replacement tube (D) so that one end sticks out of connection (A). Insert the tube as far as it will go. The tube, part number ZVP 202 851, is available from your VW dealer.

4. Push the tube clear of hole (B) and drill an $^1/_{16}$ in. hole (C) through the elbow and the tube. Fasten the tube in the elbow by fitting a sheet metal screw through the hole you just drilled.

Fuel injected gasoline engine air filter is located under the fuel mixture control unit—release clips (A) and raise control unit

The diesel air filter is mounted directly on the intake manifold

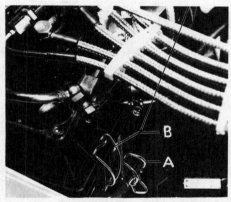

To remove late model Dasher air filter, release clip A, pull the air cleaner housing away from the bracket slightly, release clips B and open the housing until the filter can be removed

filter cut-off valve was added to various models from 1977 and is located between the charcoal filter and the air cleaner. When the engine is idling or not running, the valve is closed, preventing vapors from entering the air cleaner.

Check the components visually for cracks, broken hoses and disconnections. Also check the seal on the gas tank filler cap. Replace the cap if the seal looks worn. If any hoses are in need of replacement, use only hoses marked EVAP, available from your local automotive supply store. VW recommends that the canister be discarded and replaced every 50,000 miles.

NOTE: *The Volkswagen Rabbit Pick-up truck's canister is located under the left front fender.*

BATTERY

The battery is located at left front of the engine compartment on the Dasher Fox and Quan-

tum. Routinely check the battery electrolyte level and specific gravity. A few minutes occasionally spent monitoring battery condition is worth saving hours of frustration when your car won't start due to a dead battery. Only distilled water should be used to top up the battery, as tap water, in many areas, contains harmful minerals. Two tools which will facilitate battery maintenance are a hydrometer and a squeeze bulb filler. These are cheap and widely available at automotive parts stores, hardware stores, etc. The specific gravity of the electrolyte should be between 1.27 and 1.20. Keep the top of the battery clean, as a film of dirt can sometimes completely discharge a battery. A solution of baking soda and water may be used to clean the top surface, but be careful to flush this off with clear water and that none of the solution enters the filler holes. Clean the battery posts and clamps with a wire brush to eliminate corrosion deposits.

Special clamp and terminal cleaning brushes are available for just this purpose. Lightly coat the posts and clamps with petroleum jelly or chassis grease after cleaning them.

FLUID LEVEL (EXCEPT MAINTENANCE FREE BATTERIES)

Check the battery electrolyte level at least once a month, or more often in hot weather or during periods of extended car operation. The level can be checked through the case on translucent polypropylene batteries. The cell caps must be removed on other models. The electrolyte level in each cell should be kept filled to the split ring inside, or the line marked on the outside of the case.

If the level is low, add only distilled water, or colorless, odorless drinking water, through the opening until the level is correct. Each cell is completely separate from the others, so each must be checked and filled individually.

If water is added in freezing weather, the car should be driven several miles to allow the water to mix with the electrolyte. Otherwise, the battery could freeze.

SPECIFIC GRAVITY (EXCEPT MAINTENANCE FREE BATTERIES)

At least once a year, check the specific gravity of the battery. It should be between 1.20 and 1.26 at room temperature.

The specific gravity can be checked with the use of an hydrometer, an inexpensive instrument available from many sources, including auto parts stores. The hydrometer has a squeeze bulb at one end and a nozzle at the other. Battery electrolyte is sucked into the hydrometer until the float is lifted from its seat.

The specific gravity is then read by noting the position of the float. Generally, if after charging, the specific gravity between any two cells varies more than 50 points (0.050), the battery is bad and should be replaced.

It is not possible to check the specific gravity in this manner on sealed (maintenance free) batteries. Instead, the indicator built into the top of the case must be relied on to display any signs of battery deterioration. If the indicator is dark, the battery can be assumed to be OK. If the indicator is light, the specific gravity is low, and the battery should be charged or replaced.

CABLES AND CLAMPS

Once a year, the battery terminals and the cable clamps should be cleaned. Loosen the clamps and remove the cables, negative cable first. On batteries with posts on top, the use of a puller specially made for the purpose is recommended. These are inexpensive, and available in auto parts stores. Side terminal battery cables are secured with a bolt.

Clean the cable clamps and the battery terminal with a wire brush, until all corrosion, grease, etc. is removed and the metal is shiny. It is especially important to clean the inside of the clamp thoroughly, since a small deposit of foreign material or oxidation there will prevent a sound electrical connection and inhibit either starting or charging. Special tools are available for cleaning these parts, one type for conventional batteries and another type for side terminal batteries.

Before installing the cables, loosen the battery holddown clamp or strap, remove the battery and check the battery tray. Clear it of any debris, and check it for soundness. Rust should be wire brushed away, and the metal given a coat of anti-rust paint. Replace the battery and tighten the holddown clamp or strap securely, but be careful not to over-tighten, which will crack the battery case.

After the clamps and terminals are clean, reinstall the cables, negative cable last. Do not hammer on the clamps to install. Tighten the clamps securely, but do not distort them. Give the clamps and terminals a thin external coat of grease after installation, to retard corrosion.

Check the cables at the same time that the terminals are cleaned. If the cable insulation is cracked or broken, or if the ends are frayed, the cable should be replaced with a new cable of the same length and gauge.

NOTE: *Keep flame or sparks away from the battery. It gives off explosive hydrogen gas. Battery electrolyte contains sulphuric acid. If you should splash any on your skin or in your eyes, flush the affected area with plenty of* clear water. If it lands in your eyes, get medical help immediately.

REPLACEMENT

When it becomes necessary to replace the battery, select a battery with a rating equal to or greater than the battery originally installed. Deterioration, embrittlement and just plain aging of the battery cables, starter motor, and associated wires makes the battery's job harder in successive years. The slow increase in electrical resistance over time makes it prudent to install a new battery with a greater capacity than the old.

Drive Belts
CHECKING TENSION AND ADJUSTMENT

The belt tension on most driven components is adjusted by moving the component (alternator, power steering pump etc.) within the range of a slotted bracket(s). Some late model air conditioner compressor drive belts are adjusted by varying the number of discs between the halves of the crankshaft pulley.

Check the belt tension every 3 months or 3,000 miles. Push in on the drive belt about midway between the crankshaft pulley and the driven component. If the belt deflects more than $\frac{9}{16}$ inch or less than $\frac{3}{8}$ inch, adjustment is required.

1. Loosen the adjustment nut and bolt in the slotted bracket. Slightly loosen the pivot bolt.

2. Pull (don't pry) the component outward to increase tension. Push inward to reduce tension. Tighten the adjusting nut and bolt and the pivot bolt.

3. Components, such as the power steering pump and some air conditioner compressors, may be mounted with a double slotted adjusting bracket using a threaded bolt or bolts and locknuts to adjust and maintain tension. Loosen the locknut(s) and slightly loosen the bolt(s)

Alternator mounting bolts

Remove the filter element from the housing

in the slotted groove(s), turn the threaded adjustment bolt(s) in or out to gain correct tension. Tighten locknuts and slotted bracket bolts.

4. Recheck the drive belt tension, readjust if necessary.

5. On air conditioner compressors without a slotted bracket adjustment; remove the nuts (bolts) securing the crankshaft pulley halves.

Add or subtract spacer discs until the belt tension is correct. Secure the pulley halves.

REPLACEMENT

Belt replacement requires the loosening of the mounting and adjustment bolts as described in belt adjustment. Relax tension on the belt until removal from the pulleys is possible. Remove old belt and install new in the reverse or-

Carbureted Dasher air cleaner location

HOW TO SPOT WORN V-BELTS

V-Belts are vital to efficient engine operation—they drive the fan, water pump and other accessories. They require little maintenance (occasional tightening) but they will not last forever. Slipping or failure of the V-belt will lead to overheating. If your V-belt looks like any of these, it should be replaced.

This belt has deep cracks, which cause it to flex. Too much flexing leads to heat build-up and premature failure. These cracks can be caused by using the belt on a pulley that is too small. Notched belts are available for small diameter pulleys.

Cracking or weathering

Oil and grease on a belt can cause the belt's rubber compounds to soften and separate from the reinforcing cords that hold the belt together. The belt will first slip, then finally fail altogether.

Softening (grease and oil)

Glazing is caused by a belt that is slipping. A slipping belt can cause a run-down battery, erratic power steering, overheating or poor accessory performance. The more the belt slips, the more glazing will be built up on the surface of the belt. The more the belt is glazed, the more it will slip. If the glazing is light, tighten the belt.

Glazing

The cover of this belt is worn off and is peeling away. The reinforcing cords will begin to wear and the belt will shortly break. When the belt cover wears in spots or has a rough jagged appearance, check the pulley grooves for roughness.

Worn cover

This belt is on the verge of breaking and leaving you stranded. The layers of the belt are separating and the reinforcing cords are exposed. It's just a matter of time before it breaks completely.

Separation

Troubleshooting the Serpentine Drive Belt

Problem	Cause	Solution
Tension sheeting fabric failure (woven fabric on outside circumference of belt has cracked or separated from body of belt)	• Grooved or backside idler pulley diameters are less than minimum recommended • Tension sheeting contacting (rubbing) stationary object • Excessive heat causing woven fabric to age • Tension sheeting splice has fractured	• Replace pulley(s) not conforming to specification • Correct rubbing condition • Replace belt • Replace belt
Noise (objectional squeal, squeak, or rumble is heard or felt while drive belt is in operation)	• Belt slippage • Bearing noise • Belt misalignment • Belt-to-pulley mismatch • Driven component inducing vibration • System resonant frequency inducing vibration	• Adjust belt • Locate and repair • Align belt/pulley(s) • Install correct belt • Locate defective driven component and repair • Vary belt tension within specifications. Replace belt.
Rib chunking (one or more ribs has separated from belt body)	• Foreign objects imbedded in pulley grooves • Installation damage • Drive loads in excess of design specifications • Insufficient internal belt adhesion	• Remove foreign objects from pulley grooves • Replace belt • Adjust belt tension • Replace belt
Rib or belt wear (belt ribs contact bottom of pulley grooves)	• Pulley(s) misaligned • Mismatch of belt and pulley groove widths • Abrasive environment • Rusted pulley(s) • Sharp or jagged pulley groove tips • Rubber deteriorated	• Align pulley(s) • Replace belt • Replace belt • Clean rust from pulley(s) • Replace pulley • Replace belt
Longitudinal belt cracking (cracks between two ribs)	• Belt has mistracked from pulley groove • Pulley groove tip has worn away rubber-to-tensile member	• Replace belt • Replace belt
Belt slips	• Belt slipping because of insufficient tension • Belt or pulley subjected to substance (belt dressing, oil, ethylene glycol) that has reduced friction • Driven component bearing failure • Belt glazed and hardened from heat and excessive slippage	• Adjust tension • Replace belt and clean pulleys • Replace faulty component bearing • Replace belt
"Groove jumping" (belt does not maintain correct position on pulley, or turns over and/or runs off pulleys)	• Insufficient belt tension • Pulley(s) not within design tolerance • Foreign object(s) in grooves • Excessive belt speed • Pulley misalignment • Belt-to-pulley profile mismatched • Belt cordline is distorted	• Adjust belt tension • Replace pulley(s) • Remove foreign objects from grooves • Avoid excessive engine acceleration • Align pulley(s) • Install correct belt • Replace belt
Belt broken (Note: identify and correct problem before replacement belt is installed)	• Excessive tension • Tensile members damaged during belt installation • Belt turnover • Severe pulley misalignment • Bracket, pulley, or bearing failure	• Replace belt and adjust tension to specification • Replace belt • Replace belt • Align pulley(s) • Replace defective component and belt

Troubleshooting the Serpentine Drive Belt (cont.)

Problem	Cause	Solution
Cord edge failure (tensile member exposed at edges of belt or separated from belt body)	• Excessive tension • Drive pulley misalignment • Belt contacting stationary object • Pulley irregularities • Improper pulley construction • Insufficient adhesion between tensile member and rubber matrix	• Adjust belt tension • Align pulley • Correct as necessary • Replace pulley • Replace pulley • Replace belt and adjust tension to specifications
Sporadic rib cracking (multiple cracks in belt ribs at random intervals)	• Ribbed pulley(s) diameter less than minimum specification • Backside bend flat pulley(s) diameter less than minimum • Excessive heat condition causing rubber to harden • Excessive belt thickness • Belt overcured • Excessive tension	• Replace pulley(s) • Replace pulley(s) • Correct heat condition as necessary • Replace belt • Replace belt • Adjust belt tension

Check the belt deflection (arrow)

der. Adjust belt tension. Some late models have a front engine mount installed through the air conditioner compressor belt circle. Support the engine and remove the mount prior to belt removal and installation, reinstall mount.

Hoses

CAUTION: *Disconnect the negative battery cable. If the engine is warm, the cooling fan could operate even if the ignition switch is off.*

HOSE REPLACEMENT

To replace the hoses on your car, loosen the radiator cap AFTER the engine is cool and drain the coolant into a clean container. To drain the cooling system, remove the lower radiator hose at the radiator end connection.

NOTE: *Some early model Rabbits, Dashers*

and Sciroccos have a petcock at the bottom of the radiator for draining purposes. Check to see if yours is equipped with one.

Loosen the clamps on the hose and remove the hose by cutting it or twisting it to break its grip on the flange. Clean all connections, use fine sandpaper if necessary. When installing the new hose, don't overtighten the clamps or you may cut the hose.

After the new hose in installed and the cooling system is refilled (See Cooling System, below), run the engine up to operating temperature and check for leaks.

Air Conditioning

NOTE: *Exercise the air conditioner for a few minutes, every two weeks or so, during the cold months. This avoids the possibility of the compressor seals drying out from lack of lubrication.*

GENERAL SERVICING PROCEDURES

The most important aspect of air conditioning service is the maintenance of pure and adequate charge of refrigerant in the system. A refrigeration system cannot function properly if a significant percentage of the charge is lost. Leaks are common because the severe vibration encountered in an automobile can easily cause a sufficient cracking or loosening of the air conditioning fittings. As a result, the extreme operating pressures of the system force refrigerant out.

The problem can be understood by considering what happens to the system as it is operated with a continuous leak. Because the expansion valve regulates the flow of refrigerant to the evaporator, the level of refrigerant there is fairly constant. The receiver-drier stores any excess of refrigerant, and so a loss will first ap-

HOW TO SPOT BAD HOSES

Both the upper and lower radiator hoses are called upon to perform difficult jobs in an inhospitable environment. They are subject to nearly 18 psi at under hood temperatures often over 280°F., and must circulate nearly 7500 gallons of coolant an hour—3 good reasons to have good hoses.

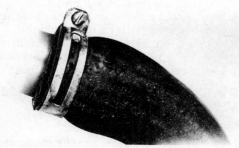

A good test for any hose is to feel it for soft or spongy spots. Frequently these will appear as swollen areas of the hose. The most likely cause is oil soaking. This hose could burst at any time, when hot or under pressure.

Swollen hose

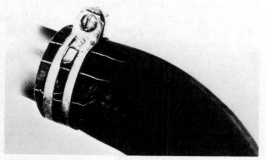

Cracked hoses can usually be seen but feel the hoses to be sure they have not hardened; a prime cause of cracking. This hose has cracked down to the reinforcing cords and could split at any of the cracks.

Cracked hose

Weakened clamps frequently are the cause of hose and cooling system failure. The connection between the pipe and hose has deteriorated enough to allow coolant to escape when the engine is hot.

Frayed hose end (due to weak clamp)

Debris, rust and scale in the cooling system can cause the inside of a hose to weaken. This can usually be felt on the outside of the hose as soft or thinner areas.

Debris in cooling system

pear there as a reduction in the level of liquid. As this level nears the bottom of the vessel, some refrigerant vapor bubbles will begin to appear in the stream of liquid supplied to the expansion valve. This vapor decreases the capacity of the expansion valve very little as the valve opens to compensate for its presence. As the quantity of liquid in the condenser decreases, the operating pressure will drop there and throughout the high side of the system. As the R-12 continues to be expelled, the pressure available to force the liquid through the expansion valve will continue to decrease, and, eventually, the valve's orifice will prove to be too much of a restriction for adequate flow even with the needle fully withdrawn.

At this point, low side pressure will start to drop, and severe reduction in cooling capacity, marked by freeze-up of the evaporator coil, will result. Eventually, the operating pressure of the evaporator will be lower than the pressure of the atmosphere surrounding it, and air will be drawn into the system wherever there are leaks in the low side.

Because all atmospheric air contains at least some moisture, water will enter the system and mix with the R-12 and the oil. Trace amounts of moisture will cause sludging of the oil, and corrosion of the system. Saturation and clogging of the filter-drier, and freezing of the expansion valve orifice will eventually result. As air fills the system to a greater and greater extend, it will interfere more and more with the normal flows of refrigerant and heat.

A list of general precautions that should be observed while doing this follows:

1. Keep all tools as clean and dry as possible.

2. Thoroughly purge the service gauges and hoses of air and moisture before connecting them to the system. Keep them capped when not in use.

3. Thoroughly clean any refrigerant fitting before disconnecting it, in order to minimize the entrance of dirt into the system.

4. Plan any operation that requires opening the system beforehand in order to minimize the length of time it will be exposed to open air. Cap or seal the open ends to minimize the entrance of foreign material.

5. When adding oil, pour it through an extremely clean and dry tube or funnel. Keep the oil capped whenever possible. Do not use oil that has not been kept tightly sealed.

6. Use only refrigerant 12. Purchase refrigerant intended for use in only automotive air conditioning system. Avoid the use of refrigerant 12 that may be packaged for another use, such as cleaning, or powering a horn, as it is impure.

7. Completely evacuate any system that has been opened to replace a component, other than when isolating the compressor, or that has leaked sufficiently to draw in moisture and air. This requires evacuating air and moisture with a good vacuum pump for at least one hour.

If a system has been open for a considerable length of time it may be advisable to evacuate the system for up to 12 hours (overnight).

8. Use a wrench on both halves of a fitting that is to be disconnected, so as to avoid placing torque on any of the refrigerant lines.

ADDITIONAL PREVENTIVE MAINTENANCE CHECKS

Antifreeze

In order to prevent heater core freeze-up during A/C operation, it is necessary to maintain permanent type antifreeze protection of +15°F (−9°C) or lower. A reading of −15°F (−26°C) is ideal since this protection also supplies sufficient corrosion inhibitors for the protection of the engine cooling system.

NOTE: *The same antifreeze should not be used longer than the manufacturer specified.*

Radiator Cap

For efficient operation of an air conditioned car's cooling system, the radiator cap should have a holding pressure which meets manufacturer's specifications. A cap which fails to hold these pressure should be replaced.

Condenser

Any obstruction of or damage to the condenser configuration will restrict the air flow which is essential to its efficient operation. It is therefore, a good rule to keep this unit clean and in proper physical shape.

NOTE: *Bug screens are regarded as obstructions.*

Condensation Drain Tube

This single molded drain tube expels the condensation, which accumulates on the bottom of the evaporator housing, into the engine compartment.

If this tube is obstructed, the air conditioning performance can be restricted and condensation buildup can spill over onto the vehicle's floor.

SAFETY PRECAUTIONS

Because of the importance of the necessary safety precautions that must be exercised when working with air conditioning systems and R-12 refrigerant, a recap of the safety precautions are outlined.

1. Avoid contact with a charged refrigera-

tion system, even when working on another part of the air conditioning system or vehicle. If a heavy tool comes into contact with a section of copper tubing or a heat exchanger, it can easily cause the relatively soft material to rupture.

2. When it is necessary to apply force to a fitting which contains refrigerant, as when checking that all system couplings are securely tightened, use a wrench on both parts of the fitting involved, if possible. This will avoid putting torque on refrigerant tubing. (It is advisable, when possible, to use tube or line wrenches when tightening these flare nut fittings.)

3. Do not attempt to discharge the system by merely loosening a fitting, or removing the service valve caps and cracking these valves. Precise control is possibly only when using the service gauges. Place a rag under the open end of the center charging hose while discharging the system to catch any drops of liquid that might escape. Wear protective gloves when connecting or disconnecting service gauge hoses.

4. Discharge the system only in a well ventilated area, as high concentrations of the gas can exclude oxygen and act as an anesthesia. When leak testing or soldering, this is particularly important, as toxic gas is formed when R-12 contacts any flame.

5. Never start a system without first verifying that both service valves are backseated, if equipped, and that all fittings are throughout the system are snugly connected.

6. Avoid applying heat to any refrigerant line or storage vessel. Charging may be aided by using water heated to less than +125°F (+51°C) to warm the refrigerant container. Never allow a refrigerant storage container to sit out in the sun, or near any other source of heat, such as a radiator.

7. Always wear goggles when working on a system to protect the eyes. If refrigerant contacts the eye, it is advisable in all cases to see a physician as soon as possible.

8. Frostbite from liquid refrigerant should be treated by first gradually warming the area with cool water, and then gently applying petroleum jelly. A physician should be consulted.

9. Always keep refrigerant can fittings capped when not in use. Avoid sudden shock to the can which might occur from dropping it, or from banging a heavy tool against it. Never carry a can in the passenger compartment of a car.

10. Always completely discharge the system before painting the vehicle (if the paint is to be baked on), or before welding anywhere near the refrigerant lines.

TEST GAUGES

Most of the service work performed in air conditioning requires the use of a set of two gauges, one for the high (head) pressure side of the system, the other for the low (suction) side.

The low side gauge records both pressure and vacuum. Vacuum readings are calibrated from 0 to 30 inches and the pressure graduations read from 0 to no less than 60 psi.

The high side gauge measures pressure from 0 to at last 600 psi.

Both gauges are threaded into a manifold that contains two hand shut-off valves. Proper manipulation of these valves and the use of the attached test hoses allow the user to perform the following services:

1. Test high and low side pressures.
2. Remove air, moisture, and contaminated refrigerant.
3. Purge the system (of refrigerant).
4. Charge the system (with refrigerant).

The manifold valves are designed so that they have no direct effect on gauge readings, but serve only to provide for, or cut off, flow of refrigerant through the manifold. During all testing and hook-up operations, the valves are kept in a close position to avoid disturbing the refrigeration system. The valves are opened only to purge the system or refrigerant or to charge it.

INSPECTION

CAUTION: *The compressed refrigerant used in the air conditioning system expands into the atmosphere at a temperature of −21.7°F (−29.8°C) or lower. This will freeze any surface, including your eyes, that it contacts. In addition, the refrigerant decomposes into a poisonous gas in the presence of a flame. Do not open or disconnect any part of the air conditioning system.*

SIGHT GLASS CHECK (REFRIGERANT LEVEL)

You can safely make a few simple checks to determine if your air conditioning system needs service. The tests work best if the temperature is warm (about 70°F).

NOTE: *This test is for the factory installed air conditioning system only. Aftermarket air conditioner testing procedures may be different. If in doubt, contact the manufacturer of your particular unit.*

1. Place the automatic transmission in Park or the manual transmission in Neutral. Set the parking brake.
2. Run the engine at a fast idle (about 2,500 rpm) either with the help of a friend, or by temporarily readjusting the idle speed screw.

Troubleshooting Basic Air Conditioning Problems

Problem	Cause	Solution
There's little or no air coming from the vents (and you're sure it's on)	• The A/C fuse is blown • Broken or loose wires or connections • The on/off switch is defective	• Check and/or replace fuse • Check and/or repair connections • Replace switch
The air coming from the vents is not cool enough	• Windows and air vent wings open • The compressor belt is slipping • Heater is on • Condenser is clogged with debris • Refrigerant has escaped through a leak in the system • Receiver/drier is plugged	• Close windows and vent wings • Tighten or replace compressor belt • Shut heater off • Clean the condenser • Check system • Service system
The air has an odor	• Vacuum system is disrupted • Odor producing substances on the evaporator case • Condensation has collected in the bottom of the evaporator housing	• Have the system checked/repaired • Clean the evaporator case • Clean the evaporator housing drains
System is noisy or vibrating	• Compressor belt or mountings loose • Air in the system	• Tighten or replace belt; tighten mounting bolts • Have the system serviced

Sight glass condition
  Constant bubbles, foam or oil streaks
  Clear sight glass, but no cold air
  Clear sight glass, but air is cold
  Clouded with milky fluid
	• Undercharged system
	• No refrigerant at all
	• System is OK
	• Receiver drier is leaking dessicant
		• Charge the system
		• Check and charge the system
		• Have system checked

Large difference in temperature of lines	• System undercharged	• Charge and leak test the system
Compressor noise	• Broken valves • Overcharged • Incorrect oil level • Piston slap • Broken rings • Drive belt pulley bolts are loose	• Replace the valve plate • Discharge, evacuate and install the correct charge • Isolate the compressor and check the oil level. Correct as necessary. • Replace the compressor • Replace the compressor • Tighten with the correct torque specification
Excessive vibration	• Incorrect belt tension • Clutch loose • Overcharged • Pulley is misaligned	• Adjust the belt tension • Tighten the clutch • Discharge, evacuate and install the correct charge • Align the pulley
Condensation dripping in the passenger compartment	• Drain hose plugged or improperly positioned • Insulation removed or improperly installed	• Clean the drain hose and check for proper installation • Replace the insulation on the expansion valve and hoses
Frozen evaporator coil	• Faulty thermostat • Thermostat capillary tube improperly installed • Thermostat not adjusted properly	• Replace the thermostat • Install the capillary tube correctly • Adjust the thermostat
Low side low—high side low	• System refrigerant is low • Expansion valve is restricted	• Evacuate, leak test and charge the system • Replace the expansion valve
Low side high—high side low	• Internal leak in the compressor—worn	• Remove the compressor cylinder head and inspect the compressor. Replace the valve plate assembly if necessary. If the compressor pistons, rings or

Troubleshooting Basic Air Conditioning Problems (cont.)

Problem	Cause	Solution
Low side high—high side low (cont.)		cylinders are excessively worn or scored replace the compressor
	• Cylinder head gasket is leaking	• Install a replacement cylinder head gasket
	• Expansion valve is defective	• Replace the expansion valve
	• Drive belt slipping	• Adjust the belt tension
Low side high—high side high	• Condenser fins obstructed	• Clean the condenser fins
	• Air in the system	• Evacuate, leak test and charge the system
	• Expansion valve is defective	• Replace the expansion valve
	• Loose or worn fan belts	• Adjust or replace the belts as necessary
Low side low—high side high	• Expansion valve is defective	• Replace the expansion valve
	• Restriction in the refrigerant hose	• Check the hose for kinks—replace if necessary
	• Restriction in the receiver/drier	• Replace the receiver/drier
	• Restriction in the condenser	• Replace the condenser
Low side and high side normal (inadequate cooling)	• Air in the system	• Evacuate, leak test and charge the system
	• Moisture in the system	• Evacuate, leak test and charge the system

3. Set the controls for maximum cold and the highest fan speed.

4. Locate the sight glass in one of the system lines and wipe it clean. Usually it is on the left alongside the top of the radiator.

5. If you see bubbles, the system must be recharged. Very likely there is a leak at some point.

6. If there are no bubbles and air coming from the vents is warm, the system needs complete charge. If there air no bubbles and the vent air is cold, the system is ok.

7. You are probably making these tests because you think there is something wrong. As a further check, check the temperature of the 2 lines going to the belt driven compressor. If they are both the same temperature, the system is empty.

8. Have an assistant in the car turn the fan control on and off to operate the compressor clutch. Watch the sight glass.

9. If bubbles appear when the clutch is disengaged and disappear when it is engaged, the system is properly charged.

10. If the refrigerant takes more than 45 seconds to bubble when the clutch is disengaged, the system is overcharged. This usually causes poor cooling at low speeds.

If it is determined that the system has a leak, it should be corrected as soon as possible. Leaks may allow moisture to enter and cause a very expensive rust problem.

TESTING THE SYSTEM

1. Connect a gauge set.
2. Close (clockwise) both gauge set valves.
3. Mid-position both service valves.
4. Park the vehicle in the shade. Start the engine, set the parking brake, place the transmission in NEUTRAL and establish an idle of 1,500 rpm.
5. Run the air conditioning system for full cooling, but NOT in the MAX or COLD mode.
6. Insert a thermometer into the center air outlet.
7. Use the accompanying performance chart for a specifications reference. If pressures are abnormal, refer to the accompanying Pressure Diagnosis Chart.

ISOLATING THE COMPRESSOR

It is not necessary to discharge the system for compressor removal. The compressor can be isolated from the rest of the system, eliminating the need for recharging.

1. Connect a manifold gauge set.

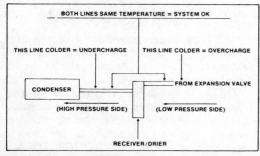

Checking refrigerant charge by line temperature

2. Close both gauge hand valves and mid-position (crack) both compressor service valves.

3. Start the engine and turn on the air conditioning.

4. Turn the compressor suction valve slowly clockwise towards the front-seated position. When the suction pressure drops to zero, stop the engine and turn off the air conditioning. Quickly front-seat the valve completely.

5. Front-seat the discharge service valve.

6. Loosen the oil level check plug to remove any internal pressure.

The compressor is now isolated and the service valves can now be removed.

DISCHARGING THE SYSTEM

1. Connect the manifold gauge set.

2. Turn both manifold gauge set hand valves to the full open (counterclockwise) position.

3. Open both service valve slightly, from the backseated position, and allow the refrigerant to discharge *slowly*.

NOTE: *If you allow the refrigerant to rush out, it will take some refrigerant oil with it!*

EVACUATING THE SYSTEM

NOTE: *This procedure requires the use of a vacuum pump.*

1. Connect the manifold gauge set.

2. Discharge the system.

3. Connect the center service hose to the inlet fitting of the vacuum pump.

4. Turn both gauge set valves to the wide open position.

5. Start the pump and note the low side gauge reading.

6. Operate the pump for a minimum of 30 minutes after the lowest observed gauge reading.

7. Leak test the system. Close both gauge set valves. Turn off the pump and note the low side gauge reading. The needle should remain stationary at the point at which the pump was turned off. If the needle drops to zero rapidly, there is a leak in the system which must be repaired.

8. If the needle remains stationary for 3 to 5 minutes, open the gauge set valves and run the pump for at least 30 minutes more.

9. Close both gauge set valves, stop the pump and disconnect the gauge set. The system is now ready for charging.

LEAK TESTING

Some leak tests can be performed with a soapy water solution. There must be at least a ½lb charge in the system for a leak to be detected. The most extensive leak tests are performed with either a Halide flame type leak tester or the more preferable electronic leak tester.

In either case, the equipment is expensive, and, the use of a Halide detector can be **extremely** hazardous!

CHARGING THE SYSTEM

1. Connect the gauge set.

2. Close (clockwise) both gauge set valves.

3. Mid-position the service valves.

4. Connect the center hose to the refrigerant can opener valve.

5. Make sure the can opener valve is closed, that is, the needle is raised, and connect the valve to the can. Open the valve, puncturing the can with the needle.

6. Loosen the center hose fitting at the pressure gauge, allowing refrigerant to purge the hose of air.

7. Open the low side gauge set valve and the can valve.

8. Start the engine and turn the air conditioner to the maximum cooling mode. The compressor will operate and pull refrigerant gas into the system.

NOTE: *To help speed the process, the can may be placed, upright, in a pan of warm water, not exceeding +125°F (+51°C).*

9. If more than one can of refrigerant is needed, close the can valve and gauge set low side valve when the can is empty and connect a new can to the opener. Repeat the charging process until the sight glass indicates a full charge. The frost line on the outside of the can will indicate what portion of the can has been used.

10. When the charging process has been completed, close the gauge set valve and can valve. Run the system for at least five minutes to allow it to normalize.

11. Back-seat (turn fully counterclockwise) both service valves.

12. Loosen both service hoses at the gauges to allow any refrigerant to escape. Remove the gauge set and install the dust caps on the service valves.

NOTE: *Multi-can dispensers are available which allow a simultaneous hook-up of up to four 1 lb. cans of R-12.*

CAUTION: *Never exceed the recommended maximum charge for the system. The maximum charge for systems using the 5-cylinder Sankyo compressor is 2 lbs.*

NOTE: *This book contains testing and charging procedures for your Volkswagen's air conditioning system. More comprehensive testing, diagnosis and service procedures can be found in CHILTON'S GUIDE TO AIR CONDITIONING SERVICE AND RE-*

PAIR, book part number 7580, available at your local retailer.

Windshield Wipers

For maximum effectiveness and longest element life, the windshield and wiper blades should be kept clean. Dirt, tree sap, road tar and so on will cause streaking, smearing and blade deterioration if left on the glass. It is advisable to wash the windshield carefully with a commercial glass cleaner at least once a month. Wipe off the rubber blades with the wet rag afterwards. Do not attempt to move the wipers by hand. Damage to the motor and drive mechanism will result.

If the blades are found to be cracked, broken or torn, they should be replaced immediately. Replacement intervals will vary with usage, although ozone deterioration usually limits blade life to about one year. If the wiper pattern is smeared or streaked, or if the blade chatters across the glass, the elements should be replaced. It is easiest and most sensible to replace the elements in pairs.

There are basically three different types of refills, which differ in their method of replacement. One type has two release buttons, approximately ⅓ of the way up from the ends of the blade frame. Pushing the buttons down releases a lock and allows the rubber filler to be removed from the frame. The new filler slides back into the frame and locks in place.

The second type of refill has two metal tabs which are unlocked by squeezing them together. The rubber filler can then be withdrawn from the frame jaws. A new refill is installed by inserting the refill into the front frame jaws and sliding it rearward to engage the remaining frame jaws. There are usually four jaws. Be certain when installing that the refill is engaged in all of them. At the end of its travel, the tabs will lock into place on the front jaws of the wiper blade frame.

The third type is a refill made from polycarbonate. The refill has a simple locking device at one end which flexes downward out of the groove into which the jaws of the holder fit, allowing easy release. By sliding the new refill through all the jaws and pushing through the slight resistance when it reaches the end of its travel, the refill will lock into position.

Regardless of the type of refill used, make sure that all of the frame jaws are engaged as the refill is pushed into place and locked. The metal blade holder and frame will scratch the glass if allowed to touch it.

Troubleshooting Basic Windshield Wiper Problems

Problem	Cause	Solution
Electric Wipers		
Wipers do not operate— Wiper motor heats up or hums	• Internal motor defect • Bent or damaged linkage • Arms improperly installed on linking pivots	• Replace motor • Repair or replace linkage • Position linkage in park and reinstall wiper arms
Wipers do not operate— No current to motor	• Fuse or circuit breaker blown • Loose, open or broken wiring • Defective switch • Defective or corroded terminals • No ground circuit for motor or switch	• Replace fuse or circuit breaker • Repair wiring and connections • Replace switch • Replace or clean terminals • Repair ground circuits
Wipers do not operate— Motor runs	• Linkage disconnected or broken	• Connect wiper linkage or replace broken linkage
Vacuum Wipers		
Wipers do not operate	• Control switch or cable inoperative • Loss of engine vacuum to wiper motor (broken hoses, low engine vacuum, defective vacuum/fuel pump) • Linkage broken or disconnected • Defective wiper motor	• Repair or replace switch or cable • Check vacuum lines, engine vacuum and fuel pump • Repair linkage • Replace wiper motor
Wipers stop on engine acceleration	• Leaking vacuum hoses • Dry windshield • Oversize wiper blades • Defective vacuum/fuel pump	• Repair or replace hoses • Wet windshield with washers • Replace with proper size wiper blades • Replace pump

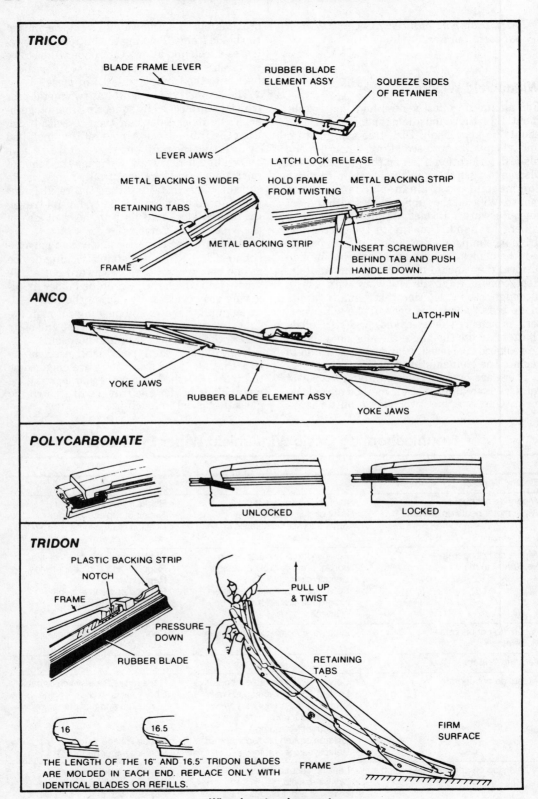

TRICO

BLADE FRAME LEVER

RUBBER BLADE ELEMENT ASSY

SQUEEZE SIDES OF RETAINER

LEVER JAWS

LATCH LOCK RELEASE

METAL BACKING IS WIDER

HOLD FRAME FROM TWISTING

METAL BACKING STRIP

RETAINING TABS

METAL BACKING STRIP

FRAME

INSERT SCREWDRIVER BEHIND TAB AND PUSH HANDLE DOWN.

ANCO

LATCH-PIN

YOKE JAWS

RUBBER BLADE ELEMENT ASSY

YOKE JAWS

POLYCARBONATE

UNLOCKED

LOCKED

TRIDON

PLASTIC BACKING STRIP

NOTCH

FRAME

PULL UP & TWIST

PRESSURE DOWN

RUBBER BLADE

RETAINING TABS

16

16.5

FIRM SURFACE

THE LENGTH OF THE 16″ AND 16.5″ TRIDON BLADES ARE MOLDED IN EACH END. REPLACE ONLY WITH IDENTICAL BLADES OR REFILLS.

FRAME

Wiper insert replacement

WIPER ARM AND BLADE REPLACEMENT

To replace the complete wiper blade, lift up on the locking lever and slide the blade off of the wiper arm.

NOTE: *There are two different styles of wiper arms. On the first, the arm pivot attaching nut is covered with a plastic cap that pulls off. On the second, the arm pivot is covered by a spring-loaded metal cap that slips back off the nut.*

Lift the blade and arm up off the windshield. Simultaneously push the arm down and lift the smaller end cap up, or pull the plastic cap off to expost the retaining nut. Remove the retaining nut and apply upward pressure to remove the wiper arm. Install the arm in the reverse order of removal.

Tires and Wheels

Buy a tire pressure gauge and keep it in the glovebox of your car. Service station air gauges are generally either not working or inaccurate and should not be relied upon. The decal on the left door post gives the recommended air pressure for the standard tires. If you are driving on replacement tires of a different type, follow the inflation recommendations of the manufacturer and never exceed the maximum pressure stated on the sidewall. Always check tire pressure when the tires are cool because air pressure increases with heat and readings will be 4–6 psi higher after the tire has been run. For continued expressway driving, increase the tire pressure by a few pounds in each tire. Never mix tires of different construction on your Volkswagen. When replacing tires, en-

Tread wear bars show up as horizontal bands across the tire when tire is worn to less than 1/16 in.

sure that the new tire(s) are the same size and type as those which will be remaining on the car. Intermixing bias ply tires with radial or bias belted can result in unpredictable and treacherous handling.

TIRE ROTATION

To equalize tire wear and thereby lengthen the mileage you obtain from your tires, rotate them every 5 or 6,000 miles. Follow the illustrations that are appropriate for the type of tires on your car.

TIRE DESIGN

For maximum satisfaction, tires should be used in sets of five. Mixing of different types (radial, bias-belted, fiberglass belted) should

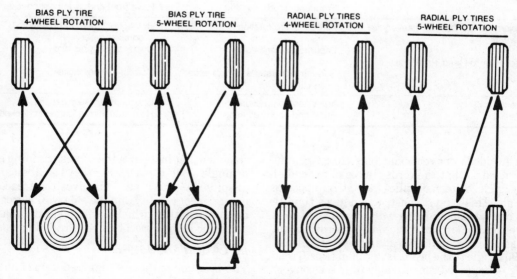

BIAS PLY TIRE
4-WHEEL ROTATION

BIAS PLY TIRE
5-WHEEL ROTATION

RADIAL PLY TIRES
4-WHEEL ROTATION

RADIAL PLY TIRES
5-WHEEL ROTATION

Tire rotation diagrams

Troubleshooting Basic Wheel Problems

Problem	Cause	Solution
The car's front end vibrates at high speed	• The wheels are out of balance • Wheels are out of alignment	• Have wheels balanced • Have wheel alignment checked/adjusted
Car pulls to either side	• Wheels are out of alignment • Unequal tire pressure • Different size tires or wheels	• Have wheel alignment checked/adjusted • Check/adjust tire pressure • Change tires or wheels to same size
The car's wheel(s) wobbles	• Loose wheel lug nuts • Wheels out of balance • Damaged wheel • Wheels are out of alignment • Worn or damaged ball joint • Excessive play in the steering linkage (usually due to worn parts) • Defective shock absorber	• Tighten wheel lug nuts • Have tires balanced • Raise car and spin the wheel. If the wheel is bent, it should be replaced • Have wheel alignment checked/adjusted • Check ball joints • Check steering linkage • Check shock absorbers
Tires wear unevenly or prematurely	• Incorrect wheel size • Wheels are out of balance • Wheels are out of alignment	• Check if wheel and tire size are compatible • Have wheels balanced • Have wheel alignment checked/adjusted

Troubleshooting Basic Tire Problems

Problem	Cause	Solution
The car's front end vibrates at high speeds and the steering wheel shakes	• Wheels out of balance • Front end needs aligning	• Have wheels balanced • Have front end alignment checked
The car pulls to one side while cruising	• Unequal tire pressure (car will usually pull to the low side) • Mismatched tires • Front end needs aligning	• Check/adjust tire pressure • Be sure tires are of the same type and size • Have front end alignment checked
Abnormal, excessive or uneven tire wear See "How to Read Tire Wear"	• Infrequent tire rotation • Improper tire pressure • Sudden stops/starts or high speed on curves	• Rotate tires more frequently to equalize wear • Check/adjust pressure • Correct driving habits
Tire squeals	• Improper tire pressure • Front end needs aligning	• Check/adjust tire pressure • Have front end alignment checked

be avoided. Conventional bias tires are constructed so that the cords run bead to bead at an angle. Alternate plies run at an opposite angle. This type of construction gives rigidity to botrh tread and side wall. Bias belted tires are similar in construction to conventional bias ply tires. Belts run at an angle and also at a 90° angle to the bead, as in radial tires. Tread life is improved considerably over the conventional bias tire. The radial tire differs in construction, but instead of the carcass running at an angle of 90° to each other they run at an angle of 90° to the bead. This gives the tread a great deal of rigidity and the side wall a gread deal of flexibility (which accounts for the characteristic bulge associated with radial tires).

INFLATION PRESSURE

Tire inflation is the most ignored item of auto maintenance. Gasoline mileage can drop as

Tire Size Comparison Chart

"Letter" sizes			Inch Sizes	Metric-inch Sizes		
"60 Series"	"70 Series"	"78 Series"	1965–77	"60 Series"	"70 Series"	"80 Series"
		Y78-12	5.50-12, 5.60-12 6.00-12	165/60-12	165/70-12	155-12
		W78-13	5.20-13	165/60-13	145/70-13	135-13
		Y78-13	5.60-13	175/60-13	155/70-13	145-13
			6.15-13	185/60-13	165/70-13	155-13, P155/80-13
A60-13	A70-13	A78-13	6.40-13	195/60-13	175/70-13	165-13
B60-13	B70-13	B78-13	6.70-13	205/60-13	185/70-13	175-13
			6.90-13			
C60-13	C70-13	C78-13	7.00-13	215/60-13	195/70-13	185-13
D60-13	D70-13	D78-13	7.25-13			
E60-13	E70-13	E78-13	7.75-13			195-13
			5.20-14	165/60-14	145/70-14	135-14
			5.60-14	175/60-14	155/70-14	145-14
			5.90-14			
A60-14	A70-14	A78-14	6.15-14	185/60-14	165/70-14	155-14
	B70-14	B78-14	6.45-14	195/60-14	175/70-14	165-14
	C70-14	C78-14	6.95-14	205/60-14	185/70-14	175-14
D60-14	D70-14	D78-14				
E60-14	E70-14	E78-14	7.35-14	215/60-14	195/70-14	185-14
F60-14	F70-14	F78-14, F83-14	7.75-14	225/60-14	200/70-14	195-14
G60-14	G70-14	G77-14, G78-14	8.25-14	235/60-14	205/70-14	205-14
H60-14	H70-14	H78-14	8.55-14	245/60-14	215/70-14	215-14
J60-14	J70-14	J78-14	8.85-14	255/60-14	225/70-14	225-14
L60-14	L70-14		9.15-14	265/60-14	235/70-14	
	A70-15	A78-15	5.60-15	185/60-15	165/70-15	155-15
B60-15	B70-15	B78-15	6.35-15	195/60-15	175/70-15	165-15
C60-15	C70-15	C78-15	6.85-15	205/60-15	185/70-15	175-15
	D70-15	D78-15				
E60-15	E70-15	E78-15	7.35-15	215/60-15	195/70-15	185-15
F60-15	F70-15	F78-15	7.75-15	225/60-15	205/70-15	195-15
G60-15	G70-15	G78-15	8.15-15/8.25-15	235/60-15	215/70-15	205-15
H60-15	H70-15	H78-15	8.45-15/8.55-15	245/60-15	225/70-15	215-15
J60-15	J70-15	J78-15	8.85-15/8.90-15	255/60-15	235/70-15	225-15
	K70-15		9.00-15	265/60-15	245/70-15	230-15
L60-15	L70-15	L78-15, L84-15	9.15-15			235-15
	M70-15	M78-15				255-15
		N78-15				

Note: Every size tire is not listed and many size comparisons are approximate, based on load ratings. Wider tires than those supplied new with the vehicle, should always be checked for clearance.

much as 0.8% for every 1 pound per square inch (psi) of under inflation.

Two items should be a permanent fixture in every glove compartment: a tire pressure gauge and a tread depth gauge. Check the tire air pressure (including the spare) regularly with a pocket type gauge. Kicking the tires won't tell you a thing, and the gauge on the service station air hose is notoriously inaccurate.

The tire pressures recommended for your car are usually found on the left door or in the owner's manual. Ideally, inflation pressure should be checked when the tires are cool. When the air becomes heated it expands and the pressure increases. Every 10° rise (or drop) in temperature means a difference of 1 psi, which also explains why the tire appears to lose air on a very cold night. When it is impossible to check the tires cold, allow for pressure build-up due to heat. If the hot pressure exceeds the cold pressure by more than 15 psi, reduce your speed, load or both. Otherwise internal heat is created in the tire. When the heat approaches the temperature at which the tire was cured, during manufacture, the tread can separate from the body.

CAUTION: *Never counteract excessive pressure build-up by bleeding off air pressure (letting some air out). This will only further raise the tire operating temperature.*

Before starting a long trip with lots of luggage, you can add about 2–4 psi to the tires to make them run cooler, but never exceed the maximum inflation pressure on the side of the tire.

TREAD DEPTH

All tires made since 1968, have 7 built-in tread wear indicator bars that show up as ½" wide smooth bands across the tire when $1/_{16}$" of tread remains. The appearance of tread wear indicators means that the tires should be replaced. In fact, many states have laws prohibiting the use of tires with less than $1/_{16}$" tread.

You can check your own tread depth with an inexpensive gauge or by using a Lincoln head penny. Slip the Lincoln penny into several tread grooves. If you can see the top of Lincoln's head in 2 adjacent grooves, the tires have less than $1/_{16}$" tread left and should be replaced. You can measure snow tires in thesame manner by using the tails side of the Lincoln penny. If you can see the top of the Lincoln memorial, it's time to replace the snow tires.

STORAGE

Store the tires at the proper inflation pressure if they are mounted on wheels. Keep them in a cool dry place, laid on their sides. If the tires are stored in the garage or basement, do not let them stand on a concrete floor. Set them on strips of wood.

BUYING NEW TIRES

When buying new tires, give some though to the following points, especially if you are considering a switch to larger tires or a different profile series:

1. All four tires must be of the same construction type. This rule cannot be violated. Radial, bias, and bias-belted tires must not be mixed.

2. The wheels should be the correct width for the tire. Tire dealers have charts of tire and rim compatibility. A mismatch will cause sloppy handling and rapid tire wear. The tread width should match the rim width (inside bead to inside bead) within an inch. For radial tires, the rim width should be 80% or less of the tire (not tread) width.

3. The height (mounted diameter) of the new tires can change speedometer accuracy, engine speed at a given road speed, fuel mileage, acceleration, and ground clearance. Tire manufacturers furnish full measurement specifications.

4. The spare tire should be usable, at least for short distance and low speed operation, with the new tires.

5. There shouldn't be any body interference when loaded, on bumps, or in turns.

NOTE: *For a more detailed description of the cooling system and servicing procedures see fluid level checks in this section.*

FLUIDS AND LUBRICANTS

LUBRICATION

Oil and Fuel Recommendations
GASOLINE ENGINES

The SAE (Society of Automotive Engineers) grade number indicates the viscosity of the engine oil, and thus its ability to lubricate at a given temperature. The lower the SAE grade number, the lighter the oil. The lower the viscosity, the easier it is to crank the engine in cold weather.

Oil viscosities should be chosen from those oils recommended for the lowest anticipated temperatures during the oil change interval.

Multi-viscosity oils (10W-30, 20W-50, etc.) offer the important advantage of being adaptable to temperature extremes. They allow easy starting at low temperatures, yet give good protection at high speeds and engine temperatures. This is a decided advantage in changeable climates or in long distance touring.

The API (American Petroleum Institute) designation indicates the classification of engine oil for use under given operating conditions. Only oils designated for use Service SE or SF should be used. Oils of the SE or SF type perform a variety of functions inside the engine in addition to the basic function as a lubricant. Through a balanced system of metallic detergents and polymeric dispersants, the oil prevents the formation of high and low temperature deposits, and also keeps sludge and dirt particles in suspension. Acids, particularly sulfuric acid, as well as other by-products of combustion, are neutralized. Both the SAE grade number and the API designation can be found on the top of the oil can.

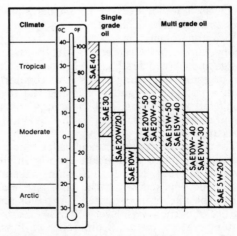

Gasoline engine oil recommendations

NOTE: *Non-detergent or straight mineral oils must never be used.*

Your VW is designed to operate on lead-free fuel. The octane ratings are listed on the inside of the fuel filler door or on the door jamb. Use of leaded gasoline will render the emission control catalyst ineffective.

Oil must be selected with regard to the anticipated temperatures during the period before the next oil change. Using the chart, select the oil viscosity prior to the next oil change for the lowest expected temperature and you will be assured of easy cold starting and sufficient engine protection. The oil you pour into your engine should have the designation 'SE' or 'SF' marked on the top of its container.

DIESEL ENGINES

The Volkswagen diesel engine is designed to run on Diesel Fuel No. 2. Since diesel fuel is generally available along major truck routes, supply is not usually a problem, though it is wise to check in advance. Several diesel station guides are available from fuel companies and are normally sold at diesel fuel stations.

Some U. S. States and Canadian provinces require purchasers of diesel fuel to obtain a special permit to buy diesel fuel. Check with your local VW dealer or fuel supplier for regulations in your area.

There is a difference between the refinement levels of Diesel fuel and home heating oil. While you may get away with running your diesel on home heating oil for a while, inevitably you will fill your tank with a filter and injector clogging batch of oil that will leave you stranded. Also, never allow diesel fuel to come in contact with any rubber hoses, as it will damage them.

Engine oils should be selected from the accompanying chart. The SAE viscosity number should be chosen for the lowest anticipated temperature at which the engine will be required to start not for the temperature at the time the oil is changed.

Use only oils designated by the API (American Petroleum Institute) for service CO 'CC' or 'CD'. The letters should appear somewhere on the oil can for example 'SE/CC' or 'SF/CD'. This indicates that the oil provides protection from rust, corrosion and high temperature deposits in diesel engines in moderate to severe service.

LEVEL CHECK

Engine oil level should be checked weekly as a matter of course. Always check the oil with the car on level ground and after the engine has been shut off for about five minutes. The oil dipstick is located on the front side of engine on the Rabbit, Golf, Jetta and Scirocco, and on the

There is approximately 1 quart between the minumum and maximum marks on the oil dipstick

Add oil through the capped opening in the valve cover

Diesel engine oil recommendations

driver's side near the fuel pump on the Dasher Fox and Quantum models.

1. Remove the dipstick and wipe it clean.
2. Reinsert the dipstick.
3. Remove the dipstick again. The oil level should be between the two marks. The difference between the marks is one quart.
4. Add oil through the capped opening on the top of the valve cover. Select oil of the proper viscosity from the chart later in this chapter.

OIL CHANGE

Change the oil according to the maintenance interval chart in this chapter. This interval is only for average driving. If your car is being used under dusty conditions, change the oil and filter sooner. The same thing goes for cars being driven in stop and go city traffic, where acid and sludge buildup is a problem.

Always drain the oil after the engine has been run long enough to bring it to the normal operating temperature. Hot oil will flow easier and more contaminants will be removed with the oil than if it were drained cold. A large capacity drain pan, which can be purchased at any automotive supply store, will be more than paid back by savings from do-it-yourself containers for the used oil. You will find that plastic bleach containers make excellent storage bottles. Two ecologically desirable solutions to the used oil disposal problem are to take it to a service station and ask to dump it into their sump tank or keep it and use it as a preservative for exposed wood around your home.

To change the oil:
1. Run the engine until it reaches the normal operating temperature.
2. Slide a drain pan under the oil pan drain plug.
3. Loosen the drain plug with a socket or box wrench, and then remove it by hand. Push in on the plug as you turn it out, so that no oil escapes until the plug is completely removed.
4. Allow the oil to drain into the pan.

5. Install the drain plug, making sure that the brass gasket is still on the plug. Tighten the plug to 22 ft.lb.
6. Refill the engine with oil. Start the engine and check for leaks.

OIL FILTER CHANGES

NOTE: *For better protection, always change the filter at oil change time if you have a diesel powered vehicle. VW recommends changing the oil filter at every other oil change, but it is more beneficial to replace the filter every time the oil is changed.*

To replace oil and filter:
1. Drain the crankcase into a pan of sufficient capacity. The plug is in the end of the pan.
2. The filter is located on the front of the engine block. Reach in and turn the filter off counterclockwise. If it's tight use a filter strap wrench.
3. Carefully lift the filter out of the engine compartment and dispose of it.
4. Clean the oil filter adapter on the engine with a clean rag.
5. On gasoline engines, lightly oil the rubber seal on the new filter and spin it on to the engine. Tighten it until the seal is flush and then give it an additional ½ to ¾ turn. On diesel engines, through mid-1982; if the oil filter

An oil cooler is used on Turbo-diesel engines. Always check the oil cooler for tightness when replacing the oil filter. If necessary, torque the nut retaining the cooler to 18 ft. lbs.

The oil drain plug is in the end of the oil pan

The oil filter (diesel shown) is on the side of the engine block that faces the front of the car on Rabbit, Jetta and Scirocco. On Dasher and Quantum, the filter is located on the driver's side

mounting surface is ridged, tighten the filter ¾ turn beyond hand tight; run engine for 3–5 minutes; stop engine and torque filter to at least 18 ft.lb. Models mid-1982 and later, having a flat filter mounting flange require the filter to be tightened following the filter manufacturers instructions.

6. Refill the engine, start the engine and check for leaks.

MANUAL TRANSAXLE

NOTE: *Volkswagen strongly suggests that manual transmission maintenance on later model VW's be left to qualified dealers.*

From 1976 on, Volkswagen claims that the Hypoid oil in the manual transaxle and the differential section of the automatic transmission does not have to be changed. They have inserted a large magnet in the bottom of the assembly to attract any gear shavings and thus keep them from causing friction among the gears. The following procedure is mainly for pre-1976 models.

The only equipment required is a drain pan, a wrench to fit the filler and drain plugs, and an oil suction gun. Gear oil can be purchased in gallon cans at the larger automotive supply stores.

LEVEL CHECK

NOTE: *Volkswagen advises that the manual transmission lubricant need never be checked or changed. VW also recommends you entrust all transmission service to the dealer.*

Dasher Fox and Quantum

The oil filler plug is located on the driver's side of the transaxle at the rear of the final drive cover. Remove the plug, if the fluid is level with the bottom of the hole, it is correct. Add 80W-90 weight GL4 lubricant if necessary.

Rabbit, Golf, Jetta, Scirocco

For Rabbit, Golf and Scirocco transmissions up to No. 06 054, check the oil at the oil control plug. Remove the plug with a 5mm allen wrench. With the car level (the front and rear wheels on level ground or raised the same height off the ground), the oil should just begin

Transmission Fluid Indications

The appearance and odor of the transmission fluid can give valuable clues to the overall condition of the transmission. Always note the appearance of the fluid when you check the fluid level or change the fluid. Rub a small amount of fluid between your fingers to feel for grit and smell the fluid on the dipstick.

If the fluid appears:	It indicates:
Clear and red colored	• Normal operation
Discolored (extremely dark red or brownish) or smells burned	• Band or clutch pack failure, usually caused by an overheated transmission. Hauling very heavy loads with insufficient power or failure to change the fluid, often result in overheating. Do not confuse this appearance with newer fluids that have a darker red color and a strong odor (though not a burned odor).
Foamy or aerated (light in color and full of bubbles)	• The level is too high (gear train is churning oil) • An internal air leak (air is mixing with the fluid). Have the transmission checked professionally.
Solid residue in the fluid	• Defective bands, clutch pack or bearings. Bits of band material or metal abrasives are clinging to the dipstick. Have the transmission checked professionally.
Varnish coating on the dipstick	• The transmission fluid is overheating

Dasher transaxle drain plug (A) and filler plug (B) locations

Oil control plug (arrow) for all manual transaxle Rabbit, Jetta and Scirocco models. For transaxles up to number 06054, the filler plug is located on the front of the transaxle case next to the backup light switch. On later models, fill through the control plug hole

to run out of the hole. If not, add SAE 80W or 80/90W GL4 gear oil through the separate filler plug located on the front of the transmission near the backup light switch. A bulb syringe or an oil squirt can should do the trick.

NOTE: *Both the transmission and the final drive gears share the same lubricant.*

For Rabbit, Golf and Scirocco transmissions from No. 07 954, and all Jetta transmissions,

you check and fill the transmission through the oil control plug, using the same weight gear oil as the earlier transmissions.

To change the oil:

1. Jack up the front of the car and support it safely on stands.

2. Slide drain pan under the transaxle.

3. Remove the filler plug and then the drain plug.

4. When the oil has been completely drained, install the drain plug. Tighten to 18 ft.lb.

5. Using the suction gun, refill the gearbox up to the level of the filler plug. Use an SAE 80W or 90W GL-4 gear oil.

6. Install and tighten the filler plug.

AUTOMATIC TRANSMISSION

The final drive section of the automatic transmission requires no attention other than an occasional level check. Top up with SAE 90 GL-5 hypoid gear oil.

VW of America recommends that the automatic transmission fluid be replaced every 30,000 miles, or 20,000 miles if you use your car for frequent trailer towing, mountain driving, or other severe service.

NOTE: *Automatic transmission is not yet available on the Fox.*

LEVEL CHECK

The automatic transmission dipstick is located at the right-side of the engine compartment near the battery on the Rabbit, Golf, Jetta and Scirocco, and on the driver's side near the front of the transmission on the Dasher and Quantum. Use the following procedure when checking the fluid level:

1. Idle the engine for a few minutes with the selector in Neutral. Apply the parking brake.

2. Remove the dipstick, wipe it clean, reinsert it, and withdraw it again.

B32-051

Dasher automatic transmission dipstick location

Rabbit, Jetta, Scirocco manual transaxle drain plug

Rabbit, Jetta and Scirocco automatic transmission dipstick location

Arrows indicate the maximum/minimum marks on the see-through brake master cylinder reservoir. Fluid is added through the capped opening

3. The fluid level should be within the two marks. Top up with Dexron® or Dexron®II automatic transmission fluid. Bear in mind that the difference between the two marks is less than one pint. Use a long-necked funnel to add the fluid. Fluid should be drained and replaced at the specified interval in the maintenance interval chart in this chapter to drain/replace the fluid, see, 'Automatic Transmission' in Chapter 6.

AUTOMATIC TRANSAXLE FINAL DRIVE

The final drive uses SAE 90W GL5 gear oil. The filler plug is located on the side of the unit directly behind the axle driveshaft. Check and add oil in the same manner as the manual transaxle.

To change the fluid:

1. Purchase 4 quarts of automatic transmission fluid (Dexron® or Dexron®II) and a pan gasket.

2. Slide a drain pan under the transmission. Jack up the front of the car and support it safely on stands.

3. Many early models are equipped with drain plugs in the pan. On later models, you must loosen the pan retaining bolts to drain the fluid.

4. On all models, remove the pan retaining bolts and drop the pan.

5. Discard the old gasket and clean the pan with solvent.

6. On models with circular oil strainers, unscrew the strainer and clean it. On models with rectangular or not perfectly circular oil strainers, the strainer cannot be cleaned and must be replaced.

NOTE: *Only replace the oil strainer if the transmission fluid is contaminated.*

7. Install the oil strained, but don't tighten the bolt too much. Specified torque is only 4 ft.lb.

8. Using a long-necked funnel, refill the transmission with fluid. Check the level with the dipstick. Run the car for a few minutes and check again.

DRIVE AXLE (FRONT)

Automatic Transmission Equipped Cars Only

The lubricant should be changed according to the schedule in the Maintenance Intervals chart.

NOTE: *This pertains to vehicles with automatic transmission only.*

FLUID RECOMMENDATIONS

Use gear oil with API classification GL-5. Viscosity should be
- SAE 90 — above 30°F
- SAE 85W — above −30°F
- SAE 80W — below 90°F

LEVEL CHECK

The lubricant level in the drive axle is checked in the same manner as the engine oil, with the engine off and the vehicle parked on a level surface. The dipstick is located to the rear of the engine oil dipstick and near the starter motor.

NOTE: *This section pertains to vehicles with automatic transmissions only.*

If the lubricant level is not at the upper mark on the dipstick additional gear oil is necessary and should be added through the dipstick filler tube. Use the proper weight oil with API classification of GL-5. Do not overfill.

DRAIN AND REFILL

1. Park the car on a level surface, turn off engine and apply the parking brake.

2. Place a container of adequate capacity beneath the drain plug, located on the lower left side of the differential case, near the left axle shaft.

3. Remove the drain plug and allow the fluid to drain.

4. After draining, replace the drain plug and gasket. Do not overtighten.

5. Remove the differential dipstick and fill the differential to the upper mark on the dipstick.

Cooling System
FLUID RECOMMENDATION

Make it a habit to periodically check the coolant level in the radiator. Ideally, this should be performed when the engine is cold. When checking the coolant level on a warm or hot engine, turn the cap to the first catch to permit pressure to be released from the system. Turn the cap off counterclockwise. A gauge plate inside the radiator aids in level checking. The coolant should be maintained at the bottom of the plate. Use only a quality ethylene glycol antifreeze to refill or top up the cooling system.

Some models are equipped with a coolant reservoir. The reservoir is translucent and can be checked without removing the cap. The reservoir has low and high level marks. The coolant must be between the two marks when the

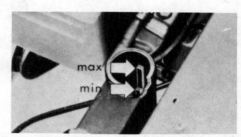

Some models have a gauge inside the radiator neck to check coolant level

On some models, the coolant level lines are on the outside of the radiator neck

Four routine level checks—brake fluid (lower left), coolant (upper left), windshield washer reservoir (upper right), and battery (lower right)—Rabbit, Scirocco engine compartment shown. Most cars with rear windshield washer have an additional reservoir in the back

engine is cold and slightly above the high mark at normal operating temperature.

Models equipped with an electric coolant warning device cause a light on the dash to flash until the coolant level is filled to the normal level.

DRAINING AND REFILLING

CAUTION: *Never attempt to drain the coolant from a warm engine. If you do, there's a good chance you'll be scalded. Always handle a warm radiator cap with a heavy rag.*

1. Turn the heater control to HOT.
2. Remove the radiator cap by turning it until it hisses. Wait for the hissing to stop, then turn it the rest of the way and remove it.
3. On early models, there is a petcock at the bottom of the radiator. Loosen it after placing a container underneath to catch the coolant. To drain the cooling system, remove the lower radiator hose at the radiator end connection. Use one of the many commercially available cleaners, that is safe to use in aluminum components, to flush out the system. These remove

rust and scale which cut down on cooling efficiency.

· 4. After all of the coolant is drained, replace or tighten the petcock, thermostat flange or hose.

5. Remove the top water hose from the radiator and fill the system with coolant. When coolant just begins to flow out of the hose, refit the hose and continue to add coolant until the system is full. See the 'Appendix' for the antifreeze/water mixture chart. A gauge plate inside the radiator or lines on the outside aid in coolant filling. Coolant should be between the lines.

NOTE: *Because of the use of aluminum in engines and cooling systems, be sure to use an antifreeze formulated to provide anticorrosion protection for all metals including aluminum. The reason for removing the water hose when filling the empty system is that air pockets often form in the block which create hot spots, causing damage. Removing the hose bleeds the air from the system.*

6. Replace the radiator cap and run the engine until it's warm, then, after it cools sufficiently, recheck the coolant level.

FLUSHING AND CLEANING THE SYSTEM

The cooling system should be drained, thoroughly flushed and refilled at least every 30,000 miles or 24 months. This operation should be done with the engine cold.

1. Remove the radiator and recovery tank caps. Run the engine till the upper radiator hose gets hot. This means that the thermostat is open and the coolant is flowing through the system.

2. Turn the engine Off and place a large container under the radiator. Open the drain valve at the bottom of the radiator. Open the block drain plugs (If equipped) to speed up the draining process.

3. Close the drain valves and the block drain plugs and add water until the system is full. Repeat the draining and filling process several times, until the liquid is nearly colorless.

4. After the last draining, fill the system with a 50/50 mixture of ethylene glycol and water. Run the engine until the system is hot and add coolant, if necessary. Replace the caps and check for leaks.

BRAKE MASTER CYLINDER

The brake fluid reservoir is located on the left-side of the engine compartment at the firewall. Brake fluid level should be maintained at the MAX line on the reservoir. Level can be checked visually without removing the cap on this translucent unit. If necessary, top up with a brand name hydraulic fluid which bears the DOT 3 or 4 marking. This information will be stamped on the can.

POWER STEERING RESERVOIR

The reservoir for the power assisted steering is located at the rear of the engine compartment on the firewall. The fluid level should be checked at regular intervals. With the engine running (transmission in Park and parking brake applied), the fluid level should be between the 'MAX' and 'Min' marks on the outside of the reservoir. Add only Dexron® or Dexron®II fluid if required. If fluid is added, make sure the filler cap is secured.

CAUTION: *Stand to the side of the car when checking the fluid. Do not stand in front when the engine is running.*

STEERING GEAR

The rack and pinion steering gear is filled with lubricant and sealed at the factory. If you notice any leaking, have it checked at the dealer.

CHASSIS GREASING

The Rabbit, Golf, Dasher, Fox, Jetta, Scirocco and Quantum require no chassis greasing and are not equipped with grease nipples. Check the axle and driveshaft and tie rod rubber boots occasionally for leaking or cracking. At the same time, squirt a few drops of oil on the parking brake equalizer (point where cables V-off to the rear brakes). The front wheel bearings do not require greasing unless they are disassembled.

Body Lubrication

Periodic lubrication will prevent squeaky, hard-to-open doors and lids. About every three months, pry the plastic caps off the door hinges and squirt in enough oil to fill the chambers. Press the plug back into the hinge after filling. Lightly oil the door check pivots. Finally, spray graphite lock lubricant onto your key and insert it into the door a few times.

Front Wheel Bearing Adjustments

There is no front wheel bearing adjustment. The bearing is pressed into the steering knuckle. The axle nut should be torqued to 174 ft.lb. on all Rabbits, Jettas and Sciroccos and either 145 ft.lb. (M18 nut) or 175 ft.lb. (M20 nut) on the Dasher Fox and Quantum. Tighten the nut with the wheels on the ground.

REMOVAL AND INSTALLATION (PACKING)

Front Axle Only

1. In order to remove the wheel bearings, the steering knuckle must be removed.
2. Jack up the vehicle and remove the wheel and tire.
3. Straighten the lockplate at the wheel hub on the constant velocity joint side, loosen the wheel hub nut, and remove the nut with the lockplate.
4. Remove the tie rod end from the knuckle arm.
5. Remove the two cotter pins, castle nuts, spring washers, and the lower arm ball joint. NOTE: *When the camber and caster adjusting cams are removed, remember the setting number for reassembly.*
6. After flattening the lockwasher, remove the nut and lockplate which joins the upper arm and the upper arm joint.
7. Remove the hub and knuckle assembly from the splined section of the axle shaft constant velocity joint side.
8. Separate the hub from the knuckle.
9. Remove the upper and lower ball joints and then remove the steering knuckle from the vehicle.
10. Straighten out the lockplate, loosen the bolt, and remove the bolt together with the spring washer and the lockplate.
11. Remove the inner oil seal from the bearing nut.
12. Remove the nut from the knuckle.
13. Remove the spacer.
14. Remove the outer oil seal from the knuckle.
15. Remove the bearing from the knuckle by pressing it out with a press. Remove the wheel bearing race using a puller with a clamping bracket.
16. Make sure that the bearings are installed in the same position as they were removed.
17. Before installing the bearing, clean and inspect it for damage. Repack the bearing with wheel bearing grease.
18. Press the outer and inner races, and the oil seal into the knuckle. Insert the outer oil seal into the knuckle. Insert the outer oil seal so that it protrudes from the knuckle end surface about 0.04 in. Coat the outer seal lip with grease when installing.
19. Insert the spacer making sure that the lip of the oil seal is not tucked up.
20. Tighten the bearing nut.
21. Align the lockplate groove with the nut groove and bend the lockplate and lock the nut.
22. Press the inner oil seal into the nut. Be careful not to damage the side lip of the oil

seal. Coat the inner oil seal lip surface with grease when installing.

23. Assemble the steering knuckle to the vehicle in the reverse order of removal.

Rear Wheel Bearing Adjustment

Before attempting to adjust the wheel bearings, tighten the adjustment nut while turning the wheel to seat the bearings. Wheel bearing clearance is correctly adjusted when the thrust washer under the adjusting nut can be moved slightly with a screwdriver. Do not twist or pry with the screwdriver. Install a new cotter pin.

REMOVAL AND INSTALLATION (PACKING)

Rear Axle Only

1. Apply parking brake and loosen (but do not remove) rear wheel nuts.
2. Jack up vehicle, support it with jack stands, block the front wheels, release the parking brake and remove the wheel and tire.
3. Remove brake drum cap from drum.
4. Flatten lock washer and loosen axle nut, then remove lock washer, washer and brake drum so as not to drop inner race of outer bearing.
NOTE: *Outer races of outer bearing and inner bearing, and oil seal can be removed together with drum.*
5. Pry up spacer with a screwdriver and remove spacer and inner bearing inner race with a puller.
6. Remove outer race of inner bearing from drum. Remove the oil seal at this time.
7. Remove outer race of outer bearing from drum.
Clean the removed parts and check them for wear, damage and corrosion. If faulty, repair or replace.
To Install:
1. Press inner race of inner bearing into drum using a taper roller bearing installer and a press.
2. Apply sufficient grease to oil seal lip. Apply approximately 4 g (0.14 oz) of grease to inner bearing. Install the bearing and oil seal into drum. Make sure that the outer end of the oil seal is flush with drum surface.
3. Press outer race of outer bearing into drum using a taper rolller bearing installer and a press.
4. Apply approximately 3 g (0.11 oz) of grease to the outer bearing. Fill the boss of drum with approximately 30 g (1.06 oz) of grease.
5. Install spacer and inner race of inner bearing onto the spindle of trailing arm.
NOTE: *Stepped surface of the spacer must be faced toward the bearing.*

6. Install drum, inner race of outer bearing, washer, lock washer and axle nut in this order onto the spindle.
NOTE: *Make sure the old lock washer is replaced with a new one.*

ADJUSTMENT

1. Temporarily tighten the axle nut to 36 ft.lb., then turn the drum back and forth alternately several times to properly seat the bearing and ascertain bearing stability.
2. Turn back nut ⅛ to ¼ turn in order to obtain correct starting torque. Measure the starting force as shown.
NOTE: *Starting force when measured at the hub bolt should be 1.87–3.20 lbs.. Make sure there is no free play in the bearing.*
3. Bend lock washer.
4. After installing O-ring to drum cap, install cap to brake drum by lightly tapping with plastic hammer.
NOTE: *Do not use a steel hammer on the drum cap and be sure to replace the old O-ring with a new one.*

TRAILER TOWING

Factory trailer towing packages are available for most vehicles. However, if you are installing a trailer hitch and wiring on your car, there are a few thing that you ought to know.

Trailer Weight

Trailer weight is the first, and most important, factor in determining whether or not your vehicle is suitable for towing the trailer you have in mind. The horsepower-to-weight ratio should be calculated. The basic standard is a ratio of 35:1. That is, 35 pounds of GVW for every horsepower.

To calculate this ratio, multiply you engine's rated horsepower by 35, then subtract the weight of the vehicle, including passengers and luggage. The resulting figure is the ideal maximum trailer weight that you can tow. One point to consider: a numerically higher axle ratio can offset what appears to be a low trailer weight. If the weight of the trailer that you have in mind is somewhat higher than the weight you just calculated, you might consider changing your rear axle ratio to compensate.

Hitch Weight

There are three kinds of hitches: bumper mounted, frame mounted, and load equalizing.

Bumper mounted hitches are those which attach solely to the vehicle's bumper. Many states prohibit towing with this type of hitch, when it attaches to the vehicle's stock bumper, since it subjects the bumper to stresses for which it was not designed. Aftermarket rear step bumpers, designed for trailer towing, are acceptable for use with bumper mounted hitches.

Frame mounted hitches can be of the type which bolts to two or more points on the frame, plus the bumper, or just to several points on the frame. Frame mounted hitches can also be of the tongue type, for Class I towing, or, of the receiver type, for classes II and III. Volkswagens should not be used for towing anything with a Class II or class III rating, as maximum towing capacity for these cars is limited to 1000 lbs gross weight.

Load equalizing hitches are usually used for large trailers. Most equalizing hitches are welded in place and use equalizing bars and chains to level the vehicle after the trailer is hooked up.

The bolt-on hitches are the most common, since they are relatively easy to install.

Check the gross weight rating of your trailer. Tongue weight is usually figured as 10% of gross trailer weight. Therefore, a trailer with a maximum gross weight of 2,000 lb. will have a maximum tongue weight of 200 lb. Class I trailers fall into this category. Class II trailers are those with a gross weight rating of 2,000–3,500 lb., while Class III trailers fall into the 3,500–6,000 lb. category. Class IV trailers are those over 6,000 lb. and are for use with fifth wheel trucks, only.

When you've determined the hitch that you'll need, follow the manufacturer's installation instructions, exactly, especially when it comes to fastener torques. The hitch will be subjected to a lot of stress and good hitches come with hardened bolts. Never substitute an inferior bolt for a hardened bolt.

Wiring

Wiring the car for towing is fairly easy. There are a number of good wiring kits available and these should be used, rather than trying to design your own. All trailers will need brake lights and turn signals as well as tail lights and side marker lights. Most states require extra marker lights for overwide trailers. Also, most states have recently required backup lights for trailers, and most trailer manufacturers have been building trailers with backup lights for several years.

Additionally, some Class I, most Class II and just about all Class III trailers will have electric brakes.

Add to this number an accessories wire, to operate trailer internal equipment or to charge the trailer's battery, and you can have as many as seven wires in the harness.

Determine the equipment on your trailer and buy the wiring kit necessary. The kit will contain all the wires needed, plus a plug adapter set which included the female plug, mounted on the bumper or hitch, and the male plug, wired into, or plugged into the trailer harness.

When installing the kit, follow the manufacturer's instructions. The color coding of the wires is standard throughout the industry.

One point to note: some domestic vehicles, and most imported vehicles, have separate turn signals. On most domestic vehicles, the brake lights and rear turn signals operate with the same bulb. For those vehicles with separate turn signals, you can purchase an isolation unit so that the brake lights won't blink whenever the turn signals are operated, or, you can go to your local electronics supply house and buy four diodes to wire in series with the brake and turn signal bulbs. Diodes will isolate the brake and turn signals. The choice is yours. The isolation units are simple and quick to install, but far more expensive than the diodes. The diodes, however, require more work to install properly, since they require the cutting of each bulb's wire and soldering in place of the diode.

One, final point, the best kits are those with a spring loaded cover on the vehicle mounted socket. This cover prevents dirt and moisture from corroding the terminals. Never let the vehicle socket hang loosely; always mount it securely to the bumper or hitch.

Cooling
ENGINE

One of the most common, if not THE most common, problems associated with trailer towing is engine overheating.

With factory installed trailer towing packages, a heavy duty cooling system is usually included. Heavy duty cooling systems are available as optional equipment on most GM vehicles, with or without a trailer package. If you have one of these extracapacity systems, you shouldn't have any overheating problems.

If you have a standard cooling system, without an expansion tank, you'll definitely need to get an aftermarket expansion tank kit, preferably one with at least a 2 quart capacity. These kits are easily installed on the radiator's overflow hose, and come with a pressure cap designed for expansion tanks.

Another helpful accessory is a Flex Fan. These fan are large diameter units are designed to provide more airflow at low speeds, with blades that have deeply cupped surfaces.

The blades then flex, or flatten out, at high speed, when less cooling air is needed. These fans are far lighter in weight than stock fans, requiring less horsepower to drive them. Also, they are far quieter than stock fans.

If you do decide to replace your stock fan with a flex fan, note that if your van has a fan clutch, a spacer between the flex fan and water pump hub will be needed.

Aftermarket engine oil coolers are helpful for prolonging engine oil life and reducing overall engine temperatures. Both of these factors increase engine life.

While not absolutely necessary in towing Class I and some Class II trailers, they are recommended for heavier Class II and all Class III towing.

Engine oil cooler systems consist of an adapter, screwed on in place of the oil filter, a remote filter mounting and a multi-tube, finned heat exchanger, which is mounted in front of the radiator or air conditioning condenser.

TRANSMISSION

An automatic transmission is usually recommended for trailer towing. Modern automatics have proven reliable and, of course, easy to operate, in trailer towing.

The increased load of a trailer, however, causes an increase in the temperature of the automatic transmission fluid. Heat is the worst enemy of an automatic transmission. As the temperature of the fluid increases, the life of the fluid decreases.

It is essential, therefore, that you install an automatic transmission cooler.

The cooler, which consists of a multi-tube, finned heat exchanger, is usually installed in front of the radiator or air conditioning compressor, and hooked inline with the transmission cooler tank inlet line. Follow the cooler manufacturer's installation instructions.

Select a cooler of at least adequate capacity, based upon the combined gross weights of the Van and trailer.

Cooler manufacturers recommend that you use an aftermarket cooler in addition to, and not instead of, the present cooling tank in your vans radiator. If you do want to use it in place of the radiator cooling tank, get a cooler at least two sizes larger than normally necessary.

One note, transmission cooler can, sometimes, cause slow or harsh shifting in the transmission during cold weather, until the fluid has a chance to come up to normal operating temperature. Some coolers can be purchased with or retrofitted with a temperature bypass valve which will allow fluid flow through the cooler only when the fluid has reached operating temperature, or above.

PUSH-STARTING AND TOWING

CAUTION: *Pushing or towing in an attempt to start a catalytic converter equipped car can cause raw gasoline to enter the converter and cause expensive damage.*

If your car is equipped with a manual transaxle, it may be push-started in an extreme emergency. It should be recognized that there is the possibility of damaging bumpers and/or fenders of both cars. Make sure that the bumpers of both cars are evenly matched. Depress the clutch pedal, select Second or Third gear, and switch the ignition On. When the car reaches a speed of approximately 10 or 15 mph, release the clutch to start the engine. DO NOT ATTEMPT TO PUSH-START AN AUTOMATIC TRANSMISSION EQUIPPED MODEL.

Both manual and automatic models may be towed short distances. Attach tow lines to the towing eye on the front suspension or the left or right bumper bracket at the rear. Automatic equipped cars must be towed in Neutral no farther than 30 miles and no faster than 30 mph, unless the front wheels are off the ground.

If you plan on towing a trailer, don't exceed 886 lb. for the Rabbit, Jetta and Scirocco, and 992 lb. for the Dasher and Quantum (trailer without brakes). Towing a trailer with an automatic equipped car places an extra load on the transmission and a few items should be made note of her. Make doubly sure that the transmission fluid is at the correct level. Change the fluid more frequently if you're doing much trailer hauling. Start out in 1 or 2 and use the lower ranges when climbing hills. Aftermarket transmission coolers are available which greatly ease the load on your automatic and one should be considered if you often pull a trailer.

JACKING

Your car is equipped with a single post, crank handle jack which fits the jacking points behind the front wheel and in front of the rear wheel. These are marked with triangular sections of the body stamping. Never use the tire changing jack for anything other than that. If you intend to use this book to perform your own maintenance, a good pair of scissors or a small hydraulic jack and two sturdy jackstands would be a wise purchase. Always

JUMP STARTING A DEAD BATTERY

The chemical reaction in a battery produces explosive hydrogen gas. This is the safe way to jump start a dead battery, reducing the chances of an accidental spark that could cause an explosion.

Jump Starting Precautions

1. Be sure both batteries are of the same voltage.
2. Be sure both batteries are of the same polarity (have the same grounded terminal).
3. Be sure the vehicles are not touching.
4. Be sure the vent cap holes are not obstructed.
5. Do not smoke or allow sparks around the battery.
6. In cold weather, check for frozen electrolyte in the battery. Do not jump start a frozen battery.
7. Do not allow electrolyte on your skin or clothing.
8. Be sure the electrolyte is not frozen.

CAUTION: *Make certain that the ignition key, in the vehicle with the dead battery, is in the OFF position. Connecting cables to vehicles with on-board computers will result in computer destruction if the key is not in the OFF position.*

Jump Starting Procedure

1. Determine voltages of the two batteries; they must be the same.
2. Bring the starting vehicle close (they must not touch) so that the batteries can be reached easily.
3. Turn off all accessories and both engines. Put both cars in Neutral or Park and set the handbrake.
4. Cover the cell caps with a rag—do not cover terminals.
5. If the terminals on the run-down battery are heavily corroded, clean them.
6. Identify the positive and negative posts on both batteries and connect the cables in the order shown.
7. Start the engine of the starting vehicle and run it at fast idle. Try to start the car with the dead battery. Crank it for no more than 10 seconds at a time and let it cool off for 20 seconds in between tries.
8. If it doesn't start in 3 tries, there is something else wrong.
9. Disconnect the cables in the reverse order.
10. Replace the cell covers and dispose of the rags.

chock the wheels when changing a tire or working beneath the car. It cannot be overemphasized.

CLIMBING UNDER A CAR SUPPORTED BY JUST THE JACK IS EXTREMELY DANGEROUS!

A jack can be safely placed under the front and rear jacking points, the engine crossmember, or the center of the rear axle beam. Take care that the jack pad is at least 4 in. square when jacking the rear axle, or you may damage it.

HOW TO BUY A USED CAR

Many people believe that a two or three year old used car is a better buy than a new car. This may be true. The new car suffers the heaviest depreciation in the first two years, but is not old enough to present a lot of costly repair problems. Whatever the age of the used car you might want to buy, this section and a little patience will help you select one that should be safe and dependable.

Typical tire repair jack. The Rabbit Pick-up has a scissor jack. Turn the handle toward A to raise, B to lower

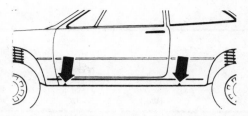

There are two jacking points on each side of the vehicle

newspaper ads. Privately owned cars are usually less expensive, however you will not get a warranty that, in most cases, comes with a used car purchased from a lot.

3. Never shop at night. The glare of the lights make it easy to miss faults on the body caused by accident or rust repair.

4. Try to get the name and phone number of the previous owner. Contact him/her and ask about the car. If the owner of the lot refuses this information, look for a car somewhere else.

A private seller can tell you about the car and

Tips

1. First decide what model you want, and how much you want to spend.

2. Check the used car lots and your local

Capacities

Year	Model	Engine Displacement Cu In (cc)	Engine Crankcase (qts)		Transaxle (pts)			Drive Axle Automatic Trans only (pts)	Fuel Tank (gals)	Cooling System (pts)
			With Filter	Without Filter	Manual 4-sp	5-sp	Automatic			
1974	Dasher	89.7 (1,471)	3.2	2.6	3.2	—	6.4	1.6	12.1	12.6
1975	Rabbit, Scirocco	89.7 (1,471)	3.7	3.2	2.6	—	6.4	1.6	12.1	9.8
1975–76	Dasher	96.8 (1,588)	3.2	2.6	3.2	—	6.4	1.6	11.9	12.6
1976	Rabbit, Scirocco	96.8 (1,588)	3.7	3.2	2.6	—	6.4	1.6	12.1	9.8
1977	Rabbit, Scirocco	96.8 (1,588)	3.7	3.2	2.6	—	6.4	1.6	12.1	9.8
1977–78	Rabbit, (diesel)	89.7 (1,471)	3.7	3.2	2.6	—	6.4	1.6	10.6	9.8
1977–80	Dasher	96.8 (1,588)	3.2	2.6	3.4	—	6.4	1.6	11.9	12.6
1978	Scirocco	88.9 (1,457)	3.7	3.2	2.6	—	6.4	1.6	10.5	9.8
1978–79	Rabbit	88.9 (1,457)	3.7	3.2	2.6	4.2	6.4	1.6	10.5	9.8
1979–80	Scirocco	97.0 (1,588)	3.7	3.2	3.2	4.2	6.4	1.6	10.6	9.8 ①
	Dasher (diesel)	89.7 (1,471)	3.7	3.2	3.2	—	6.4	1.6	11.9	11.8
	Rabbit (diesel)	89.7 (1,471)	3.7	3.2	3.2	4.2	6.4	1.6	10.6 ②	14.6

Capacities (cont.)

Year	Model	Engine Displacement Cu In (cc)	Engine Crankcase (qts)		Transaxle (pts)			Drive Axle Automatic Trans only (pts)	Fuel Tank (gals)	Cooling System (pts)
			With Filter	Without Filter	Manual 4-sp	5-sp	Automatic			
1980	Rabbit, Jetta	96.8 (1,588) ③	3.7	3.2	3.2	4.2	6.4	1.6	10.0 ④	9.8 ⑤
	Rabbit (Pick-up)	96.8 (1,588)	3.7	3.2	3.2	4.2	6.4	1.6	15.0	14.6
1981	Scirocco, Dasher Rabbit, Jetta	105.0 (1,715)	4.5	4.0	3.2	4.2	6.4	1.6	10.0 ② ⑥	9.8
1981	Dasher, Rabbit Jetta (Diesel)	97.0 (1,588)	3.7	3.2	3.2	4.2	6.4	1.6	10.0 ② ⑥	14.3 ⑦
1982–84	Rabbit, Jetta, Scirocco, Quantum	105 (1,715)	4.7	4.2	3.2	4.2	6.4	1.6	⑧	14.3
	Rabbit, Jetta Quantum (Diesel)	97.0 (1,588)	3.7	3.2	3.2	4.2	6.4	1.6	⑧	14.3
	GTI, Scirocco	109.0 (1,790)	4.7	4.2	—	4.2	—	—	10.0	13.8
	Quantum	131 (2,144)	4.8	4.3	—	—	6.4	1.6	15.8	14.3
1985–87	Golf	109 (1,781)	4.8	4.3	—	4.2	6.4	1.6	10.5	10.2
	Jetta, GTI	109 (1,781)	4.8	4.3	—	4.2	6.4	1.6	13.7	13.6
	Scirocco	97 (1,588)	4.8	4.3	—	4.2	6.4	1.6	13.7	10.2
	Quantum (Turbo Diesel)	97 (1,588)	7.0	6.0	—	4.2	6.4	1.6	16.0	13.0
1987	Fox	109 (1,781)	3.7	3.3	3.5	—	—	—	12.7	13.8

① 1980 Scirocco: 10.2 pts.
② Pick-up: 15.0 gals.
③ Fuel injected engines. Carburetor equipped engines: 88.9 Cu in. (1457 cc)
④ Jetta: 10.5 gals.
⑤ 10.2 pts. for Rabbit convertible and Jetta
⑥ Dasher: 12.0
⑦ Dasher: 12.2
⑧ 10.0 Rabbit; 10.6 Jetta, Convertible, Scirocco; 15.8 Quantum; 15 Pickup

maintenance. Remember, however, there's no law requiring honesty from private citizens selling used cars. There is a law that forbids the tampering with or turning back the odometer mileage. This includes both the private citizen and the lot owner. The law also requires that the seller or anyone transferring ownership of the car must provide the buyer with a signed statement indicating the mileage on the odometer at the time of transfer.

5. Write down the year, model and serial number before you buy any used car. Then dial 1-800-424-9393, the toll free number of the National Highway Traffic Safety Administration, and ask if the car has ever been included on any manufacturer's recall list. If so, make sure the needed repairs were made.

6. Use the Used Car Checklist in this section and check all the items on the used car you are considering. Some items are more important than others. You know how much money you can afford for repairs, and, depending on the price of the car, may consider doing any needed work yourself. Beware, however, of trouble in areas that will affect operation, safety or emission. Problems in the Used Car Checklist break down as follows:

1–8: Two or more problems in these areas

indicate a lack of maintenance. You should beware.

9–13: Indicates a lack of proper care, however, these can usually be corrected with a tune-up or relatively simple parts replacement.

14–17: Problems in the engine or transmission can be very expensive. Walk away from any car with problems in both of these areas.

7. If you are satisfied with the apparent condition of the car, take it to an independent diagnostic center or mechanic for a complete check. If you have a state inspection program, have it inspected immediately before purchase, or specify on the bill of sale that the sale is conditional on passing state inspection.

8. Road test the car. Refer to the Road Test Checklist in this section. If your original evaluation and the road test agree, the rest is up to you.

Used Car Checklist

NOTE: *The numbers on the illustrations refer to the numbers on this checklist.*

1. Mileage: Average mileage is about 12,000 miles per year. More than average mileage may indicate hard usage. 1975 and later catalytic converter equipped models may need converter service at 50,000 miles.

2. Paint: Check around the tailpipe, molding and windows for overspray indicating that the car has been repainted.

3. Rust: Check fenders, doors, rocker panels, window moldings, wheelwells, floorboards, under floormats, and in the trunk for signs of rust. Any rust at all will be a problem. There is no way to check the spread of rust, except to replace the part or panel.

4. Body appearance: Check the moldings, bumpers, grille, vinyl roof, glass, doors, trunk lid and body panels for general overall condition. Check for misalignment, loose holddown clips, ripples, scratches in glass, rips or patches in the top. Mismatched paint, welding in the trunk, severe misalignment of body panels or ripples may indicate crash work.

5. Leaks: Get down and look under the car. There are no normal leaks, other than water from the air conditioning condenser.

6. Tires: Check the tire air pressure. A common trick is to pump the tire pressure up to make the car roll easier. Check the tread wear, open the trunk and check the spare too. Uneven wear is a clue that the front end needs alignment. See the troubleshooting chapter for clues to the causes of tire wear.

7. Shock absorbers: Check the shock absorbers by forcing downward sharply on each corner of the car. Good shocks will not allow the car to bounce more than twice after you let go.

8. Interior: Check the entire interior. You're looking for an interior condition that agrees with the overall condition of the car. Reasonable wear is expected, but be suspicious of new seatcovers on sagging seats, new pedal pads, and worn armrests. These indicate an attempt to cover up hard use. Pull back the carpets and look for evidence of water leaks or flooding. Look for missing hardware, door handles, control knobs, etc. Check lights and signal operations. Make sure all accessories (air conditioner, heater, radio, etc.) work. Check windshield wiper operation.

9. Belts and Hoses: Open the hood and check all belts and hoses for wear, cracks or weak spots.

10. Battery: Low electrolyte level, corroded terminals and/or cracked case indicate a lack of maintenance.

11. Radiator: Look for corrosion or rust in the coolant indicating a lack of maintenance.

12. Air filter: A dirty air filter usually means a lack of maintenance.

13. Ignition Wires: Check the ignition wires for cracks, burned spots, or wear. Worn wires will have to be replaced.

14. Oil level: If the oil level is low, chances are the engine uses oil or leaks. Beware of water in the oil (cracked block), excessively thick oil (used to quiet a noisy engine), or thin, dirty oil with a distinct gasoline smell (internal engine problems).

15. Automatic Transmission: Pull the transmission dipstick out when the engine is running. The level should read Full, and the fluid should be clear or bright red. Dark brown or black fluid that has distinct burnt odor, signals a transmission in need of repair or overhaul.

16. Exhaust: Check the color of the exhaust smoke. Blue smoke indicates, among other problems, worn rings. Black smoke can indicate burnt valves or carburetor problems. Check the exhaust system for leaks. It can be expensive to replace.

17. Spark Plugs: Remove one of the spark plugs (the most accessible will do). An engine in good condition will show plugs with a light tan or gray deposit on the firing tip. See the color Tune-Up tips section for spark plug conditions.

Road Test Check List

1. Engine Performance: The car should be peppy whether cold or warm, with adequate power and good pickup. It should respond smoothly through the gears.

2. Brakes: They should provide quick, firm

stops with no noise, pulling or brake fade.

3. Steering: Sure control with no binding, harshness, or looseness and no shimmy in the wheel should be expected. Noise or vibration from the steering wheel when turning the car means trouble.

4. Clutch (Manual Transmission): Clutch action should give quick, smooth response with easy shifting. The clutch pedal should have about 1 to 1½ inches of free-play before it disengages the clutch. Start the engine, set the parking brake, put the transmission in first gear and slowly release the clutch pedal. The engine should begin to stall when the pedal is ½–¾ of the way up.

5. Automatic Transmission: The transmission should shift rapidly and smoothly, with no noise, hesitation, or slipping.

6. Differential: No noise or thumps should be present. Differentials have no normal leaks.

7. Driveshaft, Universal Joints: Vibration and noise could mean driveshaft problems. Clicking at low speed or coast conditions means worn U-joints.

8. Suspension: Try hitting bumps at different speeds. A car that bounces has weak shock absorbers. Clunks mean worn bushings or ball joints.

9. Frame: Wet the tires and drive in a straight line. Tracks should show two straight lines, not four. Four tire tracks indicate a frame bent by collision damage. If the tires can't be wet for this purpose, have a friend drive along behind you and see if the car appears to be traveling in a straight line.

Tune-Up and Performance Maintenance

2

Emission Standards
CO Volume (%) at idle:

		49 States US Models	California Models
1974–75 (all models)	Manual Trans.	2.0±0.5	2.0±0.5
	Auto Trans.	2.0±0.5	2.0±0.5
1976 (all models)	Manual Trans.	1.5	0.5
	Auto Trans.	1.0	0.5
1977–78 (all models)	Manual Trans.	1.5 max.	0.3 max.
	Auto Trans.	1.0 max.	0.3 max.
1979–87 (see note)	Manual Trans.	0.6+0.4 ①	0.5+0.4 ②
	Auto Trans.	0.6+0.4 ①	0.5+0.4 ②

NOTE: 1980 California and all models, 1981 and later have sealed CO screw to prevent unauthorized adjustment. Special tools (frequency counter, CO tester, etc.) are required which are usually not available to the general public.

NOTE: When adjusting CO volume, always use the percentage given on your vehicles underhood sticker.

① Measured at the tail pipe

② Measured before the catalytic converter

Diesel Tune-Up Specifications

Model	Valve Clearance (cold) ①		Intake Valve Opens (deg)	Injection Pump Setting (deg)	Injection Nozzle Pressure (psi)		Idle Speed (rpm)	Cranking Compression Pressure (psi)
	Intake (in.)	Exhaust (in.)			New	Used		
Diesel (All Models)	0.006–0.010	0.014–0.018	N.A.	Align marks	1849	1706	770–870 ②	406 minimum

① Warm clearance given—Cold clearance: Intake 0.006–0.010
Exhaust 0.014–0.018

② Volkswagen has lowered the idle speed on early models to this specification.

Valve clearance need not be adjusted unless it varies more than 0.002 in. from specification

N.A. Not Available

TUNE-UP PROCEDURES

Diesels do not require tune-ups as such. Your gasoline VW should be tuned including points and plugs, at least 12,000 mile intervals. The tune-up is a good time to take a look around the engine compartment for beginning problems and head them off before they get expensive. Look for oil and fuel leaks, deteriorating radiator or heater hoses, loose and/or frayed fan belt, etc. These little items have the tendency to develop into major headaches, so don't overlook anything.

Gasoline Engine Tune-Up Specifications

Year, Model	Engine Displacement cc (Cu in.)	Spark Plugs		Distributor		Ignition Timing (deg)	Intake Valve Opens (deg)	Compression Pressure (psi)	Idle Speed (rpm)	Valve Clearance (in.)	
		Type	Gap (in.)	Point Dwell (deg)	Point Gap (in.)					In ⑥	Ex ⑥
1974 Dasher	1,471 (90)	W175 T30 N8Y	0.024–0.028	44–50 ①	0.016	3 ATDC @ Idle	4 BTDC	142–184	850–1000	0.008–0.012	0.016–0.020
1975 Dasher	1,588 (1,471 Canada)	W200 T30 N8Y	0.024–0.028	44–50	0.016	3 ATDC @ Idle	4 BTDC	142–184	850–1000	0.008–0.012	0.016–0.020
1975 Rabbit, Scirocco	1,471 (90)	W200 T30 N8Y	0.024–0.028	44–50	0.016	3 ATDC @ Idle	4 BTDC	142–184	850–1000	0.008–0.012	0.016–0.020
1976–79 Dasher	1,588 (97)	W215 T30 N7Y	0.024–0.028	44–50	0.016	3 ATDC @ Idle	4 BTDC	142–184	850–1000	0.008–0.012	0.016–0.020
1976 Rabbit, Scirocco	1,588 (97)	W200 T30 N8Y	0.024–0.028	44–50	0.016	3 ATDC @ Idle	4 BTDC	142–184	850–1000	0.008–0.012	0.016–0.020
1977 Rabbit, Scirocco	1,588 (97)	W215 T30 N7Y	0.024–0.028	44–50	0.016	3 ATDC @ Idle	4 BTDC	142–184	850–1000	0.008–0.012	0.016–0.020
1978 Rabbit, Scirocco	1,457 (89)	W175 T30 N8Y	0.024–0.028	44–50	0.016	②	4 BTDC	142–184	850–1000	0.008–0.012	0.016–0.020
1979 Rabbit	1,457 (89)	W175 T30 N8Y	0.024–0.032	44–50	0.016	3 ATDC @ Idle	4 BTDC	142–184	850–1000	0.008–0.012	0.016–0.020
1979 Scirocco	1,588 (97)	W175 T30 N8Y	0.024–0.032	44–50	0.016	3 ATDC @ Idle	4 BTDC	142–184	850–1000	0.008–0.012	0.016–0.020
1980–81 Dasher (49 states)	1,588 (97)	W175 T30 N8Y	0.024–0.032	44–50 ⑦	0.016 ⑦	3 ATDC @ Idle	4 BTDC	142–184	850–1000 ⑧	0.008–0.012	0.016–0.020
1980–81 Dasher (California)	1,588 (97)	WR7DS N8GY	0.024–0.028	Electronic		3 ATDC @ Idle	4 BTDC	142–184	880–1000	0.008–0.012	0.016–0.020
1980–83 Rabbit, Jetta, Scirocco, Quantum (49 states)	1,588 (97) ③	W175 T30 N8Y	0.024–0.032	44–50 ⑦	0.016 ⑦	3 ATDC @ Idle ⑨	4 BTDC	142–184 ⑩	850–1000 ⑧	0.008–0.012	0.016–0.020

Year / Model	Engine Displacement cc (cu. in.)	Spark Plugs Type	Gap (in.)	Distributor	Ignition Timing @ Idle	(deg.)	Fuel Pump Pressure	Idle Speed (rpm)	Valve Clearance Intake (in.)	Valve Clearance Exhaust (in.)
1980–83 Rabbit, Jetta, Scirocco, Quantum (California)	1,588 (97) ③	WR7DS N8GY	0.024–0.028	Electronic	3 ATDC @ Idle	4 BTDC	142–184 ⑩	880–1000	0.008–0.012	0.016–0.020
1983 GTI, Scirocco	1,790 (109)	WR7DS N8GY	0.024–0.032	Electronic	6 BTDC @ Idle	—	131–174	875–1000	0.008–0.012	0.016–0.020
1983 Quantum	2,144 (131)	N8Y	0.035	Electronic	3 ATDC @ Idle	—	120–170	800–1000	0.008–0.012	0.016–0.020
1984 Rabbit, Jetta, GTI, Scirocco, Quantum (49 states)	1,715 (105.0)	W175 T30 N8Y	0.024–0.032	Electronic	6 BTDC @ Idle	4 BTDC	131–174	850–1000 ⑧	0.008–0.012	0.016–0.020
1984 Rabbit, Jetta, GTI, Scirocco, Quantum (California)	1,715 (105.0)	WR7DS N8GY	0.024–0.028	Electronic	6 BTDC @ Idle	4 BTDC	131–174	880–1000	0.008–0.012	0.016–0.020
1985 Scirocco, Golf, Jetta, GTI, (49 states)	1,780 (109)	WR7DS N8GY	0.024–0.032	Electronic	6 BTDC @ Idle	6 BTDC	123–174	850–1000	0.008–0.012	.016–.020
1985 Quantum	2,226 (136)	W7DC N9YC	0.024–0.032	Electronic	6 BTDC	6 BTDC	123–174	850–1000	.008–.012	.016–.020
1986–87 All					See Underhood Sticker					

NOTE: The underhood sticker often reflects tune-up specification changes made in production. Sticker figures must be used if they disagree with those in this chart.

① 47°–53° California
② 3 ATDC @ Idle with CIS fuel injection; 7½ BTDC @ Idle with 34 PICT-5 Carburetor
③ Non-California Rabbit with 1 barrel carburetor—1980; 1,457 cc (89 cu. in.)
④ California Rabbit
⑤ Non-California Rabbit with fuel injection
⑥ Valve clearance need not be adjusted unless it varies more than 0.002 in. from specifications.
⑦ 1981 and later have Electronic ignition
⑧ w/o Idle stabilizer
⑨ Non-Cal. Rabbit w/1 bbl. timing 7½° BTDC; 1983 w/Manual Trans; timing 6° BTDC
⑩ 1982 and later; 131–174 psi

Spark Plugs (Gasoline Engine Only)

Their primary job of igniting the air/fuel mixture aside, the spark plugs in your engine can also serve as very useful diagnostic tools. Once removed, compare your spark plugs with the samples illustrated in the "Fuel Economy and tune-Up Tips" section. typical plug conditions are shown along with their causes and remedies. Plugs which exhibit only normal wear and deposits can be cleaned, regapped, and installed. However, it is a good practice to replace them at every major tune-up.

Tool kits for spark plug changing are available at most tool outlets. The tool kit includes a spark plug socket and handle, but you will find it much more convenient to purchase a ½" drive, ¹³⁄₁₆" spark plug socket which can be turned with a ratchet handle. Using a small extension, all four plugs can be removed very quickly. Before removing the spark plug leads, number the tower on the distributor cap with tape. The firing order is 1-3-4-2 or 1-2-4-5-3 (five cylinder engine) with the No. 1 cylinder at the right of the engine on the Rabbit, Jetta and Scirocco, and at the front of the engine on the Dasher, Fox and Quantum. This prevents mixups in the case of distributor cap replacement or spark plug wire replacement.

SPARK PLUG HEAT RANGE

While spark plug heat range has always seemed to be somewhat of an obtuse subject for many people, in reality the entire subject is quite simple. Basically, it boils down to this; the amount of heat the plug absorbs is determined by the length of the lower insulator. The longer the insulator (or the farther it extends into the engine), the hotter the plug will operate; the shorter the insulator the cooler it will operate. A plug that absorbs little head and remains too cool will quickly accumulate deposits of oil and carbon since it is not hot enough to burn them off. This leads to plug fouling and consequently to misfiring. A plug that absorbs too much heat will have no deposits, but, due to the excessive heat, the electrodes will burn away quickly and in some instances, preignition may result. Preignition takes place when plug tips get so hot that they glow sufficiently to ignite the fuel/air mixture before the actual spark occurs. This early ignition will usually cause a pinging during low speeds and heavy loads. In severe cases, the heat may become high enough to start the fuel/air mixture burning throughout the combustion chamber rather than just to the front of the plug as in normal operation. At this time, the piston is rising in the cylinder making its compression stroke. The burning mass is compressed and an explo-

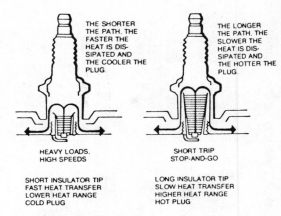

Spark plug heat range

sion results, forcing the piston back down in the cylinder while it is still trying to go up. Obviously, something must go, and it does—pistons are often damaged.

The general rule of thumb for choosing the correct heat range when picking a spark plug is: if most of your driving is long distance, high speed travel, use a colder plug; if most of your driving is stop and go, use a hotter plug. Factory installed plugs are, of course, compromise plugs, since the factory has no way of knowing what sort of driving you do. It should be noted that most people never have occasion to change their plugs from the factory recommended heat range.

REMOVAL AND INSTALLATION

1. Grasp the spark plug boot, twist and pull straight out. Don't pull on the wire. If the boot(s) are cracked, replace them.
2. Place the spark plug socket firmly on the plug. Turn the spark plug out of the cylinder head in a counterclockwise direction.

NOTE: *The cylinder head is aluminum, which is easily stripped. Remove plugs only when the engine is cold.*

If removal is difficult, loosen the plug only slightly and drip penetrating oil onto the threads. Allow the oil time enough to work and then unscrew the plug. This will prevent damaging the threads in the cylinder head. Be sure to keep the socket straight to avoid breaking the ceramic insulator.

3. Continue on and remove the remaining spark plugs.
4. Inspect the plugs using the "Tune-Up Tips" section illustrations and then clean or discard them according to condition.

New spark plugs come pre-gapped, but double check the setting or reset them if you desire a different gap. The recommended spark plug gas is listed in the "Tune-Up Specifications"

Remove the spark plug wire by grasping the boot; don't pull on the cable

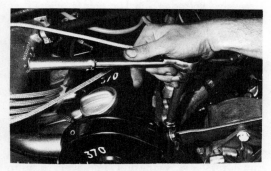

A spark plug socket, extension and ratchet will greatly speed spark plug removal

chart. Use a spark plug wire gauge for checking the gap. The wire should pass through the electrode with just a slight drag. Using the electrode bending tool on the end of the gauge, bend the side electrode to adjust the gap. Never attempt to adjust the center electrode. Lightly oil the threads of the replacement plug and install it handtight. It is a good practice to use a torque wrench to tighten the spark plugs on any car and especially since the head is aluminum. Torque is 22 ft.lb. Install the ignition wire boots firmly on the spark plugs.

CHECKING AND REPLACING SPARK PLUG CABLES

Visually inspect the spark plug cables for burns, cuts, or breaks in the insulation. Check the spark plug boots and the nipples on the distributor cap and coil. Replace any damaged wiring. If no physical damage is obvious, the wires can be checked with an ohmmeter for excessive resistance. Remove the distributor cap and leave the wires connected to the cap. Connect one lead of the ohmmeter to the corre-

sponding electrode inside the cap and the other lead to the spark plug terminal (remove it from the spark plug for the test). Replace any wire which shows over 50,000Ω. Generally speaking, however, resistance should not run over 35,000Ω and 50,000Ω should be considered the outer limits of acceptability. It should be remembered that wire resistance is a function of

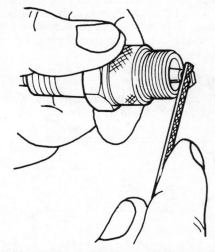

Plugs in good condition can be filed and re-used

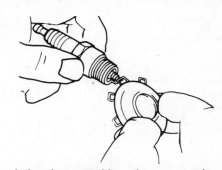

Check the plug gap with a wire gauge only

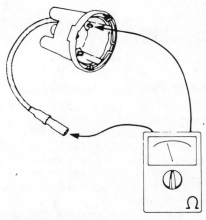

Checking plug wire resistance

length, and that the longer the cable, the greater the resistance. Thus, if the cables on your car are longer than the factory originals, resistance will be higher and quite possibly outside of these limits.

When installing a new set of spark plug cables, replace the cables one at a time so there will be no mixup. Start by replacing the longest cable first. Install the boot firmly over the spark plug. Route the wire exactly the same as the original. Insert the nipple firmly into the tower on the distributor cap. Repeat the process for each cable.

Firing Orders

NOTE: *To avoid confusion, remove and tag the wires one at a time, for replacement.*

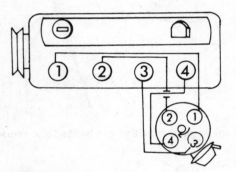

Firing order—1-3-4-2

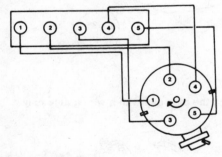

Firing order; 1-2-4-5-3

Breaker Points and Condenser

The points function as a circuit breaker for the primary circuit of the ignition system. the ignition coil must boost the 12 volts of electrical pressure supplied by the battery to as much as 25,000 volts in order to fire the plugs. To do this, the coil depends on the points and the condenser to make a clean break in the primary circuit.

The coil has both primary and secondary circuits. When the ignition is turned on, the battery supplies voltage through the coil and onto the points. The points are connected to ground, completing the primary circuit. As the current passes through the coil, a magnetic field is created in the iron center core of the coil. When the cam in the distributor turns, the points open, breaking the primary circuit of the coil then collapses and cuts through the secondary circuit windings around the iron core. Because of the physical principle called "electromagnetic induction," the battery voltage is increased to a level sufficient to fire the spark plugs.

When the points open, the electrical charge in the primary circuit tries to jump the gap created between the two open contacts of the points. If this electrical charge were not transferred elsewhere, the metal contacts of the points would start to change rapidly.

The function of the condenser is to absorb excessive voltage from the points when they open and thus prevent the points from becoming pitted or burned.

If you have ever wondered why it is necessary to tune-up your engine occasionally, consider the fact that the ignition system must complete the above cycle each time a spark plug fires. On a four cylinder, four cylinder engine, two of the four plugs must fire once for every engine revolution. If the idle speed of an engine were 800 revolutions per minute (800 rpm), the breaker points open and close two times for each revolution. For every minute the engine idles, the points open and close 1600 times (2x800 = 1600). And that is just at idle, what about at 55 mph?

There are two ways to check to check breaker point gap: with a feeler gauge or with a dwell meter. Either way you set the points, you are adjusting the amount of time (in degrees of distributor rotation) that the points will remain open. If you adjust the points with a feeler gauge, you are setting the maximum amount the points will open when the rubber block on the points is on a high point of the distributor cam. When you adjust the points with a dwell meter, you are measuring the number of degrees (of distributor cam rotation) that the points will remain closed before they start to open as a high point of the distributor cam approaches the rubbing block of the points.

There are two rules that should always be followed when adjusting or replacing the points. The points and condenser are a matched set; never replace one without replacing the other. If you change point gap or dwell of the engine, you also change the ignition timing. Therefore, if you adjust the points, you must also adjust the timing.

INSPECTION OF THE POINTS

1. Disconnect the high tension wire which runs between the distributor and the ignition coil.

2. Remove the static shield which is fitted around the distributor cap, if equipped.

3. The distributor cap is held down by two spring clips. Insert a screwdriver under their ends and release them. Lift off the cap with the spark plug wires attached. Lift off the cap with the spark plug wires attached. Wipe the inside of the cap clean with a rag and check for burned contacts, cracks or carbon tracks. Carbon tracks are dark lines running from one terminal to another. They cannot be successfully removed, so replace the cap if it has any tracks.

4. Remove the rotor from the distributor shaft by pulling it straight up. Examine the condition of the rotor, if it is cracked or if the metal tip is excessively worn or burned, it should be replaced. If not, clean the tip with a clean cloth.

CAUTION: *Do not file the contact tip on the rotor.*

5. Pry open the points with a screwdriver and check the condition of the contacts. If they are excessively worn, burned or pitted, they should be replaced.

6. If the points are in good condition, adjust them and replace the rotor and the distributor cap. If they need to be replaced, follow the replacement procedure given next.

REPLACEMENT OF THE BREAKER POINTS AND CONDENSER

1. Remove the cap and rotor as outlined in the previous section.

2. Remove the dust shield and loosen the screws securing the points (if possible, use a magnetic screwdriver for removal to avoid losing a screw down into the distributor). Slide the point wire connector off of its terminal and remove the point set.

3. The condenser is located on the outside of the distributor body. Pull the wire connector coming from the suppressor off of the condenser terminal. Remove the screw that secures the condenser assembly to the distributor body and remove the assembly.

4. Before installing the new points and condenser, place a small dab of grease on the distributor shaft a smear it evenly around the

On 1979 and later distributors, unfasten ground strap (1), suppressor lead at suppressor (2), and suppressor lead at distributor body (3) to remove distributor cap

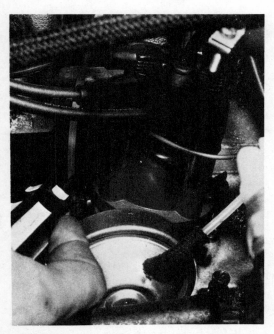

Unsnap the distributor cap retaining clips with a screwdriver

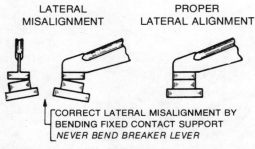

LATERAL MISALIGNMENT   PROPER LATERAL ALIGNMENT

CORRECT LATERAL MISALIGNMENT BY BENDING FIXED CONTACT SUPPORT
NEVER BEND BREAKER LEVER

Points must be correctly aligned

cam. Install the new points and condenser. Tighten the condenser mounting screw but leave the points screws loose.

5. Make sure that the faces of the points meet squarely. If not, the fixed mount can be bent slightly with a little force and a pair of needle nose pliers. Do not bend the movable contact.

6. The point gap must be adjusted next. The gap is adjusted with the rubbing block of the points resting on one of the high spots of the distributor cam. To get it there, the engine can be rotated by bumping the starter with the ignition key, or the crankshaft can be turned with a wrench on the crankshaft pulley bolt; this is easier to do with the spark plugs removed.

7. Insert a 0.017" flat feeler gauge between the points. A slight drag should be felt. If no drag can be felt, or if the gauge can't be insert-

ed at all, insert a screwdriver into the notch provided for adjustment and use it to open or close the gap between the points until it is correct.

8. When you feel the gap is set, tighten the points screws and recheck the gap. Sometimes it takes three or four times to get it corrected, so don't feel frustrated if they seem to move around on you a little. It's not easy to feel the correct gap either. To check yourself, use gauges 0.002" larger and smaller than 0.016" as a test. If the points are spread slightly by a 0.018" gauge, but not touched at all by a 0.014" gauge, the testing should be right.

9. After all the adjustments are complete, pull a clean piece of tissue or a piece of white paper between the contacts to clear away any bits of grit.

10. Replace the dust cover, the rotor and the distributor cap. Snap on the spring clips and replace the static shield. If you have a dwell meter (recommended) you should next set the dwell. Otherwise, go on to the ignition timing section.

Dwell Angle

The dwell angle is the number of degrees of distributor cam rotation through which the points remain closed (conducting electricity). Increasing the point gap decreases dwell, while decreasing the gap increases dwell.

The dwell angle may be checked with the distributor cap and rotor installed and the engine running, or with the cap and rotor removed and the engine cranking at starter speed. The meter gives a constant reading with the engine running. With the engine cranking, the meter will fluctuate between zero degrees dwell and the maximum figure for that setting. Never attempt to adjust the points when the ignition is on, or you may receive a shock.

ADJUSTMENT WITH A DWELL METER

NOTE: *The dwell angle on all cars with electronic ignition is set at the factory and is not adjustable.*

1. Connect a meter as per the manufacturer's instructions (usually one lead to the distributor's terminal of the coil and the other lead to a ground). Zero the meter, if necessary.

2. Check the dwell by either the cranking method, or with the engine running. If the setting is correct, the points must be adjusted.

CAUTION: *Keep your hands, hair and clothing clear of the engine fan and pulleys. Be sure the wires from the dwell meter are routed out of the way. If the engine is running, block the front wheels, put the transmission in Neutral, or Park, and set the parking brake.*

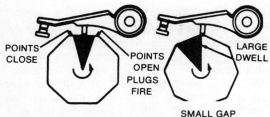

Dwell angle

3. To change the dwell angle, turn the ignition off, loosen the points hold down screw and adjust the point gap; increase the gap to decrease dwell, and vice versa. Tighten the hold down screw and check the dwell angle with the engine cranking. If it seems to be correct, replace the cap and rotor and check dwell with the engine running. Readjust as necessary.

4. Run the engine speed up to about 2,500 rpm, and then let the speed drop abruptly; the dwell reading should not change. If it does, a worn distributor shaft, bushing or cam, or a worn breaker plate is indicted. The parts must be inspected and replaced if necessary.

5. After adjusting the dwell angle, go on to the "Ignition Timing" section following.

Hall Effect Electronic Ignition System

Electronic ignition systems offer many advantages over the conventional breaker point ignition system. By eliminating the points, maintenance requirements are greatly reduced. An electronic ignition system is capable of producing much higher voltage which in turn aids starting, reduces spark plug fouling and provides better emission control.

NOTE: *This book contains simple testing procedures for your Volkswagon's electronic ignition. More comprehensive testing on this system and other electronic control systems on your Volkswagon can be found in Chilton's Guide To Electronic Engine Controls, book part number 7535, available at your local retailer*

The Hall generator produces a voltage pulse which is sent to the control unit, which in turn switches the primary ignition circuit on and off.

The Hall generator, which is located in the distributor, consists of a trigger wheel that revolves with the distributor shaft and a stationary unit called the Hall sender. The Hall sender consists of a semiconductor layer positioned on a magnetically conducting element and a permanent magnet, both of which are separated by an air gap. When the trigger wheel shutter enters the air gap, it blocks the magnetic field and the Hall sender is shut off. When this occurs, the control unit will complete the primary circuit and you have the dwell period. When the shutter leaves the air gap, the magnetic field flows again. The Hall sender generates a voltage pulse to the control unit which will then interrupt the primary ignition circuit and ignition will occur.

Because temperature changes and engine load variations caused by different electrical accessories can effect idle quality and speed, many cars equipped with the Hall generator also use an electronic idle stabilization system. This system consists of a small control unit in between the Hall generator and the main control unit. The frequency of the voltage signal sent from the Hall generator gives the idle stabilizer information on engine speed. When the idle stabilizer senses that the engine speed has dropped below a certain rpm, it will trigger the main control unit (faster than the Hall generator) which will advance the timing, causing the idle speed to increase. To check the idle stabilizer:

1. Disconnect both plugs from the idle stabilizer unit and connect them together.

NOTE: *The idle stabilizer is connected to the main control unit, at the rear of the engine compartment, under the air plenum.*

2. Start the engine.

3. Hook up a dwell/tachometer and reduce the idle speed to 750 rpm.

4. Turn the engine off, pull the two plugs apart and reconnect them to the idle stabilizer unit.

5. Start the engine. The idle speed should increase to normal (see Specifications chart). If it does not return to normal, replace the idle stabilizer.

ELECTRONIC IGNITION PRECAUTIONS

When working on the Hall ignition, observe the following precautions to prevent damage to the ignition system.

1. Connect and disconnect test equipment only when the ignition switch is OFF.

2. On the carbureted Rabbit, if you use a conventional tachometer, you will have to rig up an adapter. See below for instructions.

3. Do not crank the engine with the starter for compression tests, etc., until the high tension coil wire (terminal 4) is grounded.

4. Do not replace the original equipment coil with a conventional coil.

5. Do not install any kind of condenser to coil terminal 1.

6. Do not use a battery booster for longer than 1 (one) minute.

7. On the fuel injected models, do not tow cars with defective ignitions systems without disconnecting the plugs at the ignition control unit.

TACHOMETER ADAPTATION (CARBURET-ED RABBITS)

An adapter must be used when connecting a conventional tachometer to the Hall Effect ignition system to prevent damage to the ignition components. Use the illustration as a guide. All components will be available to you locally. Connect the positive wire of the tachometer to the adapter and the negative wire to the ground.

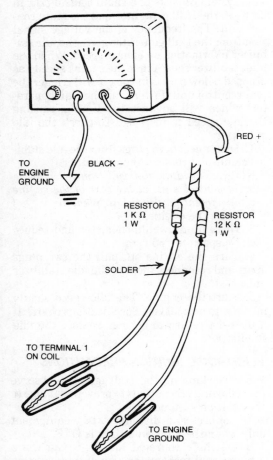

Fabricate this adapter for your tachometer on carbureted models with electronic ignition

IGNITION COIL TEST

A defective Hall ignition coil cannot be checked with standard coil testing equipment. If there is no high tension current and all other components of the ignition system check out, see if you're getting a spark from the coil wire to the distributor cap by unplugging the coil wire at the distributor, holding the end of it with insulated pliers about ½" from ground (engine block, etc.) and turning over the engine. If a weak or no spark is obtained, try replacing the coil.

HALL PICKUP UNIT TEST

1. Check for voltage on terminal 15 (+) of the ignition coil. There should be voltage with the ignition ON.

2. Ground the high tension coil wire.

3. Connect a test light (4 to 24 volts) between terminal 15(+) and terminal 1 (–).

4. Crank the engine with the starter for approximately 5 seconds. The test light should flicker. If not, replace the ignition distributor.

IGNITION CONTROL UNIT TEST

1. On fuel injected models, disconnect the plugs at the control unit and connect the plugs to each other. Ground high tension coil wire on carbureted Rabbit.

2. Turn the ignition switch on and make sure there is current at terminal 15(+) of the ignition coil. Turn the ignition OFF.

3. Disconnect the high tension wire between the ignition coil and the distributor at the distributor on fuel injected models.

4. Disconnect the wire (plug) between the control unit and the distributor at the distributor.

5. Connect the positive (+) terminal of the voltmeter to terminal 1 of the ignition coil and the negative (–) terminal to ground.

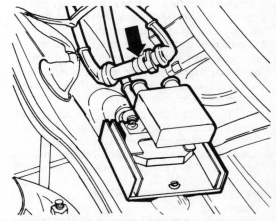

Disconnect plugs at the control unit and plug them together (electronic ignition)

Electronic Ignition Testing Specifications

Component Tested	Specification
Rotor resistance	1000 ohm; rotor must be marked R1
Ignition Timing: CIS	3° ± 2° ATDC when checking ①
	3° ± 1° ATDC when adjusting ①
Carburetor	7½° BTDC
Vacuum hoses during testing	Connected (CIS)
	Disconnect retard hose and plug (carburetor)
	TYF Carb. disconnect and plug both hoses
Ignition coil primary resistance:	0.52–0.76 ohms
Resistance between positive and negative terminals	
Ignition coil secondary resistance:	2400–3500 ohms
Resistance between negative terminal and coil tower	

① 1983–85 models with CIS and manual transmission—6° BTDC ± 2°

6. Turn the ignition ON. There must be a voltage reading of at least 12 volts. If voltage drops below 12 volts in one second, turn off the ignition. The control unit is defective and will have to be replaced.

7. Disconnect the green wire where it connects to the distributor and ground the wire.

Turn the ignition switch ON. The voltmeter should read about 12 volts. Disconnect the ground wire. The voltage should drop to 6 volts. If not, replace the control unit. Turn off the ignition.

8. On fuel injected models connect the terminals of the voltmeter to the outer connector of the control unit. Connect the positive (+) lead to the red wire and the negative (–) lead to the brown wire. Switch on the ignition. The voltmeter should read about 10 volts. If not, replace the control unit.

Ignition Timing (Gasoline Engine Only)

CAUTION: *When performing this or any other operation with the engine running, be very careful of the alternator belt and pulleys. Make sure that your timing light wires don't interfere with the belt.*

Ignition timing is an important part of the tune-up. It is always adjusted after the points are gapped (dwell angle changed), on breaker point ignitions, since altering the dwell affects the timing. Three basic types of timing lights are available, the neon, the DC, and the AC powered. Of the three, the DC light is the most frequently used by professional tuners. The bright flash put out by the DC light makes the timing marks stand out on even the brightest of days. Another advantage of the DC light is that you don't need to be near an electrical outlet. Neon timing lights are available for a few dollars, but their weak flash makes it necessary to use them in a fairly dark work area.

One neon light lead is attached to the spark plug and the other to the plug wire. The DC light attaches to the spark plug and the wire with an adapter and two clips attach to the battery posts for power. The AC unit is similar, except that the power cable is plugged into a house outlet. If your particular car has electronic ignition, you should use a timing light with an inductive pickup. The pickup simply clamps onto the No. 1 plug wire, eliminating an adapter. This type light is not susceptible to crossfiring or false triggering which may occur with a conventional light, due to the greater voltages produced by electronic ignitions.

BREAKER-POINT IGNITION SYSTEMS

1. Attach the timing light as outlined above or according to the manufacturer's instructions. Hook-up a dwell/tachometer since you'll need an rpm indication for correct timing.

2. Locate the timing mark opening in the clutch or torque converter housing at the rear of the engine directly behind the distributor. The OT mark stands for TDC or 0° advance. The other mark designates the correct timing position. Mark them with chalk so that they will be more visible. Don't disconnect the vacuum line.

3. Start the engine and allow it to reach the normal operating temperature. The engine should be running at normal idle speed.

4. Shine the timing light at the marks.

5. The light should now be flashing when the timing mark and the V-shaped pointer are aligned.

6. If not, loosen the distributor hold-down bolt and rotate the distributor very slowly to align the marks.

7. Tighten the mounting nut when the ignition timing is correct.

8. Recheck the timing when the distributor is secured.

CAUTION

Before starting to work on any part of
electrical system disconnect battery
ground strap

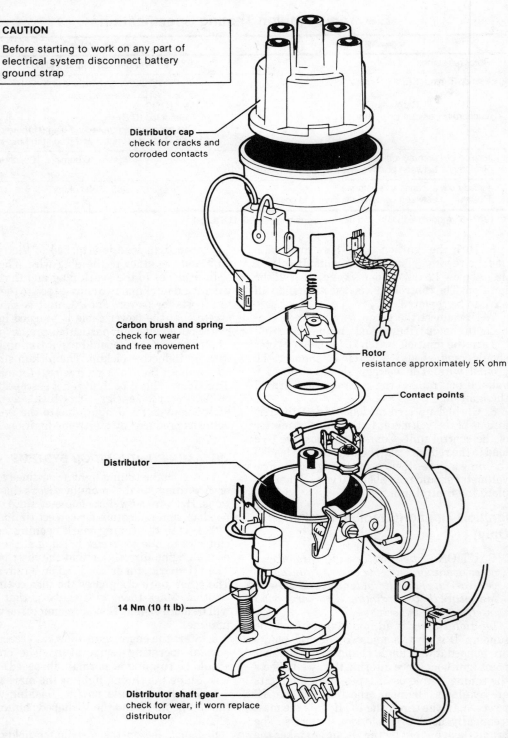

Distributor cap
check for cracks and
corroded contacts

Carbon brush and spring
check for wear
and free movement

Rotor
resistance approximately 5K ohm

Contact points

Distributor

14 Nm (10 ft lb)

Distributor shaft gear
check for wear, if worn replace
distributor

Typical breaker point type distributor

ELECTRONIC IGNITION SYSTEMS

1. Run the engine to operating temperature. Connect tachometer. See Electronic Ignition Precautions, above.

2. Stop the engine. Disconnect the idle stabilizer plugs at the control unit and plug them together. On the carbureted Rabbit, disconnect the vacuum retard hose and plug. Models with TYF carburetor, disconnect and plug both lines.

3. Check the idle speed. It should be 800–1000 rpm on carbureted Rabbit and normal on all others.

4. With your timing light attached according to manufacturers instructions, shine the light on the timing hold. The pointer in the hole must line up with the notch in the flywheel. To adjust the timing, loosen the distributor at its base and turn it.

5. On the carbureted Rabbit, reinstall the vacuum hose(s). Idle speed should drop to 600–750 rpm.

6. Stop the engine and reconnect the plugs at the control unit. On the carbureted Rabbit, start the engine and rev it a few times to activate the idle stabilizer. On the carbureted Rabbit, the idle speed should now be 850–950 rpm.

Locate the timing mark opening (arrow) in the clutch or torque converter housing. This 1980 Jetta has plastic cover over timing hole—many earlier models do not

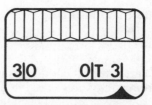

Dasher timing marks seen through opening on transmission bell housing

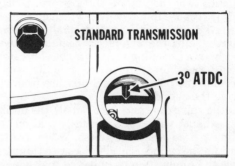

Typical timing mark for models with CIS. GTI and Scirocco (with 1.8) timed at 6° BTDC

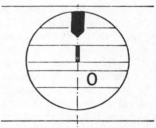

Timing mark for 1978 and 1980 34 PICT-5 Carburetor (7½° BTDC)

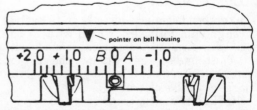

Westmoreland Rabbits with a 200 mm clutch may have a "universal" flywheel. Each timing mark is equal to 2°. Marks to the left of the 0 are BTDC, to the right ATDC

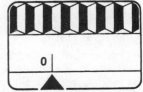

1980 electronic ignition Dashers have only one mark for correct timing (3° ATDC)

Valve Lash (All Models)

Valve adjustment is one factor which determines how far the intake and exhaust valves open into the cylinder. If the valve clearance is too large, part of the lift of the camshaft will be used in removing the excessive clearance, therefore the valves will not open far enough. This has two ill effects; one, the valve gear will become noisy as the excess clearance is taken up and, two, the engine will perform poorly. This is because intake valves which don't open the full distance will admit a smaller air/fuel mixture into the cylinders. Exhaust valves which aren't opening the full amount create a greater back pressure in the cylinder which prevents the proper air/fuel mixture from entering the cylinder.

If the valve clearance is too small, the intake and exhaust valves will not fully seat on the cylinder head when they close. When a valve seats on the cylinder head it does two things; it seals the combustion chamber so that none of the gases in the cylinder can escape and it cools itself by transferring some of the heat absorbed from the combustion process through the cylinder head and into the cooling system. Therefore, if the valve clearance is too small, the engine will run poorly (due to gases escaping from the combustion chamber), and the valves will overheat and eventually warp (since they cannot properly transfer heat unless they fully seat on the cylinder head).

While all valve adjustments must be as accurate as possible, it is better to have the valve adjustment slightly loose than tight, as burned valves can result from too tight an adjustment.

ADJUSTMENT

The overhead cam acts directly on the valves through cam followers which fit over the springs and valves. Adjustment is made with an adjusting disc which fits into the cam follower. Different thickness disc result in changes in valve clearance.

NOTE: *VW recommends that two special tools be used to remove and install the adjustment discs. One is a pry bar to compress the valve springs and the other a pair of special pliers to remove the disc. If the purchase of these tools is not possible, a flat metal plate can be used to compress the valve springs if you are careful not to gouge the camshaft lobes. The cam follower has two slots which permit the disc to be lifted out. Again, you an improvise with a then bladed screwdriver. An assistant to pry the spring down while you remove the disc would be the ideal way to perform the operation if you must improvise your own tools.*

Check the valve clearance with a feeler gauge. The camshaft lobe should not be putting pressure on the valve disc

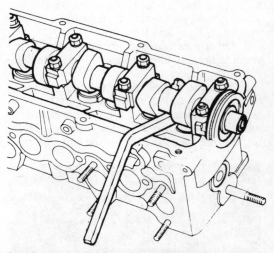

Remove the adjusting discs with special pry bar and pliers—don't press on the disc itself, but on the lip of the disc holder. Note the position of cam lobes on No. 1 cylinder. This is the correct position for measuring valve clearances

Valve clearance is checked with the engine moderately warm (coolant temperature should be about 95°F (35°C).

1. Remove the accelerator linkage (if necessary), the upper drive belt cover (if necessary), the air cleaner and any hoses or lines which may be in the way.

2. Remove the cylinder head cover. Valve clearance is checked in the firing order; 1-3-4-2 for the 4 cylinder and 1-2-4-5-3 for the 5 cylinder engines, with the piston of the cylinder being checked at TDC of the compression stroke. Both valves will be closed at this position and the cam lobes will be pointing straight up.

NOTE: *When adjusting the clearances on the diesel engine, the pistons must not be at TDC. Turn the crankshaft ¼ turn past TDC so that the valves do not contact the pistons when the tappets are depressed.*

3. Turn the crankshaft pulley bolt with a socket wrench to position the camshaft for checking.

NOTE: *There is a hole behind the front license plate, on Dasher models, through which a wrench can be used.*

CAUTION: *Do not turn the camshaft by the camshaft mounting bolt, this will stretch the drive belt. When turning the crankshaft pulley bolt, turn CLOCKWISE ONLY.*

4. With the No. 1 piston at TDC (¼ turn past for the diesel) of the compression stroke, determine the clearance with a feeler gauge. Intake clearance should be 0.008–0.012"; exhaust clearance should be 0.016–0.020" (0.006–0.010" and 0.014–0.918" for the Diesel).

5. Continue on to check the other cylinders in the firing order, turning the crankshaft to bring each particular piston to the top of the compression stroke (¼ turn for the diesel). Record the individual clearances as you go along.

6. If measured clearance is within tolerance levels (0.002"), it is not necessary to replace the adjusting discs.

7. If adjustment is necessary, the discs will have to be removed and replaced with thicker or thinner ones which will yield the correct clearance. Discs are available in 0.002" increments from 0.12" to 0.17".

NOTE: *The thickness of the adjusting discs are etched on one side. When installing, the marks must face the cam followers. Discs can be can be reused if they are not worn or damaged.*

8. To remove the discs; turn the cam followers so that the grooves are accessible when the pry bar is depressed.

9. Press the cam follower down with the pry bar and remove the adjusting discs with the special pliers or the screwdriver.

10. Replace the adjustment discs as necessary to bring the clearance within the 0.002" tolerance level. If the measured clearance is larger than the given tolerance, remove the existing disc and insert a thicker one to bring the clearance up to specification. If it is smaller, insert a thinner one.

11. Recheck all valve clearances after adjustment.

12. Install the cylinder head cover with a new gasket.

13. Install the accelerator linkage, the upper drive belt cover and any wires or lines which were removed.

Carburetor

The Dasher carburetor is a Solex 32/35 DIDTA two-barrel unit through 1974, and a Zenith 2B3 in 1975. Both have vacuum operated sec-

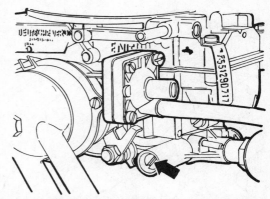

Idle speed adjusting screw—except 34 PICT (1978 and 1980) and Carter TYF

Idle mixture, carbureted 1975–76 Rabbit, Scirocco, 1975 Dasher

ondary barrels. The 1975–76 Rabbit and Scirocco use a Zenith 2B2 carburetor with a vacuum operated secondary barrel and dual floats. Some 1978 and 1980 Rabbits are equipped with the 35 PICT-5 single barrel carburetor. The various 1982 and later use a Carter TYF feedback carburetor.

IDLE SPEED ADJUSTMENT

Solex 32/35 DIDTA Carburetor, Zenith 2B2 and 2B3 Carburetors

1. Start the engine and run it until the normal operating temperature is reached.

2. Hook-up a tachometer to the engine and observe the idle speed.

3. If the idle speed is not specified, turn the curb idle screw to correct it. Make sure that you are turning the correct it. Make sure that you are turning the correct screw as shown in the illustration. Do not mistake the idle mixture screw for the curb idle screw.

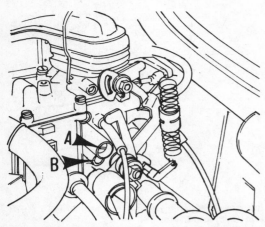

1978 34 PICT-5 idle speed screw (A) and CO screw (B)—1980 similar

Solex 34 PICT-5 Carburetor

1978 RABBIT ONLY

NOTE: *See below for 1980 Rabbit with Solex 34 PICT-5 carburetor adjustments.*

The choke must be fully open and the engine at normal operating temperature.

1. Remove the hose from the charcoal filter at the air intake elbow. Plug the hose.

2. Remove the air injection hose at the air cleaner. Plug the hose.

3. Make sure no electrical equipment is ON. In particular the cooling fan must be OFF.

4. Connect a tachometer. Adjust the idle speed to specification at the idle speed adjusting screw (A). The CO content can be adjusted at screw (B) if a CO meter is available.

5. Disconnect the tachometer and reconnect 11 hoses.

1980 RABBIT ONLY

NOTE: *See above for 1978 Rabbit with Solex 34 PICT-5 carburetor adjustments.*

1. The engine must be at operating temperature and the choke must be fully open.

2. Remove the two hoses from the carburetor air intake elbow and plug the two hose inlets in the elbow. The air intake elbow sits right on top of the carburetor.

3. Remove both of the air injection hoses at the air injection valves, located side by side in the front middle of the engine. Plug the air injection valves.

4. Shut off all electrical equipment, including the air conditioner (if installed).

5. Connect a tachometer, timing light and CO meter (if available) to the engine.

CAUTION: *See Tachometer Adaptation (Carbureted Rabbits), under the electronic ignition section above for method of connecting tachometer. If you do not follow these in-*

structions, you will damage your ignition system!

6. Start the engine. Rev the engine a few times to start the idle stabilizer.

7. Check the idle; it should be 850-950 rpm. If the idle is not correct, disconnect the plugs at the control unit and plug them together (see electronic ignition system above).

8. Remove the vacuum advance and retard hoses, then plug the hoses.

9. Adjust the idle speed to 8000–1000 rpm at the idle adjustment screw. Check the timing, see above section for procedures.

10. If the timing was off, recheck the idle speed.

11. Reconnect the advance and retard hoses.

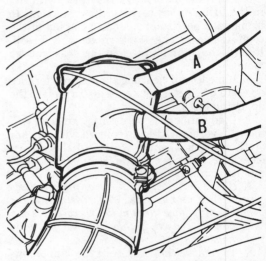

Disconnect both hoses (A) and (B) before setting idle on 1980 34 PICT-5 Rabbit. On 1978 model, disconnect only the braided charcoal filter hose

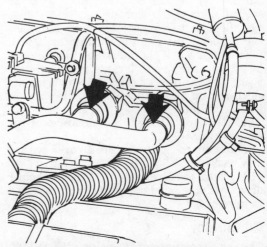

Remove air injection hoses and plug valves 1980 34 PICT-5. For 1978 34 PICT-5, remove the air injection hose at the air cleaner and plug the hose

Adjust the CO lever at the CO adjusting screw to 0.5–1.1%.

12. Reconnect the control unit.

13. Rev the engine to reactivate idle stabilizer and check the idle speed and CO. Idle speed should be 850–950 rpm, CO should be 0.5–1.5%.

14. If the idle speed is still not correct, replace the control unit or the idle stabilizer.

CARTER TYF

The Carter TYF in an electrically controlled carburetor requiring special equipment for adjustment. The adjustment procedure calls for a special duty cycle meter which is not commonly available to the backyard mechanic. Unless you have access to this meter it is suggested that the procedure be performed by an authorized service technician.

1. Run the engine till normal operating temperature, the electric cooling fan should cycle at least once. Make sure the choke is fully opened and not sticking. Remove the breather hose from the side of the valve cover. Shut off all electrical equipment including the air conditioner (if so equipped). The radiator fan must not be running for idle adjustment. Disconnect the vacuum hoses to the distributor and plug them. Check ignition timing with a timing light and adjust to 7½° BTDC if necessary. Connect hoses.

2. Connect a tachometer to the engine according to the tach manufacturer's instructions.

3. Connect the duty cycle meter to the test connector on the left strut tower.

4. Start the engine, and run at 2000 rpm for 5 seconds. Check the idle speed, it should be 850–1000 rpm. Duty cycle should be fluctuating between 20% and 50%.

5. To adjust the idle speed, disconnect both idle stabilizer plugs and connect the plugs together

6. Remove the vacuum hoses from the distributor and plug them.

7. Adjust the idle speed to 820–900 rpm by turning the idle screw at the front of the bracket mounted idle kickback switch on the side of the carburetor. Duty cycle should still be fluctuating between 20% and 50%. If the duty cycle reading is incorrect the car should be taken to a professional for adjustment, as a tamperproof plug must be removed from the carburetor body to make the required adjustment.

NOTE: *On air conditioned cars, turn the compressor on and set the controls to MAX cold and FAST fan speed before setting idle speed to 820–900 rpm.*

8. Stop engine, reconnect the idle stabilizer plugs and vacuum hoses at the distributor.

Idle Mixture Adjustment

This adjustment should only be performed if you have access to an accurate CO meter, otherwise leave it to your dealer or a service garage.

1. Run the engine until it reaches normal operating temperature.

2. Check that ignition timing and idle speed are as specified.

3. Adjust the CO level with the idle mixture screw to specifications.

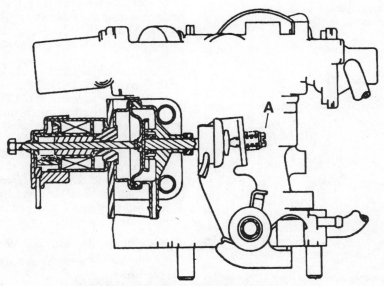

Carter TYF idle speed adjustment at screw "A"

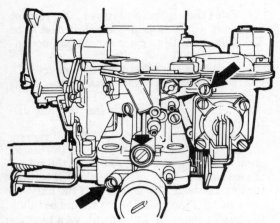

Idle mixture adjusting screw 1974 Dasher California (upper), 49 states (lower). Idle speed screw is at center

CIS Fuel Injection

IDLE SPEED AND MIXTURE ADJUSTMENT

All Except 1980 California and 1981 and Later Models

1. To adjust the idle speed; run the engine until normal operating temperature is reached.

2. Adjust the ignition timing to specifications with the vacuum hoses connected and the engine at idle.

3. With a tachometer connected following the tach manufacturer's instructions, adjust the idle speed to specifications. The idle adjustment screw is located on the throttle chamber near the accelerator linkage.

4. If a CO meter and CO adjusting tool (VW-P377) are available the CO idle mixture can be adjusted. If these special tools are not available, take your car to a qualified mechanic for adjustment.

5. To adjust CO, remove the charcoal filter

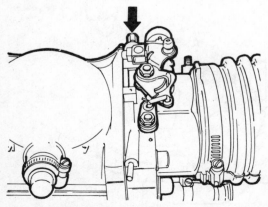

Idle speed adjusting screw (arrow)—CIS fuel injection (Rabbit shown)

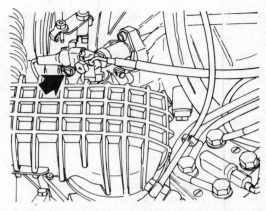

Dasher idle speed adjustment screw—CIS fuel injection

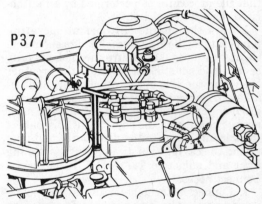

CO adjustment tool (P377)—CIS fuel injection: note plug resting on battery

hose from the air cleaner (except Canadian models). Turn on the headlights to high beam.

6. Remove the plug from the CO adjusting hole and insert CO adjusting tool (VW-P377).

CAUTION: *Do not push down on the adjusting tool or accelerate the engine with the tool in place.*

Turn the adjusting tool clockwise to raise the percentage of CO and counter-clockwise to lower the percentage of CO.

7. Remove the tool after each adjustment and accelerate the engine briefly before reading the CO value.

NOTE: *The plug covering the CO adjustment is attached to a long thin wire with a loop at the end. The plug is located next to the fuel distributor, which is identified by the four injector hoses attached at the top. Remove the plug by pulling on the wire loop.*

1980 California, 1981 and Later Models

1. The engine must be at normal operating temperature.

2. Disconnect the crankcase breather hose

Tach. Conv. Chart.

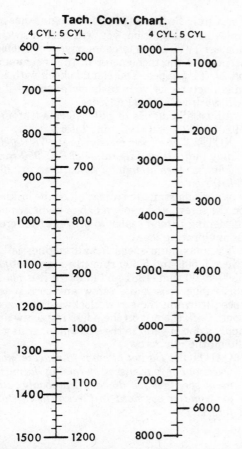

Use this chart to convert the 4 cylinder tachometer reading to true idle speed on 5 cylinder models

CIS-E Fuel Injection

IDLE SPEED AND MIXTURE ADJUSTMENT

NOTE: *Certain 1.8 Liter engines are equipped with a manual pre-heat valve located on the air cleaner housing. The valve is marked "S" (summer) and "W" (winter). When servicing, position the valve to S (unless work area is below freezing). After servicing, return the valve to the position that matches climate conditions.*

1. The engine must be at normal operating temperature.

2. Leave the crankcase breather hose open with the exception of the 5 cylinder models. Plug the hose on the 5 cylinder models.

3. Disconnect the two plugs on the idle stabilizer at the control unit and plug them together.

4. Make sure that all the electrical accessories are "OFF".

NOTE: *Only adjust the idle when the radiator fan is off. On the Quantum, remove the cap from the "T" piece in the charcoal canister vent hose near the right fender. On all others, remove the charcoal canister vent hose at the elbow below the intake boot.*

5. Connect a tachometer and timing light according to manufacturers instructions. Check the timing and adjust in the conventional manner, if necessary.

6. Using adapter hose US-4492, connect a CO meter to the CO test point on the engine.

7. Start the engine, accelerate briefly, check and/or adjust the idle speed and the timing.

8. Remove the air sensor housing plug, insert adjusting tool P377 and adjust the dwell to 38-52 degrees, by turning the mixture adjust screw.

9. Check the CO reading. If it is too high, check for leaks in the intake or exhaust systems and malfunctions in the fuel system.

10. Check the idle speed against the specifications chart or the underhood sticker. Adjust the idle at the idle adjustment screw on the throttle chamber (800-1000rpm).

11. When the adjustment is completed, reinstall the removed items and remove the test equiptment.

1985 and Later CIS and Emission Controls

1. The following must be checked prior to adjustment: engine oil temperature at normal operating 176°F, radiator fan and A/C off, no exhaust system leaks and oxygen regulator operating.

2. Clamp the idle speed boost hose tightly to prevent flow.

3. Pull the breather hoses from the cylinder

at the cam cover and plug, on models through 1982. 1983 models, except the 5 cylinder, allow hose opened to air. Plug the hose on 5 cylinder models.

3. Disconnect the two idle stabilizer plugs from the control unit and connect them together. Make sure all electrical accessories are turned off.

4. Connect a tachometer and timing light. Check the timing, adjust if necessary.

5. Check the idle speed against the specifications chart or your underhood sticker. Adjust the idle at the idle adjustment screw on the throttle chamber.

NOTE: *Only adjust the idle when the fan is not on.*

6. The CO adjustment on these engines is sealed to prevent unauthorized adjustment. The only way CO levels can be adjusted on these models is with special dealer tools which are not usually available to the general public.

head to allow fresh sir to circulation (hose at intake manifold and hose from air cleaner).

4. Remove the "T" connector from the carbon canister at the intake air boot. Turn the "T" connector 90° and insert blank side with 0.059″ restrictor into the hole in the intake boot.

5. Connect a suitable duty meter to measure ignition timing and rpm.

6. Start and run engine at idle. Check the timing (4-8 ATDC) and idle rpm (under 1000).

7. Adjust as necessary. Timing 6° ATDC. Idle rpm-900.

8. Stop the engine and remove all test equiptment. Connect all hoses removed.

Diesel Injection System

Idle Speed/Maximum Speed Adjustments

Volkswagen diesel engines have both an idle speed and a maximum speed adjustment. The maximum engine speed adjustment prevents the engine from over-revving and swallowing itself whole. The adjusters are located side by side on top of the injection pump. The screw closest to the engine is the idle speed adjuster, while the outer screw is the maximum speed adjuster.

The idle and maximum speed must be adjusted wit the engine warm (normal operating temperature). Because the diesel engine has no conventional ignition, you will need a special adapter (VW 1324) to connect your tachometer, or use the tachometer in the instrument panel, if equipped. You should check with the manufacturer of your tachometer to see if it will work with diesel engines.

Adjust all engines to 770–870 rpm (through 1980) or 800–850 (1981 and later).

NOTE: *The sticker on your pre-1978 Rabbit may indicate an idle range of 850–950 rpm. This has been altered by Volkswagen to 770–870 rpm.*

When adjustment is correct, lock the locknut on the screw, and apply a dab of paint or non-hardening thread sealer to prevent the screw from vibrating loose.

The maximum speed for all engines is between 5,500 and 5,600 rpm (through 1980) or 5300–5400 rpm (1981 and later). If it is not in this range, loosen the screw and correct the speed (turning the screw clockwise decreases rpm). Lock the nut on the adjusting screw and apply a dab of paint in the same manner as you did on the idle screw.

CAUTION: *Do not attempt to squeeze more power out of your engine by raising the maximum speed. If you do, you'll probably be in for a major overhaul in the not too distant future.*

A special adaptor (VW 1324) is necessary to hook up an external tachometer on diesel engines

Adjust diesel engine idle speed at the inner screw (arrow). Adjust the maximum speed at the outer screw (no arrow). Lock screws in place with sealer

Troubleshooting Diesel Engines

Problem	Possible Causes
Starter will not crank engine	Battery terminals loose or broken
	Battery discharged
	Starter switch damaged, or wires loose or broken
	Starter clutch or solenoid malfunction
	Starter drive locked
	Hydraulic lock, water or oil in combustion chamber
	Blow plug light still "ON" (dashboard)
Failure to start or hard starting	Correct starting procedures not being followed
	Cold start aid inoperative
	Battery low, slow cranking speed
	Starter equipment malfunctioning
	Engine oil too heavy
	Blocked exhaust system
	Air filter dirty
Failure to start or hard starting	Low engine compression due to defective valves or piston rings
	Insufficient fuel in tank
	Water or ice in fuel tank
	Excessive fuel device inoperative
	Fuel injection parts scored, poor delivery
	Advance mechanism in advance position. It should be in retarded position when engine is to be started.
	Fuel injection pump not timed properly
	Air in the fuel system
	Fuel oil filter plugged or restricted
	Fuel lift pump not operating
	Leak in high pressure delivery lines
Engine runs, but misses NOTE: *The first signs of injector trouble usually appear as:* –A knock in one or more cylinders, –Overheated engine, –Loss of power, –Smoky black exhaust, –Increased fuel consumption. The faulty injector can be located by slightly loosening the pipe joint at each injector in turn with the engine at fast idle (1000–1200 rpm). If the engine speed remains constant (does not change), after loosening the joint, the injector is faulty. Do not loosen the fuel line with the engine running, and do not remove the injector. The system is under tremendous pressure (up to 1850 psi) and is enough to cause diesel fuel to penetrate skin.	Restricted fuel lines
	Water in fuel or poor quality fuel
	Air leaks in fuel suction line
	Injectors improperly adjusted or plugged
	Low compression, intake or exhaust valves leaking
	Leaking turbocharger air connection
	Restricted drain line
Excessive vibration	Engine bearings worn
	Engine supports broken or loose
	Difference in compression pressures between cylinders
	Injector setting pressures unequal
	Unequal fuel delivery, line resistance
	Air in fuel system
Low Engine Torque NOTE: *The first signs of injector trouble usually appear as:*	Excessive exhaust back pressure
	Engine valve timing not correct

Troubleshooting Diesel Engines (cont.)

Problem	Possible Causes
–A knock in one or more cylinders, –Overheated engine, –Loss of power, –Smoky black exhaust, –Increased fuel consumption. The faulty injector can be located by slightly loosening the pipe joint at each injector in turn with the engine at fast idle (1000–1200 rpm). If the engine speed remains constant (does not change), after loosening the joint, the injector is faulty. Do not loosen the fuel line with the engine running, and do not remove the injector. The system is under tremendous pressure (up to 1850 psi) and is enough to cause diesel fuel to penetrate skin.	Fuel filters dirty High pressure fuel line leaks Poor atomization of fuel Dirty or cracked injectors Fuel injection pump to engine timing wrong Throttle stop set too low Inferior quality fuel Advance device not working Brakes binding
Engine Knocks NOTE: *The first signs of injector trouble usually appear as:* –A knock in one or more cylinders, –Overheated engine, –Loss of power, –Smoky black exhaust, –Increased fuel consumption. The faulty injector can be located by slightly loosening the pipe joint at each injector in turn with the engine at fast idle (1000–1200 rpm). If the engine speed remains constant (does not change), after loosening the joint, the injector is faulty. Do not loosen the fuel line with the engine running, and do not remove the injector. The system is under tremendous pressure (up to 1850 psi) and is enough to cause diesel fuel to penetrate the skin.	Low coolant level Engine overloaded Crankshaft vibration damper malfunction Excessive crankshaft end clearance Flywheel loose or unbalanced Broken or worn piston rings Incorrect bearing clearances Damaged or worn main or connecting rod bearings Broken tooth in engine gear train Worn or scored cylinder liners or pistons Broken valve springs Fuel injection pump timing too early Poor atomization of fuel Octane value of fuel low
Excessive Smoke *BLACK SMOKE* consists of a large number of particles of carbon; this carbon forms when the fuel is heated in oxygen-lean regions in the combustion chamber. *BLUE SMOKE* consists of a large number of particles of fuel oil; these particles are recondensed droplets of unburned fuel or incompletely burned fuel. These small particles cause blue light to be scattered. When an engine is running fast but under light load, regions of the combustion chamber may be at too low a temperature to permit ignition and blue smoke would appear. When viewed in transmitted light, the blue smoke appears brown. *WHITE SMOKE* consists of a large number of particles of fuel oil. To produce white smoke, the fuel must have time to condense into larger droplets than for blue smoke. A cold engine running at light load and low speed could produce white smoke.	Restricted air intake High exhaust back pressure Intake manifold or cylinder head gasket leakage Cracked cylinder head or block Broken or worn piston rings Engine in need of overhaul Incorrect valve timing Worn or scored cylinder liners or pistons Engine overload Low compression Inferior quality fuel Restricted fuel lines Plugged injector spray holes Incorrect injector timing Injectors improperly adjusted Fuel injection pump to engine timing retarded Injector pump improperly adjusted Broken fuel delivery valve or valve sticking
Engine gradually loses power; then stops NOTE: *The first signs of injector trouble usually appear as:* –A knock in one or more cylinders, –Overheated engine, –Loss of power,	Low compression Engine valve clearance too small Air leak at suction side of fuel lines Choked fuel filter

Troubleshooting Diesel Engines (cont.)

Problem	Possible Causes
−Smoky black exhaust, −Increased fuel consumption. The faulty injector can be located by slightly loosening the pipe joint at each injector in turn with the engine at fast idle (1000−1200 rpm). If the engine speed remains constant (does not change), after loosening the joint, the injector is faulty. Do not loosen the fuel line with the engine running, and do not remove the injector. The system is under tremendous pressure (up to 1850 psi) and is enough to cause diesel fuel to penetrate the skin.	Damaged control linkage Fuel tank vent clogged Leak off line blocked Nozzle and delivery valve stuck open
Engine cannot reach maximum speed	Poor condition of engine Throttle stop improperly adjusted Maximum speed setting to low Broken or wrong type governor springs Dirty air filter
Excessive fuel consumption NOTE: *The first signs of injector trouble usually appear as:* −A knock in one or more cylinders, −Overheated engine, −Loss of power, −Smoky black exhaust, −Increased fuel consumption. The faulty injector can be located by slightly loosening the pipe joint at each injector in turn with the engine at fast idle (1000−1200 rpm). If the engine speed remains constant (does not change), after loosening the joint, the injector is faulty. Do not loosen the fuel line with the engine running, and do not remove the injector. The system is under tremendous pressure (up to 1850 psi) and is enough to cause diesel fuel to penetrate the skin.	Restricted air intake High exhaust back pressure Engine overloaded Engine in need of overhaul Inferior quality fuel Restricted fuel lines or filter Fuel leaks external or internal Plugged injector spray holes Injectors not adjusted properly Cracked injector body or cap
Excessive oil consumption	Broken or worn piston rings Worn or scored cylinder liners or piston External or internal oil leaks Faulty cylinder oil control Wrong grade oil for conditions Engine in need of overhaul Loose crankcase breather vent
Low oil pressure	Incorrect bearing clearances Engine overloaded Insufficient coolant Worn water pump Coolant thermostat not working Loose fan belts Clogged coolant passages Clogged oil cooler Radiator core openings restricted Air in cooling system Leaking coolant hoses, connections or gaskets Insufficient radiator capacity Oil suction line restricted or cracked Oil pickup screen blocked Crankcase oil level too low

Troubleshooting Diesel Engines (cont.)

Problem	Possible Causes
	Wrong grade of oil for conditions
	Engine in need of overhaul
Overheating (high coolant temperature) NOTE: *The first signs of injector trouble usually appear as:*	Low coolant level
	Air leaks in suction line
–A knock in one or more cylinders, –Overheated engine, –Loss of power, –Smoky black exhaust, –Increased fuel consumption. The faulty injector can be located by slightly loosening the pipe joint at each injector in turn with the engine at fast idle (1000–1200 rpm). If the engine speed remains constant (does not change), after loosening the joint, the injector is faulty. Do not loosen the fuel line with the engine running, and do not remove the injector. The system is under tremendous pressure (up to 1850 psi) and is enough to cause diesel fuel to penetrate the skin.	Low coolant level
	Engine overloaded
	Injectors not properly adjusted
	Injector pipe partially clogged
	Faulty injectors
	Injector timing too early
	Worn or scored cylinder liners or pistons
	Broken valve springs
	Crankshaft vibration damper faulty
	Excessive crankshaft end clearance
	Flywheel loose or unbalanced
	Broken or worn piston rings
	Incorrect bearing clearances
	Engine in need of overhaul
	Broken tooth in engine gear train

Troubleshooting Basic Charging System Problems

Problem	Cause	Solution
Noisy alternator	• Loose mountings • Loose drive pulley • Worn bearings • Brush noise • Internal circuits shorted (High pitched whine)	• Tighten mounting bolts • Tighten pulley • Replace alternator • Replace alternator • Replace alternator
Squeal when starting engine or accelerating	• Glazed or loose belt	• Replace or adjust belt
Indicator light remains on or ammeter indicates discharge (engine running)	• Broken fan belt • Broken or disconnected wires • Internal alternator problems • Defective voltage regulator	• Install belt • Repair or connect wiring • Replace alternator • Replace voltage regulator
Car light bulbs continually burn out— battery needs water continually	• Alternator/regulator overcharging	• Replace voltage regulator/alternator
Car lights flare on acceleration	• Battery low • Internal alternator/regulator problems	• Charge or replace battery • Replace alternator/regulator
Low voltage output (alternator light flickers continually or ammeter needle wanders)	• Loose or worn belt • Dirty or corroded connections • Internal alternator/regulator problems	• Replace or adjust belt • Clean or replace connections • Replace alternator or regulator

Troubleshooting Basic Starting System Problems

Problem	Cause	Solution
Starter motor rotates engine slowly	• Battery charge low or battery defective	• Charge or replace battery
	• Defective circuit between battery and starter motor	• Clean and tighten, or replace cables
	• Low load current	• Bench-test starter motor. Inspect for worn brushes and weak brush springs.
	• High load current	• Bench-test starter motor. Check engine for friction, drag or coolant in cylinders. Check ring gear-to-pinion gear clearance.
Starter motor will not rotate engine	• Battery charge low or battery defective	• Charge or replace battery
	• Faulty solenoid	• Check solenoid ground. Repair or replace as necessary.
	• Damage drive pinion gear or ring gear	• Replace damaged gear(s)
	• Starter motor engagement weak	• Bench-test starter motor
	• Starter motor rotates slowly with high load current	• Inspect drive yoke pull-down and point gap, check for worn end bushings, check ring gear clearance
	• Engine seized	• Repair engine
Starter motor drive will not engage (solenoid known to be good)	• Defective contact point assembly	• Repair or replace contact point assembly
	• Inadequate contact point assembly ground	• Repair connection at ground screw
	• Defective hold-in coil	• Replace field winding assembly
Starter motor drive will not disengage	• Starter motor loose on flywheel housing	• Tighten mounting bolts
	• Worn drive end busing	• Replace bushing
	• Damaged ring gear teeth	• Replace ring gear or driveplate
	• Drive yoke return spring broken or missing	• Replace spring
Starter motor drive disengages prematurely	• Weak drive assembly thrust spring	• Replace drive mechanism
	• Hold-in coil defective	• Replace field winding assembly
Low load current	• Worn brushes	• Replace brushes
	• Weak brush springs	• Replace springs

Engine and Engine Overhaul

3

ENGINE ELECTRICAL

Ignition Coil (Breaker Point Ignitions Only)

PRIMARY RESISTANCE CHECK

1. Disconnect all wires from the coil terminals.
2. Measure the resistance between terminal 15 (+) and terminal 1 (–). Resistance should be 1.7–2.1Ω.
3. If not, replace the coil.

SECONDARY RESISTANCE CHECK

1. Disconnect all wires from the coil.
2. Measure the resistance between terminal 1(–) and the coil wire terminal (terminal 4).
3. Resistance should be 7,000–12,000Ω.
4. If not, replace the ignition coil.

REMOVAL AND INSTALLATION

1. Tag and disconnect the negative and positive terminal wires from the top of the coil.
2. Remove the coil wire from the coil.
3. Using a flat screwdriver, loosen the adjusting screw which secures the coil inside the clamp.
4. Remove the coil from the vehicle.
5. Install in the reverse order.

Ballast Resistor

CHECKING

All 1976 and later Dashers and other later models, have replaced the ballast resistor with a resistor wire which runs from terminal 15 (+) of the ignition coil to terminal C15 at the back of the fuse block/relay panel. The color of the resistor wire is usually clear with violet stripes.

To test the resistor wire, disconnect it from the ignition coil and unplug multipin connector C from the back of the fuse/relay panel.

Connect an ohmmeter to each end of the resistor wire (resistor wire is terminal C15 at the fuse/relay panel). The resistance should be between 0.85–0.95 ohm for the Rabbit, Golf, Jetta and Scirocco, 0.52–0.76 ohm for the Fox and approximately 1Ω for Dasher and Quantum. The old type ballast resistor can also be checked using this method. Before checking, disconnect all wires from the ballast resistor.

Distributor

NOTE: *If your car is equipped with an electronic Hall Effect distributor, refer to Chapter 2 for all troubleshooting and maintenance procedures except removal and installation.*

All distributors incorporate both centrifugal advance and vacuum advance and retard ignition timing mechanisms. Centrifugal advance is controlled by two weights located beneath the breaker plate. As engine speed increases, centrifugal force moves the weights out from the distributor shaft and advances the ignition by changing the position of the cam in relation to the shaft. This advanced positioning of the cam will then open the breaker points sooner and ignite the air fuel mixture quickly enough in relation to piston speed. Centrifugal advance is necessary because as engine speed increases, the time period available to ignite the mixture decreases. At idle speed, the ignition setting is, say, 3° ATDC. This is adequate for the spark plug to ignite the mixture at 925 rpm, but not at 2,500 rpm. The weights, governed by spring, move out at a predetermined rate to advance the timing to match engine speed.

Centrifugal advance is not completely sufficient to provide the proper advance under all conditions, and so we also have vacuum advance/retard. Under light load conditions, such as very gradual acceleration and low

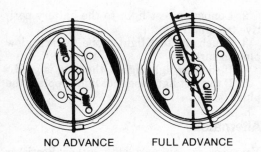

NO ADVANCE   FULL ADVANCE

Centrifugal advance weight operation

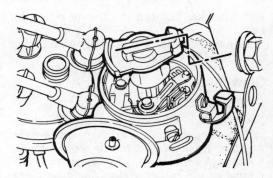

Rotor/distributor alignment for No. 1 cylinder

speed cruising, the throttle opening is not sufficient to draw enough air/fuel mixture into the cylinder. Vacuum advance is used to provide the extra spark advance needed to ignite the smaller mixture. The round can on the side of the distributor is the vacuum advance/retard unit. The rubber hose supplies vacuum from the intake manifold to draw on the diaphragm in the unit which is connected by a link to the breaker plate in the distributor. Under part throttle operation, the vacuum advance moves the breaker plate as necessary to provide the correct advance for efficient operation. At idle, the vacuum retard unit retards the timing to reduce exhaust emission.

The distributor is gear driven by an intermediate shaft which also drives the fuel pump. The distributor is gear driven by an intermediate shaft which also drives the fuel pump. The distributor shaft also turns the oil pump. The distributor is located toward the rear of the engine on the left side and is easily accessible.

REMOVAL AND INSTALLATION

NOTE: *Aside from replacing the cap, rotor, breaker points, and the condenser, refer all distributor repair to a VW dealer or ignition specialty shop. They are equipped with a distributor test machine which permits diagnosis of any problems.*

1. Disconnect the coil high tension wire from the distributor. This is the large wire which goes into the center of the cap.

2. Detach the smaller primary wire which also connects from the coil to the distributor or unfasten the spring clip and disconnect the connector plug at the distributor housing.

3. Unsnap the clips and remove the distributor cap. Position it out of the way.

4. Use the crankshaft pulley nut or bump the starter to turn the engine until the rotor aligns with the index mark on the outer edge of the distributor and the engine timing marks

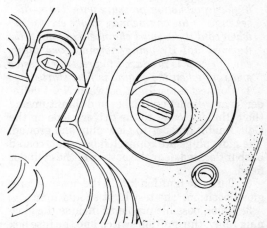

Oil pump driveshaft slot must be parallel to the crankshaft

are aligned. Matchmark the bottom of the distributor housing and its mounting flange on the engine. This is extra insurance that you'll get the distributor back in correctly.

5. Loosen and remove the hex bolt and lift off the retaining flange. Lift the distributor straight out of the engine.

If the engine has not been disturbed while the distributor was out i.e., the crankshaft was not turned, then reinstall the distributor in the reverse order of removal. Carefully align the matchmarks.

If the engine has been rotated while the distributor was out, then proceed as follows:

1. Turn the crankshaft so that the No. 1 piston is on its compression stroke and the OT timing marks are aligned with the V-shaped pointer.

2. Turn the distributor so that the rotor points approximately 15° before the No. 1 cylinder position on the distributor.

3. Insert the distributor and, using a long screwdriver, turn the pump shaft so that it is parallel to the centerline of the crankshaft.

4. Install the distributor, aligning the

matchmarks. Tighten the flange retaining nut.

5. Install the cap. Adjust the ignition timing as outlined in Chapter 2.

Glow Plug

SYSTEM CHECK

NOTE: *The 1982 and later diesels (except Turbo models) have a new type quick-glow system. Nominal glow time is seven seconds. Although the wiring for this system is the same as the earlier system, the glow plugs and relay cannot be paired or interchanged with earlier parts or vice versa. Because of the higher combustion pressure with Turbo-diesel engines the engine may smoke excessively when cold if the swirl chambers are not fully warmed up. By using normal glow plugs enough heat is produced to prevent excessive smoking when the engine is first started.*

1. Connect a test light between No. 4 cylinder (rear cylinder on Dasher and Quantum and the cylinder closest to the driver's side on the Golf, Rabbit and Jetta) glow plug and ground. The glow plugs are connected by a flat, coated busbar (located near the bottom of the cylinder head).

2. Turn the ignition key to the heating (pre-glow) position. The test light should light.

3. If not, possible problems include the glow plug relay, the ignition switch and the fuse box relay plater and the glow plug fuse or a break in the wire to the relay terminal.

INDIVIDUAL GLOW PLUG TEST

1. Remove the wire and busbar from the glow plugs.

2. Connect a test light to the battery positive terminal.

3. Touch the test light probe to each glow plug in turn.

4. If the test light lights, the plug is good.

5. If the test light does not light, replace the plug.

Alternator

Your car is equipped with either Bosch or Motorola alternators, which produce alternating current (AC), as opposed to generators, which produce direct current (DC). The regulators on these alternators are contained on the alternator housing, therefore no adjustments are possible.

ALTERNATOR PRECAUTIONS

To prevent damage to the alternator and regulator, the following precautionary measures must be taken when working with the electrical system.

1. Never reverse battery connections. Always check the battery polarity visually. This is to be done before any connections are made to be sure that all of the connections correspond to the battery ground polarity of the car.

2. Booster batteries for starting must be connected properly. Make sure that the positive cable of the booster battery is connected to the positive terminal of the battery which is getting the boost.

3. Disconnect the battery cables before using a fast charger; the charger has a tendency to force current through the diodes in the opposite direction for which they were designed. This burns out the diodes.

No. 4 cylinder glow plug

4. Never use a fast charger as a booster for starting the vehicle.

5. Never disconnect the voltage regulator while the engine is running.

6. Do not ground the alternator output terminal.

7. Do not operate the alternator on an open circuit with the field energized.

8. Do not attempt to polarize an alternator.

9. Disconnect the battery cables before using an electric arc welder on the car.

REMOVAL AND INSTALLATION

The alternator and voltage regulator are combined in one housing. No voltage adjustment can be made with this unit. As with the distributor, repairs to the alternator should be made by an authorized VW dealer. The regulator can be replaced without removing the alternator, just unbolt it from the rear.

1. Disconnect the battery cables.

2. Remove the multiconnector retaining

bracket and unplug the connector from the rear of the alternator.

3. Loosen and remove the top mounting nut and bolt.

4. Using a hex socket inserted through the timing belt cover (it is not necessary to remove the cover), loosen the lower mounting bolt.

5. Slide the alternator over and remove the alternator belt.

6. Remove the lower nut and bolt. Don't lose the spacers or rubber isolators.

7. Remove the alternator.

NOTE: *Remember when installing the alternator that it is not necessary to polarize the system.*

8. Install the alternator with the lower bolt. Don't tighten at this point.

9. Install the alternator belt over the pulleys.

10. Loosely install the top mounting bolt and pivot the alternator over until the belt is correctly tensioned as explained in the next procedure.

CAUTION

Before starting to work on any part of electrical system disconnect battery ground strap

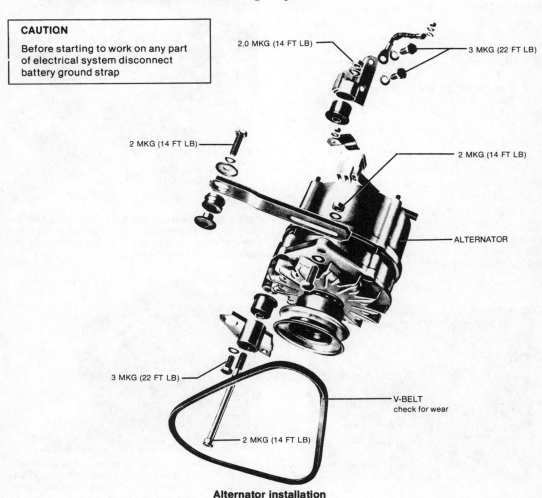

Alternator installation

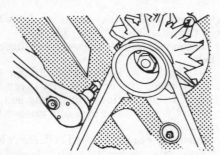

Remove the lower alternator bolt through the timing cover

11. Finally tighten the top and bottom bolts to 14 ft.lb.
12. Connect the alternator and battery wires.

Battery

REMOVAL AND INSTALLATION

CAUTION: *Battery electrolyte (acid) is highly corrosive and can damage both you and the paintwork. Be careful when lifting the battery in and out of the engine compartment.*
1. Disconnect the battery cables, negative cable first.
2. Put on heavy work gloves.
3. Loosen the retaining clamp bolt and remove the clamp.
4. Disconnect the small electrical lead for the computer sensor.
5. Lift the battery carefully out of the tray.
6. Clean all corrosion deposits from the battery tray and the retaining plate. Spray them with rust preventive paint.
7. Install the battery in reverse order of removal. Polish the inside of the cables and give them a coat of petroleum jelly before installation. Don't trap or crimp the cables when installing the battery.

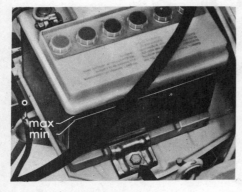

The battery is retained by a clamp

Starter

REMOVAL AND INSTALLATION

All Models Except Dasher Diesel

1. Disconnect the battery ground cable.
2. Jack up the right front of the car and support on jackstands.
3. Mark with tape and then disconnect the two small wires from the starter solenoid. One wire connects to the ignition coil and the second to the ignition switch through the wiring harness.
4. Disconnect the large cable, which is the positive battery cable, from the solenoid.
5. Remove the starter retaining nuts.
6. Unscrew the socket head bolt. Pull the starter straight out.
7. Installation of the starter is carried out in reverse order of removal.

Rabbit and Scirocco old type manual transmission starter installation—be sure bolts (2) have enough clearance in the elongated holes of the bracket (1) so there is no strain

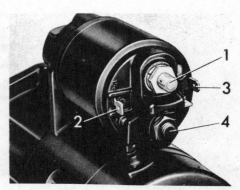

Rabbit, Jetta, Scirocco starter installation—(1) from battery (+) terminal, (2) from terminal 15A to ignition coil terminal 15, (3) from starter switch and (4) field winding connection

NEW TYPE   OLD TYPE

New and old type starter motors

Dasher Diesel

1. Disconnect the battery ground cable.
2. Support the weight of the engine with either Volkswagen special tool 10-222 or use a jack with a block of wood under the oil pan. Don't jack the engine too high, just take the weight off the motor mounts. Be careful not to bend the oil pan.

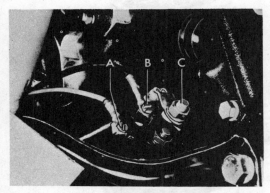

Dasher starter installation—(A) from starter switch, (B) from terminal 15 on coil, (C) from battery (+) terminal

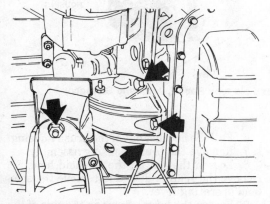

Dasher diesel starter removal—remove the engine mount and carrier on the starter side (arrows)

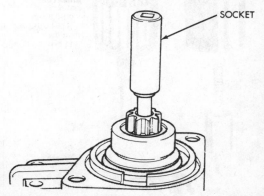

SOCKET

On Dasher and old type Rabbit, Jetta and Scirocco starters, remove the stop ring over the circlip with a socket

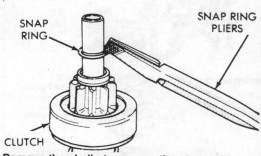

SNAP RING

SNAP RING PLIERS

CLUTCH

Remove the circlip to remove the starter drive

3. Remove the engine/transmission cover plate.
4. Unbolt and remove the starter side motor mount and carrier.
5. Disconnect and mark the starter wiring.
6. Remove the bolts holding the starter and remove the starter.
7. Install the starter and tighten the nuts and bolt to 14 ft.lb.
8. Install the engine mount and carrier.
9. Install and attach remaining components. Don't forget to reconnect the battery cable.

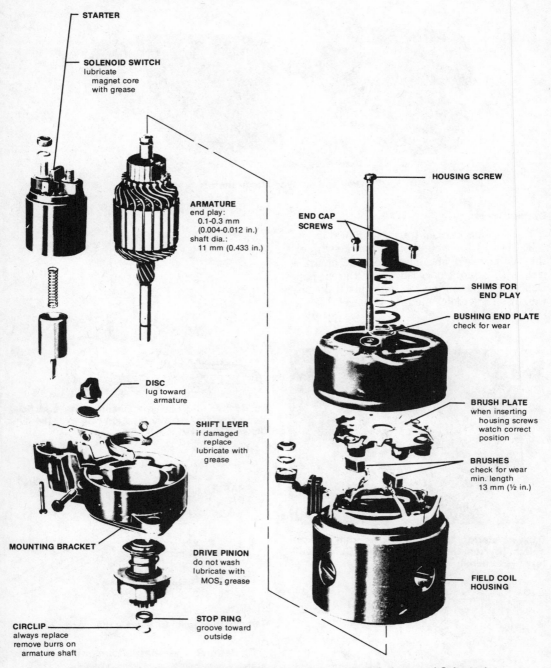

STARTER

SOLENOID SWITCH
lubricate
magnet core
with grease

ARMATURE
end play:
0.1-0.3 mm
(0.004-0.012 in.)
shaft dia.:
11 mm (0.433 in.)

DISC
lug toward
armature

SHIFT LEVER
if damaged
replace
lubricate with
grease

MOUNTING BRACKET

CIRCLIP
always replace
remove burrs on
armature shaft

DRIVE PINION
do not wash
lubricate with
MOS₂ grease

STOP RING
groove toward
outside

HOUSING SCREW

END CAP
SCREWS

SHIMS FOR
END PLAY

BUSHING END PLATE
check for wear

BRUSH PLATE
when inserting
housing screws
watch correct
position

BRUSHES
check for wear
min. length
13 mm (½ in.)

FIELD COIL
HOUSING

Exploded view of typical starter (Dasher and old type Rabbit, Jetta and Scirocco)

OVERHAUL

1. Remove the solenoid.
2. Remove the end bearing cap.
3. Loosen both of the long housing screws.
4. Remove the lockwasher and spacer washers.
5. Remove the long housing screws and remove the end cover.
6. Pull the brushes out of the brush housing.
7. Remove the brush housing assembly.
8. Loosen the nut on the solenoid housing, remove the sealing disc, and remove the solenoid operating lever.
9. Loosen the large screws on the side of the starter body and remove the field coil along with the brushes. Brushes should be ½" long.

Battery and Starter Specifications

(All models use 12 volt, negative ground system)

Year	Model	Battery Amp Hour Capacity	Lock Test			No Load Test			Brush Spring Tension (oz)	Minimum Brush Length (in)
			Amps	Volts	Torque (ft. lbs.)	Amps	Volts	RPM		
1974–87	All	45/54*	280–370	7.5	2.42	33–55	11.5	6000–8000	35.5	0.5

*w/AC

NOTE: *If the brushes require replacement, the field coil and brushes and/or the brush housing and its brushes must be replaced as a unit. Have the armature commutator turned at a machine shop if it is out-of-round, scored, or grooved.*

10. If the starter drive is being replaced, push the stop ring down and remove the circlip at the end of the shaft. Remove the snapring and starter drive.

11. Assemble the starter in the reverse order. Use a new snapring and circlip if necessary.

SOLENOID REPLACEMENT

1. Remove the starter.

2. Remove the nut which secures the connector strip on the end of the solenoid.

3. Take out the two retaining screws on the mounting bracket and withdraw the solenoid after it has been unhooked from the operating lever.

4. Installation is the reverse of removal. In order to facilitate engagement of the lever the pinion should be pulled out as far as possible when inserting the solenoid.

ENGINE MECHANICAL

Overhaul

Most engine overhaul procedures are fairly standard. In addition to specific parts replacement procedures and complete specifications for your individual engine, this chapter also is a guide to accepted rebuilding procedures. Examples of standard rebuilding practice are shown and should be used along with specific details concerning your particular engine.

Competent and accurate machine shop services will ensure maximum performance, reliability and engine life. Procedures marked with the symbol shown above should be performed by a competent machine shop, and are provided so that you will be familiar with the procedures necessary to a successful overhaul.

In most instances it is more profitable for the do-it-yourself mechanic to remove, clean and inspect the component, buy the necessary parts and deliver these to a shop for actual machine work.

On the other hand, much of the rebuilding work (crankshaft, block, bearings, piston rods, and other components) is well within the scope of the do-it-yourself mechanic.

Tools

The tools required for an engine overhaul or parts replacement will depend on the depth of your involvement. With a few exceptions, they will be the tools found in a mechanic's tool kit (see Chapter 1). More in-depth work will require any or all of the following:
• A dial indicator (reading in thousandths) mounted on a universal base
• Micrometers and telescope gauges
• Jaw and screw-type pullers
• Scraper
• Valve spring compressor
• Ring groove cleaner
• Piston ring expander and compressor
• Ridge reamer
• Cylinder hone or glaze breaker
• Plastigage®
• Engine stand
Use of most of these tools is illustrated in this chapter. Many can be rented for a one-time use from a local parts jobber or tool supply house specializing in automotive work.

Occasionally, the use of special tools is called for. See the information on Special Tools and Safety Notice in the front of this book before substituting another tool.

Inspection Techniques

Procedures and specifications are given in this chapter for inspecting, cleaning and assessing the wear limits of most major components. Other procedures such as Magnaflux and Zyglo can be used to locate material flaws and stress cracks. Magnaflux is a magnetic process applicable only to ferrous materials. The Zyglo process coats the material with a flourescent dye penetrant and can be used on any material Check for suspected surface cracks can be more readily made using spot check dye. The dye is sprayed onto the suspected area, wiped off and the area sprayed with a developer. Cracks will show up brightly.

Overhaul Tips

Aluminum has become extremely popular for use in engines, due to its low weight. Observe the following precautions when handling aluminum parts:

• Never hot tank aluminum parts (the caustic hot-tank solution will eat the aluminum.

• Remove all aluminum parts (identification tag, etc.) from engine parts prior to the tanking.

• Always coat threads lightly with engine oil or antiseize compounds before installation, to prevent seizure.

• Never over-torque bolts or spark plugs especially in aluminum threads.

Stripped threads in any component can be repaired using any of several commercial repair kits (Heli-Coil®, Microdot®, Keenserts®, etc.).

When assembling the engine, any parts that will be frictional contact must be prelubed to provide lubrication at initial start-up. Any product specifically formulated for this purpose can be used, but engine oil is not recommended as a prelube.

When semi-permanent (locked, but removable) installation of bolts or nuts is desired, threads should be cleaned and coated with Loctite® or other similar, commercial nonhardening sealant.

Repairing Damaged Threads

Several methods of repairing damaged threads are available. Heli-Coil® (shown here), Keenserts® and Microdot® are among the most widely used. All involve basically the same principle—drilling out stripped threads, tapping the hole and installing a prewound insert—making welding, plugging and oversize fasteners unnecessary.

Two types of thread repair inserts are usually supplied—a standard type for most Inch Coarse, Inch Fine, Metric Course and Metric Fine thread sizes and a spark lug type to fit most spark plug port sizes. Consult the individual manufacturer's catalog to determine

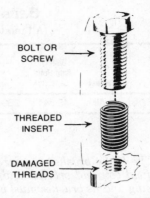

Damaged bolt holes can be repaired with thread repair inserts

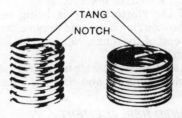

Standard thread repair insert (left) and spark plug thread insert (right)

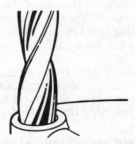

Drill out the damaged threads with specified drill. Drill completely through the hole or to the bottom of a blind hole

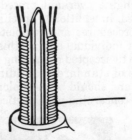

With the tap supplied, tap the hole to receive the thread insert. Keep the tap well oiled and back it out frequently to avoid clogging the threads

exact applications. Typical thread repair kits will contain a selection of prewound threaded inserts, a tap (corresponding to the outside diameter threads of the insert) and an installa-

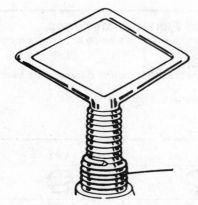

Screw the threaded insert onto the installation tool until the tang engages the slot. Screw the insert into the tapped hole until it is ¼–½ turn below the top surface. After installation break off the tang with a hammer and punch

The screw-in type compression gauge is more accurate

tion tool. Spark plug inserts usually differ because they require a tap equipped with pilot threads and a combined reamer/tap section. Most manufacturers also supply blister-packed thread repair inserts separately in addition to a master kit containing a variety of taps and inserts plus installation tools.

Before effecting a repair to a threaded hole, remove any snapped, broken or damaged bolts or studs. Penetrating oil can be used to free frozen threads; the offending item can be removed with locking pliers or with a screw or stud extractor. After the hole is clear, the thread can be repaired, as follows:

CHECKING ENGINE COMPRESSION

A noticeable lack of engine power, excessive oil consumption and/or poor fuel mileage measured over an extended period are all indicators of internal engine war. Worn piston rings, scored or worn cylinder bores, blown head gaskets, sticking or burnt valves and worn valve seats are all possible culprits here. A check of each cylinder's compression will help you locate the problems.

As mentioned in the "Tools and Equipment" section of Chapter 1, a screw-in type compression gauge is more accurate that the type you simply hold against the spark plug hole, although it takes slightly longer to use. It's worth it to obtain a more accurate reading. Follow the procedures below for gasoline and diesel engined cars.

Gasoline Engines

1. Warm up the engine to normal operating temperature.
2. Remove all spark plugs.

3. Disconnect the high tension lead from the ignition coil.
4. On carbureted cars, fully open the throttle either by operating the carburetor throttle linkage by hand or by having an assistant "floor" the accelerator pedal. On fuel injected cars, disconnect the cold start valve and all injector connections.
5. Screw the compression gauge into the No. 1 spark plug hole until the fitting is snug.
NOTE: *Be careful not to crossthread the plug hole. On aluminum cylinder heads use extra car, as the threads in these heads are easily ruined.*
6. Ask an assistant to depress the accelerator pedal fully on both carbureted and fuel injected cars. Then, while you read the compression gauge, ask the assistant to crank the engine two or three times in short bursts using the ignition switch.
7. Read the compression gauge at the end of each series of cranks, and record the highest of these readings. Repeat this procedure for each of the engine's cylinders. Compare the highest reading of each cylinder to the compression pressure specification in the "Tune-Up Specifications" chart in Chapter 2. The specs in this chart are maximum values.

A cylinders compression pressure is usually acceptable if it is not less than 80% of maximum. The difference between each cylinder should be no more than 12–14 pounds.

8. If a cylinder is unusually low, pour a tablespoon of clean engine oil into the cylinder through the spark plug hole and repeat the compression test. If the compression comes up after adding the oil, it appears that the cylinder's piston rings or bore are damaged or worn. If the pressure remains low, the valves may not be seating properly (a valve job is needed), or the head gasket may be blown near that cylinder. If compression in any two adjacent cylinders is low, and if the addition of oil doesn't help the compression, there is leakage past the head gasket. Oil and coolant water in the com-

Standard Torque Specifications and Fastener Markings

In the absence of specific torques, the following chart can be used as a guide to the maximum safe torque of a particular size/grade of fastener.
- There is no torque difference for fine or coarse threads.
- Torque values are based on clean, dry threads. Reduce the value by 10% if threads are oiled prior to assembly.
- The torque required for aluminum components or fasteners is considerably less.

U.S. Bolts

SAE Grade Number	1 or 2			5			6 or 7		
Number of lines always 2 less than the grade number.									
Bolt Size (Inches)—(Thread)	Maximum Torque			Maximum Torque			Maximum Torque		
	Ft./Lbs.	Kgm	Nm	Ft./Lbs.	Kgm	Nm	Ft./Lbs.	Kgm	Nm
¼—20	5	0.7	6.8	8	1.1	10.8	10	1.4	13.5
—28	6	0.8	8.1	10	1.4	13.6			
⁵⁄₁₆—18	11	1.5	14.9	17	2.3	23.0	19	2.6	25.8
—24	13	1.8	17.6	19	2.6	25.7			
⅜—16	18	2.5	24.4	31	4.3	42.0	34	4.7	46.0
—24	20	2.75	27.1	35	4.8	47.5			
⁷⁄₁₆—14	28	3.8	37.0	49	6.8	66.4	55	7.6	74.5
—20	30	4.2	40.7	55	7.6	74.5			
½—13	39	5.4	52.8	75	10.4	101.7	85	11.75	115.2
—20	41	5.7	55.6	85	11.7	115.2			
⁹⁄₁₆—12	51	7.0	69.2	110	15.2	149.1	120	16.6	162.7
—18	55	7.6	74.5	120	16.6	162.7			
⅝—11	83	11.5	112.5	150	20.7	203.3	167	23.0	226.5
—18	95	13.1	128.8	170	23.5	230.5			
¾—10	105	14.5	142.3	270	37.3	366.0	280	38.7	379.6
—16	115	15.9	155.9	295	40.8	400.0			
⅞—9	160	22.1	216.9	395	54.6	535.5	440	60.9	596.5
—14	175	24.2	237.2	435	60.1	589.7			
1—8	236	32.5	318.6	590	81.6	799.9	660	91.3	894.8
—14	250	34.6	338.9	660	91.3	849.8			

Metric Bolts

Relative Strength Marking	4.6, 4.8			8.8		
Bolt Markings						
Bolt Size Thread Size x Pitch (mm)	Maximum Torque			Maximum Torque		
	Ft./Lbs.	Kgm	Nm	Ft./Lbs.	Kgm	Nm
6 x 1.0	2–3	.2–.4	3–4	3–6	.4–.8	5–8
8 x 1.25	6–8	.8–1	8–12	9–14	1.2–1.9	13–19
10 x 1.25	12–17	1.5–2.3	16–23	20–29	2.7–4.0	27–39
12 x 1.25	21–32	2.9–4.4	29–43	35–53	4.8–7.3	47–72
14 x 1.5	35–52	4.8–7.1	48–70	57–85	7.8–11.7	77–110
16 x 1.5	51–77	7.0–10.6	67–100	90–120	12.4–16.5	130–160
18 x 1.5	74–110	10.2–15.1	100–150	130–170	17.9–23.4	180–230
20 x 1.5	110–140	15.1–19.3	150–190	190–240	26.2–46.9	160–320
22 x 1.5	150–190	22.0–26.2	200–260	250–320	34.5–44.1	340–430
24 x 1.5	190–240	26.2–46.9	260–320	310–410	42.7–56.5	420–550

bustion chamber can result from this problem. There may be evidence of water droplets on the engine dipstick when a had gasket has blown.

Diesel Engines

Checking cylinder compression on diesel engines is basically the same procedure as on gasoline engines except for the following:

1. A special compression gauge adaptor suitable for diesel engines (because these engines have much greater compression pressures) must be used.

2. Remove the injector tubes and remove the injectors from each cylinder.

NOTE: *Don't forget to remove the washer underneath each injector, otherwise, it may get lost when the engine is cranked.*

3. When fitting the compression gauge adaptor to the cylinder head, make sure the bleeder of the gauge (if equipped) is closed.

4. When reinstalling the injector assemblies, install new washers underneath each injector.

Design

GASOLINE ENGINE

Rabbit, Golf, Scirocco, Jetta

The engine is an inline 4-cyl. with single overhead camshaft. The engine is inclined 30° to the rear. The center of gravity is in front of the

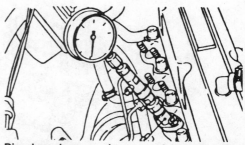

Diesel engines require a special compression gauge adaptor

axle, thereby providing lighter steering and better handling. The crankshaft runs in five bearings with thrust being taken on the center bearing. The cylinder block is cast iron. A steel reinforced belt drives the intermediate shaft and camshaft. The intermediate shaft drives the oil pump, distributor, and fuel pump.

The cylinder head is lightweight aluminum alloy. The intake and exhaust manifolds are mounted on the same side of the cylinder head. The valves are opened and closed by the camshaft lobes operating on cupped cam followers which fit over the valves and springs. This design results in lighter valve train weight and fewer moving parts. The Rabbit, Golf, Jetta and Scirocco engine combines low maintenance and high power output along with low emissions and excellent fuel mileage.

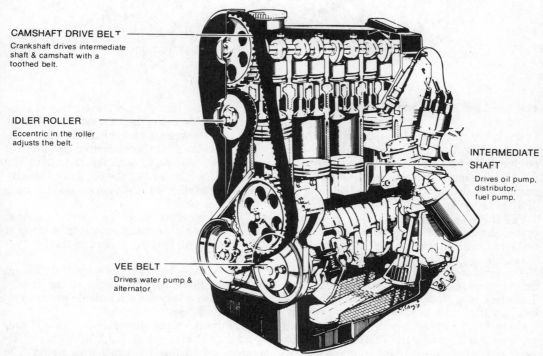

CAMSHAFT DRIVE BELT
Crankshaft drives intermediate shaft & camshaft with a toothed belt.

IDLER ROLLER
Eccentric in the roller adjusts the belt.

INTERMEDIATE SHAFT
Drives oil pump, distributor, fuel pump.

VEE BELT
Drives water pump & alternator

Cutaway view of gasoline engine. The diesel engine is very similar, using many parts from the gasoline engine

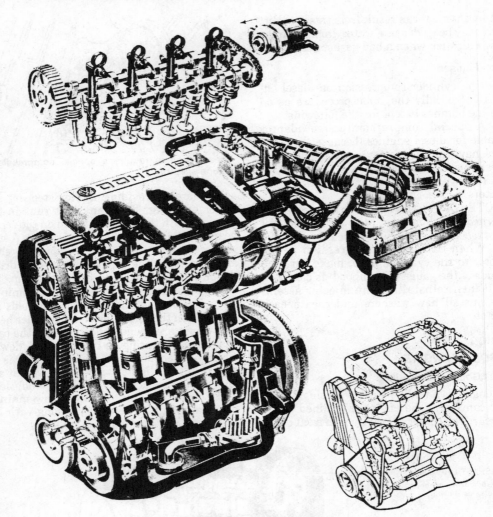

Cut-away view, 16V DOHC engine

1986 and Later Sirocco and GTI (16V DOHC)

In the latter part 1986 Volkswagen introduced its 1.8L, DOHC, 16 valve, fuel injected 4cyl. engine in the Sorocco, as an option to the standard 1.8L, single overhead cam engine. This engine will also be offered in the GTI as of the 1987 model year.

The DOHC and 16 valve engine design can propel the Sorocco from 0–60 mph in 7.7 seconds, reach a top speed of 125 mph, and still gets 25.0 mpg in normal driving.

The cylinder head has a cross flow design and is made of light weight aluminum allow. The block is a standard Volkswagon inline 4 cyl., modified with greater oil pump capacity, and special piston cooling oil jets. In addition to these modifications the DOHC engine gets new pistons to create a 10.0:1 ccompression ratio, a bhp of 123 at 5800 rpm, and a torque of 120 ft.lb. at 4250 rpm.

The combustion chamber is contained completely within the cylinder head. The exhaust valves are vewrtical with the intake valves angled 25° to the engines centerline. This helps to provide a narrow combustion chamber. The spark plug is located in the center of the combustion chamber which allows a shorter ignition flame path.

When combined with the narrow combustion chamber, this results in rapid burning of the fuel air mixture and less potential for ignition knock.

The cylinder head is lightweight aluminum silicone alloy. The 25° angle of the intake valves also allows for a relatively narrow cylinder head design.

The intake valve diameter is 1.25″ (32mm) and the exhaust valves are 1.10″ (28mm). The valves are surface hardened with stelite. The valve seats in the cylinder head are made from sintered steel.

The exhaust valve stems are partially filled with sodium to inprove heat dissipation. At normal operating temperatures, the sodium is in liquid form. The motion of the valves causes the sodium to travel back and forth from the valve head area to the stem. The liquid sodium acts as a medium to remove heat from the valve head area and transfer it to the valve stem where it is rewmoved through the valve guide to the cylinder head coolant jacket. Under no circumstances should either the intake or the exhaust valves be resurfaced. If these valves show signs of wear or damage they must be replaced and the old valves disposed of properly to prevent personal injury. Refer disposal of the valves to a qualified machine shop technician.

The camshafts are driven by a single toothed belt. The belt drives the exhaust camshaft in an arrangement similar to the normal 1.8L engine. The exhaust camshaft then drives the intake camshaft through a single roller chain and sprockets attached to the backs of the camshafts.

The camshafts and pulleys must be installed together in the cylinder head so the timing marks line up as pictured

The camshaft drive belt and all pulleys have been widened from 0.748″ (19mm) to 0.984″ (25mm). The tooth pitch of the belt and pulleys are also deeper.

Dasher, Fox and Quantum

The 4-cylinder engine is identical to the Rabbit or Scirocco engine except for the way it is mounted. While the Rabbit and Scirocco engine is transverse, or mounted sideways in the engine compartment, the Dasher and Fox engine is mounted straight ahead in the traditional fashion. Engines are inclined 30° to the right.

The Quantum 5-cylinder engine is an inline engine with a single overhead camshaft and fuel injection. The engine is installed in the straight ahead manner and tilted to the right.

The crankshaft runs in six main bearings, the cylinder block is made of cast iron and the cylinder head is light weight aluminum alloy. The oil pump is driven by the crankshaft, while the distributor is camshaft driven.

DIESEL ENGINE

VW introduced the diesel engine option on 1977 Rabbit models and 1979 Dashers.

The key difference between the gasoline and diesel engine is that the diesel has no carburetor and no electrical ignition system. There are no plugs, points or coil to replace. Combustion occurs when a fine mist of diesel fuel is sprayed into hot compressed air (1,650°F) under high pressure (850 psi). The air is heated by the compression as the piston moves up on the compression stroke. The diesel engine has a compression ration of 23.5:1 compared to the gasoline engine's compression ration of 8.2:1.

VW's diesel block, flywheel, bearings and crankshaft are identical to those in the Rabbit gasoline engine. The connecting rod wrist pins were strengthened and new pistons and cylinder head, made of aluminum for lightness, were designed.

The cylinder head has an overhead camshaft to actuate the valves and the cam is driven by a flexible toothed belt which also operates the fuel injection pump.

The Volkswagen diesel has a spherical precombustion chamber in which combustion begins. The burning fuel/air mixture is given a swirl pattern by the chamber's shape. The swirl promotes more complete combustion as the combustion process continues in the main combustion chamber. Using the swirl chamber has other advantages: it reduces the peak load which the force of combustion would normally exert on pistons, rods, bearings and crankshaft, enabling VW to use many standard components, and it also permits the VW diesel to be revved to the relatively high speed of 500 rpm.

Warm weather starts and warm engine

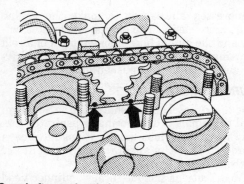

Camshaft sprocket timing marks at TDC

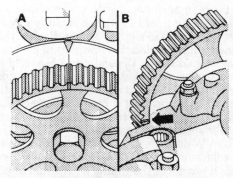

Exhaust camshaft pulley timing mark at TDC

Valve Specifications

Year/Model	Seat Angle (deg)	Face Angle (deg)	Stem to Guide Clearance (in.)		Stem Diameter (in.)	
			Intake	Exhaust	Intake	Exhaust
1974–87	45	45	0.039 max.①	0.051 max.	0.314	0.313

NOTE: Exhaust valves must be ground by hand.
NOTE: Specifications for the 16V DCHC engine were not available at time of publication
① Outer spring, inner spring test pressure is 46–51 lbs. @ 0.72 in.
 Diesels: 0.051 max.

Crankshaft and Connecting Rod Specifications
(All measurements are given in inches)

Year/Model	Crankshaft				Connecting Rod		
	Main Brg. Journal Dia.	Main Brg. Oil Clearance	Shaft End/Play	Thrust on No.	Journal Diameter	Oil Clearance	Side Clearance (max.)
1974–87	2.126①	0.001–0.003②	0.003–0.007	3③	1.811⑥	0.001–0.003④	0.015⑤

NOTE: Main connecting rod bearings are available in three undersizes
① 5 cylinder—2.2834
② 5 cylinder—0.0006–0.003
③ 5 cylinder—No. 4
④ 5 cylinder—.0006–.002
⑤ 5 cylinder—.016
⑥ 1.8 liter; 1.912

Piston and Ring Specifications
(All measurements in inches)

Year/Model	Piston Clearance	Ring Gap			Ring Side Clearance		
		Top Compression	Bottom Compression	Oil Control	Top Compression	Bottom Compression	Oil Control
1974–87 All Gasoline Engines	0.001①– 0.003	0.012–② 0.018	0.012–② 0.018	0.010–② 0.016	0.001–③ 0.002	0.001–③ 0.002	0.001–③ 0.002
1977–87 All Diesel Engines	0.001– 0.003	0.012– 0.020	0.012– 0.020	0.010–④ 0.016	0.002– 0.004	0.002– 0.003	0.001– 0.002

NOTE: Three piston sizes are available to accommodations over-bores up to 0.040 in.
① 5 cylinder; .0011
② 5 cylinder; .010–.020
③ 5 cylinder; .0008–.003
④ 1985; 0.010–0.018

starts are immediate, as with a a gasoline version. Starting a cold engine on a chilly day is different and takes slightly longer. Each of the cylinders has an electric glow plug to preheat them for cold starts. Depending on how cold it is, the driver must wait from 15 to 60 seconds before starting. A light on the dashboard indicates when preheating is completed. Once the engine is warmed up, there is no need to preheat for subsequent restarting.

The VW diesel is also equipped with a manual cold start device that looks like a choke knob. It advances the timing for the fuel injection so that the fuel is injected into the hot compressed air earlier to make the engine start more easily. The engine accelerates better and the puff of blue smoke typical of a cold starting diesel is reduced. Once the car is driven away, the knob is pushed in.

TURBO DIESEL ENGINE

The turbo diesel engine shares the basic design and principals of the normally aspirated diesel, however various modifications have been made to suit the special requirements of turbocharging.

Modifications include: a new cylinder head alloy, new materials used in the valves, valve

Torque Specifications
(All readings in ft. lbs.)

Year	Model	Cylinder Head Bolts	Rod Rearing Bolts ④	Main Bearing Bolts	Crankshaft Pulley Bolt	Flywheel To Crankshaft Bolts	Manifold	
							Intake	Exhaust
'74–'80	Dasher	65 ①	33	47	58	54	18	18
'80–'84	Gas	③	33 ⑥ ⑧	47	58 ⑦	54 ②	18	18
	Diesel	⑤	33 ⑧	47	56 ⑦	54 ②	18	18
'85–'87	Gas	③	33 ⑧	47	145 ⑦	72	18	18
	Diesel	⑤	33 ⑧	47	130	72	18	18

① Torque in 5 steps:
  1st step—36 ft/lbs.
  2nd step—51 ft/lbs.
  3rd step—65 ft/lbs.
  4th step—run engine until fan starts to run.
  5th step—retorque to 65 ft/lbs.
  After 1,000 miles, head bolts must be loosen 30° and retorqued to 65 ft/lbs.
② Pressure plate to crankshaft bolts
③ With 12 points (polygon) head bolts
  Torque in 4 steps:
  1st step—29 ft/lbs.
  2nd step—43 ft/lbs.
  3rd step—additional ½ turn (180°) further in one movement (two 90° turns are permissible)
  Note tightening sequence
  Do not retorque at 1,000 miles

  With 6 point (hex) head bolts
  Torque in steps to 54 ft/lbs. with engine cold, when engine is warmed up, torque to 61 ft/lbs.
  Head bolts must be retorqued after 1,000 miles.
④ Always use new bolts
⑤ Rabbit/Jetta/Quantum
  Torque in 6 steps
  1st step—29 ft/lbs.
  2nd step—43 ft/lbs.
  3rd step—additional ½ turn (180°) further in one movement (two 90° turns are permissible)
  Note tightening sequence
  4th step—run engine until oil temp is 50°C.
  5th step—tighten bolts ¼ turn more.
  Head bolts must be retorqued after 1,000 miles.
⑥ 5 cylinder—36 ft. lbs.
⑦ '83–'87 w/14mm bolt; 145 ft. lbs. 5 cylinder—253 ft. lbs.
⑧ Stretch bolts: 22 ft. lbs. plus ¼ (90°) turn

seats and swirl chambers–all of which improve heat resistance. A new cylinder head gasket is used to provide better heat resistance and sealing. The engine block has been reinforced to accept 12mm stretch type cylinder head bolts. Piston cooling jets have been installed in the block to provide a spray of oil to help cool the pistons and internal temperatures. The pistons have been modified and strengthened, while the piston rings have been redesigned to provide better sealing and wear characteristics. The surface of the crankshaft connecting rod journals have been hardened to increase torsional rigidity and the front crank pulley size has been increased to help reduce vibration.

Engine
REMOVAL AND INSTALLATION

NOTE: *A good rule to follow when removing engines from all models is to label all hoses, electrical wires, and linkages and their connections with tape. Number each tape tag and the place it connects; this should help eliminate the hassles of "Where does this go?" during installation.*

Dasher and Quantum
GASOLINE ENGINES

1. Disconnect the battery cables.
2. Remove the exhaust manifold heater hose and breather hose from the air cleaner.

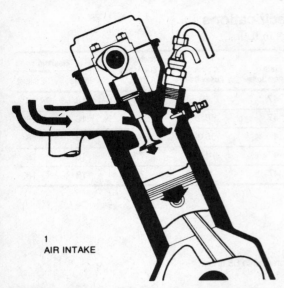

1
AIR INTAKE

Rotation of the crankshaft drives a toothed belt which turns the camshaft, opening the intake valve. As the piston moves down, a vacuum is created, sucking fresh air into the cylinder, past the open intake valve

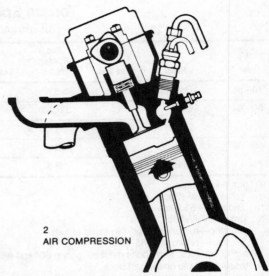

2
AIR COMPRESSION

As the piston moves up, both valves are closed and the air is compressed about 23 times smaller than its original volume. The compressed air reaches a temperature of about 1650° F., far above the temperature needed to ignite diesel fuel

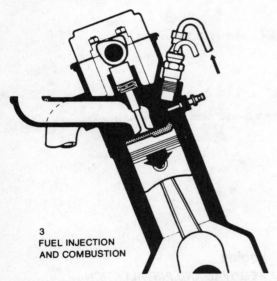

3
FUEL INJECTION
AND COMBUSTION

As the piston reaches the top of the stroke, the air temperature is at its maximum. A fine mist of fuel is sprayed into the prechamber where it ignites and the flame front spreads rapidly into the combustion chamber. The piston is forced downward by the pressure (about 500 psi) of expanding gasses

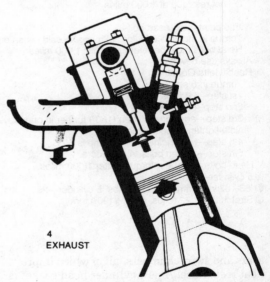

4
EXHAUST

As the energy of combustion is spent and the piston begins to move upward again, the exhaust valve opens and burned gasses are forced out past the open valve. As the piston starts down, the exhaust valve closes, intake valve opens, and the air intake stroke begins again

Diesel Engine Power Cycle

3. Remove the air cleaner assembly.

4. On carbureted models, pull the clip off the accelerator cable and detach the cable. On fuel injected models, disconnect the electrical connector for the fuel injection, cold start valve, oxygen sensor and frequency valve (if equipped), and detach the control pressure regulator lines.

5. Loosen the upper adjustment nut on the clutch cable and detach it. (On Quantum, re-

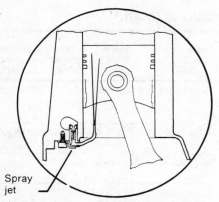

Spray jet for engine oil on turbo-diesel engines

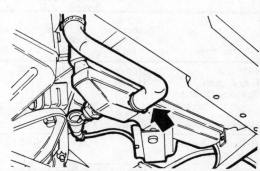

Remove the bottom hose on models without drain plugs to drain the radiator

General Engine Specifications

Year Model	Engine Displacement Cu in. (cc)	Carburetor Type	Horsepower @ rpm (SAE)	Torque @ rpm (ft. lbs.) (SAE)	Bore x Stroke (in)	Compression Ratio	Oil Pressure @ rpm (psi)
1974 Dasher	89.7 (1,471)	2 bbl Solex	75 @ 5,800 ⑦	81 @ 4,000	3.01 x 3.15	8.5:1	40 @ 2,500
1975 Dasher	96.8 (1,588) ⑤	2 bbl Zenith	81 @ 5,500 ⑥	90 @ 3,300	3.13 x 3.15	8.0:1	40 @ 2,500
1975 Rabbit, Scirocco	89.7 (1,471)	2 bbl Zenith	70 @ 6,000	81 @ 3,500	3.01 x 3.15	8.2:1	40 @ 2,500
1976 Rabbit, Scirocco	96.8 (1,588)	2 bbl Zenith	71 @ 5,600	82 @ 3,300	3.13 x 3.15	8.2:1	40 @ 2,500
1976–77 Dasher	96.8 (1,588)	CIS Fuel inj.	79 @ 5,500 ⑧	90 @ 3,300	3.13 x 3.15	8.0:1	40 @ 2,500
1977 Rabbit, Scirocco	96.8 (1,588)	CIS Fuel inj.	78 @ 5,500 ①	90 @ 3,300	3.13 x 3.15	8.0:1	40 @ 2,500
1977–80 Rabbit (Diesel)	89.7 (1,471)	Fuel inj.	48 @ 5,000	56.5 @ 3,000	3.01 x 3.15	23.5:1	27 @ 2,000
1978 Scirocco	88.9 (1,457)	CIS Fuel inj.	73 @ 5,800	73 @ 3,500 ④	3.13 x 2.89	8.0:1	28 @ 2,000
1978–79 Dasher	97.0 (1,588)	CIS Fuel inj.	78 @ 5,500 ①	84 @ 3,200 ②	3.13 x 3.15	8.0:1	28 @ 2,000
1978–79 Rabbit	88.9 (1,457)	CIS Fuel inj. ⑨	71 @ 5,800 ③	73 @ 3,500 ④	3.13 x 2.89	8.0:1	28 @ 2,000
1979 Scirocco	97.0 (1,588)	CIS Fuel inj.	78 @ 5,500 ①	84 @ 3,200 ②	3.13 x 3.15	8.0:1	28 @ 2,000
1979–80 Dasher (Diesel)	89.7 (1,471)	Fuel inj.	48 @ 5,000	56.5 @ 3,000	3.01 x 3.15	23.5:1	28 @ 2,000
1980 Dasher	97.0 (1,588)	CIS Fuel inj.	76 @ 5,500	83 @ 3,200	3.13 x 3.15	8.2:1	40 @ 2,500
1980 Rabbit	89.0 (1,457)	1 bbl Solex	62 @ 5,400	76.6 @ 3,000	3.13 x 2.89	8.0:1	28 @ 2,000
1980 Rabbit, Jetta, Scirocco	97.0 (1,588)	CIS Fuel inj.	71 @ 5,500 ⑩	83 @ 3,200 ⑪	3.13 x 3.15	8.2:1	28 @ 2,000

General Engine Specifications (cont.)

Year Model	Engine Displacement Cu in. (cc)	Carburetor Type	Horsepower @ rpm (SAE)	Torque @ rpm (ft. lbs.) (SAE)	Bore x Stroke (in)	Compression Ratio	Oil Pressure @ rpm (psi)
1981–83 Rabbit, Jetta, Scirocco, Quantum	105.0 (1,715)	CIS ⑬ Fuel inj.	74 @ 5,000	90 @ 3,000	3.13 x 3.40	8.2:1	28 @ 2,000
1983 Rabbit, Scirocco	109.0 (1,780)	CIS Fuel inj.	90 @ 5,500	100 @ 3,000	3.19 x 3.40	8.5:1	28 @ 2,000
1983 Turbo-diesel	97.0 (1,588)	Fuel inj.	68 @ 4,500	98 @ 2,800	3.0 x 3.40	23.0:1	⑫
1981–83 Diesel	97.0 (1,588)	Fuel inj.	52 @ 4,800	72 @ 2,000	3.01 x 3.40	23.0:1	28 @ 2,000
1983 Quantum	130.8 (2,144)	Fuel inj.	100 @ 5,100	112 @ 3,000	3.12 x 3.40	8.2:1	28 @ 2,000
'84–'87 Jetta, Quantum	109.0 (1,780)	CIS Fuel inj.	88 @ 5,500	96 @ 3,250	3.19 x 3.40	9.0:1	28 @ 2,000
'85–'87 GTI, Jetta	109.0 (1,780)	CIS Fuel inj.	100 @ 5,500	107 @ 3,000	3.20 x 3.40	10.0:1	28 @ 2,000
'85–'87 Cabriolet Scirocco	109.0 (1,780)	CIS Fuel inj.	90 @ 5,500	100 @ 3,000	3.19 x 3.40	8.5:1	28 @ 2,000
'85–'87 Golf	109.0 (1,780)	CIS Fuel inj.	85 @ 5,250	98 @ 3,000	3.20 x 3.40	8.5:1	28 @ 2,000
'85–'87 Golf (Diesel)	97 (1,588)	Fuel inj.	52 @ 4,800	70 @ 2,000	3.01 x 3.40	23:1	20 @ 2,000
'82–'84 Rabbit (Diesel)	97 (1,588)	Fuel inj.	52 @ 4,800	97 @ 2,800 ⑨	3.01 x 3.40	23:1	20 @ 2,000
'83–'84 Rabbit (GTI)	109.0 (1,780)	CIS Fuel inj.	90 @ 5,500	100 @ 3,000	3.19 x 3.40	8.5:1	28 @ 2,000
1987 Fox	109.0	CIS Fuel inj.	81 @ 5,500	93 @ 3,250	3.20 x 3.40	9.0:1	28 @ 2,000
'86–'87 Scirocco 16V	109.0	CIS Fuel inj.	123 @ 5,800	120 @ 4,250	3.20 x 3.40	10.0:1	28 @ 2,000

① 76 @ 5,000—California
② 83 @ 3,200—California
③ 70 @ 5,800—California
④ 72 @ 3,500—California
⑤ 1,471 cc engine for Canada
⑥ 71 @ 5,800—Canada
⑦ 71 @ 5,800—California
⑧ 77 @ 5,500—California
⑨ Some 1978 Rabbits are equipped with a Solex 1 bbl carburetor
⑩ Canada: 76 hp
⑪ Canada: 92 ft. lbs.
⑫ 7 psi @ idle; 74 psi @ 5,000 rpm
⑬ Carter TYF carburetor used on some models

move clip on clutch cable and unhook cable).

6. On carbureted models only, disconnect the fuel line from the fuel pump, plug it, and place it out of the way. On fuel injected models, disconnect the air duct. Remove the cold start valve. Remove the fuel injectors from the head (protect the ends with caps) and the accelerator cable. Remove the air flow sensor with the fuel distributor and place out of the way.

7. Detach emission control hoses. Remove power steering pump and V-belts, if equipped.

8. Disconnect the wiring from the alternator.

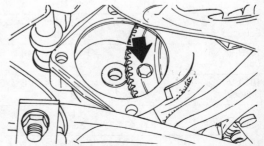

On automatic transmissions, remove the converter to flywheel bolts through the starter mounting hole (Dasher and Quantum)

9. Detach the clip and remove the heater cable.

CAUTION: *Do not disconnect refrigerant lines on cars equipped with air conditioning.*

10. On cars with air conditioning:

a. Remove the horn, compressor and condenser assesmblies.

b. Move the compressor and condensers out of the way, without disconnecting the refrigerant lines.

c. Disconnect the vacuum hoses and brake booster hose, if equipped.

11. Disconnect the front engine mounts and remove the mount bracket.

12. Drain the coolant from the radiator. The plug is located near the lower hose, or remove the hose on models without the drain plug. Drain the cylinder block at the plug near the starter.

13. Disconnect the electrical wire from the coil and distributor, oil pressure and temperature sending units, fan and the thermal switch on the radiator.

14. Disconnect the radiator and heater hoses from the engine. Detach the heater valve cable.

15. Loosen the radiator shroud retainers. Remove the mounting bolts and nuts and lift out the radiator and fan.

16. Raise the front of the car and safely support it.

17. Remove the starter.

18. Disconnect the exhaust pipe from the manifold.

19. Detach the engine side mounts.

20. Loosen the upper engine-to-transmission bolts. Remove the lower bolts. If the car is equipped with an automatic transmission, remove the three torque converter-to-flywheel bolts by working through the starter hole. Use a bar to hold the flywheel. Also disconnect the automatic transmission vacuum hose.

21. Support the transmission with a floor jack.

22. Lower the car until the wheels are on the ground.

23. Attach the hoist to the engine lift points.

24. Raise the engine/transmission until the transmission touches the steering rack.

25. Adjust your jack or support so that the transmission is held firmly.

26. Remove the upper engine-to-transmission bolts.

27. Pry the engine and transmission apart and remove the intermediate plate. Install a bar or cable to the torque converter housing on automatic cars to prevent the converter from falling out.

28. Remove the engine by slowly lifting and turning simultaneously.

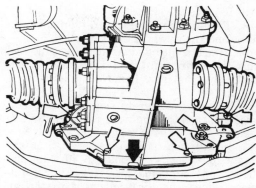

Remove the lower engine/transmission bolts and flywheel cover (arrows)

CAUTION: *Do this very carefully to avoid damaging the halfshafts or transmission.*

29. Installation is the reverse of removal. Be careful not to damage the input shaft of the transmission during installation. Install new torque converter mounting bolts. Tighten the torque converter bolts to 25 ft.lb., engine to transaxle bolts to 40 ft.lb., and the engine mount bolts to 32 ft.lb.

DIESEL ENGINES

1. Remove the negative battery cable.

2. Set the heat control to hot. Remove the lower radiator hose and remove the thermostat to drain the coolant. Remove the thermoswitch electrical connector and the radiator brace at the bottom of the radiator, remove the top radiator shroud, upper hose, radiator mounting bolts, and remove the radiator and fan.

3. Remove the supply and return lines from the injection pump. Disconnect the throttle cable from the pump and remove the cable mounting bracket. Disconnect the cold start cable at the pin, and remove the electrical connector from the fuel shut-off solenoid.

4. Disconnect the electrical connectors from the oil pressure switch, coolant temperature sensor and glow plugs. Remove the radiator hose from the head and the vacuum hose from the vacuum pump.

5. Loosen the adjusting nuts and unhook the clutch cable from the lever.

6. Remove the hose from the water pump.

7. Unbolt the rear of the turbocharger (if equipped) from the exhaust system.

8. Loosen the right engine mount.

9. Remove the alternator after tagging the wires for installation.

10. Remove the front engine mounts.

11. Disconnect the exhaust pipe from the manifold, and the pipe bracket from the transmission.

12. Loosen the left engine mount.

13. Remove the starter.

14. Remove the engine-to-transmission bolts, and the flywheel cover bolts.

15. Attach a lifting chain to the engine and raise the engine until the transmission touches the steering rack. Remove the left engine mount.

16. Support the transmission with a jack and raise and turn the engine at the same time to remove.

17. Installation is the reverse. Tighten the engine-to-transmission bolts to 40 ft.lb. and the engine mount bolts to 29 ft.lb. After installation adjust the throttle and cold starting cables.

Rabbit, Golf, Jetta, GTI and Scirocco with Manual Transmission

GASOLINE ENGINES

The engine and transmission are removed as an assembly.

1. Disconnect the battery ground cable and remove the battery.

2. Drain the coolant by unbolting the lower water pump flange or by removing the hoses.

CAUTION: *Do not disconnect or loosen any refrigerant hose connections during engine removal on cars equipped with air conditioning.*

3. On cars equipped with air conditioning:

  a. Loosen the compressor support bolts and remove the compressor.

  b. Remove the radiator cooling fan, air ducts and radiator.

  c. Remove the condenser.

  d. Place the air conditioning compressor and condenser out of the way without disconnecting any refrigerant lines.

4. Remove the radiator with the air ducts and fan.

Disconnect (1) front mount, (2) clutch cable, and (3) speedometer cable—manual transmission Rabbit, Jetta, Scirocco

5. Detach and label all the electrical wires connecting the engine to the body.

6. Disconnect and plug the fuel line at the fuel pump. Detach the coolant hoses at the left end of the engine. Disconnect the accelerator cable and remove the air cleaner.

7. Disconnect the speedometer cable from the transmission. Detach the clutch cable.

8. Remove the engine support to the right of the starter.

9. Remove the headlight caps inside the engine compartment.

10. Unbolt the driveshafts from the transmission and wire them up.

11. Unbolt the exhaust pipe from the manifold and unbolt the exhaust pipe brace.

NOTE: *On the sixteen valve, four cylinder engine, you will have to unbolt and remove the intake manifold in order to remove the engine.*

12. Unbolt the transmission rear mount from the body (alongside the tunnel).

13. Detach the ground strap from the transmission and body.

14. Remove the shift linkage.

15. Attach a chain sling to the alternator bracket and the lifting eye at the left end of the engine. Lift the engine and transmission slightly.

16. Detach the engine carrier from the body and remove the left transmission carrier.

17. Slightly lower and tilt the engine and transmission, then lift the engine/transmission assembly, turning slightly at the same time, carefully out of the car.

18. To separate the engine and transmission, turn the flywheel to align the lug on the flywheel (to the left of TDC) with the pointer in the opening. The engine and transmission can only be separated in this position. Remove the cover plate over the driveshaft flange and remove the engine to transmission bolts and the transmission housing cover plate.

19. To attach the transmission to the engine, the recess in the flywheel edge must be at 3:00 o'clock (facing the left end of the engine). Torque the engine to transmission bolts to 40 ft.lb. Lift the engine/transmission assembly into place. Loosen the bolts for the engine and transmission mounts. Move the engine assembly from side to side until the rear transmission mount is straight. Center the left and right transmission mounts and tighten all transmission bolts. Push the front mount upward to center the rubber cone, then tighten the mount. Loosen the exhaust pipe clamps, release any strain, then tighten the clamps. Torque the 10mm bolts to 29 ft.lb. Torque the driveshaft flange bolts to 32 ft.lb. Refill the cooling system.

Disconnect (1) exhaust pipe bracket, (2) exhaust pipe, and (3) rear transmission mount

Rabbit, Golf, Jetta and Sirocco with Automatic Transmission

GASOLINE ENGINES

The engine and transmission are removed as an assembly.

1. Shift the transmission into "Park." Disconnect both battery cables.

2. Drain the coolant by unbolting the lower water pump flange or by removing the hoses.

CAUTION: *Do not disconnect or loosen any refrigerant hose connections during engine removal on cars quipped with air conditioning.*

3. On cars equipped with air conditioning proceed as follows:

   a. Loosen the compressor support bolts and remove the compressor.

   b. Remove the radiator cooling fan, air ducts, and radiator.

   c. Remove the condenser.

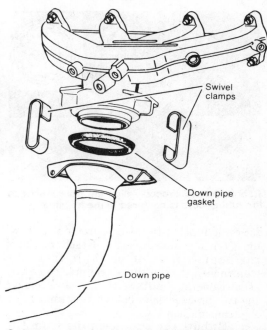

Swivel clamps

Down pipe gasket

Down pipe

Swivel type exhaust pipe mounting on 1983 models

   d. Place the air conditioning components out of the way without disconnecting any refrigerant lines.

4. Remove the radiator with the air ducts and fan.

5. Remove the air cleaner.

6. Detach the speedometer cable from the transmission.

7. Detach and label all electrical wires connecting the engine to the body. Detach and label all heater and coolant hoses.

8. Remove the screws holding the accelera-

When installing Rabbit, Jetta, Scirocco engine, align engine/transmission mounts at front mount (A), left mount (B) and rear mount (C)

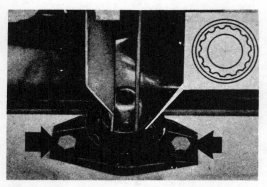

Rabbit, Jetta, Scirocco—align the front mount so the rubber core is centered in the housing

tor cable bracket to the carburetor float bowl (do not disassemble linkage), detach the end of the gearshift selector cable from the transmision, detach the accelerator cable and pedal cable at the transmission, and remove the two bracket bolts behind this linkage on the transmission.

9. Unbolt the exhaust pipe from the manifold.

10. Remove the rear transmission mount. Unbolt the driveshafts and wire them up and out of the way.

NOTE: *On the sixteen valve, four cylinder engine, you will have to unbolt and remove the intake manifold in order to remove the engine.*

11. Remove the converter cover plate and remove the three torque converter to drive plate bolts.

12. Attain a chain sling to the alternator bracket and the lifting eye at the left end of the engine. It may be necessary to remove the alternator. Lift the engine and transmission slightly.

13. Detach the engine front mounting support. Remove the left transmission carrier and the right engine carrier.

14. Slightly lower and tilt the engine and transmission, then lift the engine/transmission assembly, turning slightly at the same time, carefully out of the car.

15. The transmission can now be detached from the engine.

16. The engine to transmission bolts should be torqued to 40 ft.lb. Lift the engine/transmission assembly into place and install the left transmission carrier, tightening first the body, the the transmission bolts. Lower the assembly to attach the engine carrier to the body, tightening the bolts to 40 ft.lb. Install the engine mounting support. Check that all mounts and clamps are free of strain. Torque converter bolts should be torqued to 21 ft.lb. and driveshaft bolts to 32 ft.lb. Refill the cooling system.

Check the adjustment of transmission and carburetor linkages.

DIESEL ENGINES

The diesel engine is removed with the transmission attached.

1. Disconnect the battery.

2. Disconnect the radiator hoses and drain the coolant. It can be saved for reuse, if it's not too old.

3. Remove the radiator complete with fan.

CAUTION: *Do not disconnect any refrigerant hose connections during engine removal on cars equipped with air conditioning.*

4. Remove the alternator.

5. Disconnect the fuel filter and set it aside near the windshield washer reservoir.

6. Detach the supply and return lines from the injection pump.

7. Disconnect the accelerator cable from the lever on the injection pump and remove the injection pump complete with bracket.

8. Disconnect the cold start cable from the pump.

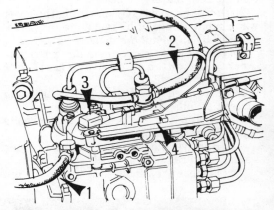

Detach and mark the fuel lines at the injection pump. (1) fuel supply line, (2) return line, (3) accelerator cable and (4) remove bracket—diesel

Move the engine/transmission front to rear to center the left and right transmission mounts in the brackets—Rabbit, Jetta, Scirocco

9. Disconnect and label all electrical wires and leads.

10. Remove the front transmission mount.

11. Disconnect the clutch cable.

12. Remove the relay rod and connecting rod from the transmission and turn the relay lever shaft to the rear.

13. Disconnect the selector rod.

14. Unbolt the driveshafts and wire them up out of the way. Remove the rear support.

15. Disconnect the exhaust pipe at the manifold and remove the rear transmission mount. Unbolt the rear of the turbocharger (if equipped) from the exhaust system.

16. Attach a lifting sling to the engine and take the weight from the engine mounts. Remove the left and right transmission mounts.

17. Carefully guide the engine out of the car while turning it slightly.

18. To separate the engine from the transmission, unscrew the plug from the TDC sensor opening and turn the flywheel to align the mark on the flywheel with the pointer. The engine/transmission can only be separated in this position.

19. Remove the cover plate over the drive-

Move the engine/transmission assembly side to side so that the rear mount is straight—Rabbit, Jetta, Scirocco

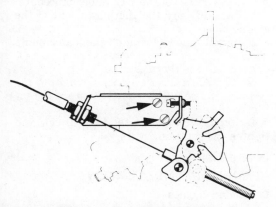

Remove the accelerator cable bracket screws (arrows) without disturbing the settings

shaft flange and remove the engine-to-transmission belts.

20. Press the engine off the transmission.

21. Installation is the reverse of removal. Turn the flywheel so that the recess in the flywheel is level with the driveshaft flange. Lower the engine into the car and attach the left transmission mount to the transmission first. Align the rear transmission mount, center the engine/transmission and center the front transmission mount. Adjust the accelerator and cold start cables and bleed the injection system.

Fox

GASOLINE ENGINE

The engine is lifted out of the vehicle after seperation from the transmission.

1. Disconnect the battery ground cable and remove the battery.

2. Open the heating valve and the cap on the coolant expansion tank. Drain the coolant by removing the hoses. Then seperate the electrical connector from the radiator fan.

CAUTION: *Do not disconnect or loosen any refrigerant hose connections during engine removal on cars equipped with air conditioning.*

3. On cars equipped with air conditioning:

   a. Loosen the compressor support bolts and remove the compressor.

   b. Remove the radiator cooling fan, air ducts and radiator.

   c. Remove the condenser.

   d. Place the air conditioning compressor and condenser out of the way without disconnecting any refrigerant lines.

4. Disconnect the radiator thermo switch and remove the radiator cover. Disconnect the motor mount and remove the rubber bushing. Remove the radiator with the air ducts and fan.

5. Detach and label all the electrical wires connecting the engine to the body.

6. Disconnect and plug the fuel line at the fuel pump. Detach the coolant hoses at the left end of the engine. Disconnect the accelerator cable and remove the air cleaner.

7. Disconnect the speedometer cable from the transmission. Detach the clutch cable.

8. Remove the vacuum hoses. Remove the wire from the ignition coil, the vacuum unit hose, and the plug for the Hall system from the distributor.

9. Remove the fuel injectors and install protective caps and plugs.

10. Remove the cold start valve leaving the fuel line connected.

11. Loosen the charcoal filter clamp and

move the filter to the rear of the engine compartment.

12. Remove the upper engine to transmission bolts.

13. Remove the left and right engine mounting bolts.

14. Remove the engine stop and the air duct from the intake manifold.

15. Disconnect and lable the starter cables. Then remove the starter mounting bolts and the starter.

16. Remove the two lower engine to transmission bolts. Then remove the cover plate bolts and the cover plate.

17. Disconnect the exhaust pipe from the manifold at the flange. Then remove the bolt from the exhaust pipe support and remove the exhaust pipe from the manifold.

18. Install transmission support bar (VW 758/1) with slight preload.

19. Install chain (US 1105) on the engine lifting eyes, located on the left side of the cylinder head.

20. Lift the engine until its weight is taken off the engine mounts.

21. Adjust the support bar to contact the transmission.

22. Seperate the engine and transmission.

23. Carefully lift the engine out of the engine compartment so as not to damage the transmission main shaft, clutch and body.

To install: Proceed in the reverse order of removal and note the following.

24. Lubricate the clutch release bearing and transmission main shaft splines with MoS_2 grease or an equvalent. Do Not lubricate the guide sleeve for the clutch release bearing.

25. Carefully guide the engine into the vehicle and attach to the transmission while keeping weight off of the motor mounts.

26. Install and tighten the upper engine to transmission bolts.

27. Remove the transmission support bar and lower the engine onto the engine mounts.

28. Reconnect and tighten the starter cables, being carefull not to let the cables touch the engine, causing a short circuit and possibly a fire.

29. The remainder of the engines installation is the reverse of the removal procedure.

NOTE: *Tighten the engine mounts and subframe bolts with the engine running at idle speed.*

30. Torque the cold start valve, the radiator mount bolts, and the engine to transmission cover plate bolts to 7 ft.lb.

31. Torque the engine to transmission bolts to 42 ft.lb., the engine mount bolts to 26 ft.lb., the engine stop to body bolck and exhaust pipe support bolts to 18 ft.lb., the exhaust pipe to

manifold bolts to 22 ft.lb. and the starter bolts to 15 ft.lb.

Camshaft (Valve) Cover
REMOVAL AND INSTALLATION

Remove air cleaner asssembly or loosen and relocate the air cleaner snorkel or box (depending on year and model). Disconnect the fuel line and accelerator cable (if necessary) and any other vacuum lines or hoses that will interfere with the cover removal. Disconnect the crankcase breather hose from the cover connection. Remove the cover retaining bolts and the cover. Clean all mounting surfaces. Install a new cover gasket and seal. Install the cover in the reverse order of removal.

Thermostat
REMOVAL AND INSTALLATION
4-Cylinder

The thermostat is located in the bottom radiator hose neck on the water pump.

1. Drain the cooling system.

2. Remove the two retaining bolts from the lower water pump neck.

NOTE: *It's not necessary to disconnect the hose.*

3. Move neck, with hoses attached, out of the way.

4. Remove the thermostat.

5. Install a new seal on the water pump neck.

6. Install the thermostat with the spring end up.

7. Replace the water pump neck and tighten the two retaining bolts.

5-Cylinder

The thermostat is located in the lower radiator hose neck, on the left side of the engine block, behind the water pump housing.

Follow Steps 1–3 of the 4-Cylinder procedure.

1. Carefully pry the thermostat out of the engine block.

2. Install a new O-ring on the water pump neck.

3. Install the thermostat.

NOTE: *When installing the thermostat, the spring end should be pointing toward the engine block.*

4. Reposition the water pump neck and tighten the retaining bolts.

Intake Manifold
REMOVAL AND INSTALLATION
Carbureted Engines

1. Remove the air cleaner. Drain the cooling system.

2. Disconnect the accelerator cable.
3. Disconnect the EGR valve connections.
4. Detach all electrical leads.
5. Disconnect the coolant hoses.
6. Disconnect the fuel line from the carburetor.
7. Remove the vacuum hoses from the carburetor.
8. Loosen and remove the six retaining bolts and lift off the manifold.
9. Install a new gasket. Fit the manifold and tighten the bolts from the inside out. Tightening torque is 18 ft.lb.
10. Install the remaining components in the reverse order of removal. Refill the cooling system.
NOTE: *See Throttle Linkage Adjustment in chapter 4, Emission Controls and Fuel System for correct adjustment of the throttle cable.*

Fuel Injected Engines

1. Disconnect the air duct from the throttle valve body. Drain the cooling system.
2. Disconnect the accelerator cable.
3. Remove the injectors and disconnect the line from the cold start valve.
4. Disconnect all coolant hoses.
5. Disconnect all vacuum and emission control hoses. Label all hoses for installation.
6. Remove the auxiliary air regulator.
7. Disconnect all electrical lines. Label all wires for installation.
8. Disconnect the EGR line from the exhaust manifold.
9. Loosen and remove the retaining bolts and lift off the manifold.
10. Install a new gasket. Install the manifold and tighten the bolts to 18 ft.lb.
11. Install the remaining components in the reverse order of removal.

Diesel Engines

1. Disconnect the negative battery cable.
2. Drain the cooling system.
3. Disconnect the hose that runs between the air duct and the turbocharger.
4. Remove the air cleaner.
5. Disconnect and plug all lines coming from the brake booster vacuum pump and remove the pump.
6. Disconnect the PCV line.
7. Disconnect and remove the blow-off valve and then disconnect the hose which runs from the intake manifold to the turbocharger (turbo-diesel only).
8. Remove the manifold.
9. Installation is in the reverse order of removal.
NOTE: *When installing the manifolds,*

tighten the bolts from the center towards the ends, alternating from center.

Exhaust Manifold
REMOVAL AND INSTALLATION

1. Disconnect the EGR tube from the exhaust manifold (if equipped).
2. Remove the air pump components which are in the way, if vehicle is so equipped.
3. Remove the air cleaner hose from the exhaust manifold.
4. Disconnect the intake manifold support.
5. Separate the exhaust pipe from the manifold or turbocharger.
6. Remove turbocharger. Remove the eight retaining nuts and remove the manifold.
7. Clean the cylinder head and manifold mating surfaces.
8. Using a new gasket, install the exhaust manifold.
9. Tighten the nuts to 18 ft.lb. Work from the inside out.
10. Install the remaining components in the reverse order of removal. Use a new manifold flange gasket.

Turbocharger
REMOVAL AND INSTALLATION

1. Disconnect the negative battery cable and ground strap.
2. Remove the engine and transmission cover shield to gain access to the turbocharger.
3. Loosen the stabilizer bar clamps on both sides of the stabilizer and push the bar down out of the way.
4. Loosen the oil return connector bolt at the bottom of the turbocharger. Remove the side support bolt. Have a container ready to catch the oil when disconnecting bottom adapter.
5. Remove the turbocharger heat shield mounting nuts and the oil return line.
6. Remove both hoses, turbocharger to intake manifold and air cleaner. Loosen and remove the oil supply line to the turbocharger.
7. Remove the exhaust pipe to turbocharger mounting bolts and the turbocharger exhaust manifold mounting bolts. Remove the turbocharger.
8. To install, position the turbocharger on the exhaust manifold and hand tighten the two mounting bolts. Install the lower vertical oil return connector mounting bolt and lower side support bolt, tighten hand tight. Torque the mounting bolts in the following sequence:
• Manifold-to-turbocharger: 50 ft.lb.
• Lower oil connection: 18 ft.lb.
• Lower side mount: 18 ft.lb.
9. Fill the upper oil supply connection on

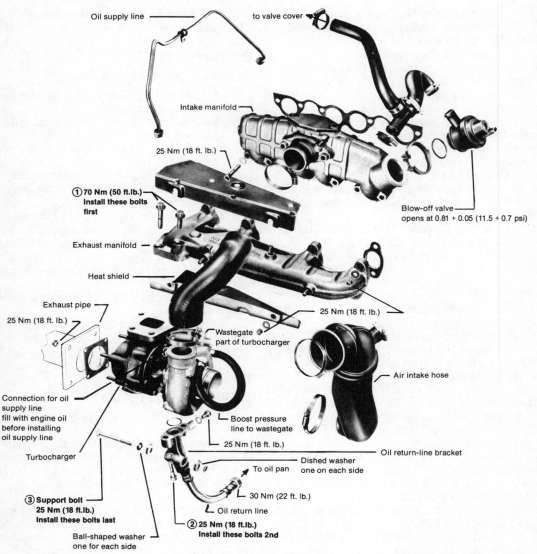

Oil supply line

to valve cover

Intake manifold

25 Nm (18 ft. lb.)

① **70 Nm (50 ft.lb.)**
Install these bolts
first

Blow-off valve
opens at 0.81 + 0.05 (11.5 + 0.7 psi)

Exhaust manifold

Heat shield

Exhaust pipe
25 Nm (18 ft. lb.)

25 Nm (18 ft. lb.)

Wastegate
part of turbocharger

Air intake hose

Connection for oil
supply line
fill with engine oil
before installing
oil supply line

Boost pressure
line to wastegate

25 Nm (18 ft. lb.)

Oil return-line bracket

Turbocharger

Dished washer
one on each side

To oil pan

③ **Support bolt**
25 Nm (18 ft.lb.)
Install these bolts last

30 Nm (22 ft. lb.)

Oil return line

② **25 Nm (18 ft.lb.)**
Install these bolts 2nd

Ball-shaped washer
one for each side

Turbocharger mounting

NEW
POLYGON

OLD
HEXAGON

New and old style head bolts

the turbocharger with oil. Install the remaining turbocharger connections, shields, etc., in the reverse order of removal.

10. When installation is complete, start the engine and allow to idle for several minutes. Do not increase engine speed above idle until the turbocharger oil supply system has had a chance to fill.

Air Conditioning Compressor
REMOVAL AND INSTALLATION

1. Remove the compressor clutch.
2. Remove the camshaft drive belt cover.
3. Remove the compressor mounting bracket bolts.

4. Remove the diagional and support braces.

5. Remove the compressor mounting bracket bolts.

6. Remove the brackets from the engine and tie the compressor back out of the way in such a manner that there is no stress on the refrigerant lines.

NOTE: *Compressor mounting brackets can be removed without disconnecting the refrigerant lines.*

7. installation is the reverse of the removal procedure.

Radiator and Fan
REMOVAL AND INSTALLATION
4-Cylinder

1. Drain the cooling system.

NOTE: *Various late models have the radiator retained by locating tabs at the bottom and two mounting brackets at the top. Disconnect hoses and wiring connectors, disconnect top brackets and remove radiator and fan assembly.*

2. Remove the inner shroud mounting bolts.

3. Disconnect the lower radiator hose.

4. Disconnect the thermo-switch lead.

5. Remove the lower radiator shroud.

6. Remove the lower radiator mounting units.

7. Disconnect the upper radiator hose.

8. Detach the upper radiator shroud.

9. Disconnect the heater and intake manifold hoses.

10. Remove the side mounting bolts and top clip and lift the radiator and fan out as an assembly.

11. Installation is the reverse of removal.

5-Cylinder

1. Drain the cooling system.

2. Remove the three pieces of the radiator cowl and the fan motor assembly. Take care in removing the fan motor connectors to avoid bending them.

3. Remove the upper and lower radiator hoses and the coolant tank supply hose.

4. Disconnect the coolant temperature switch located on the lower right side of the radiator.

5. Remove the radiator mounting bolts and lift out the radiator.

6. Installation is the reverse of removal. Torque radiator mounting bolts to 14 ft.lb. and cowl bolts to 7 ft.lb.

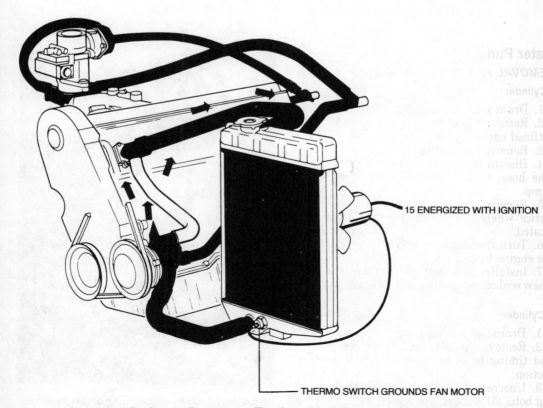

15 ENERGIZED WITH IGNITION

THERMO SWITCH GROUNDS FAN MOTOR

Carbureted Dasher cooling system. The thermo switch controls fan operation

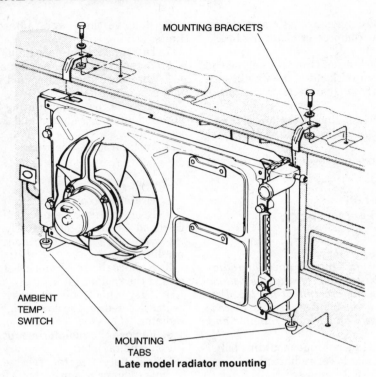

MOUNTING BRACKETS

AMBIENT
TEMP.
SWITCH

MOUNTING
TABS
Late model radiator mounting

Water Pump
REMOVAL AND INSTALLATION
4-Cylinder

1. Drain the cooling system.
2. Remove the alternator and drive belt as outlined earlier in this chapter.
3. Remove the timing belt cover.
4. Disconnect the lower radiator hose, engine hose, and heater hose from the water pump.
5. Remove the four pump retaining bolts. Notice where the different length bolts are located.
6. Turn the pump slightly and lift it out of the engine block.
7. Installation is the reverse of removal. Use a new seal on the mating surface of the engine.

5-Cylinder

1. Drain the cooling system.
2. Remove the V-belts, timing belt covers and timing belts as outlined earlier in this section.
3. Unscrew the water pump pulley retaining bolts (3) and remove the pulley.
4. Unscrew the intermediate shaft drive

Check the condition of the O-ring before installing the water pump

Water pump installation. The long bolt goes in the location shown

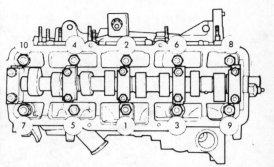
Cylinder head torque sequence—installing. Reverse sequence when removing

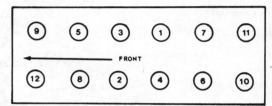
5 cylinder head bolt tightening sequence

sprocket retaining bolt and remove the sprocket.

5. Unscrew the water pump retaining bolts and remove the pump from its housing.

6. Always replace the old gasket with a new one.

7. Installation is in the reverse order of removal.

Cylinder Head

REMOVAL AND INSTALLATION

Carbureted Engines

The engine should be cold before the cylinder head can be removed. The head is retained by 10 socket head bolts. It can be removed without removing the intake and exhaust manifolds.

NOTE: *Beginning approximately July 1977, 12 point socket head bolts were used in place of 6 point older version. These should be used in complete sets only and need not be retorqued after the mileage interval.*

1. Rotate the crankshaft to set No. 1 cylinder at TDC with timing marks aligned. Disconnect the battery ground cable.

2. Drain the cooling system.

3. Remove the air cleaner. Disconnect the fuel line.

4. Disconnect the radiator, heater, and choke hoses.

5. Disconnect all electrical wires. Remove the spark plug wires.

CAUTION: *Remove air conditioner compressor with lines attached and place out of the way. Do not disconnect any lines.*

6. Separate the exhaust manifold from the exhaust pipe.

7. Disconnect the EGR line from the exhaust manifold. Remove the EGR valve and filter from the intake manifold.

8. Remove the carburetor.

9. Disconnect the air pump fittings.

10. Remove the timing belt cover and belt.

11. Loosen the cylinder head bolts in the sequence of 10 to 1 as shown in the illustration.

12. Remove the bolts and lift the cylinder head straight off.

13. Install the new cylinder head gasket with the word Top or OBEN up.

14. Install bolts Nos. 10 and 8 first, these holes are smaller and will properly locate the gasket and cylinder head.

15. Install the remaining bolts. Tighten them in three stages in the 1 through 10 sequence shown. Cylinder head tightening torque is 54 ft.lb. 12 point bolts should be tightened to 54 ft.lb., then tightened ¼ turn more.

NOTE: *After approximately 1000 miles, retighten the cylinder head bolts. Torque them, with the engine hot (operating temperature) to 61 ft.lb. This is for six point bolts only, 12 point bolts do not have to be retorqued.*

16. Install the remaining components in the reverse order of removal.

Fuel Injected Engines

The cylinder head is retained by Allen Bolts. When installing the head gasket, the TOP or OBEN goes up. Install No. 10 and 8 bolts (4-cylinder) first; these are shorter and will locate the head and gasket.

NOTE: *Beginning approximately July 1977, 12 point socket had bolts were used in place of the older six point bolts. These should be used in complete sets only and need not be retorqued after the mileage interval.*

1. Rotate the crankshaft to set No. 1 cylinder at TDC with timing marks aligned. Disconnect the battery ground cable.

2. Drain the cooling system.

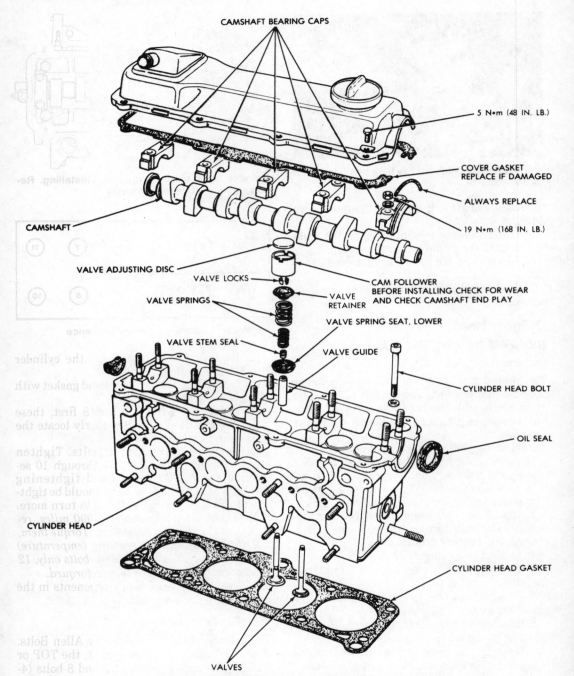

CAMSHAFT BEARING CAPS

5 N•m (48 IN. LB.)

COVER GASKET REPLACE IF DAMAGED

ALWAYS REPLACE

19 N•m (168 IN. LB.)

CAMSHAFT

VALVE ADJUSTING DISC

VALVE LOCKS

VALVE SPRINGS

VALVE RETAINER

CAM FOLLOWER
BEFORE INSTALLING CHECK FOR WEAR
AND CHECK CAMSHAFT END PLAY

VALVE SPRING SEAT, LOWER

VALVE STEM SEAL

VALVE GUIDE

CYLINDER HEAD BOLT

OIL SEAL

CYLINDER HEAD

CYLINDER HEAD GASKET

VALVES

Exploded view of gasoline engine camshaft and cylinder head

3. Disconnect the air duct from the throttle valve assembly.

4. Disconnect the throttle cable from the throttle valve assembly.

5. Remove the injectors and disconnect the line from the cold start valve.

6. Disconnect the radiator and heater hoses.

7. Disconnect the vacuum and PCV lines. Label lines for installation.

8. Remove the auxiliary air regulator from the intake manifold.

9. Disconnect all electrical lines and remove the spark plugs. Label all lines and wires for installation.

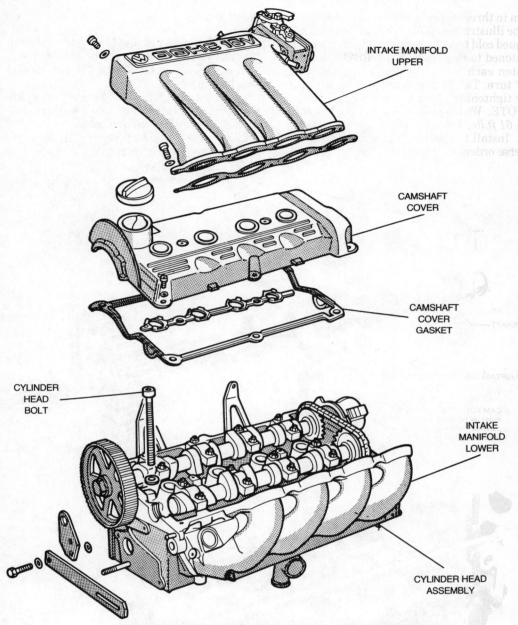

Exploded view, 16V DOHC cylinder head and intake manifold

CAUTION: *Remove air conditioner compressor with lines attached and place out of the way. Do not disconnect any lines.*

10. Separate the exhaust manifold from the exhaust pipe.

11. Remove the EGR line from the exhaust manifold.

12. Remove the intake manifold.

13. Remove the timing belt cover and belt.

14. Loosen the cylinder had bolts in the reverse of the tightening sequence.

15. Remove the bolts and lift the head straight off.

16. Check the flatness of the cylinder block.

17. Install the new cylinder head gasket with the TOP or OBEN facing upward.

CAUTION: *Do not reuse stretch type head bolts.*

18. Install bolts No. 10 and 8 on 4 cylinder engines first; these holes are smaller and will properly locate the gasket and cylinder head.

19. Install the remaining bolts. Tighten

them in three stages using the sequence shown in the illustration. Cylinder head bolts must be torqued cold to 54 ft.lb. 12 point bolts should be tightened to first 29 ft.lb., then 43 ft.lb., then tighten each bolt, in sequence, an additional 180° turn. Two 90° turns are permissible. Further tightening is not necessary.

NOTE: *With 6-point bolts, retorque the bolts to 61 ft.lb., hot, after 100 miles of driving.*

20. Install the remaining components in the reverse order of removal.

Diesel Engines

The head is retained by Allen bolts. The engine should be cold when the head is removed. The word TOP or OBEN on the new gasket should face up.

1. Rotate the crankshaft to set No. 1 cylinder at TDC with timing marks aligned. Disconnect the battery ground cable.

2. Drain the cooling system.

3. Remove the air cleaner.

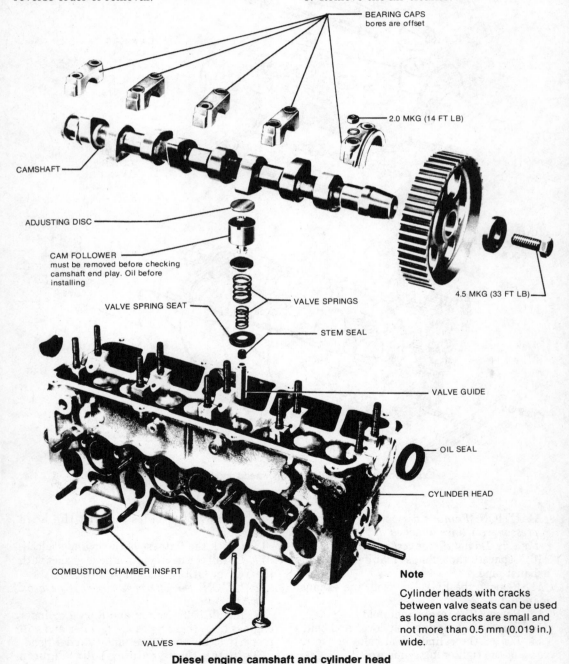

Note

Cylinder heads with cracks between valve seats can be used as long as cracks are small and not more than 0.5 mm (0.019 in.) wide.

Diesel engine camshaft and cylinder head

4. Disconnect the fuel lines. Disconnect and tag all electrical wires and leads.

CAUTION: *Remove air conditioner compressor with lines attached and place out of the way. Do not disconnect any lines.*

5. Separate the exhaust manifold or turbocharger from the pipe. Disconnect the radiator and heater hoses.

6. Remove the timing cover and belt (See timing belt replacement).

7. Loosen the cylinder head bolts in the reverse order of the tightening sequence.

8. Remove the head. Do not lay the head on the gasket surface with the injectors installed. Support it at the ends on strips of wood.

NOTE: *Turbo diesel or engines using 12mm stretch type cylinder head bolts require a new set of head bolts whenever the head is removed.*

CAUTION: *Do not reuse stretch type head bolts.*

9. Install the cylinder head with a new gasket. Be sure the new gasket has the same number of notches and the same identifying number as the old one, unless the pistons were also replaced. In this case, see Piston Replacement.

Install bolts 8 and 10 first to locate the head on the block. Install remaining bolts. Torque the head bolts in the proper sequence first to 29 ft.lb., then to 43 ft.lb., and finally give each head bolt a 108° turn tighter. Two 90° turns are permissible. Then, run the engine to normal operating temperature and give each head bolt, in sequence, an additional 90° turn tighter.

After about 1,000 miles, with the engine either cold or warm, give each head bolt, in sequence, an additonal 90° turn tighter.

CLEANING AND INSPECTION

CAUTION: *Do not place a diesel cylinder head down in the normal position until the injectors and inserts are removed or damage to the injectors an result. Inserts are removed by placing a drift through the injector hole and tapping the insert out.*

1. Remove the intake and exhaust manifolds if still mounted. Remove all water hose connections, and the injectors combustion chamber inserts and glow plugs if diesel engine.

2. Place the head on wooden blocks and remove the camshaft, cam followers and end seals.

NOTE: *Keep the valve adjusting shims and cam followers in order from the valves they were removed from for reinstallation.*

3. Working in a suitable area, use spray solvent or brush cleaning solvent on the cylinder head top, sides and combustion chamber surfaces to remove any grease, dirt or oil, and help soften carbon deposits. After cleaning with solvent, wash the head with hot water and wipe dry.

4. Turn the head so the combustion chambers are facing up. Support the head on wooden blocks so damage to the cam bearing cap mounting studs will not occur.

5. Mount a rotary wire carbon cleaning brush in an electric drill and clean the combustion chambers and valve heads.

6. Use a dull scraper to remove any old cylinder head gasket material remaining on the gasket surface. Use fine sandpaper on a sanding block to clean the head gasket surface. Use safe solvent on a rag to wipe the combustion chambers and gasket surface, wipe dry with a clean rag.

7. A complete inspection of the cylinder head (combustion chambers, valves, guides etc.) can be done after the valves and springs are removed.

RESURFACING

After the head gasket mounting surface has been cleaned, check the head for flatness.

Place a straightedge across the gasket surface. Using feeler gauges, determine the clearance between the straightedge and head surface. Measure along the length at the center and across both diagonals. Check clearance at several points along the straightedge. The allowable distortion of the cylinder head is 0.004 inch. If clearance is greater the head will have to be resurfaced. VW cautions that the diesel cylinder head cannot be resurfaced, and if over specs., must be replaced. The gasoline engine cylinder head should not be resurfaced to a point where measurement from the valve cover to head gasket mounting surfaces is less than 5.2185 inches. Cylinder head replacement is indicated if measurement is less than specified.

Cylinder head resurfacing can be handled by most local automative machine shops.

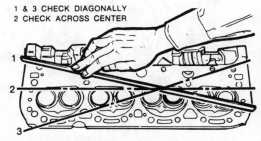

Check the cylinder head for warpage

Valves and Springs

REMOVAL AND INSTALLATION

1. Number the valve heads (in order) with a permanent marker for reinstallation identification.

2. Block the head on wooden supports in a position that permits use of the type of valve spring removing tool you are going to use. VW uses tool VW 541, although you should be able to perform the job with several other available removers, the locking C-clamp type is popular.

3. Compress the valve springs and remove the stem locks and retainers. Remove the valve springs. Keep the parts from each valve separate and in order for reinstallation. Remove the lower valve spring seats and valve stem oil seals. Remove the valves, keep them in order in case the identification marking wears off.

4. Clean valve faces, tips and combustion chambers with a rotary wire brush or bench grinder wire wheel. Do not wire brush the valve stems, take care not to damage the valve seats. Remove the carbon, do not just burnish. If a stubborn carbon deposit is encountered, use a blunt drift to break the carbon loose. Again use caution around the valve seat.

5. Use a valve guide cleaning brush and safe solvent to clean the valve guides.

6. If a water leak is suspected, or the valve seats, guides or valves need machine work, take the head and parts to the machine shop.

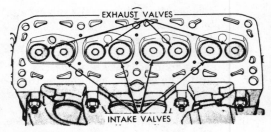

Valve identification

Now is also a good time to have the head super cleaned in a cold parts cleaner, the machine shop can handle the job. However, never allow the aluminum head to be hot tanked, this will damage the head and make replacement necessary.

7. After all machine work has been done, any required new parts on hand, reassemble the head in the reverse order. Always install new valve guide oil seals using the protectors provided to prevent damage to the seal.

8. Refer to the following sections for details on machine work and cylinder head component checking.

9. Valve adjustment can be done after the head is reassembled and the cam followers, shims and camshaft installed. Refer to Chapter 2 for necessary tools and procedure. Be sure the heel of the camshaft lobe (greatest clearance) is over the valve (cam follower) you are checking.

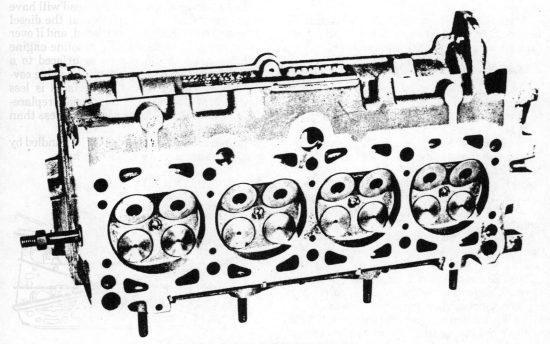

Cylinder head, 16V DOHC

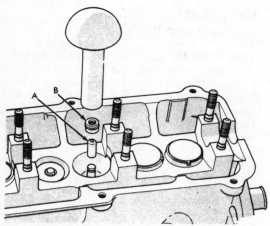

Use protector (A) when installing valve stem seal (B). Installation tool is above seal

INSPECTION

After all cylinder head parts have been removed and cleaned, examine them for any visual signs of wear. Badly worn parts should be replaced, slightly grooved or burnt valves or seats can be machined. Check the valve-stem-to guide clearance. Having a new intake or exhaust valve around would make the job easier, however if they are not on hand proceed with the following. Insert the valve into the guide it came from Lift the head of the valve away from the valve seat slightly. Wiggle the valve from side to side. A small amount of play is usual, a large amount of play indicates wear in either the valve stem, guide or both. Measure the valve stem with a micrometer and compare the reading to original "specs" to determine whether the stem or guide is responsible for the excessive clearance. Compare the valve springs, obvious length difference indicates wear. Cracked, broken or damaged spring should be replaced. Examine the valve spring seats, retainers and locks for grooves or wear, replace as necessary.

REFACING VALVES AND SEATS

Valve and valve seat refacing requires special equipment, the automotive machine shop can handle the job for you.

CAUTION: *Under no circumstances should either the exhaust or the intake valves in the 16 valve 1.8L engine be resurfaced. These valves are sodium filled and may explode if the sodium filling is exposed to extreme heat or water. These valves must be replaced with new ones, and properly disposed of, if there are any signs of wear. Proper disposal of the sodium filled valves should be refered to a qualified machine shop technician.*

VW recommends that the exhaust valves not be refaced on a machine and should be hand lapped only.

Intake valves are refaced to the angle shown on the specifications chart in this chapter. Both intake and exhaust valves are available having shorter stems which provide the use of maximum thickness valve adjusting discs if too much material has been removed from the valve seats when they are refaced. Valve seats can be refaced with either grinding stones or reamers. A true valve seat can not be machined unless the valve guide is within specifications, and not worn. Valve guides are replaceable, but if the valve seat is damaged and cannot be repaired a new cylinder head is required. Consult your machine shop for their advice.

HAND LAPPING VALVES

Invert the cylinder head, lightly lubricate the valve stem and install the valves in the head as numbered. Slightly raise the valve from the valve seat and apply a small amount of valve grinding compound to the valve seat.

Moisten the suction cup on the lapping tool and attach to the valve head. Rotate the lapping tool and valve between the palms of your hands, change position and lift the tool often to prevent grooving. Lap the valve, until a smooth polished surface is evident on the valve

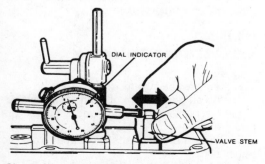

Check the valve guide to stem clearance

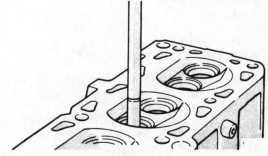

Use a press to install new valve guides

and valve seat. Remove the valve from the head and clean away all traces of lapping compound from the valve and valve seat.

VALVE SPRING CHECKING

Place the cleaned valve spring on a flat surface. Measure the height of the spring and rotate it against a carpenter's square. If the spring height varies $1/16''$ (by comparison) or if distortion of more than $1/16''$ is present when the spring is rotated, replace the spring. After the valve and spring is installed, measure the distance between the lower spring pad and lower edge of the upper retainer. Check the measurement with the specifications chart. If the installed height is incorrect, add special shim washers between the spring pad and the spring. Use only washers designed for this purpose.

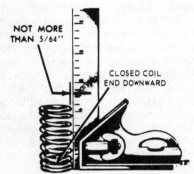

NOT MORE THAN 5/64"

CLOSED COIL END DOWNWARD

Check the valve spring free length and squareness

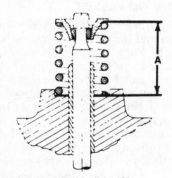

Valve spring installed height (A)

Valve Seats

REMOVAL AND INSTALLATION

Valve seats which are worn or burnt can usually be machined to the correct angle and width. VW recommends that if the seat can not be saved by machine work the head should be replaced. In some cases a new seat can be installed, consult the automotive machine shop for their advice.

Valve Guides

REMOVAL AND INSTALLATION

Worn valve guides can be replaced by the automotive machine shop. The job requires special equipment which they have. In some cases a worn valve guide can be knurled which is a process where metal is displaced and raised, thereby reducing clearance. Consult the machine shop for their advice.

Oil Pan

REMOVAL AND INSTALLATION

Dasher Fox & Quantum

1. Drain the oil pan. Loosen the motor mounts.
2. Support and slightly raise the engine with an overhead hoist.
3. Gradually loosen the engine crossmember mounting bolts. Remove the left and right side engine mounts.
4. Lower the crossmember very carefully.
5. Loosen and remove the oil pan retaining bolts.
6. Lower the pan from the car.
7. Install the pan using a new gasket and sealer.
8. Tighten the retaining bolts in a crosswise pattern. Tighten the hex head bolts to 14 ft.lb., or the Allen head bolts to 7 ft.lb.
9. Raise the crossmember. Tighten the crossmember bolts to 42 ft.lb. and the engine mounting bolts to 32 ft.lb.
10. Refill the engine with oil. Start the engine and check for leaks.

Rabbit, Golf, Scirocco, Jetta, GTI

1. Drain the oil pan.
2. Loosen and remove the socket head, oil pan retaining bolts.
3. Lower the pan from the car.
4. Install the pan using a new gasket and sealer.
5. Tighten the hex headed bolts to 14 ft.lb., or Allen bolts to 7 ft.lb. in a crosswise pattern.
6. Refill the engine with oil. Start the engine and check for leaks.

Oil Pump

REMOVAL AND INSTALLATION

1. Remove the oil pan.
2. Remove the two mounting bolts.
3. Pull oil pump down and out of the engine.
4. Unscrew the two bolts and separate the pump halves.
5. Remove the driveshaft and gear from the upper body.
6. Clean the bottom half in solvent. Pry up

the metal edges to remove the filter screen for cleaning.

7. Examine the gears and driveshaft for wear or damage. Replace them if necessary.

8. Reassemble the pump halves.

9. Prime the pump with oil and install in the reverse order of removal.

Timing Belt Cover

REMOVAL AND INSTALLATION

1. Loosen the alternator mounting bolts and if equipped, the power steering pump and air conditioner compressor bolts if their drive belts will interfere with cover removal.

2. Pivot the alternator or driven component and slip the drive belt from the pulleys.

3. Unscrew the belt cover retaining nuts and remove the cover. On some models with two piece covers, it may be necessary to remove the crankshaft pulley.

4. Reposition the spacers and nuts on the mounting studs so they will not get lost.

5. Service vehicle as necessary and reinstall the belt cover in the reverse order of removal.

Timing Belt

NOTE: *The timing belt is designed to last for more than 60,000 miles and normally does not require tension adjustment. If the belt is removed, breaks or is replaced, the basic valve timing must be checked and the belt retensioned.*

Work the belt off the gear

REMOVAL AND INSTALLATION

Gasoline Engines

NOTE: *Timing belt installation will be less confusing if the engine is set for No. l cylinder at TDC (top dead center) prior to belt removal or replacement.*

1. Remove front belt cover(s).

2. Turn the engine until the 0° mark on the flywheel is aligned with the stationary pointer on the bell housing. On 4 cylinder engines, turn the camshaft until the mark on the rear of the sprocket is aligned with the upper edge of the rear drive belt cover, at the left side of the engine. On 5 cylinder engines, turn the camshaft until the mark on the sprocket lines up with the left side edge of the camshaft housing. The notch on the crankshaft pulley should align with the dot on the intermediate shaft sprocket and the distributor rotor (remove distributor cap) should be pointing toward the mark on the rim of the distributor housing.

3. Remove the crankshaft accessories drive pulley(s).

4. On 4-cylinder engines, hold the large nut on the tensioner pulley and loosen the smaller

Belt tension is correct when the belt can be twisted 90°

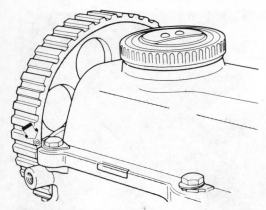

Align the camshaft timing mark with the edge of the cylinder head

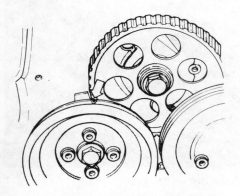

Align the timing marks on crankshaft and intermediate shaft

pulley lock nut. Turn the tensioner counterclockwise to relieve the tension on the timing belt.

5. On 5-cylinder engines, loosen the water pump bolts and turn the pump clockwise to relieve timing belt tension.

6. Slide the timing belt from the pulleys.

7. Install timing belt and retension with pulley or water pump. Reinstall the crankshaft pulley(s). Recheck alignment of timing marks.

CAUTION: *If the timing marks are not correctly aligned with the No. 1 piston at TDC of the compression stroke and the belt is installed, valve timing will be incorrect. Poor performance and possible engine damage can result from improper valve timing.*

8. Check the timing belt tension. The tension is when the belt can be twisted 90° with the thumb and index finger along the straight run between the camshaft sprocket and the water pump.

9. Turn the engine two complete revolutions (clockwise rotation) and align the flywheel mark at TDC. Recheck belt tension and timing marks. Readjust as required.

10. Reinstall the cam belt cover and drive belts in the reverse order of removal.

Diesel Engine

NOTE: *This procedure will require a number of special tools and a certain expertise with diesel engines. You may wish to have the work performed by an authorized service technician.*

TO CHECK VALVE AND INJECTOR PUMP TIMING

1. Remove the camshaft (valve) cover and the timing belt cover(s).

NOTE: *The drive belt must be checked for proper tension and must be centered in the sprockets before checking timing.*

2. Turn the engine so that No. 1 cylinder is at TDC. The No. 1 cylinder camshaft lobes should be pointing upward and the TDC mark on the flywheel should be aligned with the bellhousing mark.

3. Fix the camshaft in position with tool VW 2065 or 2065A. Align the tool as follows:

Turn the camshaft until one end of the tool touches the cylinder head. Measure the gap at the other end of the tool with a feeler gauge. Take half of the measurement and insert a feeler gauge of that thickness between the tool and the cylinder head. Turn the camshaft so the tool rests on the feeler gauge. Insert a feeler gauge of the same thickness on the other side, between the tool and the cylinder head.

4. Lock the injector pump sprocket in position with pin 2064.

5. Check that the marks on the sprocket, pump and mounting plate are approximately aligned. Check that the TDC mark on the flywheel is aligned with the bellhousing mark.

To Adjust:

1. Refer to Steps 1 through 4 of above procedure.

2. After the camshaft is set in position and the timing at TDC (flywheel and bellhousing marks aligned) loosen the camshaft sprocket mounting bolt 1 turn.

3. Tap the back of sprocket with a rubber hammer to loosen. Hand tight the bolt to remove endplay.

4. Loosen the belt adjuster and remove the belt from the injector pump sprocket.

5. Turn the injector pump sprocket until the marks on the sprocket, pump and mounting bracket align. Insert pin 2064 through the hole in the sprocket and mounting bracket to lock in position.

6. Reinstall the camshaft drive belt. Tighten the camshaft mounting bolt to 33 ft.lb. Remove the camshaft setting bar and the lock pin from the injector pump sprocket. Install VW tool VW210 (Belt tension gauge).

Timing Belt Wear

| *DESCRIPTION* | *FLAW CONDITIONS* |

1. Hardened back surface rubber

Back surface glossy. Non-elastic and so hard that even if a finger nail is forced into it, no mark is produced.

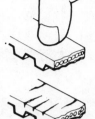

2. Cracked back surface rubber

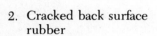

3. Cracked or exfoliated canvas

4. Badly worn teeth (initial stage)

Canvas on load side tooth flank worn (Fluffy canvas fibers, rubber gone and color changed to white, and unclear canvas texture)

Flank worn (On load side)

5. Badly worn teeth (last stage)

Canvas on load side tooth flank worn down and rubber exposed (tooth width reduced)

Rubber exposed

6. Cracked tooth bottom

Crack

7. Missing tooth

Tooth missing and canvas fiber exposed

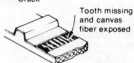

8. Side of belt badly worn

Rounded belt side

Abnormal wear (Fluffy canvas fiber)

NOTE: *Normal belt should have clear-cut sides as if cut by a sharp knife.*

9. Side of belt cracked

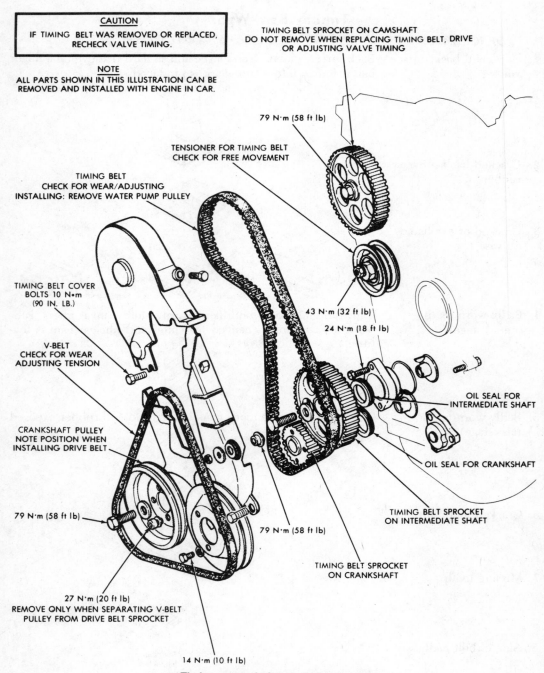

CAUTION
IF TIMING BELT WAS REMOVED OR REPLACED, RECHECK VALVE TIMING.

NOTE
ALL PARTS SHOWN IN THIS ILLUSTRATION CAN BE REMOVED AND INSTALLED WITH ENGINE IN CAR.

TIMING BELT SPROCKET ON CAMSHAFT
DO NOT REMOVE WHEN REPLACING TIMING BELT, DRIVE OR ADJUSTING VALVE TIMING

79 N·m (58 ft lb)

TENSIONER FOR TIMING BELT
CHECK FOR FREE MOVEMENT

TIMING BELT
CHECK FOR WEAR/ADJUSTING
INSTALLING: REMOVE WATER PUMP PULLEY

TIMING BELT COVER
BOLTS 10 N•m
(90 IN. LB.)

43 N·m (32 ft lb)
24 N·m (18 ft lb)

V-BELT
CHECK FOR WEAR
ADJUSTING TENSION

OIL SEAL FOR
INTERMEDIATE SHAFT

CRANKSHAFT PULLEY
NOTE POSITION WHEN
INSTALLING DRIVE BELT

OIL SEAL FOR CRANKSHAFT

79 N·m (58 ft lb)

TIMING BELT SPROCKET
ON INTERMEDIATE SHAFT

79 N·m (58 ft lb)

TIMING BELT SPROCKET
ON CRANKSHAFT

27 N·m (20 ft lb)
REMOVE ONLY WHEN SEPARATING V-BELT
PULLEY FROM DRIVE BELT SPROCKET

14 N·m (10 ft lb)

Timing gears, belts—gasoline engine

7. Adjust tension by turning the tensioner clockwise, reading on the tension gauge should be 12–13. Lock tensioner in position.

8. Turn the crankshaft 2 complete turns (clockwise rotation) and recheck belt tension. Strike the drive belt once with a rubber hammer between the camshaft and injector pump sprockets to eliminate play.

9. Recheck timing, readjust if necessary.
To install the belt:

1. Refer to Steps 1–5 of the Valve and Injector Pump Timing procedure.

2. Align all timing marks as described. Release tension on timing belt and remove belt from engine.

3. Install new belt and adjust tension.

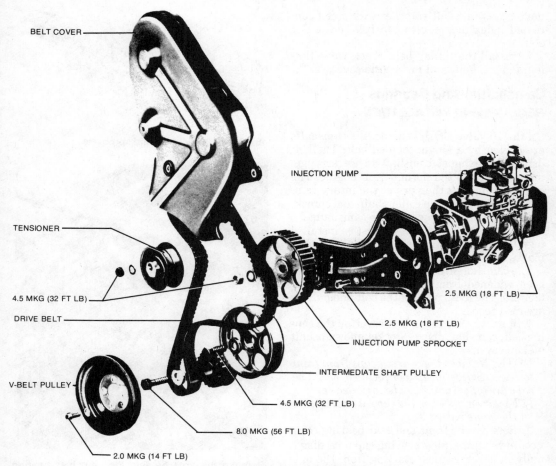

BELT COVER

INJECTION PUMP

TENSIONER

4.5 MKG (32 FT LB)

DRIVE BELT

V-BELT PULLEY

2.0 MKG (14 FT LB)

8.0 MKG (56 FT LB)

4.5 MKG (32 FT LB)

INTERMEDIATE SHAFT PULLEY

INJECTION PUMP SPROCKET

2.5 MKG (18 FT LB)

2.5 MKG (18 FT LB)

Timing belt installation—diesel engine

Lock the injection pump in position with special pin—diesel

Check and adjust timing as described in the previous section. Reinstall belt cover(s) and driven component belts.

Timing Sprockets

REMOVAL AND INSTALLATION

All Engines

Depending on year and model, the timing sprockets are located on the shaft by a key, a self-contained drive lug, or in the case of diesel engine camshaft, a tapered fit. All sprockets are retained by a bolt. To remove any or all sprockets, removal of the timing belt cover(s) and belt is required.

NOTE: *When removing the crankshaft pulley, it is not necessary to remove the four bolts which hold the outer component drive pulley to the timing belt sprocket. Remove the component drive belt, center retaining bolt and crankshaft pulley.*

1. Remove the center retaining bolt.

2. Gently pry the sprocket off the shaft.

3. If the sprocket is stubborn in coming off, use a gear puller. Don't hammer on the sprocket. On diesel engine camshafts, loosen the center bolt 1 turn and tap the rear of the sprocket with a rubber hammer. When the sprocket loosens, remove bolt and sprocket.

4. Remove the sprocket and key.

5. Install the sprocket in the reverse order of removal.

6. Tighten the center bolt to 58 ft.lb. Models

having a crankshaft sprocket with a self contained index lug require 145 ft.lb. on center bolt.

7. Install the timing belt, check valve timing, tension belt, and install the cover.

Camshaft(s) And Bearings

REMOVAL AND INSTALLATION

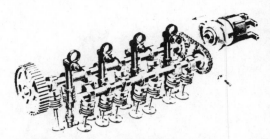

16V DOHC, roller chain and sprockets

On the 16 valve DOHC engine, the camshafts are driven by a single toothed belt. The belt drives the exhaust camshaft in an arrangement similar to the normal 1.8L engine. The exhaust camshaft then drives the intake camshaft through a single roller chain and sprockets attached to the backs of the camshafts.

The camshafts and pulleys must be installed together in the cylinder head so the timing marks line up as pictured

The camshaft drive belt and all pulleys have been widened from 0.748″ (19mm) to 0.984″ (25mm). The tooth pitch of the belt and pulleys are also deeper.

1. Remove the timing belt cover(s), the timing belt, camshaft drive sprocket and camshaft (valve) cover.

NOTE: *Number the bearing caps from front to back. Scribe an arrow facing front. The caps are off-set and must be installed correctly. Factory number on the caps are not always on the same side.*

2. Remove the front and rear bearing caps. Loosen the remaining bearing cap nuts diagonally in several steps, starting from the outside caps near the ends of the head and work toward the center. Remember, the camshaft is under pressure from the valve spring.

3. Remove the bearing caps. On the 16 valve engine, remove the single roller chain and sprockets attached to the backs of the camshafts. Then remove the camshaft(s).

4. Install new oil seal and end plug in cylinder head. Lightly coat the camshaft(s) bearing journals and lobes with a film of assembly lube or heavy engine oil. On the 16 valve engine, in-

Remove the nuts holding the camshaft bearing caps

stall the single roller chain and sprockets attached to the backs of the camshafts. Install bearing caps in the reverse order of removal. Tighten cap nuts diagonally and in several steps until they are torqued to 14 ft.lb.

5. Install the drive sprocket and timing belt. Check valve clearance and adjust if necessary. Install remaining parts in reverse order of removal.

Camshaft sprocket timing marks at TDC

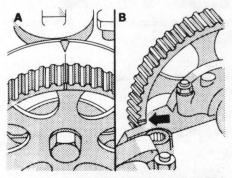

Exhaust camshaft pulley timing mark at TDC

The camshaft bearings are numbered for identification (arrows)

CHECKING CAMSHAFT(S)

Degrease the camshaft using a safe solvent. Visually inspect the cam lobes and bearing journals for excessive wear. If a lobe is questionable or a bearing journal scored, the camshaft should be replaced. Check the lobes and journals with a micrometer. Measure the lobes from nose to heel. If all intake or all exhaust lobes do not measure the same, replace the camshaft. If the lobes and journals appear intact, place the front and rear journals in V-blocks. Position a dial indicator on the center journal and rotate the camshaft. If deviation exceeds 0.0004″ replace the camshaft.

Intermediate Shaft
REMOVAL AND INSTALLATION

1. Remove timing belt cover(s), timing belt and intermediate shaft drive sprocket.
2. Remove fuel pump and distributor (gasoline engines). Remove drive key from the intermediate shaft.
3. Remove the mounting flange retaining bolts. Reinstall sprocket bolt and remove the flange and shaft by pulling on the sprocket bolt.
4. Remove flange from the intermediate shaft and install new oil seal.
5. Install in reverse order of removal. Lubricate the oil seal lips. When installing the mounting flange be sure the oil return hole is at the bottom. Tighten the flange mounting bolts to 18 ft.lb.

Pistons and Connecting Rods — Gasoline Engines
REMOVAL AND INSTALLATION

1. Follow the instructions under Timing Belt and Cylinder Head removal.
2. Remove the oil pan as described later in this Chapter.
3. Turn the crankshaft until the piston to be removed is at the bottom of travel.
4. Make sure the connecting rod and cap are marked for reference as to cylinder location and position match (scribe across rod end and cap so cap will be installed in mating position). Mark piston heads from front to back, in order, for reinstallation identification.
5. Place a rag down the cylinder bore on the head of the piston to be removed. Remove the cylinder top ridge and carbon deposits with a ridge reamer, following the instructions of the reamer's manufacturer.
CAUTION: *Do not cut too deeply or remove more than* $\frac{1}{32}$″ *from the ring travel area when removing the ridge.*
6. Remove the rag and metal cuttings from the cylinder bore. Remove the connecting rod cap and bearing insert.
7. Push the connecting rod up the bore slightly and remove the upper bearing insert.
8. Push the connecting rod and piston assembly up and out of the cylinder with a hammer handle.
9. Wipe any dirt or oil from the connecting rod bearing saddle and rod cap. Install the

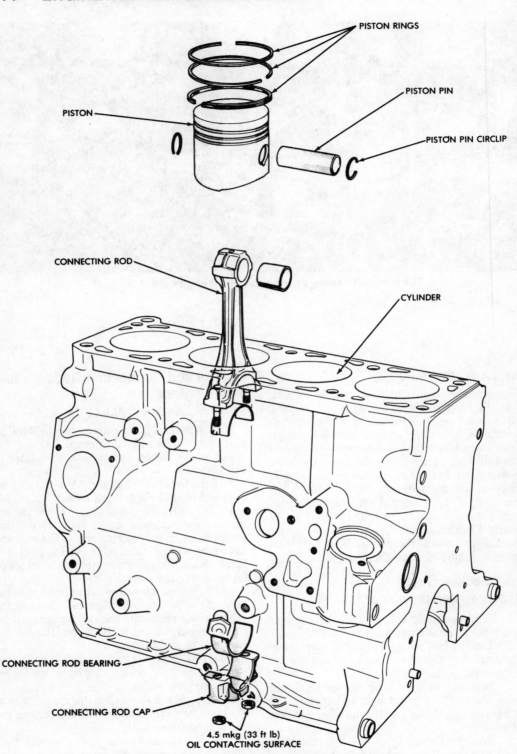

Cylinder block, pistons, connecting rods and bearings

bearing inserts (if to be reused) in the connecting rod and cap. Install cap and secure with rod bolts.

10. Remove the rest of the rod and piston assemblies in a like manner.

CAUTION: *When removing the pistons, take care not to score the crankshaft journals or cylinder walls.*

11. Lubricate the piston, rings and cylinder wall. Install and lubricate the upper bearing insert. Install a piston ring compressor over the rings and top of the piston. Be sure the piston ring ends are staggered (See following section). Lower the piston and rod assembly into the cylinder bore with the arrow on the piston head facing the front of the engine. When the ring compressor contacts the top of the engine block, use a wooden hammer handle to tap the piston into the bore.

NOTE: *If unusual resistance is encountered when starting the piston into the cylinder bore, it is possible that a ring slipped out of the compressor and is caught at the top of the cylinder. Remove the piston and reinstall compressor.*

12. Guide the connecting rod down the cylinder bore and over the crankshaft journal taking care not to score the wall or shaft. Install the lower bearing insert into the connecting rod cap. Lubricate the insert and mount the cap on the rod with matchmarks aligned. Install rod bolts and tighten to specifications.

NOTE: *Engines (GTI) using rod bolts with a smooth surface between threads and short*

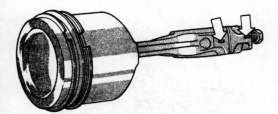

Matchmark the connecting rod and cap before disassembly

RING COMPRESSOR
Installing the piston

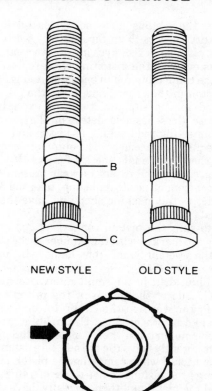

NEW STYLE   OLD STYLE

"Stretch" type rod bolt identification

knurled shank and having a round head containing six notches are stretch type bolts and cannot be reused. Always use new bolts when servicing.

13. Install remaining piston and rod assemblies in a like manner, turn the crankshaft each time so the crank journal of the piston being installed is at the bottom of travel.

CLEANING AND INSPECTION

After removing the piston and rod assemblies from the engine, take and assembly and clamp the connecting rod into a vise with the lower edge of the piston just resting on the vise jaws. Use a ring expanding tool and remove the piston rings from the piston. Save the top compression ring and tag with cylinder location number. The old ring can be used later to check the cylinder bore for wear. Clean the top of the piston with a dull scraper, use care not to gouge the piston when removing the carbon deposits. Clean the ring grooves using an appropriate groove cleaning tool. A broken piston ring can be used if a groove cleaner is not available. Once again, use care not to cut too deeply or gouge the ring seat. After all the pistons have had the rings removed and grooves cleaned, soak them in safe solvent. Do not use a wire brush or caustic solvent on the pistons.

After the pistons have been cleaned and wiped dry inspect them for scuffing, scoring, cracks, pitting or excessive ring groove wear. If wear is evident, the piston must be replaced. Hold the connecting rod in one hand and grasp the piston in the other hand, twist the piston and rod in opposite directions. If excessive clearance (looseness) is detected, the piston pin, connecting rod bushing or piston and rod may require replacement. The automotive machine shop can handle the job for you. If you are not sure of the extent of wear present or what component needs replacing, take the assemblies to the machine shop and have them checked.

Make sure the piston, connecting rod and rod cap are marked with the number of the cylinder the assembly came from. Remove the piston from the connecting rod by inserting a small blunt drift in the small cutout provided on each side of the piston at the piston pin ends. Pry upward on the circlip to compress, and remove both circlips. Use a blunt drift slightly smaller than the diameter of the piston pin to gently drive the pin out. If resistance is encountered when removing the piston pin, submerge the pistons in hot water of 140°F to expand the metal and then carefully drive the pin out. Inspect the piston pin, connecting rod bushing and piston pin bore for galling, scoring or excessive wear. If wear is evident, consult the machine shop for advice as to what repair is necessary.

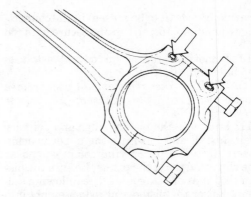

When assembling the connecting rod and cap, align the forged marks

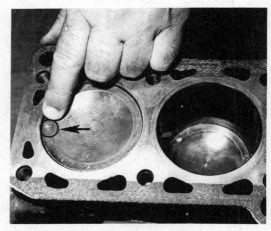

The arrow on the piston must face the camshaft drive belt

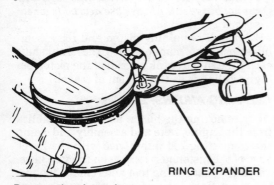

RING EXPANDER

Remove the piston rings

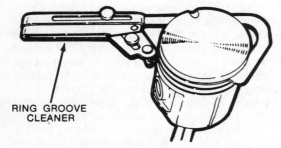

RING GROOVE CLEANER

Clean the piston ring grooves

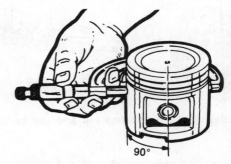

90°

Measure the piston at a point 90° from the wrist pin boss

Measure, or have the machine shop measure the piston with a micrometer. Turn the piston upside down and take a measurement at a point 5/8" below the lower edge of the piston, 90° away from the piston pin holes. Compare the reading to specifications, replace piston as needed.

Check the cylinder bore (see following section) to determine if wear indicates excessive clearance requiring cylinder boring and oversize piston installation. If the original pistons are to be reused, lubricate the piston pin and rod bushing and reinstall the connecting rod. Make sure the matchmarks you made on the connecting rod are on the same side of the piston (arrow facing front) as they were before removal. Factory forge marks at the bottom of the connecting rod and cap face must be mounted on the intermediate shaft side of the engine when the arrow mark on the piston head is facing front. Install pistons on connecting rods in the reverse order of removal.

CYLINDER BORE

Measurements can be made with a special dial indicator, telescope gauge and micrometer, or with an old compression ring taken from the piston removed from the cylinder being checked.

Measurements should be taken at a number of places in each cylinder: at the top, middle and bottom at two points at each location: that is, at a point 90° from the crankshaft, as well as a point parallel to the crankshaft. The difference between the greatest measurement of the cylinder wall and the diameter measurement of the piston (see Cleaning and Inspection) is the piston clearance. If slightly excessive clearance is indicated and the cylinder is not tapered too much, finish honing of the cylinder and a slightly larger (oversize) piston may be all that is required. A great amount of wear will require cylinder boring and standard oversize pistons.

If the necessary precision tools to check the bore are not on hand and the engine is out of the car and disassembled, have the machine shop check it out for you. One way to get an idea of cylinder wear, when no instruments are available, is to use an old compression ring taken from the cylinder being checked. Place the piston ring into the bore just below the removed ridge. Make sure the ring is square in the bore (push into place with the piston head). Take a set of feeler gauges and measure the gap between the ends of the ring. Push the ring down the bore to the end of the piston travel and take a measurement. The taper of the cylinder is roughly 0.3 times the difference of the ring gap readings. The amount of taper should not exceed 0.007–0.009 inches. If it does, the block probably requires reboring. Consult the machine shop for their advice.

CYLINDER HONING

Honing or deglazing the cylinder walls helps new piston rings seat faster for oil control. Refer to the instruction sheet packaged with the new rings that will be installed for the manufacturer's recommendation. If no special instructions are given, chuck a flexible drive hone into a power drill, lubricate the stones and insert into cylinder. Start the hone and move it up and down in the cylinder at a rate that will produce a 60° crosshatch pattern. Take care not to extend the hone below cylinder bore, or to withdraw it from the bore when operating. After developing the pattern wash the cylinder with a detergent and water solution to remove abrasive dust. Dry cylinder wall and wipe several times with a clan rag soaked in engine oil.

PISTON RINGS

After the cylinder bore has been finish honed, or determined to be in satisfactory condition, ring end gap clearance can be checked. Compress the piston rings to be used in each cylinder, one at a time, into that cylinder. Press the ring down the bore to a point about one inch below the top with an inverted piston. Measure the distance between the two ends (ring gap) of the ring with feeler gauges and compare to specifications. Pull the ring from the cylinder and file the ends with a fine file to gain required clearance, if necessary. Roll the outside of the ring around the piston groove it will be installed in to check for burrs or unremoved carbon deposits. Dress the groove with a fine file if necessary. Hold the ring in the groove and measure between top of ring and groove with a set of feeler gauges to check side clearance. If clearance is excessive, a new piston may be required or, in some cases, a spacer can be installed. Consult the machine shop for their advice.

Install the piston rings on the piston start-

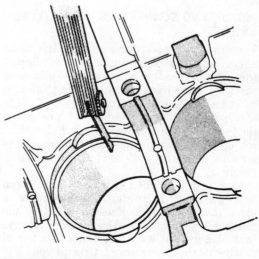

Measuring the ring gap

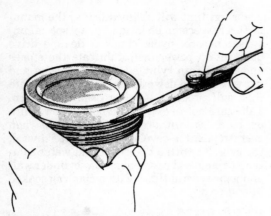

Measuring the ring side clearance

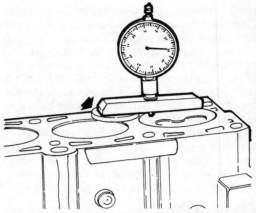

Piston projection measurement on diesel engines—note spacer (arrow)

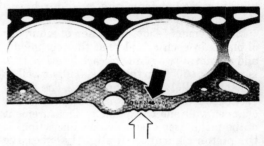

Diesel engine cylinder head gaskets are identified by a number (black arrow) and notches (white arrow)

ing with the lower oil control ring. Always refer to the ring manufacturer's instruction sheet for guidance. Be sure, when installing a three piece expander type oil ring, that the ends of the expander are butted together and do not overlap. Hold the butter edges together and install the lower rail first. Install with the ring gap about ¾" away from the butter point of the expander. Install the upper rail on the opposite side, ¾ away from the butted point of the expander. Use a ring expander and install the compression rings, second ring first. Most compression rings will have a top mark of some kind, be sure the mark is facing up.

NOTE: *Before installing the piston ring compressor, while assembling the engine, be sure the piston ring locations are staggered. The end gaps should be at three equal spacings, never in a straight line. Avoid installing the rings with their ends in line with the piston pin bosses and the thrust direction.*

PISTON AND CONNECTING RODS—DIESEL ENGINE

The same basic procedures apply to the diesel engine as the gasoline engine. The one important difference is that whenever new pistons or short block are installed, the piston projection must be checked.

A spacer (VW385/17) and bar with micrometer (VW 382/7) are necessary, and should be set up as shown to measure the maximum amount of piston projection above the deck height.

After piston height has been determined, a head gasket of suitable thickness must be used. Head gasket thickness is coded by the number of notches located on the edge. Always install a gasket with the same number of notches as the one removed. Consult your VW dealer if new pistons are installed.

Rear Main Oil Seal

NOTE: *The front crankshaft oil seal can be changed after the crank pulley and drive sprocket have been removed. A special tool from VW is required.*

REPLACEMENT

The rear main oil seal is located in a housing on the rear of the cylinder block. To replace the seal on the Dasher or Quantum, it is necessary to remove the transmission and perform the work from underneath the car or remove the engine and perform the work on an engine stand or work bench. See Transmission Removal and Installation section in chapter 6.

On the Golf, Rabbit, Fox, Jetta and Scirocco, the engine should be removed from the car.

1. Remove the transmission and flywheel.
2. Using a screwdriver, very carefully pry the old seal out of the support ring.
3. Remove the seal.
4. Lightly oil the replacement seal and then press it into place using a canister top or other circular piece of flat metal. Be careful not to damage the seal or score the crankshaft.

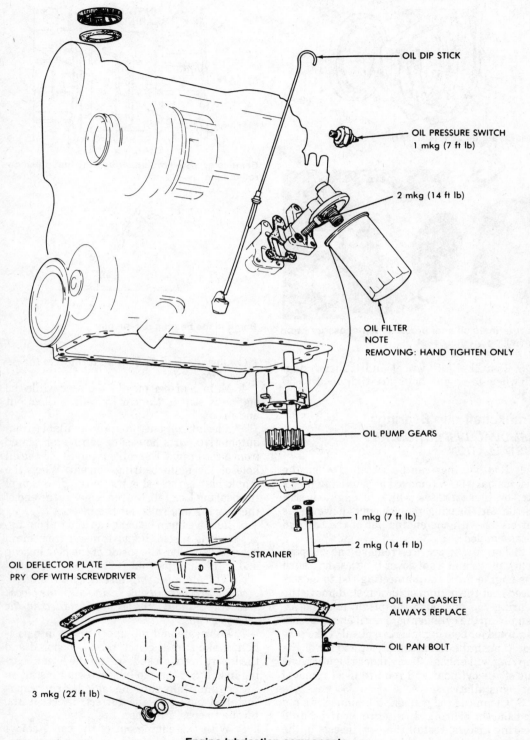

OIL DIP STICK

OIL PRESSURE SWITCH
1 mkg (7 ft lb)

2 mkg (14 ft lb)

OIL FILTER
NOTE
REMOVING: HAND TIGHTEN ONLY

OIL PUMP GEARS

1 mkg (7 ft lb)

2 mkg (14 ft lb)

STRAINER

OIL DEFLECTOR PLATE
PRY OFF WITH SCREWDRIVER

OIL PAN GASKET
ALWAYS REPLACE

OIL PAN BOLT

3 mkg (22 ft lb)

Engine lubrication components

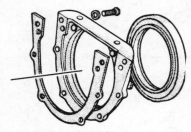

Rear main oil seal (circular)

A rear main oil seal protector is necessary when installing the new seal

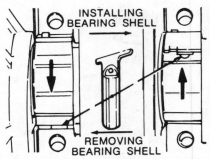

Remove or install the upper bearing insert using a roll-out pin

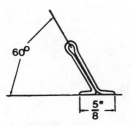

Home-made bearing roll-out pin

5. Install the flywheel and transmission. Flywheel-to-engine bolts are tightened to 36 ft.lb.

Crankshaft and Bearings

REMOVAL, INSPECTION, AND INSTALLATION

1. Rod bearings can be installed when the pistons have been removed for servicing (rings etc.) or, in most cases, while the engine is still in the car. Bearing replacement, however, is far easier with the engine out of the car and disassembled.

2. For in car service, remove the oil pan, spark plugs and front cover if necessary. Turn the engine until the connecting rod to be serviced is at the bottom of its travel. Remove the bearing cap and push the piston and rod assembly up the cylinder bore until enough room is gained for bearing insert removal. Take care not to push the rod assembly up too far or the top ring will engage the cylinder ridge or come out of the cylinder and require head removal for reinstallation.

3. Clean the rod journal, the connecting rod end and the bearing cap after removing the old bearing inserts. Install the new inserts in the rod and bearing cap, lubricate them with oil. Position the rod over the crankshaft journal and install the rod cap. Make sure the cap and rod numbers match, torque the rod bolts to specifications.
   NOTE: *See note under Step 11 of Piston and*

Connecting Rod Section pertaining to the reuse of rod bolts.

4. Main bearings may be replaced while the engine is still in the car by rolling them out and in.

5. Special roll-out pins are available from automotive parts houses or can be fabricated from a cotter pin. The roll out pin fits in the oil hole of the main bearing journal. When the crankshaft is rotated opposite the direction of the bearing lock tab, the pin engages the end of the bearing and rolls out the insert.

6. Remove main bearing cap and roll out upper bearing insert. Remove insert from main bearing cap. Clan the inside of the bearing cap and crankshaft journal.
   NOTE: *Main bearing inserts with the lubrication grooves must be installed in the block. Inserts without grooves are installed in the baring caps.*

7. Lubricate and roll upper insert into position, make sure the lock tab is anchored and the insert is not cocked. Install the lower bearing insert into the cap lubricate and install on the engine. Make sure the main bearing cap is installed facing in the correct direction and torque to specifications.

8. With the engine out of the car. Remove the manifolds, cylinder head, front cover, timing belt and gears, oil pan, oil pump, flywheel, front and rear main seals and brackets.

9. Remove the piston and rod assemblies. Remove the main bearing caps after marking them for position and direction.

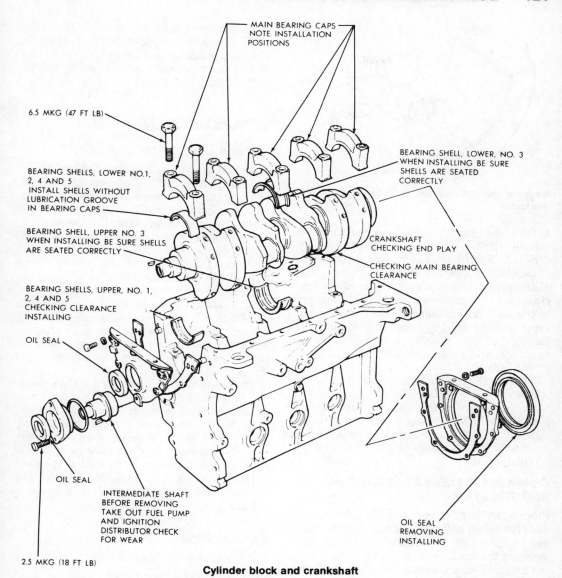

MAIN BEARING CAPS
NOTE INSTALLATION
POSITIONS

6.5 MKG (47 FT LB)

BEARING SHELL, LOWER, NO. 3
WHEN INSTALLING BE SURE
SHELLS ARE SEATED
CORRECTLY

BEARING SHELLS, LOWER NO.1,
2, 4 AND 5
INSTALL SHELLS WITHOUT
LUBRICATION GROOVE
IN BEARING CAPS

BEARING SHELL, UPPER NO. 3
WHEN INSTALLING BE SURE SHELLS
ARE SEATED CORRECTLY

CRANKSHAFT
CHECKING END PLAY

CHECKING MAIN BEARING
CLEARANCE

BEARING SHELLS, UPPER, NO. 1,
2, 4 AND 5
CHECKING CLEARANCE
INSTALLING

OIL SEAL

OIL SEAL

INTERMEDIATE SHAFT
BEFORE REMOVING
TAKE OUT FUEL PUMP
AND IGNITION
DISTRIBUTOR CHECK
FOR WEAR

OIL SEAL
REMOVING
INSTALLING

2.5 MKG (18 FT LB)

Cylinder block and crankshaft

10. Remove the crankshaft and bearing inserts. Clean the engine block and cap bearing saddles. Clean the crankshaft and inspect for wear. Check the bearing journals with a micrometer for out-of-round condition and to determine what size rod and main bearing inserts to install.

11. Install the main bearing upper inserts into the engine block. (See previous Note.)

12. Lubricate the bearing inserts and the crankshaft journals. Slowly and carefully lower the crankshaft into position.

13. Install the baring inserts into the bearing caps, install the caps working from the middle out. Torque cap bolts to specifications in stages, rotate the crankshaft after each torque stage.

14. Remove bearing caps, one at a time and check the oil clearance with Plastigage®. Reinstall if clearance is within specifications. Check the crankshaft endplay, if within specifications install connecting rod and piston assemblies with new rod bearing inserts. Check connecting rod bearing oil clearance and rod side play, if correct and assemble the rest of the engine.

BEARING OIL CLEARANCE

Remove cap from the bearing to be checked. Using a clan, dry rag, thoroughly clean all oil from crankshaft journal and bearing insert.

NOTE: *Plastigage® is soluble in oil. Therefore, oil on the journal or bearing could result in erroneous readings.*

Place a piece of Plastigage® along the full

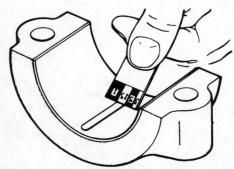

Measure the Plastigage® to determine bearing clearance

width of the insert, reinstall cap, and torque to specifications.

NOTE: *Specifications are given in the engine specifications earlier in this chapter.*

Remove bearing cap, and determine bearing clearance by comparing width of Plastigage® to the scale on Plastigage® envelope. Journal taper is determined by comparing width of the Plastigage® strip near its ends. Rotate crankshaft 90° and retest, to determine journal eccentricity.

NOTE: *Do not rotate crankshaft with Plastigage® installed. If bearing insert and journal appear intact, and are within tolerances, no further main bearing service is required. If bearing or journal appear defective, cause of failure should be determined before replacement.*

CRANKSHAFT ENDPLAY/CONNECTING ROD SIDE PLAY

Place a pry bar between a main bearing cap and crankshaft casting taking care not to damage any journals. Pry backward and forward measure the distance between the thrust baring and crankshaft with a feeler gauge. Compare reading with specifications. If too great a clearance is determined, a larger thrust bearing or crank machining may be required. Check with an automotive machine shop for their advice.

Connecting rod clearance between the rod and crank throw casting can be checked with a feeler gauge. Pry the rod carefully to one side as far as possible and measure the distance on the other side of the rod.

CRANKSHAFT REPAIRS

If a journal is damaged on the crankshaft, repair is possible by having the crankshaft machined to a standard undersize.

In most cases, however, since the crankshaft must be removed from the engine, some thought should be given to replacing the damaged crankshaft with a reground shaft kit. A reground crankshaft kit contains the necessary main and rod bearings for installation. The shaft has been ground and polished to undersize specifications and will usually hold up well if installed correctly.

EXHAUST SYSTEM

General Discription

The exhaust system is suspended by hangers and clamps attached to the frame member. Annoying rattles and noise vibrations in the exhaust system are usually caused by misalignment of parts. When aligning the system, leave all bolts and nuts loose until all parts are properly aligned, then tighten from front to rear. Make sure that you are wearing some form of eye protection when removing or installing the exhaust system, to prevent eye injury. Never work on the exhaust system of a vehicle that has been recently used. Exhaust systems reach extreamly high temperatures and can cause severe burns. Allways allow the car to cool down before starting any repairs to the exhaust.

The Catalytic Converter is an emission control device added to a gasoline engines exhaust system to reduce hydrocarbon and carbon monoxide pollutants in the exhaust gas stream. The catalyst in the converter is not servicable.

Periodic maintence of the exhaust system is not required. However, if the vehicle is raised for other service, it is advisable to check the general condition of the catalytic converter, exhaust pipes and muffler.

Exhaust Pipe

REMOVAL AND INSTALLATION

Front Exhaust Pipe (Non-Turbo)

1. Disconnect the O_2 sensor harness.
2. Remove the air duct from the upper shell cover.
3. Loosen (Do not remove) the nuts which hold the front exhaust pipe to the exhaust port of the engine.
4. Disconnect the front and rear exhaust pipes.
5. Disconnect the front exhayst pipe and bracket.
6. While holding the front exhaust pipe with one hand, remove the nuts which hold the front exhaust pipe to the exhaust port. The front exhaust pipe can then be disconnected.
7. Installation is in the reverse order of the removal procedure.

NOTE: Be sure to install a new gasket at the exhaust port. Use only nuts specified by the manufacturer. Do not remove the gasket placed between the front and rear exhaust pipes. When the front exhaust pipe needs to be replaced, the gasket must be replaced also.

Front Exhaust Pipe (Turbocharged Models)

1. Remove the turbocharger covers, and disconnect the center exhaust pipe. Remove the turbocharger unit.

2. Remove the nuts which hold the turbocharger bracket to the front exhaust pipe.

3. Remove undergaurd and right undercover.

4. Loosen the engine mount bracket and pitching stopper. Then slightly raise the engine until the bolts protrude beyond the surface of the crossmember.

5. Disconnect the front exhaust pipe from the engines exhaust port, and remove through the clearence between the crossmember and the cylinder head.

CAUTION: *Do not damage the power steering pipe which is located along the crossmember.*

NOTE: *Be sure to remove the bolts only after the engine has cooled off.*

6. Install the gasket onto the stud bolts at the engine's exhaust port with its flat surface facing the engine. If the gasket is tilted, it may catch on a thread and then will not drop down over the bolt.

NOTE:Be sure to install a new gasket.

7. Temporarily tighten the front exhaust pipe to engine's exhaust port with the nuts.

NOTE: *Use only nuts designed by the manufacturer.*

8. Lower the engine. Tighten the engine mount bracket and properly adjust the pitching stopper.

9. Install the underguard and right undercover.

10. Connect the front exhaust pipe to the turbocharger bracket.

NOTE: *Use only bolts designed by the manufacturer. Be sure to install a new gasket on the inlet of the turbocharger.*

11. Properly tighten the front exhaust pipe at the engine's exhaust port.

12. Connect the O_2 sensor connector.

13. Install the turbocharger unit, center the exhaust pipe and turbocharger covers.

Center Exhaust Pipe
REMOVAL
Turbo Vehicles Only

1. Remove turbocharger covers A and B.
2. Disconnect the O_2 sensor connector.

3. Remove the flange nuts which hold the center exhaust pipe to turbocharger unit.

NOTE: *Before removing the flang nuts, allow the turbocharger unit and exhaust pipe to cool.*

4. Remove the flange nuts from the transmission side.

5. Disconnect the center and rear exhaus pipes.

6. Disconnect the center exhaust pipe from the bracket located on the lower side of the transmission.

7. Remove the center exhaust pipe from the body.

CAUTION: *Do not allow the turbocharger cover mounting bracket to interfear with the brake pipe cover located in the front toeboard. Be sure not to damage the steering universal joint. Do not damage the gasket used on the lower side of the turbocharger unit or turbocharger cover.*

8. Install the gasket onto the stud bolts on the turbocharger unit. Connect the center exhaust pipe flange and temporarily tighten it with nuts.

CAUTION: *Be sure not to damage the gasket used on the lower side of the turbocharger unit and turbocharger cover.*

NOTE: *Use only nuts and bolts designed by the manufacturer and be sure to install a new gasket.*

9. Tamporarily connect the center exhaust pipe and bracket located on the transmission side.

10. Temporarily connect the center and rear exhaust pipes, and center exhaust pipe to the bracket located on the lower side of the transmission with new nuts.

11. Tighten the nuts and bolts at the turbocharger unit bracket, (on the transmission side) and the bracket (on the lower side of the transmiossion), in that order, to specified torque.

NOTE: *Gasket used between the center and rear exhaust pipes may be reused but not removed. When a new center exhaust pipe is installed, replace the old gasket with a new one.*

12. Install turbocharger covers.

Rear Exhaust Pipe
REMOVAL

1. Dicconnect the ASV hose from the ASV (49 state 2WD carburetor model only).

2. Disconnect the rear exhaust pipe from the front exhaust pipe (Non-Turbo), center exhaust pipe (turbocharged models).

3. Disconnect the rear exhaust pipe from the muffler assembly. To prevent damage to the

bumber or rear skirt by the muffler, wrap a cloth around the tail pipe.

4. Remove rear exhaust pipe from the rubber cushion.

INSTALLATION

1. Temporarily connect the rear exhaust pipe and the muffler assembly.

2. Temporarily connect the rear exhaust pipe and the front exhaust pipe (Non-Turbo), center exhaust pipe (turbocharged models).

3. Insert exhaust pipe bracket into the rubber cushion.

4. Adjust the clearence between the temporarily installed parts and tighten to specified torque.

NOTE: *Be sure to install bolts, springs, and self locking nuts in the order indicated in the figure. Always install new self locking nuts.*

Muffler Assembly

REMOVAL AND INSTALLATION

1. Remove the bolts and self locking nuts which hold the rear exhaust pipe to the muffler assembly.

2. Remove the left and right rubber cushions from the muffler assembly and detach the muffler assembly.

3. Installation is in the reverse order of the removal procedure.

NOTE: *Be sure to install new self locking nuts and gaskets.*

ADJUSTMENTS

1. After installing exhaust system parts, check to make sure clearences between parts and car body are larger than specified values.

2. If any clearence is not, loosen all connections.

3. Adjust when necessary to obtain proper clearences.

4. Tighten all connections to specified torque.

Troubleshooting Engine Performance

Problem	Cause	Solution
Hard starting (engine cranks normally)	• Binding linkage, choke valve or choke piston	• Repair as necessary
	• Restricted choke vacuum diaphragm	• Clean passages
	• Improper fuel level	• Adjust float level
	• Dirty, worn or faulty needle valve and seat	• Repair as necessary
	• Float sticking	• Repair as necessary
	• Faulty fuel pump	• Replace fuel pump
	• Incorrect choke cover adjustment	• Adjust choke cover
	• Inadequate choke unloader adjustment	• Adjust choke unloader
	• Faulty ignition coil	• Test and replace as necessary
	• Improper spark plug gap	• Adjust gap
	• Incorrect ignition timing	• Adjust timing
	• Incorrect valve timing	• Check valve timing; repair as necessary
Rough idle or stalling	• Incorrect curb or fast idle speed	• Adjust curb or fast idle speed
	• Incorrect ignition timing	• Adjust timing to specification
	• Improper feedback system operation	• Refer to Chapter 4
	• Improper fast idle cam adjustment	• Adjust fast idle cam
	• Faulty EGR valve operation	• Test EGR system and replace as necessary
	• Faulty PCV valve air flow	• Test PCV valve and replace as necessary
	• Choke binding	• Locate and eliminate binding condition
	• Faulty TAC vacuum motor or valve	• Repair as necessary
	• Air leak into manifold vacuum	• Inspect manifold vacuum connections and repair as necessary
	• Improper fuel level	• Adjust fuel level
	• Faulty distributor rotor or cap	• Replace rotor or cap

Troubleshooting Engine Performance (cont.)

Problem	Cause	Solution
Rough idle or stalling (cont.)	• Improperly seated valves	• Test cylinder compression, repair as necessary
	• Incorrect ignition wiring	• Inspect wiring and correct as necessary
	• Faulty ignition coil	• Test coil and replace as necessary
	• Restricted air vent or idle passages	• Clean passages
	• Restricted air cleaner	• Clean or replace air cleaner filler element
	• Faulty choke vacuum diaphragm	• Repair as necessary
Faulty low-speed operation	• Restricted idle transfer slots	• Clean transfer slots
	• Restricted idle air vents and passages	• Clean air vents and passages
	• Restricted air cleaner	• Clean or replace air cleaner filter element
	• Improper fuel level	• Adjust fuel level
	• Faulty spark plugs	• Clean or replace spark plugs
	• Dirty, corroded, or loose ignition secondary circuit wire connections	• Clean or tighten secondary circuit wire connections
	• Improper feedback system operation	• Refer to Chapter 4
	• Faulty ignition coil high voltage wire	• Replace ignition coil high voltage wire
	• Faulty distributor cap	• Replace cap
Faulty acceleration	• Improper accelerator pump stroke	• Adjust accelerator pump stroke
	• Incorrect ignition timing	• Adjust timing
	• Inoperative pump discharge check ball or needle	• Clean or replace as necessary
	• Worn or damaged pump diaphragm or piston	• Replace diaphragm or piston
	• Leaking carburetor main body cover gasket	• Replace gasket
	• Engine cold and choke set too lean	• Adjust choke cover
	• Improper metering rod adjustment (BBD Model carburetor)	• Adjust metering rod
	• Faulty spark plug(s)	• Clean or replace spark plug(s)
	• Improperly seated valves	• Test cylinder compression, repair as necessary
	• Faulty ignition coil	• Test coil and replace as necessary
	• Improper feedback system operation	• Refer to Chapter 4
Faulty high speed operation	• Incorrect ignition timing	• Adjust timing
	• Faulty distributor centrifugal advance mechanism	• Check centrifugal advance mechanism and repair as necessary
	• Faulty distributor vacuum advance mechanism	• Check vacuum advance mechanism and repair as necessary
	• Low fuel pump volume	• Replace fuel pump
	• Wrong spark plug air gap or wrong plug	• Adjust air gap or install correct plug
	• Faulty choke operation	• Adjust choke cover
	• Partially restricted exhaust manifold, exhaust pipe, catalytic converter, muffler, or tailpipe	• Eliminate restriction
	• Restricted vacuum passages	• Clean passages
	• Improper size or restricted main jet	• Clean or replace as necessary
	• Restricted air cleaner	• Clean or replace filter element as necessary
	• Faulty distributor rotor or cap	• Replace rotor or cap
	• Faulty ignition coil	• Test coil and replace as necessary
	• Improperly seated valve(s)	• Test cylinder compression, repair as necessary

Troubleshooting Engine Performance (cont.)

Problem	Cause	Solution
Faulty high speed operation (cont.)	• Faulty valve spring(s)	• Inspect and test valve spring tension, replace as necessary
	• Incorrect valve timing	• Check valve timing and repair as necessary
	• Intake manifold restricted	• Remove restriction or replace manifold
	• Worn distributor shaft	• Replace shaft
	• Improper feedback system operation	• Refer to Chapter 4
Misfire at all speeds	• Faulty spark plug(s)	• Clean or replace spark plug(s)
	• Faulty spark plug wire(s)	• Replace as necessary
	• Faulty distributor cap or rotor	• Replace cap or rotor
	• Faulty ignition coil	• Test coil and replace as necessary
	• Primary ignition circuit shorted or open intermittently	• Troubleshoot primary circuit and repair as necessary
	• Improperly seated valve(s)	• Test cylinder compression, repair as necessary
	• Faulty hydraulic tappet(s)	• Clean or replace tappet(s)
	• Improper feedback system operation	• Refer to Chapter 4
	• Faulty valve spring(s)	• Inspect and test valve spring tension, repair as necessary
	• Worn camshaft lobes	• Replace camshaft
	• Air leak into manifold	• Check manifold vacuum and repair as necessary
	• Improper carburetor adjustment	• Adjust carburetor
	• Fuel pump volume or pressure low	• Replace fuel pump
	• Blown cylinder head gasket	• Replace gasket
	• Intake or exhaust manifold passage(s) restricted	• Pass chain through passage(s) and repair as necessary
	• Incorrect trigger wheel installed in distributor	• Install correct trigger wheel
Power not up to normal	• Incorrect ignition timing	• Adjust timing
	• Faulty distributor rotor	• Replace rotor
	• Trigger wheel loose on shaft	• Reposition or replace trigger wheel
	• Incorrect spark plug gap	• Adjust gap
	• Faulty fuel pump	• Replace fuel pump
	• Incorrect valve timing	• Check valve timing and repair as necessary
	• Faulty ignition coil	• Test coil and replace as necessary
	• Faulty ignition wires	• Test wires and replace as necessary
	• Improperly seated valves	• Test cylinder compression and repair as necessary
	• Blown cylinder head gasket	• Replace gasket
	• Leaking piston rings	• Test compression and repair as necessary
	• Worn distributor shaft	• Replace shaft
	• Improper feedback system operation	• Refer to Chapter 4
Intake backfire	• Improper ignition timing	• Adjust timing
	• Faulty accelerator pump discharge	• Repair as necessary
	• Defective EGR CTO valve	• Replace EGR CTO valve
	• Defective TAC vacuum motor or valve	• Repair as necessary
	• Lean air/fuel mixture	• Check float level or manifold vacuum for air leak. Remove sediment from bowl
Exhaust backfire	• Air leak into manifold vacuum	• Check manifold vacuum and repair as necessary
	• Faulty air injection diverter valve	• Test diverter valve and replace as necessary
	• Exhaust leak	• Locate and eliminate leak

Troubleshooting Engine Performance (cont.)

Problem	Cause	Solution
Ping or spark knock	• Incorrect ignition timing	• Adjust timing
	• Distributor centrifugal or vacuum advance malfunction	• Inspect advance mechanism and repair as necessary
	• Excessive combustion chamber deposits	• Remove with combustion chamber cleaner
	• Air leak into manifold vacuum	• Check manifold vacuum and repair as necessary
	• Excessively high compression	• Test compression and repair as necessary
	• Fuel octane rating excessively low	• Try alternate fuel source
	• Sharp edges in combustion chamber	• Grind smooth
	• EGR valve not functioning properly	• Test EGR system and replace as necessary
Surging (at cruising to top speeds)	• Low carburetor fuel level	• Adjust fuel level
	• Low fuel pump pressure or volume	• Replace fuel pump
	• Metering rod(s) not adjusted properly (BBD Model Carburetor)	• Adjust metering rod
	• Improper PCV valve air flow	• Test PCV valve and replace as necessary
	• Air leak into manifold vacuum	• Check manifold vacuum and repair as necessary
	• Incorrect spark advance	• Test and replace as necessary
	• Restricted main jet(s)	• Clean main jet(s)
	• Undersize main jet(s)	• Replace main jet(s)
	• Restricted air vents	• Clean air vents
	• Restricted fuel filter	• Replace fuel filter
	• Restricted air cleaner	• Clean or replace air cleaner filter element
	• EGR valve not functioning properly	• Test EGR system and replace as necessary
	• Improper feedback system operation	• Refer to Chapter 4

Troubleshooting the Ignition Switch

Problem	Cause	Solution
Ignition switch electrically inoperative	• Loose or defective switch connector	• Tighten or replace connector
	• Feed wire open (fusible link)	• Repair or replace
	• Defective ignition switch	• Replace ignition switch
Engine will not crank	• Ignition switch not adjusted properly	• Adjust switch
Ignition switch wil not actuate mechanically	• Defective ignition switch	• Replace switch
	• Defective lock sector	• Replace lock sector
	• Defective remote rod	• Replace remote rod
Ignition switch cannot be adjusted correctly	• Remote rod deformed	• Repair, straighten or replace

TROUBLESHOOTING BASIC POINT-TYPE IGNITION SYSTEM PROBLEMS

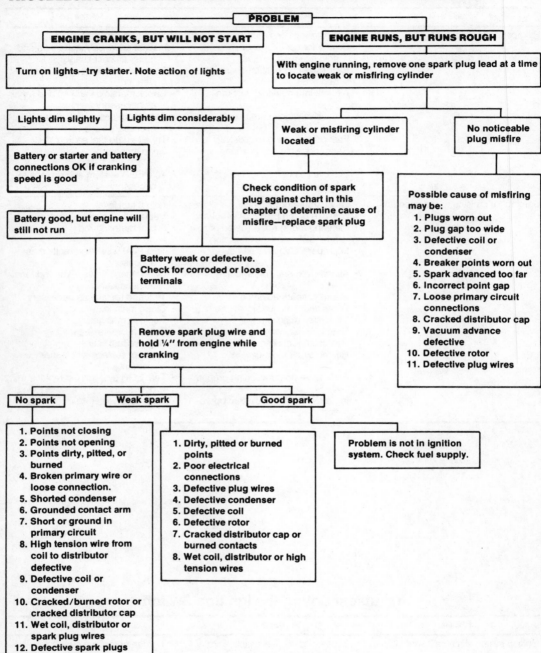

Troubleshooting Engine Mechanical Problems

Problem	Cause	Solution
External oil leaks	• Fuel pump gasket broken or improperly seated	• Replace gasket
	• Cylinder head cover RTV sealant broken or improperly seated	• Replace sealant; inspect cylinder head cover sealant flange and cylinder head sealant surface for distortion and cracks
	• Oil filler cap leaking or missing	• Replace cap
	• Oil filter gasket broken or improperly seated	• Replace oil filter
	• Oil pan side gasket broken, improperly seated or opening in RTV sealant	• Replace gasket or repair opening in sealant; inspect oil pan gasket flange for distortion
	• Oil pan front oil seal broken or improperly seated	• Replace seal; inspect timing case cover and oil pan seal flange for distortion
	• Oil pan rear oil seal broken or improperly seated	• Replace seal; inspect oil pan rear oil seal flange; inspect rear main bearing cap for cracks, plugged oil return channels, or distortion in seal groove
	• Timing case cover oil seal broken or improperly seated	• Replace seal
	• Excess oil pressure because of restricted PCV valve	• Replace PCV valve
	• Oil pan drain plug loose or has stripped threads	• Repair as necessary and tighten
	• Rear oil gallery plug loose	• Use appropriate sealant on gallery plug and tighten
	• Rear camshaft plug loose or improperly seated	• Seat camshaft plug or replace and seal, as necessary
	• Distributor base gasket damaged	• Replace gasket
Excessive oil consumption	• Oil level too high	• Drain oil to specified level
	• Oil with wrong viscosity being used	• Replace with specified oil
	• PCV valve stuck closed	• Replace PCV valve
	• Valve stem oil deflectors (or seals) are damaged, missing, or incorrect type	• Replace valve stem oil deflectors
	• Valve stems or valve guides worn	• Measure stem-to-guide clearance and repair as necessary
	• Poorly fitted or missing valve cover baffles	• Replace valve cover
	• Piston rings broken or missing	• Replace broken or missing rings
	• Scuffed piston	• Replace piston
	• Incorrect piston ring gap	• Measure ring gap, repair as necessary
	• Piston rings sticking or excessively loose in grooves	• Measure ring side clearance, repair as necessary
	• Compression rings installed upside down	• Repair as necessary
	• Cylinder walls worn, scored, or glazed	• Repair as necessary
	• Piston ring gaps not properly staggered	• Repair as necessary
	• Excessive main or connecting rod bearing clearance	• Measure bearing clearance, repair as necessary
No oil pressure	• Low oil level	• Add oil to correct level
	• Oil pressure gauge, warning lamp or sending unit inaccurate	• Replace oil pressure gauge or warning lamp
	• Oil pump malfunction	• Replace oil pump
	• Oil pressure relief valve sticking	• Remove and inspect oil pressure relief valve assembly
	• Oil passages on pressure side of pump obstructed	• Inspect oil passages for obstruction

Troubleshooting Engine Mechanical Problems (cont.)

Problem	Cause	Solution
No oil pressure (cont.)	• Oil pickup screen or tube obstructed	• Inspect oil pickup for obstruction
	• Loose oil inlet tube	• Tighten or seal inlet tube
Low oil pressure	• Low oil level	• Add oil to correct level
	• Inaccurate gauge, warning lamp or sending unit	• Replace oil pressure gauge or warning lamp
	• Oil excessively thin because of dilution, poor quality, or improper grade	• Drain and refill crankcase with recommended oil
	• Excessive oil temperature	• Correct cause of overheating engine
	• Oil pressure relief spring weak or sticking	• Remove and inspect oil pressure relief valve assembly
	• Oil inlet tube and screen assembly has restriction or air leak	• Remove and inspect oil inlet tube and screen assembly. (Fill inlet tube with lacquer thinner to locate leaks.)
	• Excessive oil pump clearance	• Measure clearances
	• Excessive main, rod, or camshaft bearing clearance	• Measure bearing clearances, repair as necessary
High oil pressure	• Improper oil viscosity	• Drain and refill crankcase with correct viscosity oil
	• Oil pressure gauge or sending unit inaccurate	• Replace oil pressure gauge
	• Oil pressure relief valve sticking closed	• Remove and inspect oil pressure relief valve assembly
Main bearing noise	• Insufficient oil supply	• Inspect for low oil level and low oil pressure
	• Main bearing clearance excessive	• Measure main bearing clearance, repair as necessary
	• Bearing insert missing	• Replace missing insert
	• Crankshaft end play excessive	• Measure end play, repair as necessary
	• Improperly tightened main bearing cap bolts	• Tighten bolts with specified torque
	• Loose flywheel or drive plate	• Tighten flywheel or drive plate attaching bolts
	• Loose or damaged vibration damper	• Repair as necessary
Connecting rod bearing noise	• Insufficient oil supply	• Inspect for low oil level and low oil pressure
	• Carbon build-up on piston	• Remove carbon from piston crown
	• Bearing clearance excessive or bearing missing	• Measure clearance, repair as necessary
	• Crankshaft connecting rod journal out-of-round	• Measure journal dimensions, repair or replace as necessary
	• Misaligned connecting rod or cap	• Repair as necessary
	• Connecting rod bolts tightened improperly	• Tighten bolts with specified torque
Piston noise	• Piston-to-cylinder wall clearance excessive (scuffed piston)	• Measure clearance and examine piston
	• Cylinder walls excessively tapered or out-of-round	• Measure cylinder wall dimensions, rebore cylinder
	• Piston ring broken	• Replace all rings on piston
	• Loose or seized piston pin	• Measure piston-to-pin clearance, repair as necessary
	• Connecting rods misaligned	• Measure rod alignment, straighten or replace
	• Piston ring side clearance excessively loose or tight	• Measure ring side clearance, repair as necessary
	• Carbon build-up on piston is excessive	• Remove carbon from piston

Troubleshooting Engine Mechanical Problems (cont.)

Problem	Cause	Solution
Valve actuating component noise	• Insufficient oil supply	• Check for: (a) Low oil level (b) Low oil pressure (c) Plugged push rods (d) Wrong hydraulic tappets (e) Restricted oil gallery (f) Excessive tappet to bore clearance
	• Push rods worn or bent	• Replace worn or bent push rods
	• Rocker arms or pivots worn	• Replace worn rocker arms or pivots
	• Foreign objects or chips in hydraulic tappets	• Clean tappets
	• Excessive tappet leak-down	• Replace valve tappet
	• Tappet face worn	• Replace tappet; inspect corresponding cam lobe for wear
	• Broken or cocked valve springs	• Properly seat cocked springs; replace broken springs
	• Stem-to-guide clearance excessive	• Measure stem-to-guide clearance, repair as required
	• Valve bent	• Replace valve
	• Loose rocker arms	• Tighten bolts with specified torque
	• Valve seat runout excessive	• Regrind valve seat/valves
	• Missing valve lock	• Install valve lock
	• Push rod rubbing or contacting cylinder head	• Remove cylinder head and remove obstruction in head
	• Excessive engine oil (four-cylinder engine)	• Correct oil level

Troubleshooting the Cooling System

Problem	Cause	Solution
High temperature gauge indication—overheating	• Coolant level low	• Replenish coolant
	• Fan belt loose	• Adjust fan belt tension
	• Radiator hose(s) collapsed	• Replace hose(s)
	• Radiator airflow blocked	• Remove restriction (bug screen, fog lamps, etc.)
	• Faulty radiator cap	• Replace radiator cap
	• Ignition timing incorrect	• Adjust ignition timing
	• Idle speed low	• Adjust idle speed
	• Air trapped in cooling system	• Purge air
	• Heavy traffic driving	• Operate at fast idle in neutral intermittently to cool engine
	• Incorrect cooling system component(s) installed	• Install proper component(s)
	• Faulty thermostat	• Replace thermostat
	• Water pump shaft broken or impeller loose	• Replace water pump
	• Radiator tubes clogged	• Flush radiator
	• Cooling system clogged	• Flush system
	• Casting flash in cooling passages	• Repair or replace as necessary. Flash may be visible by removing cooling system components or removing core plugs.
	• Brakes dragging	• Repair brakes
	• Excessive engine friction	• Repair engine
	• Antifreeze concentration over 68%	• Lower antifreeze concentration percentage
	• Missing air seals	• Replace air seals
	• Faulty gauge or sending unit	• Repair or replace faulty component
	• Loss of coolant flow caused by leakage or foaming	• Repair or replace leaking component, replace coolant
	• Viscous fan drive failed	• Replace unit

Troubleshooting the Cooling System (cont.)

Problem	Cause	Solution
Low temperature indication—undercooling	• Thermostat stuck open • Faulty gauge or sending unit	• Replace thermostat • Repair or replace faulty component
Coolant loss—boilover	• Overfilled cooling system • Quick shutdown after hard (hot) run • Air in system resulting in occasional "burping" of coolant • Insufficient antifreeze allowing coolant boiling point to be too low • Antifreeze deteriorated because of age or contamination • Leaks due to loose hose clamps, loose nuts, bolts, drain plugs, faulty hoses, or defective radiator • Faulty head gasket • Cracked head, manifold, or block • Faulty radiator cap	• Reduce coolant level to proper specification • Allow engine to run at fast idle prior to shutdown • Purge system • Add antifreeze to raise boiling point • Replace coolant • Pressure test system to locate source of leak(s) then repair as necessary • Replace head gasket • Replace as necessary • Replace cap
Coolant entry into crankcase or cylinder(s)	• Faulty head gasket • Crack in head, manifold or block	• Replace head gasket • Replace as necessary
Coolant recovery system inoperative	• Coolant level low • Leak in system • Pressure cap not tight or seal missing, or leaking • Pressure cap defective • Overflow tube clogged or leaking • Recovery bottle vent restricted	• Replenish coolant to FULL mark • Pressure test to isolate leak and repair as necessary • Repair as necessary • Replace cap • Repair as necessary • Remove restriction
Noise	• Fan contacting shroud • Loose water pump impeller • Glazed fan belt • Loose fan belt • Rough surface on drive pulley • Water pump bearing worn • Belt alignment	• Reposition shroud and inspect engine mounts • Replace pump • Apply silicone or replace belt • Adjust fan belt tension • Replace pulley • Remove belt to isolate. Replace pump. • Check pulley alignment. Repair as necessary.
No coolant flow through heater core	• Restricted return inlet in water pump • Heater hose collapsed or restricted • Restricted heater core • Restricted outlet in thermostat housing • Intake manifold bypass hole in cylinder head restricted • Faulty heater control valve • Intake manifold coolant passage restricted	• Remove restriction • Remove restriction or replace hose • Remove restriction or replace core • Remove flash or restriction • Remove restriction • Replace valve • Remove restriction or replace intake manifold

NOTE: *Immediately after shutdown, the engine enters a condition known as heat soak. This is caused by the cooling system being inoperative while engine temperature is still high. If coolant temperature rises above boiling point, expansion and pressure may push some coolant out of the radiator overflow tube. If this does not occur frequently it is considered normal.*

Troubleshooting Basic Fuel System Problems

Problem	Cause	Solution
Engine cranks, but won't start (or is hard to start) when cold	· Empty fuel tank · Incorrect starting procedure · Defective fuel pump · No fuel in carburetor · Clogged fuel filter · Engine flooded · Defective choke	· Check for fuel in tank · Follow correct procedure · Check pump output · Check for fuel in the carburetor · Replace fuel filter · Wait 15 minutes; try again · Check choke plate
Engine cranks, but is hard to start (or does not start) when hot— (presence of fuel is assumed)	· Defective choke	· Check choke plate
Rough idle or engine runs rough	· Dirt or moisture in fuel · Clogged air filter · Faulty fuel pump	· Replace fuel filter · Replace air filter · Check fuel pump output
Engine stalls or hesitates on acceleration	· Dirt or moisture in the fuel · Dirty carburetor · Defective fuel pump · Incorrect float level, defective accelerator pump	· Replace fuel filter · Clean the carburetor · Check fuel pump output · Check carburetor
Poor gas mileage	· Clogged air filter · Dirty carburetor · Defective choke, faulty carburetor adjustment	· Replace air filter · Clean carburetor · Check carburetor
Engine is flooded (won't start accompanied by smell of raw fuel)	· Improperly adjusted choke or carburetor	· Wait 15 minutes and try again, without pumping gas pedal · If it won't start, check carburetor

Emission Controls and Fuel System

EMISSION CONTROLS

Most of the following emission control procedures and, in fact, assemblies, are for gasoline engines. Volkswagen claims that most of the diesel engine emissions are controlled by the virtually complete burning of the diesel fuel in the cylinders. For the most part, emission control maintenance on the diesel is restricted to checking the crankcase ventilation hoses, the air cleaner, and the fuel tank lines and connections for leaks and wear. Replace the fuel filter at regular intervals and have your dealer give the engine a compression test.

Emission Equipment Used

GOLF, GTI, JETTA, SCIROCCO, FOX, RABBIT AND QUANTUM

- Positive crankcase ventilation
- Evaporative emission control
- Dual diaphragm distributor
- Exhaust gas recirculation
- Air injection (Carbureted Rabbit only)
- Catalytic converter
- Oxygen sensor

Required Emission Control Maintenance

NOTE: *The following information is being published from the latest information available at the time of publication. If the information contained herein differs from that which is listed on the vehicles emission label, use the specifications given on the label.*

POSITIVE CRANKCASE VENTILATION (PCV)

Every 15,000 miles, check the PCV valve. Every 30,000 miles replace the PCV valve. Inspect and clean all hoses and connections. Replace any that show signs of deterioration.

EVAPORATIVE EMISSION CONTROL SYSTEM

Make a visual check of all system hoses and filters every 10,000 miles. Replace the charcoal filter every 50,000 miles.

DUAL DIAPHRAGM DISTRIBUTOR

Check the condition of the vacuum lines every 10,000 miles.

EXHAUST GAS RECIRCULATION SYSTEM

Inspect and check the hoses regularly. Reset the mileage switch if equipped, as necessary. Replace the EGR filter every 30,000 miles.

AIR INJECTION

Visually inspect the pump, control valve and hoses every 10,000 miles. Clean the pump filter every 10,000 miles. Replace the pump filter every 20,000 miles or 2 years.

CATALYTIC CONVERTER

Check for damage and tight connections every 30,000 miles. Reset the indicator light as necessary.

AIR CLEANER

Replace the air cleaner element every 15,000 miles.

Crankcase Ventilation

The purpose of the crankcase ventilation system is twofold. It keeps harmful vapor byproducts of combustion from escaping into the atmosphere and prevents the building of crankcase pressure which in turn causes gasket failure and oil leaks. Crankcase vapors are recirculated from the camshaft cover through a hose to the air cleaner. Here they are mixed with the air/fuel mixture and burned in the combustion chamber.

NOTE: *1975–76 Rabbits and Sciroccos are*

equipped with either a PCV valve on the hose between the valve cover and the air cleaner, or a restrictor inserted inside this hose. Volkswagen suggests that the models with the restrictors would be less prone to carburetor icing if the restrictor were removed and replaced with a PCV valve. See chapter one under PCV valve for replacement procedures.

SERVICE

Service the crankcase ventilation valve at the interval suggested in Chapter 1. Remove the crankcase ventilation valve, if so quipped which is connected to the camshaft cover, and clean it in solvent. At every tune-up, examine the hoses for clogging or deterioration. Clean or replace the hoses as necessary.

Evaporative Emission Control System

This system prevents the escape of raw fuel vapors (unburned hydrocarbons or HC) into the atmosphere. The system consists of a sealed carburetor, unvented fuel tank filler cap, fuel tank expansion chamber, an activated charcoal filter canister and connector hoses. Fuel vapors which reach the filter deposit hydrocarbons on the surface of the charcoal filter element. Fresh air enters the filter when the engine is running and forces the hydrocarbons to the air cleaner where they join the air/fuel mixture and are burned. Many 1979 and later models are equipped with a charcoal filter valve which prevents vapors from escaping from the canister when the engine is not running.

SERVICE

Maintenance of the system consists of checking the condition of the various connector hoses and the charcoal filter at 10,000 mile intervals. The charcoal filter should be replaced at 50,000 mile intervals.

Dual Diaphragm Distributor

The purpose of the dual diaphragm distributor is to improve exhaust emissions during one of the engine's dirtier operating modes, idling. The distributor has a vacuum retard diaphragm, in addition to a vacuum advance diaphragm. A temperature valve shuts off vacuum from the carburetor when coolant temperature is below 130°F.

TESTING

Advance Diaphragm

1. Connect a timing light to the engine. Check the ignition timing as described in Chapter 2.
2. Remove the retard (inner) hose from the distributor and plug it. Increase the engine speed. The ignition timing should advance. If it doesn't, then the vacuum unit is faulty and must be replaced.

Temperature Valve

1. Remove the temperature valve and place the threaded portion in hot water.
2. Create a vacuum by sucking on the angled connection.
3. The valve must be open above approximately 130°F.

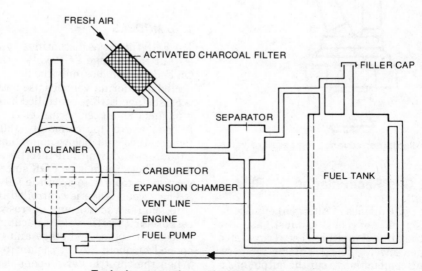

Typical evaporative emission control system

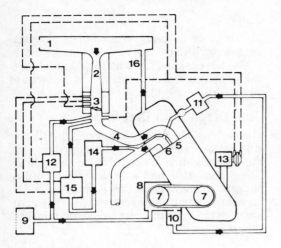

1. Air cleaner
2. Carburetor
3. Throttle plate
4. Intake manifold
5. Intake valve
6. Exhaust valve
7. Air pump belt
8. Air pump
9. Air pump air cleaner
10. High pressure valve
11. Check valve
12. Control valve
13. Distributor
14. EGR filter
15. EGR valve
16. Crankcase ventilation

═══════════════ Exhaust and air lines
─ ─ ─ ─ ─ ─ Vacuum control lines

Dasher emission control system—1974–75

Checking distributor advance temperature valve

Exhaust Gas Recirculation (EGR)

To reduce NOx (oxides of nitrogen) emissions, metered amounts of cooled exhaust gases are added to the air/fuel mixture. The recirculated exhaust gas lowers the peak flame temperature during combustion to cut the output of oxides of nitrogen. Exhaust gas from the mani-

fold passes through a filter where it is cleaned. The EGR valve controls the amount of this exhaust gas which is allowed into the intake manifold. There is no EGR at idle, partial at slight throttle and full EGR at mid-throttle.

1974–75 MODELS

1974–75 models have an EGR filter and a 2-stage EGR valve. The first stage is controlled by the temperature valve. The second stage is controlled by the microswitch on the carburetor throttle valve. The switch opens the valve when the throttle valve is open between 30°–67°F (manual transmission) or 23°–63°F(automatic transmission).

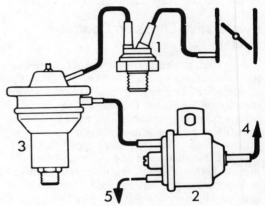

1. Temperature valve
2. Two-way valve
3. EGR valve
4. To brake booster
5. To micro switch

EGR operation—to 1975

1976 MODELS

The EGR filter was discontinued on 1976 models but the 2-stage EGR valve was retained. On Federal vehicles, only the first stage is connected; California vehicles use both stages.

First stage EGR is controlled by engine vacuum and coolant temperature. The EGR valve is open above approximately 120°F. coolant temperature and below approximately 80°F. (At idle and during full throttle acceleration (engine hot), there is no EGR since the engine vacuum is too low to open the valve.

The second stage is controlled by temperature, engine vacuum and microswitch on the carburetor throttle valve. Vacuum is always present at the second stage and the valve is opened at about 120°F. coolant temperature. When the throttle valve opens between 25°F and 67°F, the microswitch activates the 2-way

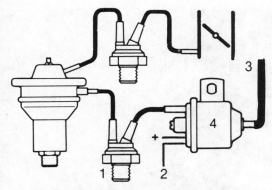

1. Temperature valve for EGR 2nd stage
2. To micro switch on throttle valve
3. Vacuum hose to brake booster
4. Two way valve

Two stage EGR operation—1976 and later

valve and allows engine vacuum to reach the second stage.

1976 AND LATER MODELS

The EGR valve on fuel injected models is controlled by a temperature valve and a vacuum amplifier. The valve is located on the intake manifold.

TESTING

EGR Valve, Checking the First Stage, (1974–76) Carbureted Engines

1. Disconnect the vacuum line from the end of the EGR valve.
2. Disconnect the vacuum hose from the distributor vacuum unit and extend hose.
3. Start the engine and allow it to idle.
4. Connect the line from the anti-backfire valve to the EGR valve. The engine should stumble or stall.
5. If the idle stays even, the EGR line is clogged or the EGR valve is defective, or the filter is clogged.

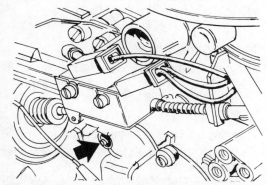

Manually operate micro-switch (arrow) to check 2nd stage EGR valve

EGR Valve, Checking the Second Stage, (1974–76) Carbureted Engines

The EGR valve second stage is on all 1974–75 USA and California models and on 1976 California Rabbits and Sciroccos only. The system includes a microswitch located on the side of the carburetor near the throttle valve. To check the system, manually operate the switch with the engine at idle. If the engine speed drops or the engine stalls, the switch is operating correctly. If not, check the microswitch, the EGR filter and the EGR return lines for blockage.

EGR Valve—Fuel Injected Models

Be sure the vacuum lines are not leaking. Replace any that are leaking or cracked.
1. Warm the engine to normal operating temperature.
2. Run the engine at idle.
3. Remove the vacuum hose from the EGR valve.
4. Remove the vacuum hose from the vacuum retard on the distributor and connect it to the EGR valve.
5. If the engine speed does not change, the EGR valve is clogged or damaged.

EGR Temperature Valve (1974–76)

1. Remove the temperature valve and place the threaded portion in hot water.
2. Create a vacuum by sucking on the angled connection. The valve should be closed below approximately 120°F.

EGR Temperature Valve—Fuel Injected Models

Warm the engine to normal operating temperature. With the engine at idle, attach a vacuum gauge between the EGR temperature control valve and the EGR valve. The valve should be replaced if the gauge shows less than 2 in.Hg.

EGR Deceleration Valve (1976 and Later)

NOTE: *1976 USA models, except California manual transmission Dashers are equipped with deceleration valves. No automatic transmission Volkswagens have deceleration valves. Rabbits and Sciroccos first received deceleration valves in 1977.*
1. Remove the hose from the deceleration valve. Plug the hose.
2. Run the engine for a few seconds at 3,000 rpm.
3. Snap the throttle valve closed.
4. With your finger, check for suction at the hose connection.
5. Remove the hose from the connector.

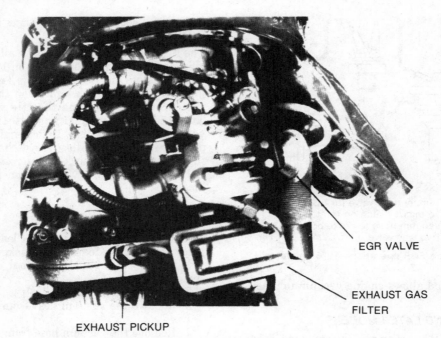

EGR VALVE

EXHAUST GAS
FILTER

EXHAUST PICKUP

EGR system components—carbureted engine

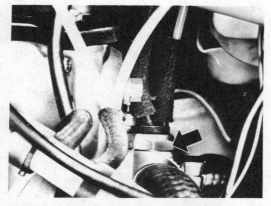

Checking EGR temperature valve (fuel injected engines)

Checking EGR deceleration valve (fuel injected engines)

6. Run the engine at about 3,000 rpm. No suction should be felt.

EGR Vacuum Amplifier (1976 and Later)

NOTE: *1976 Dashers are equipped with EGR Vacuum Amplifiers, while Rabbits and Sciroccos first received them in 1977.*

1. Run the engine at idle.
2. Connect a vacuum gauge between the vacuum amplifier and the throttle valve port.
3. The gauge should read 0.2–0.3 in.Hg. If not, check the throttle plate for correct position or check the port for obstruction.
4. Connect a vacuum gauge between the vacuum amplifier and the temperature valve.
5. Replace the vacuum amplifier if the gauge reads less than 2 in.Hg.

MAINTENANCE

The only maintenance is to replace the EGR filter (1974–75 models only) and to reset the EGR elapsed mileage switch.

Resetting the Elapsed Mileage Switch

The EGR reminder light in the speedometer should light up every 15,000 miles as a reminder for maintenance. To reset the light switch, press the white button (arrow). The speedometer light should go out.

Reset the EGR light switch

Oxygen sensor reset button

FILTER REPLACEMENT

1. Disconnect the filter EGR line fittings.
2. Remove the filter and discard.
3. Install the new filter into the EGR lines and securely tighten fittings.

REMOVAL AND INSTALLATION

EGR Valve

1. Disconnect the vacuum hose from the EGR valve.
2. Unbolt the EGR line fitting on the opposite side of the valve.
3. Remove the two retaining bolts and lift the EGR valve from the intake manifold.
4. Install the EGR valve in the reverse order of removal. Use a new gasket at the intake manifold.

Dashpot

Adjustments

See appropriate section under Carburetor, in this chapter for dashpot adjustments.

Oxygen Sensor System

Various fuel injected models are equipped with an oxygen sensor system which lowers toxic exhaust emissions while increasing fuel economy. In effect, the sensor system monitors the oxygen content in the exhaust system and, through a control unit and frequency valve. makes adjustments to the air/fuel mixture to achieve maximum fuel efficiency over a wide range of operating conditions. The system consists of the following.

Oxygen Sensor: located in the exhaust manifold. Unscrew to replace.
Control Unit: located behind the glove compartment cover.
Frequency Valve: located next to the fuel distributor.

Thermoswitch: located in the coolant system.
Oxygen Sensor System Relay: white colored relay located in the fuse/relay panel.
Elapsed Mileage Switch: located on the firewall.
Warning Light: marked OXS and located in the instrument panel. Comes on when the oxygen sensor must be replaced (every 30,000 miles).

RESETTING THE ELAPSED MILEAGE SWITCH

After replacing the oxygen sensor, reset the elapsed mileage switch by pushing the white button on the front of the switch.

Air Injection

The air injection system used on most carbureted engines, except the 1978 and 1980 Rabbit with 34 PICT-5 carburetor and later models equipped with a TYF carburetor, includes a belt driven air pump, filter, check valve, antibackfire valve or gulp valve, and connecting

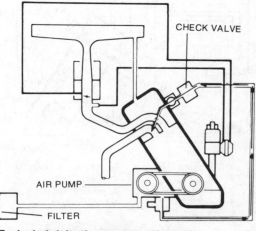

Typical air injection system schematic

1978–1980 Rabbit with 34 PICT-4 Carburetor check valves (arrows) and silencer (1) in air injection system. If valves turn blue, replace them

hoses and air lines. The system reduces exhaust emissions by pumping fresh air to the exhaust manifold or directly behind the exhaust valves where it combines with the hot exhaust gas to burn away excess hydrocarbons and reduce carbon monoxide.

The air injection systems on the 1978, 1980,

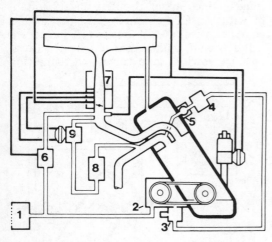

1. Air pump filter
2. Air pump
3. Relief valve
4. Check valve
5. Air manifold
6. Anti-backfire valve
7. Carburetor
8. EGR filter
9. EGR valve

Typical air injection and EGR systems schematic

1982 and later Rabbits do not have air pumps. Instead, air is drawn from the air cleaner through a silencer to two check valves. The valves turn blue when overheated. If the valves are blue, replace them.

MAINTENANCE

Required maintenance on the air pump consists of visually checking the pump, control valves, hoses and lines every 10,000 miles. Clean the air pump filter element at this interval. The filter element should be replaced every 20,000 miles or two years.

TESTING AND SERVICE

Air Pump and Hoses

1. Disconnect the hose from the check valve and plug the valve opening.
2. With the engine idling, check for air flow from the hose. If no air flows from the hose, the hoses are kinked or damaged, the diverter valve is defective or the air pump is defective (it cannot be repaired, only replaced).

Diverter Valve

1. Disconnect the vacuum hose from the F or 1 connection.
2. Disconnect the hose from the S or 2 connection and connect it to F or 1.
3. With the engine idling, if no air comes from the muffler on the diverter valve the hos-

Checking air pump and hoses

Checking the anti-backfire valve

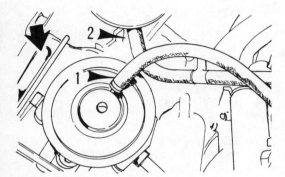

Checking Dasher diverter valve

Anti-Backfire Valve

A defective antibackfire valve could be indicated by the engine backfiring while coasting.

1. Disconnect the hose from the valve.
2. Start the engine and run it briefly at higher than normal fast idle.
3. Snap the throttle valve closed. As the throttle snaps shut, suction should be felt at the valve for about 1–3 seconds. If not, the vacuum hose is kinked or blocked, the hose between manifold and valve is kinked or blocked or the valve is defective.

Catalytic Converter

Many models are equipped with catalytic converters located in the exhaust system. This device contains noble metals acting as catalysts to convert hydrocarbons and carbon monoxide into harmless water and carbon dioxide. Required maintenance on the catalytic converter involves checking the condition of the ceramic insert every 30,000 miles. As this interval is reached, an indicator light on the dash will glow. Once service to the converter is performed, the warning light must be reset.

NOTE: *Not all models are equipped with warning lights.*

CAUTION: *Never attempt to remove the converter from a just-run or warm engine. Catalytic temperatures can reach 1,900°F, so be careful!*

Checking Rabbit, Scirocco diverter valve

es are kinked or damaged or the air pump is defective. If air flows, the diverter valve is OK.

2-Way Valve

1. Idle the engine and pull the electrical lead from the 2-way valve.
2. Ground the valve and connect a test wire directly from the battery to the valve.
3. Increase the engine rpm and check for air output at the diverter valve.
4. If no air flows from the diverter valve, the vacuum line is kinked or disconnected or the diverter valve is bad. If air flows, the 2-way valve is OK.

TESTING AND SERVICE

CAUTION: *Do not drop or strike the converter assembly or damage to the ceramic insert will result.*

Damage and overheating of the catalytic converter, indicated by the flickering of the "CAT" warning light, can be caused by the following:

1. Engine misfire caused by faulty spark plug, ignition wires and so on.
2. Improper ignition timing.
3. CO valve set too high.
4. Faulty air pump diverter valve.
5. Faulty temperature sensor.
6. Engine under strain caused by trailer hauling, high speed driving in hot weather, etc.

A faulty converter is indicated by one of the following symptoms:

1. Poor engine performance.
2. The engine stalls.
3. Rattling in the exhaust system.
4. A CO reading greater than 0.4% at the tail pipe.

Check or replace the converter as follows:

1. Disconnect the temperature sensor.
2. Loosen and remove the bolts holding the converter to the exhaust system and the chassis.
3. Remove the converter.
4. Hold the converter up to a strong light and look through both ends, checking for blockages. If the converter is blocked, replace it.
5. Install the converter in the reverse order of removal.

RESETTING THE CAT WARNING LIGHT

The CAT warning light in the speedometer should come on at 30,000 mile intervals to remind you to have the converter serviced.

The light can be reset by pushing the button marked CAT on the switch. The light on the speedometer should go out.

Reset the catalytic converter elapsed mileage odometer

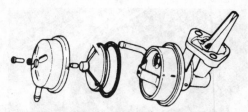

Exploded view of fuel pump showing filter screen

CARBURETED FUEL SYSTEM

Mechanical Fuel Pump

CLEANING

The filter screen can be removed from the pump and cleaned.

1. Remove the center screw.
2. Remove the screen and gasket. Clean the screen in a safe solvent.
3. Replace the screen.
4. Install a new gasket and replace the cover.

NOTE: *Make sure that the depression in the pump cover engages the projection on the body of the pump.*

REMOVAL AND INSTALLATION

The fuel pump cannot be repaired and must be replaced when defective.

1. Disconnect and plug both fuel lines.
2. Remove the two socket head retaining bolts.
3. Remove the fuel pump and its plastic flange.
4. Replace the pump in the reverse order of removal. Use a new flange seal.

Carburetor

The 1974 Dasher uses a Solex 32/35 DIDTA two barrel carburetor with a vacuum operated secondary throttle. The 1975 Dasher uses a Zenith 2B3 two barrel carburetor. It too, has a vacuum operated secondary throttle. The Rabbit and Scirocco carburetor is a Zenith 2B2 two barrel which also has a vacuum operated secondary throttle.

Some 1978 and 1980 Rabbits are equipped with a single barrel Solex 34 PICT-5 carburetor. 1982 and later carburetor equipped models use a Carter TYF feedback model.

REMOVAL AND INSTALLATION

1. Remove the air cleaner.
2. Disconnect the fuel line, being careful not to spill any fuel on the hot engine components.
3. Drain some of the coolant and then disconnect the choke hoses.
4. Disconnect all vacuum lines.
5. Disconnect all electrical leads.

OLD TYPE (1975)
PT. NO. 055 129 281A

NEW TYPE (1976)
PT. NO. 049 129 281

New and old style carburetor gaskets are not interchangeable. 1975 Dashers, Rabbits and Sciroccos use old type: 1976 Rabbits and Sciroccos use new types

6. Remove the clip which secures the throttle linkage to the carburetor. Detach the linkage, being careful not to lose any washers or bushings.

7. Unbolt the carburetor from the manifold and remove it.

8. Use a new gasket when replacing the carburetor. Don't overtighten the nuts.

ADJUSTMENTS

Solex 32/35DIDTA Carburetor 1974 Dasher

THROTTLE GAP ADJUSTMENT (BASIC SETTING)

This adjustment is made at the adjuster screw located in the linkage on the carburetor, below and to the right of the automatic choke unit.

1. Open the choke and close the throttle.

2. Turn the first stage adjusting screw out until there is a gap between it and its stop. The first stage throttle valve should be fully closed now.

Second stage adjusting screw (Arrow)—1974 Dasher

3. Turn the adjusting screw in until it just touches its stop.

4. Turn the screw in ¼ turn more and lock it.

5. The second stage throttle (secondary) should only be adjusted when it is definitely maladjusted.

   a. Loosen the adjusting screw until the secondary throttle closes.

   b. Turn the screw in 12 turn and lock it.

   c. Adjust the idle mixture after this adjustment.

FUEL LEVEL ADJUSTMENT

This adjustment is made with the carburetor installed on the engine. Incorrect fuel level can cause stalling or high speed miss.

1. Remove the air cleaner.

2. Remove the five carburetor cover mounting screws.

3. Plug the fuel inlet with a finger and lift off the carburetor cover and gasket. Set them to the side, leaving the linkages attached.

4. On models with the original equipment float, which is shaped like a child's top, with the float in the up, or closed, position, the distance from the edge of the float rim to the carburetor surface (minus the gasket) should be $5/8-11/16''$ (16–17mm).

5. Adjust the float by varying the thickness of the fiber sealing ring under the float needle valve.

6. On models with the modified float, which is more rectangular in shape, with the float in the up, or closed, position, measure from the top edge of the float closest to the throttle chambers down to the carburetor surface (minus the gasket). The distance should be $1^{15}/_{32}-1^{17}/_{32}''$ (37–39mm).

7. Adjust the float by bending the tab that contacts the needle valve.

NOTE: *For added accuracy, when measuring the float level, make all measurements with the carburetor top at a 45° angle so that the stop ball in he needle valve is not unnaturally pushed down by the weight of the float.*

FAST IDLE ADJUSTMENT

It will be necessary to remove the carburetor from the engine to perform this operation.

1. Turn the carburetor upside down and drain the fuel from it.

2. With the carburetor upside down, close the choke tightly and measure the gap between the lower edge of the throttle valve and the housing wall with a drill. The measurement should be: All Except Calif. Manual Trans. 0.030–0.034″ (0.75–0.85mm); Calif. Manual Trans. 0.024–0.028″ (0.60–0.70mm).

Fast idle adjuster (arrow)—1974 Dasher

Adjust the choke gap by bending the lever (a)

3. Adjust the fast idle speed at the eyebolt fitted in the choke lever attachment.

CHOKE VALVE GAP ADJUSTMENT

1. Remove the automatic choke cover with the water hoses still attached.
2. Push the plunger rod down into its seat, then move the choke valve toward the fully closed position.
3. With an appropriate size drill measure the gap between the choke valve and the carburetor housing. It should be: all Except Calif. 0.142–0.154" (3.55–3.85mm); Calif. 0.134–0.146" (3.35–3.65mm).
4. Adjust the choke gap by bending the lever arm attached to the plunger rod.
NOTE: *When installing the choke spring inside the choke cover, the loop in the spring must go over the protruding choke lever. Insert the spring so that it uncoils in a clockwise direction (facing you).*

Automatic Choke Adjustment

Align the mark on the automatic choke cover with the mark on the carburetor by loosing the three retaining screws and turning the choke cover with the hoses still attached.

1974 Dasher dashpot adjustment

Dashpot Adjustment

The purpose of the dashpot is to keep the throttle from snapping shut and stalling the engine. The dashpot has a plunger that extends when the throttle is closed suddenly. The plunger contacts a tab on the throttle lever and holds the throttle open slightly for a second, then closes the throttle slowly over the period of another second or so.
NOTE: *Not all models have dashpots.*
1. Close the throttle valve and make sure the choke is fully open. You may have to run the car up to operating temperature.
2. Press the dashpot plunger in as far as it will go.
3. Measure the gap between the plunger and its striking surface. It should be 0.04" (1mm).
4. Adjust by loosening the lock nut and moving the dashpot on its threads.
NOTE: *There is a dashpot kit available. The kit includes special washers which fit between the dashpot spring and the plunger mount.*

Zenith 2B3 Carburetor, 1975 Dasher
THROTTLE GAP ADJUSTMENT

To adjust first stage throttle gap:
1. The choke must be open and the first stage (primary) throttle closed.
2. Turn the first stage throttle valve stop screw until there is a gap between it and the lever moves.
3. Turn the screw in until it just touches the lever.
4. Turn screw in ¼ turn more.
5. Adjust the idle speed and CO level.
To adjust the second stage (secondary) throttle gap, proceed as follows.
6. The choke must be open and the first stage throttle must be closed.
7. Turn the second stage (secondary) adjusting screw until there is no clearance in the lever it is mounted on.

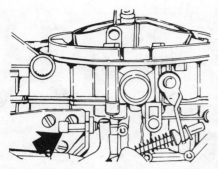

First stage throttle gap adjustment—1975 Dasher, 1975–76 Rabbit, Scirocco

Second stage throttle gap adjustment (A)—1975 Dasher, 1975–76 Rabbit, Scirocco

8. From this position, turn the screw out ¼ turn. There should be noticeable clearance at the lever.

FUEL LEVEL ADJUSTMENT

Remove the top of the carburetor. You may not haves to remove the entire carburetor from the engine to perform this operation.

1. With the carburetor top upside down and canted at a 45° angle to prevent the damping ball in the needle valve from settling too deeply due to the weight of the float, measure from the highest tip of the first stage float to the carburetor surface (minus the gasket). The distance for the first stage float should be 1.10″ ± 0.02″ (30mm ± 0.5mm).

2. Adjust the second stage float in the same manner. The distance for the second stage float should be 1.20 ± 0.02″ (30mm ± 0.5mm).

3. Adjust the float level by bending the float bracket.

CAUTION: *Do not scratch the float skin or the float may absorb fuel and sink.*

If float height must be adjusted, remove the float from the carburetor to prevent damage to the needle valve.

Checking the float level—1975 Dasher, 1975–76 Rabbit, Scirocco

FAST IDLE ADJUSTMENT

It will be necessary to remove the carburetor from the engine to perform this procedure.

1. Turn the carburetor upside down and drain the fuel from it.

2. With the carburetor upside down, close the choke tightly and measure the gap between the lower edge of the throttle valve and the housing wall with a drill. The measurement should be: 0.018–0.020″ (0.45–0.50mm).

3. Adjust the gap at the adjusting screw (beside the first stage valve) which is facing up when the carburetor is upside down.

Fast idle adjustment (a) gap, (b) adjuster screw—1975 Dasher, Rabbit, Scirocco

CHOKE VALVE GAP ADJUSTMENT

1. Remove the automatic choke cover. You should be able to remove the cover without unfastening the water hoses.

2. Open and close the choke to make sure its internal spring is working. If not, remove the vacuum cover at the side of the choke assembly and check the spring.

3. Push the choke lever to its stop (arrow) and hold the rod there with a rubber band.

4. Equalize the bushing and lever clearances by pushing the choke valve slightly open (see arrow B).

Checking the choke gap—1975 Dasher, Rabbit, Scirocco

Choke gap adjustment—1975 Dasher, Rabbit, Scirocco

5. Check the choke gap with an appropriate size drill. The gap should be between 0.152 and 0.168 (3.8–4.2mm).

6. Adjust the choke valve gap by turning the screw in the end of the vacuum unit at the side of the choke assembly. Lock the adjusting screw by dabbing a little paint over its end.

NOTE: *When installing the automatic choke cover, the choke lever (protruding part) must fit in the loop on the coiled spring.*

AUTOMATIC CHOKE ADJUSTMENT

Align the mark on the automatic choke cover with the mark on the carburetor by loosening the three retaining across and turning the choke with the hoses still attached.

DASHPOT ADJUSTMENT

For explanation of dashpot function, see 1974 Dasher dashpot procedure.

NOTE: *Not all models are equipped with dashpots.*

1. Close the throttle valve and make sure the choke is fully open. You may have to run the car up to the operating temperature.

2. Push the plunger in as far as it will go and measure the gap between the end of the

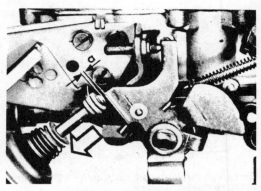

Dashpot adjustment—1975 Dasher, 1975–76 Rabbit, Scirocco

plunger and its striking surface. The gap should be 0.122″ (3mm).

3. Adjust by loosening the lock nut and moving the dashpot on its threads.

Zenith 2B2 Carburetor, 1975–76 Rabbit & Scirocco

THROTTLE GAP ADJUSTMENT

See 1975 Dasher Zenith 2B3 section, above, for throttle gap adjustment procedures.

FUEL LEVEL ADJUSTMENT

This fuel level adjustment is the same as the procedures followed for the Zenith 2B3 Carburetor used in the 1975 Dasher. See above for procedures.

1975 FAST IDLE ADJUSTMENT

See 1975 Dasher 2B3 Carburetor section, above, for fast idle gap adjustment.

1976 FAST IDLE ADJUSTMENT

On these models it is not necessary to remove the carburetor. The engine must be at normal operating temperature.

1. Set the ignition timing.

2. Disconnect and plug the hose from the choke pull-down unit.

3. Open the throttle valve slightly and close the choke valve.

4. Close the throttle valve. The choke valve should be fully open again.

Fast idle adjustment—1976 Rabbit, Scirocco

5. Set the stop screw of the fast idle cam on the highest step. Start the engine.

6. Adjust the speed with the screw (arrow) to: 3,150–3,250 rpm manual transmission or 3,350–3,450 rpm automatic transmission.

CHOKE GAP ADJUSTMENT

NOTE: *See 1975 Dasher 2B3 Carburetor section for 1975 Rabbit Scirocco choke gap adjustment illustration.*

1. Remove the automatic choke cover.

2. Close the choke valve and push the choke rod to the stop (arrow).

3. Hold the choke in position with a rubber band (a).

4. Push the choke lever (b) down slightly to equalize the clearances.

5. Check the choke gap between the edge of the carburetor wall and the edge of the valve with a drill. It should be:

- 1975: 0.19″ with vacuum delay valve.
- 1976: 0.14″ primary activated.
- 0.20″ secondary activated.

6. Adjust the gap by turning the screw on the choke vacuum unit in to decrease the gap or out to increase the gap.

Choke gap adjustment—1976 Rabbit, Scirocco

AUTOMATIC CHOKE

Align the mark on the automatic choke cover with the mark on the carburetor.

AUTOMATIC CHOKE TEMPERATURE SWITCH

The temperature switch must be removed from the carburetor and checked with an ohmmeter. Connect an ohmmeter across the 2 blades. It should read 0Ω below 107°F, and infinity above 136°F.

DASHPOT ADJUSTMENT

Dashpot adjustments are the same as those for Zenith 2B3 Carburetor (1975 Dasher), above.

Solex 34 PICT-5, 1978 Rabbit Only

THROTTLE VALVE BASIC ADJUSTMENT

You need a vacuum gauge to set the throttle valve. The stop screw (1) is set at the factory,

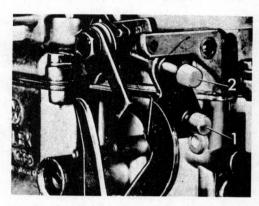

Basic throttle adjustment—1978 carbureted Rabbit

and should not be moved. If the screw is accidentally turned, proceed as follows. Make no adjustment at screw (2).

1. Run the engine at idle.

2. Remove the vacuum advance hose at the carburetor and connect a vacuum gauge.

3. Remove the plastic screw cap and turn the stop screw in until the gauge indicates vacuum.

4. Turn the stop screw out until the gauges indicates no vacuum. Turn the screw an additional ¼ turn and install the plastic cap.

5. Adjust the idle and CO.

CHOKE VALVE ADJUSTMENT

1. Remove the cover from the automatic choke and fully close the choke.

2. Push the choke rod in the direction of the arrow and check the gap between the choke valves and the air horn wall. It should be 0.11–0.13″.

3. Adjust the gap with the adjusting screw (2).

4. Reassemble the choke cover. There is an index mark on the choke housing and another on the choke cover.

Adjusting the choke valve—1978 carbureted Rabbit. Adjusting screw (2) is the same on the 1980 carbureted Rabbit

FAST IDLE ADJUSTMENT

The engine should be at normal operating temperature.

1. Run the engine with the screw on the 3rd step of the fast idle cam. The speed should be 2,350–2,450 rpm. Adjust this speed with the adjusting screw.

2. Stop the engine. Open the choke valve fully and check the gap between the adjusting screw and fast idle cam. It should be 0.008″.

ALTITUDE CORRECTION

Cars that are generally operated above 3,600 feet may require altitude correction, which is

Fast idle adjustment—1978 carbureted Rabbit. 1980 carbureted Rabbit similar

Adjust fast idle gap—1978 carbureted Rabbit

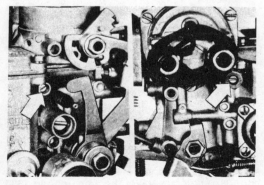

Altitude adjustment—1978 carbureted Rabbit

made by backing out the 2 screws (arrows) until they are flush with the carburetor body. Adjust the idle and CO content.

Solex 34 PICT-5, 1980 RABBIT

PART THROTTLE HEATER

This carburetor is equipped with a heating element which partly pre-heats the throttle channel while the engine temperature is below 167°F. This allows the engine to run smoother during warm-up time and prevents excessive use of the choke valve.

To test the part throttle heater, disconnect its wire and connect a test light between the throttle heater lead and the positive battery terminal. The heating element is working if the test light lights up. If the light fails to light, the element is bad and must be replaced.

MAIN JET SHUT-OFF SYSTEM

The shut-off valve is vacuum activated by the vacuum control unit, located on the fender inside the engine compartment next to the brake master cylinder. A relay is activated via terminal 15 of the fuse panel and shuts off the fuel flow to the main jet if voltage is less than 5 volts at terminal 15 or when the ignition is cut-off.

To test the system, proceed as follows:

1. Run the engine at idle and disconnect the electrical connector from the front of the vacuum control unit.

2. The engine should stall. If not, check the vacuum tubes for blockage and check the vacuum control unit (see below for procedures). If these are not the problem, replace the main jet cut-off valve.

IDLE SHUT-OFF VALVE

1. Run the engine at idle.

2. Pull the electrical connector from the idle shut-off valve.

3. The engine should stall. If not, replace the idle shutoff valve.

AUTOMATIC CHOKE

The automatic choke is operated by the electrical heating element inside the choke and coolant temperature. When coolant temperature is below 61°F, the electrical heating element in the choke receives current from thermoswitch 1 and the resistor wire. Approximately 9 volts of current is applied at this point.

When the engine temperature (coolant) is between 61°F and 167°F, the resistor wire is bypassed by thermoswitch 2 and the heating element in the choke receives full battery voltage (12 volts).

When the coolant temperature exceeds 167°F, all electrical activation of the choke

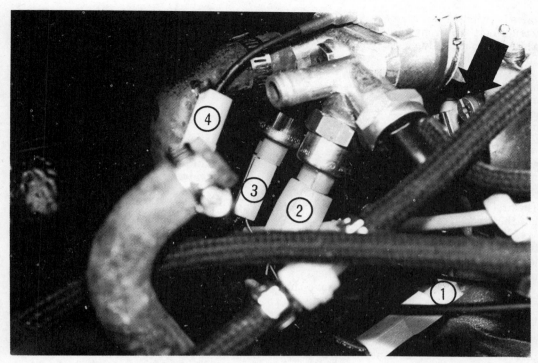

1980 Rabbit carburetor (1) part throttle heater connection (2) thermoswitch 1, (3) thermoswitch 2, (4) choke heater connection. Large black arrow indicates idle jet

Second view of 1980 Rabbit carburetor (1) cold start valve, (2) main jet cutoff valve, (3) Idle shutoff valve

valve is switched off, thermoswitch 1 opens interrupting the current to the heating element while the choke fully opens.

To test the choke system, proceed as follows:

1. Unplug the choke heating element connector and connect the positive lead of a voltmeter to the female part of the connector (part leading into the wiring harness). Connect the negative lead of the voltmeter to the carburetor ground wire. Turn on the ignition.

2. With the coolant temperature below 59°F, record the voltage.

3. Run the engine up above 131°F and check the voltage again. Compare the two readings. The first reading should be one or two volts below the second reading.

4. With the engine at operating temperature (the cooling fan must have come on at least once), the voltmeter should have no reading. If it does, check the thermoswitches.

To test the thermoswitches, remove the switches and connect an ohmmeter between the terminals on each thermoswitch. Thermoswitch 1 opens when the temperature reaches 167°F and closes when the temperature drops to 149°F. Thermoswitch 2 closes when the temperature reaches 131°F and opens when the temperature drops to 61°F.

SETTING THE CHOKE VALVE GAP

1. Set the cold idle speed adjuster screw in its upper notch.

2. Connect a manually operated vacuum pump to the connection on the pulldown unit and build up vacuum.

3. Close the choke valve by hand with the lever and check the choke valve gap with a drill. The gap should be 3.3–3.7mm.

4. Adjust the gap using the adjusting screw on the pulldown unit. After adjusting, lock the screw with sealant.

SETTING THE FAST IDEL SPEED

1. Run the engine up to operating temperature and make sure the ignition setting and the idle adjustment are correct.

2. Run the engine at idle and set the adjusting screw on its third notch on the choke valve lever.

3. Open the choke valve fully by hand using the choke valve lever.

4. Connect a tachometer and check the rpm, or use the tachometer in the car, if equipped.

CAUTION: *See Electronic Ignition Precaution in chapter two for warning about connecting tachometers to electronic ignition systems.*

5. The fast idle speed should be between 2,350–2,450 rpm. If not, adjust with fast idle

adjustment screw. Lock screw with safety cap after adjustment.

Cold Start Valve

The cold start valve enriches the air/fuel mixture when engine temperature is below 60°F by injecting fuel into the throttle chamber through a passage parallel to the main jet. Test the valve for continuity with a test light or ohmmeter. The test light should light and the ohmmeter should reach 80Ω. If test light fails to light and ohmmeter reads infinity, replace the valve.

THROTTLE KICKER (AIR CONDITIONED VEHICLES ONLY)

The throttle kicker increases the idle speed to prevent stalling when the air conditioner is engaged. To test, proceed as follows:

1. Run the engine up to operating temperature and check the ignition timing (see chapter two). Unplug the idle stabilizer (control unit) and plug the two plugs together (see electronic ignition section in chapter two). Remove the retard and advance vacuum hoses and plug them. Make sure the basic idle speed and CO adjustments areas correct (See chapter two).

2. Reconnect the advance and retard hoses and reconnect the plugs for the idle stabilizer (control unit).

3. Rev the engine to start the idle stabilizer (control unit) and note the ignition timing at idle.

4. Switch on the air conditioner (coldest temperature setting, highest fan speed), the ignition timing should not change.

5. If the timing changes, adjust the throttle kicker screw where it contacts the throttle valve lever until the correct setting (no timing change) is reached. Seal the screw with Loctite®.

VACUUM CONTROL VALVE

The vacuum control unit has two functions. It houses both the relay for the main jet cutoff valve and the relay for the throttle kicker on air conditioner equipped vehicles.

To test the main jet cutoff valve relay, perform the steps under the heading Main Jet Cutoff Valve, above. If the engine continues to run and you are sure the vacuum lines are not clogged and the valve is working replace the relay inside the vacuum control unit.

To test the throttle kicker relay, run the engine and turn the air conditioner on and then turn it off. The kicker should move in and out. If it doesn't connect the vacuum retard hose from the distributor to the throttle kicker vacuum connector. If the kicker moves, replace the relay. If the kicker does not move, replace the throttle kicker.

1980 Rabbit 34 PICT-5 vacuum control unit (arrow)

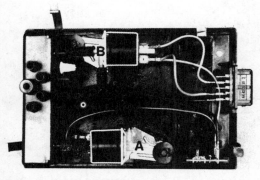

1980 carbureted Rabbit vacuum control unit: (A) main jet cutoff valve relay, (B) throttle kicker relay (air conditioned cars only)

Carter TYF — 1982 and Later

THROTTLE GAP ADJUSTMENT

Throttle gap is set at the factory and should not be tampered with.

FAST IDLE ADJUSTMENT

1. Run the engine until it reaches normal operating temperature. Make sure that the timing and idle speed are set to specifications.

2. Run the engine at idle and set the fast idle adjustment screw to the second step of the fast idle cam.

3. Disconnect the purge valve. Disconnect and plug the vacuum hose at the EGR valve.

4. Connect a tachometer as per the manufacturer's instructions and check that the engine speed is 2,800–3,200 rpm. If not, turn the fast idle screw until it is.

5. Reconnect the purge valve and the vacuum hose at the EGR valve.

CHOKE GAP ADJUSTMENT

1. Set the cold idle speed adjuster screw in its upper notch.

2. Connect a manually operated vacuum pump to the connection on the pulldown unit and build up vacuum.

3. Close the choke valve by hand with the lever and check the choke valve gap with a drill. The gap should be 3.3–3.7mm: 3.9mm for 1982: 4.2mm for 1983.

4. Adjust the gap using the adjusting screw in the end of the vacuum unit at the side of the choke unit. After adjusting, lock the screw with sealant.

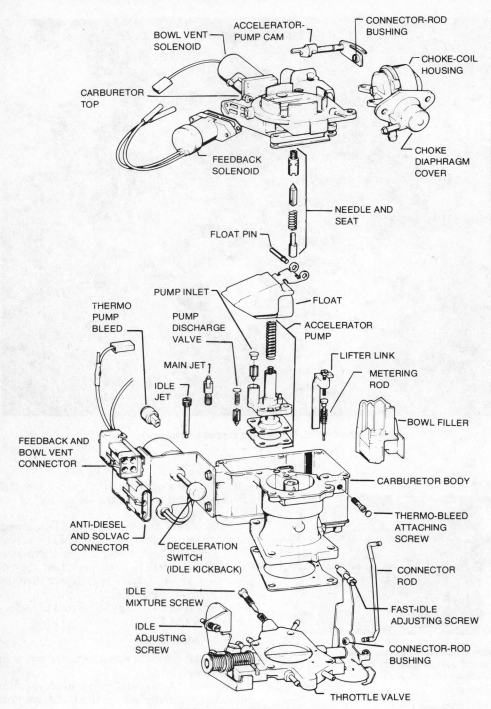

BOWL VENT SOLENOID

ACCELERATOR-PUMP CAM

CONNECTOR-ROD BUSHING

CARBURETOR TOP

CHOKE-COIL HOUSING

CHOKE DIAPHRAGM COVER

FEEDBACK SOLENOID

NEEDLE AND SEAT

FLOAT PIN

PUMP INLET

FLOAT

THERMO PUMP BLEED

PUMP DISCHARGE VALVE

ACCELERATOR PUMP

MAIN JET

LIFTER LINK

METERING ROD

IDLE JET

BOWL FILLER

FEEDBACK AND BOWL VENT CONNECTOR

CARBURETOR BODY

THERMO-BLEED ATTACHING SCREW

ANTI-DIESEL AND SOLVAC CONNECTOR

DECELERATION SWITCH (IDLE KICKBACK)

CONNECTOR ROD

IDLE MIXTURE SCREW

FAST-IDLE ADJUSTING SCREW

IDLE ADJUSTING SCREW

CONNECTOR-ROD BUSHING

THROTTLE VALVE

Typical Carter TYF style carburetor

THROTTLE LINKAGE ADJUSTMENT

All Models (Carburetor Equipped)

Throttle linkage adjustments are not normally required. However, it is a good idea to make sure that the throttle valve(s) in the carbure- tor open all the way when the accelerator pedal is held in the wide-open position. Only the primary (first stage) throttle valve will open when the pedal is pushed with the engine off: the secondary throttle on Volkswagen 2-barrel carburetors is vacuum operated.

CHILTON'S
FUEL ECONOMY
& TUNE-UP TIPS

Tune-up • Spark Plug Diagnosis • Emission Controls

Fuel System • Cooling System • Tires and Wheels

General Maintenance

CHILTON'S FUEL ECONOMY & TUNE-UP TIPS

Fuel economy is important to everyone, no matter what kind of vehicle you drive. The maintenance-minded motorist can save both money and fuel using these tips and the periodic maintenance and tune-up procedures in this Repair and Tune-Up Guide.

There are more than 130,000,000 cars and trucks registered for private use in the United States. Each travels an average of 10-12,000 miles per year, and, and in total they consume close to 70 billion gallons of fuel each year. This represents nearly ⅔ of the oil imported by the United States each year. The Federal government's goal is to reduce consumption 10% by 1985. A variety of methods are either already in use or under serious consideration, and they all affect you driving and the cars you will drive. In addition to "down-sizing", the auto industry is using or investigating the use of electronic fuel delivery, electronic engine controls and alternative engines for use in smaller and lighter vehicles, among other alternatives to meet the federally mandated Corporate Average Fuel Economy (CAFE) of 27.5 mpg by 1985. The government, for its part, is considering rationing, mandatory driving curtailments and tax increases on motor vehicle fuel in an effort to reduce consumption. The government's goal of a 10% reduction could be realized — and further government regulation avoided — if every private vehicle could use just 1 less gallon of fuel per week.

How Much Can You Save?

Tests have proven that almost anyone can make at least a 10% reduction in fuel consumption through regular maintenance and tune-ups. When a major manufacturer of spark plugs sur-

TUNE-UP

1. Check the cylinder compression to be sure the engine will really benefit from a tune-up and that it is capable of producing good fuel economy. A tune-up will be wasted on an engine in poor mechanical condition.

2. Replace spark plugs regularly. New spark plugs alone can increase fuel economy 3%.

3. Be sure the spark plugs are the correct type (heat range) for your vehicle. See the Tune-Up Specifications.

Heat range refers to the spark plug's ability to conduct heat away from the firing end. It must conduct the heat away in an even pattern to avoid becoming a source of pre-ignition, yet it must also operate hot enough to burn off conductive deposits that could cause misfiring.

The heat range is usually indicated by a number on the spark plug, part of the manufacturer's designation for each individual spark plug. The numbers in bold-face indicate the heat range in each manufacturer's identification system.

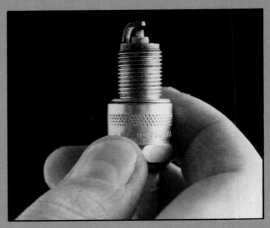

Periodically, check the spark plugs to be sure they are firing efficiently. They are excellent indicators of the internal condition of your engine.

Manufacturer	Typical Designation
AC	R **45** TS
Bosch (old)	WA **145** T30
Bosch (new)	HR **8** Y
Champion	RBL **15** Y
Fram/Autolite	**4**15
Mopar	P-**62** PR
Motorcraft	BRF-**42**
NGK	BP **5** ES-15
Nippondenso	W **16** EP
Prestolite	14GR **5** 2A

On AC, Bosch (new), Champion, Fram/Autolite, Mopar, Motorcraft and Prestolite, a higher number indicates a hotter plug. On Bosch (old), NGK and Nippondenso, a higher number indicates a colder plug.

4. Make sure the spark plugs are properly gapped. See the Tune-Up Specifications in this book.

5. Be sure the spark plugs are firing efficiently. The illustrations on the next 2 pages show you how to "read" the firing end of the spark plug.

6. Check the ignition timing and set it to specifications. Tests show that almost all cars have incorrect ignition timing by more than 2°.

veyed over 6,000 cars nationwide, they found that a tune-up, on cars that needed one, increased fuel economy over 11%. Replacing worn plugs alone, accounted for a 3% increase. The same test also revealed that 8 out of every 10 vehicles will have some maintenance deficiency that will directly affect fuel economy, emissions or performance. Most of this mileage-robbing neglect could be prevented with regular maintenance.

Modern engines require that all of the functioning systems operate properly for maximum efficiency. A malfunction anywhere wastes fuel. You can keep your vehicle running as efficiently and economically as possible, by being aware of your vehicle's operating and performance characteristics. If your vehicle suddenly develops performance or fuel economy problems it could be due to one or more of the following:

PROBLEM	POSSIBLE CAUSE
Engine Idles Rough	Ignition timing, idle mixture, vacuum leak or something amiss in the emission control system.
Hesitates on Acceleration	Dirty carburetor or fuel filter, improper accelerator pump setting, ignition timing or fouled spark plugs.
Starts Hard or Fails to Start	Worn spark plugs, improperly set automatic choke, ice (or water) in fuel system.
Stalls Frequently	Automatic choke improperly adjusted and possible dirty air filter or fuel filter.
Performs Sluggishly	Worn spark plugs, dirty fuel or air filter, ignition timing or automatic choke out of adjustment.

Check spark plug wires on conventional point type ignition for cracks by bending them in a loop around your finger.

Be sure that spark plug wires leading to adjacent cylinders do not run too close together. (Photo courtesy Champion Spark Plug Co.)

7. If your vehicle does not have electronic ignition, check the points, rotor and cap as specified.

8. Check the spark plug wires (used with conventional point-type ignitions) for cracks and burned or broken insulation by bending them in a loop around your finger. Cracked wires decrease fuel efficiency by failing to deliver full voltage to the spark plugs. One misfiring spark plug can cost you as much as 2 mpg.

9. Check the routing of the plug wires. Misfiring can be the result of spark plug leads to adjacent cylinders running parallel to each other and too close together. One wire tends to pick up voltage from the other causing it to fire "out of time".

10. Check all electrical and ignition circuits for voltage drop and resistance.

11. Check the distributor mechanical and/or vacuum advance mechanisms for proper functioning. The vacuum advance can be checked by twisting the distributor plate in the opposite direction of rotation. It should spring back when released.

12. Check and adjust the valve clearance on engines with mechanical lifters. The clearance should be slightly loose rather than too tight.

SPARK PLUG DIAGNOSIS

Normal

APPEARANCE: This plug is typical of one operating normally. The insulator nose varies from a light tan to grayish color with slight electrode wear. The presence of slight deposits is normal on used plugs and will have no adverse effect on engine performance. The spark plug heat range is correct for the engine and the engine is running normally.

CAUSE: Properly running engine.

RECOMMENDATION: Before reinstalling this plug, the electrodes should be cleaned and filed square. Set the gap to specifications. If the plug has been in service for more than 10-12,000 miles, the entire set should probably be replaced with a fresh set of the same heat range.

Oil Deposits

APPEARANCE: The firing end of the plug is covered with a wet, oily coating.

CAUSE: The problem is poor oil control. On high mileage engines, oil is leaking past the rings or valve guides into the combustion chamber. A common cause is also a plugged PCV valve, and a ruptured fuel pump diaphragm can also cause this condition. Oil fouled plugs such as these are often found in new or recently overhauled engines, before normal oil control is achieved, and can be cleaned and reinstalled.

RECOMMENDATION: A hotter spark plug may temporarily relieve the problem, but the engine is probably in need of work.

Incorrect Heat Range

APPEARANCE: The effects of high temperature on a spark plug are indicated by clean white, often blistered insulator. This can also be accompanied by excessive wear of the electrode, and the absence of deposits.

CAUSE: Check for the correct spark plug heat range. A plug which is too hot for the engine can result in overheating. A car operated mostly at high speeds can require a colder plug. Also check ignition timing, cooling system level, fuel mixture and leaking intake manifold.

RECOMMENDATION: If all ignition and engine adjustments are known to be correct, and no other malfunction exists, install spark plugs one heat range colder.

Photos Courtesy Fram Corporation

Carbon Deposits

APPEARANCE: Carbon fouling is easily identified by the presence of dry, soft, black, sooty deposits.

CAUSE: Changing the heat range can often lead to carbon fouling, as can prolonged slow, stop-and-start driving. If the heat range is correct, carbon fouling can be attributed to a rich fuel mixture, sticking choke, clogged air cleaner, worn breaker points, retarded timing or low compression. If only one or two plugs are carbon fouled, check for corroded or cracked wires on the affected plugs. Also look for cracks in the distributor cap between the towers of affected cylinders.

RECOMMENDATION: After the problem is corrected, these plugs can be cleaned and reinstalled if not worn severely.

MMT Fouled

APPEARANCE: Spark plugs fouled by MMT (Methycyclopentadienyl Maganese Tricarbonyl) have reddish, rusty appearance on the insulator and side electrode.

CAUSE: MMT is an anti-knock additive in gasoline used to replace lead. During the combustion process, the MMT leaves a reddish deposit on the insulator and side electrode.

RECOMMENDATION: No engine malfunction is indicated and the deposits will not affect plug performance any more than lead deposits (see Ash Deposits). MMT fouled plugs can be cleaned, regapped and reinstalled.

High Speed Glazing

APPEARANCE: Glazing appears as shiny coating on the plug, either yellow or tan in color.

CAUSE: During hard, fast acceleration, plug temperatures rise suddenly. Deposits from normal combustion have no chance to fluff-off; instead, they melt on the insulator forming an electrically conductive coating which causes misfiring.

RECOMMENDATION: Glazed plugs are not easily cleaned. They should be replaced with a fresh set of plugs of the correct heat range. If the condition recurs, using plugs with a heat range one step colder may cure the problem.

Ash (Lead) Deposits

APPEARANCE: Ash deposits are characterized by light brown or white colored deposits crusted on the side or center electrodes. In some cases it may give the plug a rusty appearance.

CAUSE: Ash deposits are normally derived from oil or fuel additives burned during normal combustion. Normally they are harmless, though excessive amounts can cause misfiring. If deposits are excessive in short mileage, the valve guides may be worn.

RECOMMENDATION: Ash-fouled plugs can be cleaned, gapped and reinstalled.

Detonation

APPEARANCE: Detonation is usually characterized by a broken plug insulator.

CAUSE: A portion of the fuel charge will begin to burn spontaneously, from the increased heat following ignition. The explosion that results applies extreme pressure to engine components, frequently damaging spark plugs and pistons.

Detonation can result by over-advanced ignition timing, inferior gasoline (low octane) lean air/fuel mixture, poor carburetion, engine lugging or an increase in compression ratio due to combustion chamber deposits or engine modification.

RECOMMENDATION: Replace the plugs after correcting the problem.

Photos Courtesy Champion Spark Plug Co.

EMISSION CONTROLS

13. Be aware of the general condition of the emission control system. It contributes to reduced pollution and should be serviced regularly to maintain efficient engine operation.

14. Check all vacuum lines for dried, cracked or brittle conditions. Something as simple as a leaking vacuum hose can cause poor performance and loss of economy.

15. Avoid tampering with the emission control system. Attempting to improve fuel econ-

FUEL SYSTEM

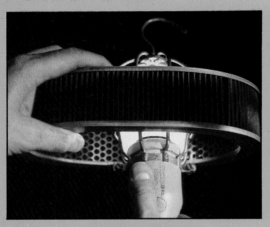

Check the air filter with a light behind it. If you can see light through the filter it can be reused.

Extremely clogged filters should be discarded and replaced with a new one.

18. Replace the air filter regularly. A dirty air filter richens the air/fuel mixture and can increase fuel consumption as much as 10%. Tests show that ⅓ of all vehicles have air filters in need of replacement.

19. Replace the fuel filter at least as often as recommended.

20. Set the idle speed and carburetor mixture to specifications.

21. Check the automatic choke. A sticking or malfunctioning choke wastes gas.

22. During the summer months, adjust the automatic choke for a leaner mixture which will produce faster engine warm-ups.

COOLING SYSTEM

29. Be sure all accessory drive belts are in good condition. Check for cracks or wear.

30. Adjust all accessory drive belts to proper tension.

31. Check all hoses for swollen areas, worn spots, or loose clamps.

32. Check coolant level in the radiator or expansion tank.

33. Be sure the thermostat is operating properly. A stuck thermostat delays engine warm-up and a cold engine uses nearly twice as much fuel as a warm engine.

34. Drain and replace the engine coolant at least as often as recommended. Rust and scale

TIRES & WHEELS

38. Check the tire pressure often with a pencil type gauge. Tests by a major tire manufacturer show that 90% of all vehicles have at least 1 tire improperly inflated. Better mileage can be achieved by over-inflating tires, but never exceed the maximum inflation pressure on the side of the tire.

39. If possible, install radial tires. Radial tires deliver as much as ½ mpg more than bias belted tires.

40. Avoid installing super-wide tires. They only create extra rolling resistance and decrease fuel mileage. Stick to the manufacturer's recommendations.

41. Have the wheels properly balanced.

omy by tampering with emission controls is more likely to worsen fuel economy than improve it. Emission control changes on modern engines are not readily reversible.

16. Clean (or replace) the EGR valve and lines as recommended.

17. Be sure that all vacuum lines and hoses are reconnected properly after working under the hood. An unconnected or misrouted vacuum line can wreak havoc with engine performance.

23. Check for fuel leaks at the carburetor, fuel pump, fuel lines and fuel tank. Be sure all lines and connections are tight.

24. Periodically check the tightness of the carburetor and intake manifold attaching nuts and bolts. These are a common place for vacuum leaks to occur.

25. Clean the carburetor periodically and lubricate the linkage.

26. The condition of the tailpipe can be an excellent indicator of proper engine combustion. After a long drive at highway speeds, the inside of the tailpipe should be a light grey in color. Black or soot on the insides indicates an overly rich mixture.

27. Check the fuel pump pressure. The fuel pump may be supplying more fuel than the engine needs.

28. Use the proper grade of gasoline for your engine. Don't try to compensate for knocking or "pinging" by advancing the ignition timing. This practice will only increase plug temperature and the chances of detonation or pre-ignition with relatively little performance gain.

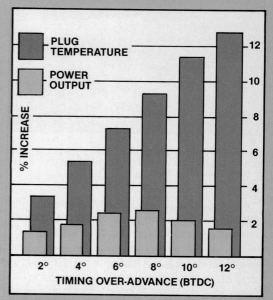

Increasing ignition timing past the specified setting results in a drastic increase in spark plug temperature with increased chance of detonation or preignition. Performance increase is considerably less. (Photo courtesy Champion Spark Plug Co.)

that form in the engine should be flushed out to allow the engine to operate at peak efficiency.

35. Clean the radiator of debris that can decrease cooling efficiency.

36. Install a flex-type or electric cooling fan, if you don't have a clutch type fan. Flex fans use curved plastic blades to push more air at low speeds when more cooling is needed; at high speeds the blades flatten out for less resistance. Electric fans only run when the engine temperature reaches a predetermined level.

37. Check the radiator cap for a worn or cracked gasket. If the cap does not seal properly, the cooling system will not function properly.

42. Be sure the front end is correctly aligned. A misaligned front end actually has wheels going in differed directions. The increased drag can reduce fuel economy by .3 mpg.

43. Correctly adjust the wheel bearings. Wheel bearings that are adjusted too tight increase rolling resistance.

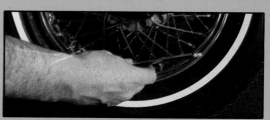

Check tire pressures regularly with a reliable pocket type gauge. Be sure to check the pressure on a cold tire.

GENERAL MAINTENANCE

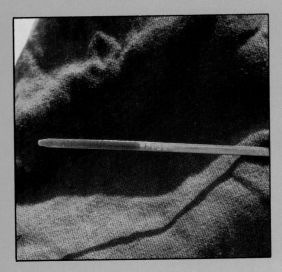

Check the fluid levels (particularly engine oil) on a regular basis. Be sure to check the oil for grit, water or other contamination.

A vacuum gauge is another excellent indicator of internal engine condition and can also be installed in the dash as a mileage indicator.

44. Periodically check the fluid levels in the engine, power steering pump, master cylinder, automatic transmission and drive axle.

45. Change the oil at the recommended interval and change the filter at every oil change. Dirty oil is thick and causes extra friction between moving parts, cutting efficiency and increasing wear. A worn engine requires more frequent tune-ups and gets progressively worse fuel economy. In general, use the lightest viscosity oil for the driving conditions you will encounter.

46. Use the recommended viscosity fluids in the transmission and axle.

47. Be sure the battery is fully charged for fast starts. A slow starting engine wastes fuel.

48. Be sure battery terminals are clean and tight.

49. Check the battery electrolyte level and add distilled water if necessary.

50. Check the exhaust system for crushed pipes, blockages and leaks.

51. Adjust the brakes. Dragging brakes or brakes that are not releasing create increased drag on the engine.

52. Install a vacuum gauge or miles-per-gallon gauge. These gauges visually indicate engine vacuum in the intake manifold. High vacuum = good mileage and low vacuum = poorer mileage. The gauge can also be an excellent indicator of internal engine conditions.

53. Be sure the clutch is properly adjusted. A slipping clutch wastes fuel.

54. Check and periodically lubricate the heat control valve in the exhaust manifold. A sticking or inoperative valve prevents engine warm-up and wastes gas.

55. Keep accurate records to check fuel economy over a period of time. A sudden drop in fuel economy may signal a need for tune-up or other maintenance.

Make note of the following:

a. Always be careful not to kink or twist the cables during installation or adjustment. This can cause rapid wear and binding.

b. On the Rabbits and Sciroccos, the accelerator cable will only bend one way, make sure you install it with the bends in the right positions.

c. On 1974–75 Dashers, when installing new accelerator cable, the hole in the fire wall must be enlarged to 5/8″. Adjust these cables at the pedal clamp.

NOTE: *When installing new cables, all bends should be as wide as possible, and fittings between which the inner cable is exposed must be aligned.*

OVERHAUL

Efficient carburetion depends greatly on careful cleaning and inspection during overhaul since dirt, gum, water, or varnish in or on the carburetor parts are often responsible for poor performance.

NOTE: *Specific directions and specifications for carburetor overhaul are usually contained in the rebuilding kit.*

Overhaul your carburetor in a clean, dustfree area. Carefully disassemble the carburetor, referring often to the exploded views. Keep all similar and lookalike parts segregated during disassembly and cleaning to avoid accidentally interchange during assembly. Make a note of all jet sizes.

When the carburetor is disassembled, wash all parts (except diaphragms, electric choke units, pump plunger, and any other plastic, leather, fiber, or rubber parts) in clean carburetor solvent. Do not leave parts in the solvent any longer than is necessary to sufficiently loosen the deposits. Excessive cleaning may remove the special finish from the float bowl and choke valve bodies, leaving these parts unfit for service. Rinse all parts in clean solvent and blow them dry with compressed air or allow them to air dry. Wipe clean all cork, plastic, leather, and fiber parts with a clean, lint-free cloth.

Blow out all passages and jets with compressed air and be sure that there are no restrictions or blockages. Never use wire or similar tools to clean jets, fuel passages, or air bleeds. Clean all jets and valves separately to avoid accidental interchange.

Check all parts for wear or damage. If wear or damage is found, replace the defective parts. Especially check the following:

1. Check the float needle and seat for wear. If wear is found, replace the complete assembly.

2. Check the float hinge pin for wear and

the float(s) for dents or distortion. Replace the float if fuel has leaked into it.

3. Check the throttle and choke shaft bores for wear or an out-of-round condition. Damage or wear to the throttle arm, shaft, or shaft bore will often require replacement of the throttle body. These parts require a close tolerance of fit. Wear may allow air leakage, which could adversely affect starting and idling.

NOTE: *Throttle shafts and bushings are not included in overhaul kits. They can be purchased separately.*

4. Inspect the idle mixture adjusting needles for burrs or grooves. Any such condition requires replacement of the needle, since you will not be able to obtain a satisfactory idle.

5. Test the accelerator pump check valves. They should pass air one way but not the other. Test for proper seating by blowing and sucking on the valve. Replace the valve if necessary. If the valve is satisfactory, wash the valve again to remove breath moisture.

6. Check the bowl cover for warped surfaces with a straightedge.

7. Closely inspect the valves and seats for wear and damage, replacing as necessary.

8. After the carburetor is assembled, check the choke valve for freedom of operation.

Carburetor overhaul kits are recommended for each overhaul. These kits contain all gaskets and new parts to replace those that deteriorate most rapidly. Failure to replace all parts supplied with the kit (especially gaskets) can result in poor performance later.

Some carburetor manufacturers supply overhaul kits of three basic types: minor repair; major repair; and gasket kits. Basically, they contain the following:

Minor Repair Kits
- All gaskets
- Float needle valve
- Volume control screw
- All diaphragms
- Spring for the pump diaphragm

Major Repair Kits
- All jets and gaskets
- All diaphragms
- Float needle valve
- Volume control screw
- Pump ball valve
- Float
- Complete intermediate rod
- Intermediate pump lever
- Some cover holddown screws and washers

Gasket Kits
- All gaskets

After cleaning and checking all components, reassemble the carburetor, using new parts and referring to the exploded view. When reassembling, make sure that all screws and jets

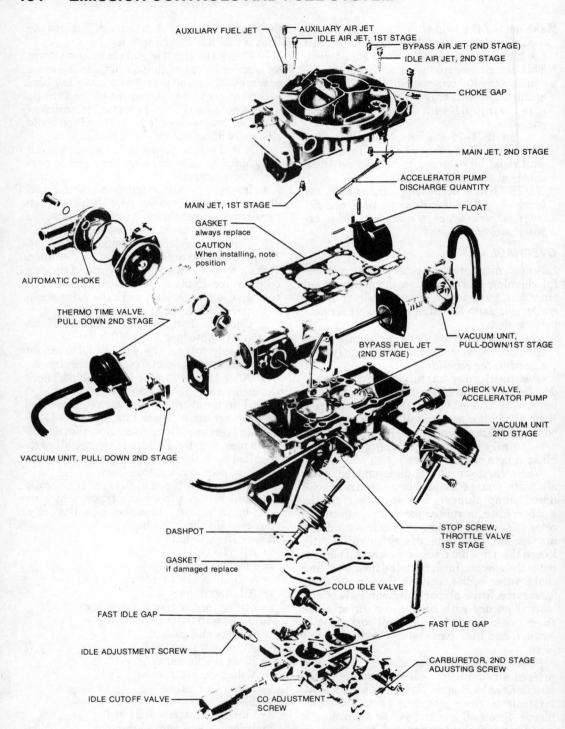

AUXILIARY FUEL JET
AUXILIARY AIR JET
IDLE AIR JET, 1ST STAGE
BYPASS AIR JET (2ND STAGE)
IDLE AIR JET, 2ND STAGE
CHOKE GAP
MAIN JET, 2ND STAGE
ACCELERATOR PUMP DISCHARGE QUANTITY
MAIN JET, 1ST STAGE
FLOAT
GASKET always replace
CAUTION When installing, note position
AUTOMATIC CHOKE
THERMO TIME VALVE, PULL DOWN 2ND STAGE
BYPASS FUEL JET (2ND STAGE)
VACUUM UNIT, PULL-DOWN/1ST STAGE
CHECK VALVE, ACCELERATOR PUMP
VACUUM UNIT 2ND STAGE
VACUUM UNIT, PULL DOWN 2ND STAGE
DASHPOT
STOP SCREW, THROTTLE VALVE 1ST STAGE
GASKET if damaged replace
COLD IDLE VALVE
FAST IDLE GAP
FAST IDLE GAP
IDLE ADJUSTMENT SCREW
CARBURETOR, 2ND STAGE ADJUSTING SCREW
IDLE CUTOFF VALVE
CO ADJUSTMENT SCREW

Zenith 2B2 carburetor—Rabbit, Scirocco. 1975 Dasher similar

are tight in their seats, but do not overtighten, as the tips will be distorted. Tighten all screws gradually, in rotation. Do not tighten needle valves into their seats; uneven jetting will result. Always use new gaskets. Be sure to adjust the float level when reassembling.

GASOLINE (CIS) FUEL INJECTION SYSTEM

The Continuous Injection Systems (CIS) is an independent mechanical system. That is, no pump or other component is driven by the en-

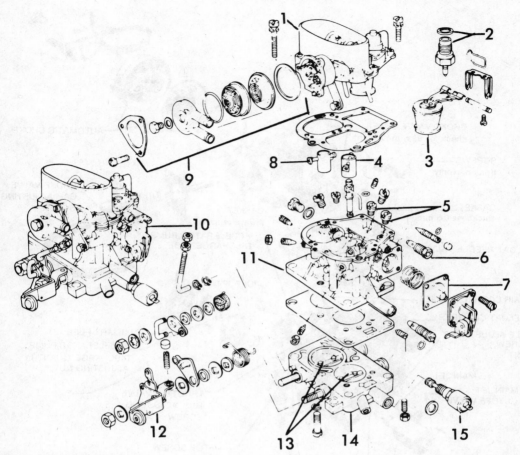

1. Top housing
2. Float needle valve assembly
3. Float
4. Venturi
5. Main jets
6. Idle jet
7. Accelerator pump assembly
8. Venturi
9. Automatic choke assembly
10. Assembled view of carburetor
11. Carburetor bowl assembly
12. Throttle lever assembly
13. Throttle valves
14. Throttle plate
15. By-pass cutoff valve

1974 Dasher carburetor

gine. The basic operating principle is to continuously inject fuel into the intake side of the engine by means of an electric pump. The amount of fuel delivered is metered by an air flow measuring device. CIS is a mechanical system, there is no electronic brain deciding when or how much fuel to inject.

The primary fuel circuit consists of an electric pump, which pulls fuel from the tank. Fuel then passes through an accumulator. The accumulator is basically a container in the fuel line. It houses a spring-loaded diaphragm that provides fuel damping and delays pressure build-up when the engine is first started. When the engine is shut down, the expanded chamber in the accumulator keeps the system under enough pressure for good hot restarts with no vapor locking. Fuel flows through a large, paper element filter to the mixture control assembly.

The mixture control assembly is the CIS heart. It houses the air flow sensor and the fuel distributor. The air sensor is a round plate attached to a counterbalanced lever. The plate and lever are free to move up-and-down on a fulcrum. Accelerator pedal linkage connects to a throttle butterfly, which is upstream (closer to the manifold and intake valves) of the air sensor. If you're following this far, stepping on the gas opens the throttle valve. Increased air, demanded by the engine, is sucked through the air cleaner and around the air sensor plate.

In the air funnel, where the air sensor plate is located, the quantity of intake air lifts the plate until an equilibrium is reached between air flow and hydraulic counterpressure acting on the lever through a plunger. This is the control plunger. In this balanced position, the plunger stays at a level in the fuel distributor to open small metering slits, one for each cylin-

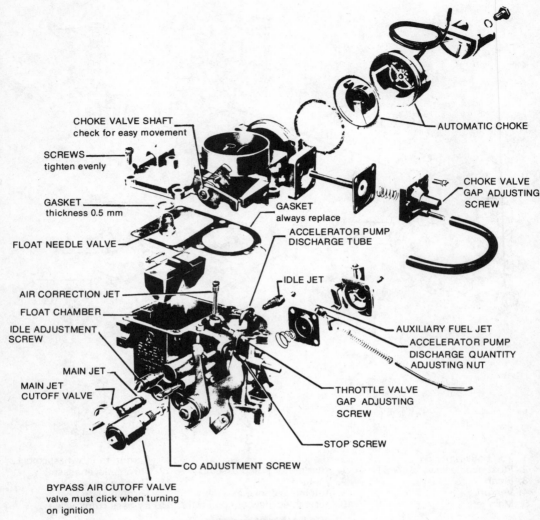

CHOKE VALVE SHAFT
check for easy movement

SCREWS
tighten evenly

GASKET
thickness 0.5 mm

FLOAT NEEDLE VALVE

AIR CORRECTION JET

FLOAT CHAMBER

IDLE ADJUSTMENT
SCREW

MAIN JET

MAIN JET
CUTOFF VALVE

BYPASS AIR CUTOFF VALVE
valve must click when turning
on ignition

CO ADJUSTMENT SCREW

STOP SCREW

THROTTLE VALVE
GAP ADJUSTING
SCREW

ACCELERATOR PUMP
DISCHARGE QUANTITY
ADJUSTING NUT

AUXILIARY FUEL JET

IDLE JET

ACCELERATOR PUMP
DISCHARGE TUBE

GASKET
always replace

CHOKE VALVE
GAP ADJUSTING
SCREW

AUTOMATIC CHOKE

1978 Rabbit carburetor

der in the engine. Fuel under controlled pressure from the pump goes through the slits to the injectors. The slit determines the right amount of fuel.

In order to maintain a precise fuel pressure, a pressure regulator, or pressure relief valve, is located in the primary fuel circuit of the fuel distributor. Excess fuel is diverted back to the tank through a return line. To make sure the amount of fuel going through the control plunger slits depends only on their area, an exact pressure differential must always be maintained at the openings. This pressure is controlled by a differential-pressure valve. There's one valve for each cylinder. The valve consists of a spring loaded steel diaphragm and an outlet to the injectors. The diaphragm separates the upper and lower chambers.

The valve keeps an exact pressure differen-

tial of 1.42 psi between upper chamber pressure and lower chamber pressure. Both pressures act on the spring loaded steel diaphragm which opens the outlet to the injectors. The size of the outlet opening is always just enough to maintain that 1.42 psi pressure differential at the metering slit. The diaphragm opens more if a larger amount of fuel flows. If less fuel enters the upper chamber, the diaphragm opens less and less fuel goes to the injectors. An exact pressure differential between upper and lower chamber is kept constant. Diaphragm movement is actually only a few thousandths of an inch.

A warm-up regulator can alter the pressure on the control plunger according to engine and outside air temperature. For warm-up running, it lowers the pressure so that the air sensor plate can go higher for the same air flow.

Carburetor Specifications

Year	Model	Carburetor Type	Main Jet Primary	Main Jet Secondary	Air Correction Jet Primary	Air Correction Jet Secondary	Idle Fuel Jet Primary	Idle Fuel Jet Secondary	Idle Air Jet Primary	Idle Air Jet Secondary	Accelerator Pump Discharge (cm³/stroke) Fast	Accelerator Pump Discharge (cm³/stroke) Slow
1974	Dasher (Calif. M/T)	Solex 32/35	x122.5	x142.5	130	140	g45	g45	180	180	0.3–0.5	0.75–1.05
	Dasher (Calif. A/T)	Solex 32/35	x120	x145	140	140	g45	g45	180	180	0.3–0.5	0.75–1.05
	Dasher (Fed. M/T)	Solex 32/35	x135	x140	150	150	g52.5	g52.5	180	180	0.3–0.5	0.75–1.05
	Dasher (Fed. A/T)	Solex 32/35	x130	x140	140	140	g52.5	g52.5	180	180	0.3–0.5	0.75–1.05
1975	Dasher (US all)	Zenith 2B3	x117.5	x137.5	140	92.5	52.5	65	130	110	—	0.75–1.05
	Rabbit, Scirocco (US all)	Zenith 2B2	x115	x115	140	92.5	52.5	70	135	100	—	0.75–1.05
1976	Rabbit, Scirocco (US all)	Zenith 2B2	x117.5	x110	130	92.5	52.5	65	135	140	1.3–1.7 [1]	0.6–0.9 [2]
1978	Rabbit	34 PICT-5	x127.5	—	120Z	—	52.5	—	120	—	[3]	[3]
1980	Rabbit	34 PICT-5	x127.5	—	120Z	—	[4]	—	120	—	[5]	[5]

[1] Cold
[2] Warm
[3] Rate given as 0.85–1.15 cm³/stroke
[4] Come in sizes 50.0/55.0/57.5/ The jet size is stamped on the float housing next to plug on front of carburetor
[5] Rate given as 0.8–1.2 cm³/stroke
M/T Manual trans.
A/T Automatic trans.
Fed. Non-California USA car.
NOTE: Refer to instruction sheet with carburetor rebuilding kit for "specs"—1981 and later models

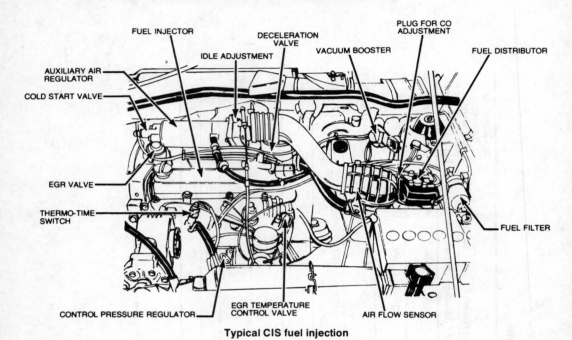

Typical CIS fuel injection

This exposes more metering slit area, and more fuel flows for a richer mixture. An auxiliary air valve passes extra air to create a richer (than throttle valve position calls for) mixture. For cold starts, a separate injector is used to squirt fuel into the intake manifold. This injector is electronically controlled. A thermo-time switch, screwed into the engine, limits the amount of time the valve is open and at higher temperatures, cuts it off.

Electric Fuel Pump

Volkswagen uses a continuous injection system (CIS) in its fuel injected gasoline engines. The system includes an electric fuel pump mounted in front of the right rear axle on Fox, Rabbit and Scirocco, and mounted below the fuel accumulator near the rear wheel on Dashers and in the gas tank on Quantum models. The fuel pump on the Rabbit Pick-up truck is mounted on the passenger's side near the front of the fuel tank, which is located near the center of the vehicle. The Jetta fuel pump is on the passenger's side in front of the rear wheel and is accessible through a cover plate.

ELECTRICAL TESTING

1. Have an assistant operate the starter. Listen near the fuel pump location to determine if the pump is running.
2. If the pump is not running, check the wiring and the fuse on the front of the fuel pump relay.

3. If the fuse is good, replace the fuel pump relay.
4. If the fuel pump still does not operate, and you're sure there are no loose connections in the wiring, the fuel pump is faulty and must be replaced.

TESTING FUEL PUMP DELIVERY RATE

1. Check the condition of the fuel filter. Make sure it is clean and that fuel flows through the lines freely.
2. Connect a jumper wire between the No. 1 terminal on the ignition coil and ground.
3. Disconnect the return fuel line and hold it in a measuring container with a capacity of more than 1 quart or 1,000cc.
4. Have an assistant run the starter for 30 seconds while watching the quantity of fuel delivered.

The minimum allowable flow for the 1975–78 Rabbit and Scirocco is 750cc in 30 seconds; 900cc in 30 seconds for 1979 and later Rabbits, Jettas and Sciroccos; 900cc in 30 seconds for 1987 and later Fox.

For Dashers with the type A fuel pump, identified by the fuel inlet and outlet ports being at opposite end of the pump, the pump must delivery 1,000cc (1 quart) of fuel in 32 seconds. For Dashers with the type B fuel pump, identified by the inlet and outlet ports forming a 90° angle through the center of the pump, the pump must delivery 1,000 cc (1 quart) of fuel in 40 seconds. Quantum fuel

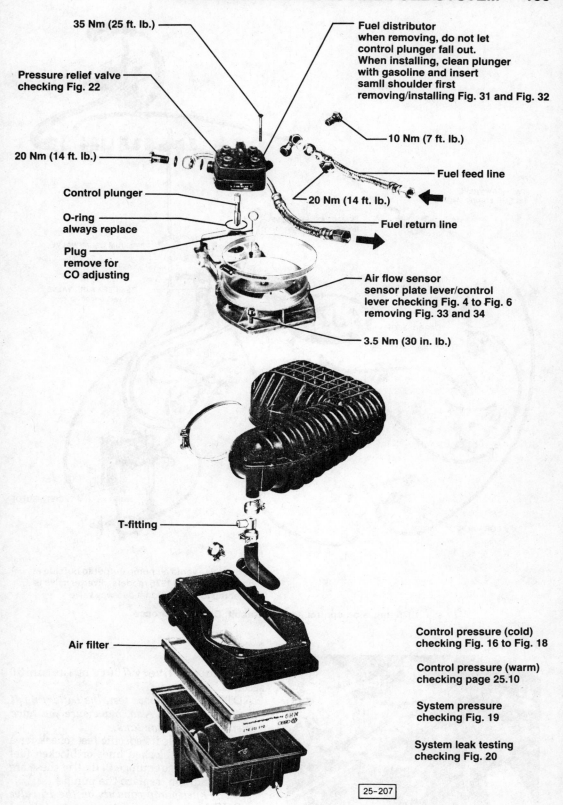

35 Nm (25 ft. lb.)

Fuel distributor
when removing, do not let
control plunger fall out.
When installing, clean plunger
with gasoline and insert
samll shoulder first
removing/installing Fig. 31 and Fig. 32

Pressure relief valve
checking Fig. 22

10 Nm (7 ft. lb.)

20 Nm (14 ft. lb.)

Fuel feed line

Control plunger

20 Nm (14 ft. lb.)

O-ring
always replace

Fuel return line

Plug
remove for
CO adjusting

Air flow sensor
sensor plate lever/control
lever checking Fig. 4 to Fig. 6
removing Fig. 33 and 34

3.5 Nm (30 in. lb.)

T-fitting

Air filter

Control pressure (cold)
checking Fig. 16 to Fig. 18

Control pressure (warm)
checking page 25.10

System pressure
checking Fig. 19

System leak testing
checking Fig. 20

25-207

Typical Cis Air/Fuel Distributor

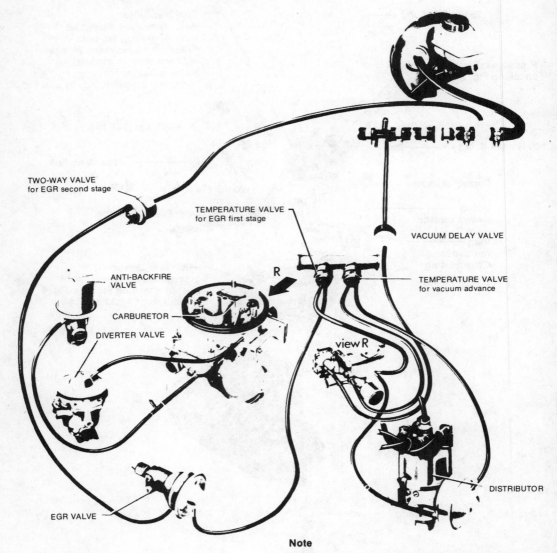

TWO-WAY VALVE
for EGR second stage

TEMPERATURE VALVE
for EGR first stage

VACUUM DELAY VALVE

R

ANTI-BACKFIRE VALVE

TEMPERATURE VALVE
for vacuum advance

CARBURETOR

DIVERTER VALVE

view R

DISTRIBUTOR

EGR VALVE

Note

Diverter valve vents air pump output to outside at
high rpm. On some 1975 models, diverter valve is
connected to an additional two-way valve

1975 emission control hoses—Rabbit, Dasher, Scirocco

Fuel pump mounting

pump must delivery 700cc of fuel in 30
seconds.

  NOTE: *For the above test, the battery must
  be fully charged. Also, make sure you have
  plenty of fuel in the tank.*

If your pump fails its specific test, check for a
dirty fuel filter, blocked lines or blocked fuel
tank strainer (if so equipped). If all of these are
in good condition, replace the pump.

  NOTE: *Fuel pump capacity on the 16 valve
  DOHC 4 cylinder engine was not available at
  the time of publication of this book.*

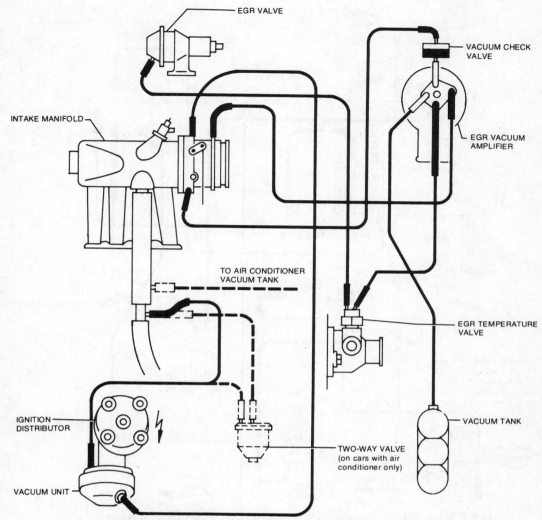

EGR VALVE

VACUUM CHECK
VALVE

INTAKE MANIFOLD

EGR VACUUM
AMPLIFIER

TO AIR CONDITIONER
VACUUM TANK

EGR TEMPERATURE
VALVE

IGNITION
DISTRIBUTOR

VACUUM TANK

VACUUM UNIT

TWO-WAY VALVE
(on cars with air
conditioner only)

Emission control hoses—1976–77 with CIS California automatic transmission

REMOVAL AND INSTALLATION

All Models Except Quantum

1. Raise the vehicle and support it on jack stands. Disconnect the battery ground cable.

2. Remove the right rear wheel on all cars. On the Rabbit Pick-up truck, you will probably have an easier go of it if you raise all four wheels off the ground and support the vehicle on jackstands.

3. Remove the gas tank filler cap to release the fuel pressure.

4. Clamp off the line between the fuel pump and the fuel tank with a pair of soft jawed vise grips or other suitable lock pliers. Don't clamp the line too tightly or you may damage it.

5. Disconnect the clamped line from the fuel pump. There's bound to be a little gas in the line, so be careful.

6. If your vehicle has an accumulator mounted next to the fuel pump, disconnect the fuel lines from the accumulator. Disconnect the wiring from the fuel pump and remove all other lines after marking them for assembly.

7. Loosen and remove the retaining nuts and remove the fuel pump on Dashers and pre '79 Rabbits and Sciroccos. On 1979 and later Rabbits, Jettas, GTIs and Sciroccos, including the Rabbit Pick-up, and on 1987 Foxs, remove the nuts on the lower bracket, loosen the nut on the upper slotted bracket where it connects to the body and slide the pump out.

8. Install the new fuel pump in the reverse order of removal. Make sure that the new seal washers are installed on the fuel discharge line.

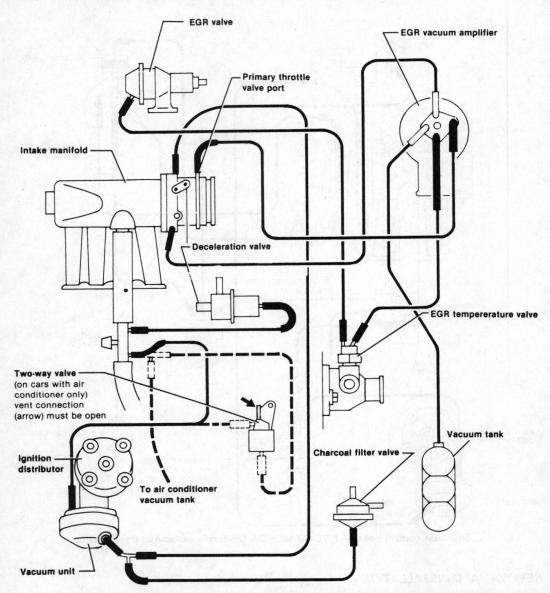

Emission control hoses—1979 and later CIS USA except California manual transmission

Quantum

1. Pull up carpet under rear cargo area, revealing fuel pump access.

2. Remove cover over sending unit.

3. Detach fuel return hose, fuel supply hose, and vent hose from top of fuel pump.

4. Disconnect electrical wire from sending unit and fuel pump.

5. Loosen fuel pump attaching screws and pull fuel pump out in one motion.

6. Installation is the reverse of removal.

Troubleshooting

WATER IN THE FUEL

Water in the fuel, and the resulting rust, are the number one enemies of any fuel injection system, especially CIS. Because normal operating pressure on CIS systems ranges from 65–85 psi, the fuel pump usually pushes any water right through the fuel filter. A little plastic filter in the center of the fuel distributor traps the water. The trapped water then rusts out

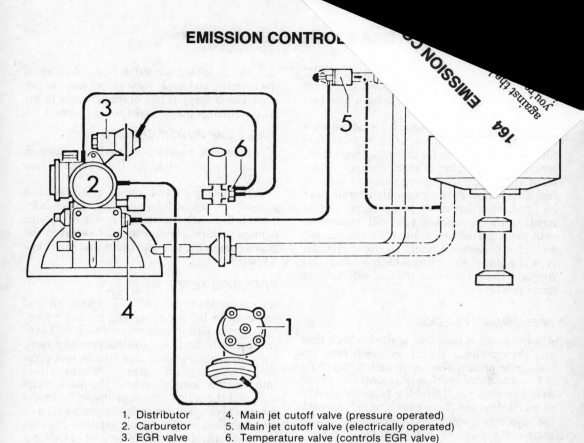

1. Distributor
2. Carburetor
3. EGR valve
4. Main jet cutoff valve (pressure operated)
5. Main jet cutoff valve (electrically operated)
6. Temperature valve (controls EGR valve)

Emission control hoses—1978 carbureted Rabbit

the fuel distributor! Not only will the rust block the tiny metering slits in the fuel distributor, it can also flow into the injectors and warm-up compensator. So if you find rust in one part, you can bet there's rust in the other. When rust particles block a metering slit, the cylinder fed by that slit will either die com-

pletely or else develop an intermittent misfire closely resembling the conditions created by a bad spark plug. If the spark plugs are known to be good, look for rust or water in the fuel. Disconnect the injector lines and spread some fresh white paper towels on the workbench. Remove the entire fuel distributor and tap it

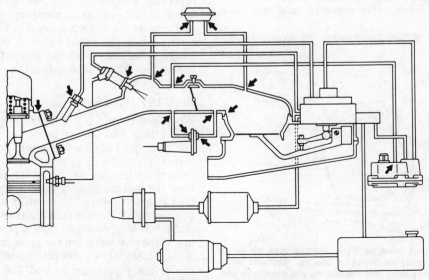

Check the CIS for vacuum leaks at arrows

bench. Shake it and tap it again. If
able to shake rust particles out of those
injector line openings, it's time for a new fuel
distributor.

Water contamination can be prevented with
regular, and the emphasis is on regular, fuel
filter changes. Filters for these cars are expensive, but a fresh filter is much cheaper than a
set of injectors, warm-up regulator, or worse, a
fuel distributor. A rusty fuel distributor can't
be fixed, and they're very expensive. Not to
mention the headaches you will experience
with lousy performance, intermittent cut-out,
and other nonsense. Change the filter regularly, add water-chasing fuel additives, and don't
frequent cheapo gas stations that sell watered
down fuel.

PRELIMINARY CHECKS

Always make a complete ignition check first
and then perform all the injection pressure
tests in sequence. The worst return you could
get on the time spent hooking up the gauge
would be that you'll find the problem quickly
or you'll discover there's nothing wrong with
the injection system. The cause of many CIS
complaints is the old fashioned vacuum leak.
Vacuum leaks fool the fuel metering system
and foul up the mixture. This gives poor gas
economy and poor performance. Look for leaks
at:
  1. EGR valve
  2. Intake manifold
  3. Cold start valve.
  4. Air sensor boot
  5. Brake booster vacuum lines
  6. Air ducts
And, don't forget the less obvious vacuum
limiter, evaporative canister, and A/C door
actuator.

To quick test the system for leaks, discon-

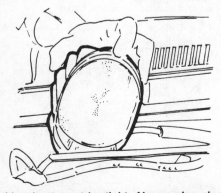

Rubber boot must be tight. Always give air ducts
the once-over for leaks or cracks. Vacuum leaks
will upset system and the engine will never run correctly

nect the auxiliary air valve hose, block open
the throttle, and apply shop air pressure to the
hose. Use a spray bottle of soapy water to hit
all the fittings where leaks could occur.

FUEL PUMP POWER CHECK

All K-Jetronic pumps are fused someplace in
the car, usually right in the vehicle's fuse
panel.

If the pump's dead, check the fuse, the
ground, and try bridging the relay, which is located inline with the pump's power wire, with
a jumper. During winter months, water in the
gas can cause the pump to freeze and then blow
a fuse.

PRESSURE TESTS

It's impossible to test any CIS system without
an accurate 100 psi gauge and a 3-way valve.

Diagnose CIS in this order: check cold control pressure first, hot control pressure next,
then primary pressure, and finally rest pressure. The gauge for testing CIS always tees
into the line running between the fuel distributor and the warm-up compensator. With the
3-way valve open, the gauge remains teed-in
and therefore reads control pressure. Remember that control pressure is derived or fed from
the primary circuit pressure so a pressure
change in one circuit means a change in the
other.

Closing the valve shuts off fuel flow to the
warm-up compensator and forces the gauge to
read only one circuit — the primary circuit.

When you shut the engine off and leave the
3-way valve open, the teed-in gauge should
show the system's holding pressure. This residual pressure is called rest pressure. The valve
functions are: valve open — control pressure;
valve closed — primary pressure; valve open
and engine off-rest pressure. On CIS, all you
have to do is close that valve on the pressure
gauge to isolate a leak inside the feed side of
the system from a leak inside the return side.

PRIMARY PRESSURE

When you close the 3-way valve with the engine idling and the primary pressure reads
low, you could have a fuel pump problem or a
primary regulator problem. To isolate one
from the other, locate the return line leading
from the fuel distributor back to the gas tank.
Now plug the return line securely at some convenient point. Have an assistant switch on the
pump just long enough to get a pressure reading. If the pump is good, the pressure will jump
almost instantly to 100 psi or higher. Should
the primary pressure exceed 116 psi during
this momentary test, the check valve in the in-

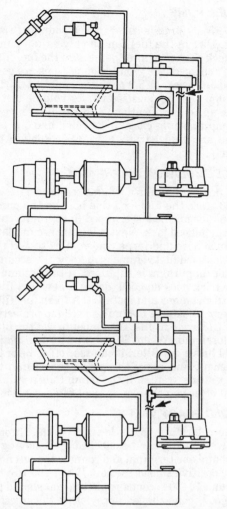

Fuel pressure test points with push valve (top) and without push valve (bottom). In general, vehicles since 1978 have push valves, recognizable by 2 fuel lines connected to the warm-up regulator

take side of the fuel pump will vent the pressure back into the gas tank.

If the fuel pump produces good pressure with the return line plugged, then you know that the primary pressure regulator is causing your low primary pressure reading. If that little O-ring you find around the inboard end of the primary regulator starts leaking or becomes dislodged, it'll lower primary pressure. Install a primary regulator repair kit from your Bosch supplier. If installing this kit doesn't bring primary pressure within specs, you'll have to shim the primary pressure regulator. For every 0.1mm shim you install, the primary pressure should increase about 2 psi (0.15 bar.) Some suppliers stock these shims and import car dealers should stock shims for the fuel distributors on any CIS equipped cars they sell. If

you can't get the shims, you'll have to replace the entire fuel distributor.

What if primary pressure is higher than specs? The car probably won't run, but look for a kinked fuel return line under the car.

Rest Pressure

Good rest pressure enables a CIS engine to start easily when it's hot. If the system loses rest pressure for any reason, the injector lines will literally vapor lock. Then the driver has to crank the engine until the pump can replenish the lines with liquid fuel. Suppose you shut off the engine and the rest pressure drops off too quickly. Start the engine and run it long enough to build the system pressure back up. Then kill the engine, pull the electrical connector off the cold start injector and remove the injector from the intake manifold. If the cold start injector is dripping, replace it and recheck rest pressure.

If the cold-start valve is holding pressure, reinstall it and run the engine again to build up pressure. Kill the engine and close the 3-way valve. If the pressure reading remains steady now, you know the return side of the system, the warm-up compensator, is leaking. Replace the compensator.

If the rest pressure still drops, rapidly after you've closed the 3-way valve, the leak's in the feed side of the system. This could mean a bad fuel pump, bad accumulator, or a bad primary pressure regulator. Shoot for the easy stuff first. The fuel pump's intake hose is flexible. Clamp this hose shut and recheck rest pressure. If the system holds pressure, then the check ball in the output side of the pump is leaking.

A sharp eye and a healthy ear will help you isolate a bad accumulator. Watch your pressure gauge as your helper shuts off the engine. If the accumulator's good, the pressure will drop, stop for a second, and then the gauge needle will actually rise—pressure will increase for a moment—before the pressure stabilizes. If you don't see that slight upward needle movement, the accumulator is leaking rest pressure. Furthermore, a bad accumulator will cause a loud, tell-tale groaning noise at the fuel pump. If you're still in doubt about that accumulator, try blocking off its return line.

The same primary pressure regulator that can cause low primary pressure can also leak rest pressure. If you've eliminated the fuel pump and the accumulator, then install a primary regulator repair kit.

AIR FLOW SENSOR PLATE

The air flow sensor plate in the fuel distributor must operate smoothly in order to do a good job

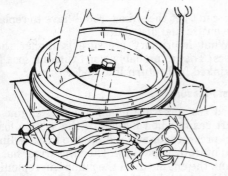

When the sensor plate moves, fuel is delivered. Check the sensor plate for free movement. You should feel even resistance through full travel

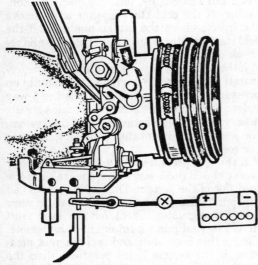

Throttle valve provides full load enrichment when at wide opened throttle on 1.8 CIS engines. To check—disconnect wire on switch and connect test light between battery and contact on throttle switch. Push throttle valve in direction of open throttle until test light lights up. Adjust contact gap to .047 ins.

of measuring air. Remove the air boot and check the sensor plate movement. When released, the plate should fall freely with one or two bounces. If the plate sticks, loosen the mounting screws and retighten them uniformly. If it feels as if the plunger is sticking, remove it and clean it in solvent. Be very careful not to drop it. Clean the funnel and sensor plate too, as these can get dirty from PCV fumes.

The sensor plate should sit flat and rest even in the narrowest part of the funnel. It shouldn't touch the sides of the funnel. If it's out of position, loosen the center screw and using a guide plate or 0.10mm feeler gauge, center the plate.

FUEL PUMP

The fuel pump is sometimes a source of trouble. Dirt in the fuel can quickly ruin a pump. Check the pump after being sure the fuel filter isn't clogged, the ground connections are good, and at least 11.5 volts are supplied to the pump. See previous section for volume test. If not up to specifications and the filter's good, pump's getting close to 12 volts, and the fuel line and tank strainer are OK. Replace the pump.

ACCUMULATOR DIAPHRAGM

If the pump flunks a volume test, raise the car and trace the fuel feed line back to the pump. Look for mashed or crimped lines from a carelessly placed jack. Next, plug the accumulator return hose and repeat the volume test. If this yields good fuel volume, you know the accumulator diaphragm is ruptured. If the accumulator trick does no good, douse a new fuel filter with clean gas and install it. A fresh fuel filter every 10,000–12,000 miles is cheap protection for CIS system. Just remember to wet the filter beforehand. When 80 psi worth of incoming fuel hits a dry filter, it can tear off some of the element and carry the paper debris into the rest of the system. If the pump fails a volume test after you change the fuel filter, replace it.

COLD START VALVE

The cold start valve, located on the throttle valve housing can be checked by removing it. Ground one terminal and connect the second to the positive side of the coil. When you run the pump, 10–30 seconds is plenty, you should get a good, cone-shaped spray. Dry the injector, disconnect your jumpers, and energize the pump again. There shouldn't be any fuel. If it drips, replace it. Check the thermo-time switch when it's below 95°F. Disconnect the cold start valve and hook up a test light across its connector. Ground No. 1 coil terminal and run the starter. The light should glow for several seconds and then go out. If not, replace the thermo-time switch.

INJECTOR SPRAY PATTERN

A bad injection valve can cause a number of problems:
1. Hot restart troubles
2. Rough idle
3. Hesitation
4. Poor power.

Hot starting complaints can come from an injector or injectors that are leaking fuel droplets when they're supposed to be completely shut. The next three problems can be caused by a bad spray pattern from one or more of the injectors. Dribble patterns, fire hose shots, and

UNEVEN SPRAY

FIRE HOSE

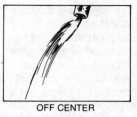

OFF CENTER

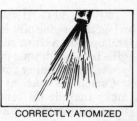

CORRECTLY ATOMIZED

Fuel injector spray patterns

uneven sprays will produce hesitation, stumbling and general lack of power.

On-Car Testing

With care, you can check injectors without a tester, but if you suspect injector problems, it's worth having them checked on a test stand. To watch spray patterns on the car, switch the ignition on, pull an injector out of the head, and lift the air sensor plate with your fingers (carefully). When you let the plate down quickly, you should get a fine, cone-shaped spray of fuel. If not, the injector should come off and be cleaned or replaced. Repeat the test for each injector. Hot start complaints call for a different procedure. Crank the starter and pull each injector in turn. If an injector drips fuel, it's defective and should be replaced.

Off-Car Testing

Testing injectors out of the car is the most accurate method for determining whether or not they're causing performance problems. Individual injectors are expensive items, and immediately trashing suspect injection valves is not wise. New and old injectors can be mixed in the set for that engine, so only defective units need be replaced.

Bosch manufactures a valve tester KDJE 7452. This tester is only for CIS injectors. The CIS only tester reads to 142.2 psi and comes with a hand pump, pressure gauge, test-fluid bottle, and test line. All you need do is bolt it to a stand.

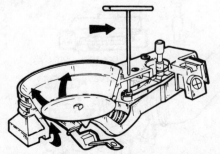

Mixture control on CIS is especially critical, since it affects the air/fuel ratio throughout the operating range, not just at idle. Adjustment is made with allen wrench (arrow)

On the test stand, you can operate the valve as much as you like and watch the pattern. Use kerosene as a test fluid, not gasoline! With the injector filled with fluid and bled, tighten the test line fitting. Slowly work the handle, without going over 21 psi. Pressure should build up and the injector shouldn't leak. Next, build up pressure with the test valve open until the injector squirts. Opening pressure for all CIS cars is 35–52 psi.

Injector

REMOVAL AND INSTALLATION

1. Grasp injector body. DO NOT grasp and pull on fuel line. Pull injector straight out of manifold.

2. Protect injector tip. It is a precision instrument and is easily damaged. Proceed to next injector and so on.

3. Moisten a new rubber seal with gasoline before installing injectors.

4. Press each injector in fully until seated.

Adjustments

IDLE SPEED

The idle speed screw (called a by-pass screw by some manufacturers) on the throttle body housing of the CIS system bleeds air into the manifold when you increase idle speed, or cuts it off to slow the engine down. When you change idle speed, the idle mixture always changes to some degree, and vice-versa. Therefore, you'll have to juggle the speed and mixture adjustments back and forth to get the specified idle speed within the right range of CO. Tweak that mixture screw a wee bit at a time. It's so sensitive that you can just touch it with the 3mm Allen wrench and the CO changes! And unlike a carburetor, changing the idle CO changes the mixture throughout the entire rpm range. Never rev the engine with the Allen wrench sitting in the mixture screw or you may damage the air sensor plate.

Engine oil temperature is the most critical factor in getting an accurate CO adjustment on any CIS system. Don't touch the mixture screw until the oil temperature is between 140–

176°F (60–80°C). If you try adjusting mixture when the engine oil's hotter than 176°F, you'll end up with a clean-running engine. If the engine is too cold, your mixture setting will give you a rich-running guzzler.

Companies such as Sun Electric and Siemens include oil temperature probes with their equipment. These probes slip into the dipstick tube. Final advice? Other than servicing the primary pressure regulator, don't fool around with a fuel distributor! Opening a fuel distributor would be like opening Pandora's Box all over again.

ACCELERATOR THROTTLE CABLE ADJUSTMENT

Throttle cable slack adjustments are made at the two locknuts where the cable is mounted on the valve cover.

1. Check that the throttle valve is closed (in the idle position).

2. If adjustment is necessary, loosen locknut and turn the adjusting nut until the throttle cable is free of slack or tension.

NOTE: *On automatic transmission models, make sure the throttle cable levers on the transmission are moved the whole way into their rest positions. Some models do not use transmission cables.*

Closed Loop System

With the advent of the 3-way catalytic converter, the CIS system has undergone modification. Three new components have been integrated with the system, an oxygen sensor, an electronic control unit (ECU), and a frequency valve. These convert CIS into a closed loop fuel system. In order for the 3-way converter to work effectively, the air/fuel mixture must be kept within a very precise range. Between 15 and 14 parts of air to one part of fuel, there's an ideal ratio called stoichiometric where HC,

CO, and NOx emissions are all at a minimum. Bosch calls this ratio, or point, Lambda. Combined with an oxygen, or Lambda, sensor, the air/fuel ratio in a fuel injected system can be controlled within a tolerance of 0.02%.

The oxygen sensor in the exhaust system monitors the oxygen content of the exhaust gases. It produces a small amount of voltage that varies depending on the amount of oxygen present in the exhaust. This voltage signal is sent to the ECU. The ECU, in turn, then signals the frequency valve to enrichen or lean the mixture. The voltage signal is approximately one volt. The frequency valve is located between the fuel distributor and the fuel return line. It does not change control pressure in the K-Jetronic system. It alters system pressure in the lower chamber of the fuel distributor for each cylinder's differential pressure valve.

DUTY CYCLE

When the oxygen sensor signals a rich mixture to the ECU, it will close the frequency valve. This causes pressure in the lower chamber of the fuel distributor to increase and push the diaphragm up to reduce fuel quantity. If the air/fuel mixture is too lean, the frequency valve will be open and reduce pressure in the lower chamber. The diaphragm is then pushed down and the amount of fuel is increased. The valve opens and closes many times per second. The average pressure is determined by the ratio of valve openings and closings. A higher open-to-closed ratio would provide a richer mixture, a lower open-to-closed ratio would give a leaner mixture. This is called the duty cycle of the frequency valve.

Bosch makes a tester for the Lambda system that measures the open-to-closed ratio, or duty cycle. The Bosch KDJE 7453 tester reads out the duty cycle on a percentage meter. A read-

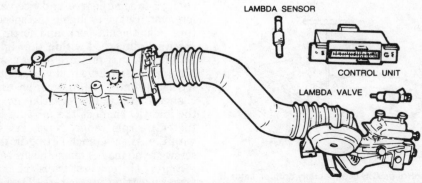

CIS in its Lambda guise. Components are similar to early CIS with the addition of an electronic control unit (ECU), oxygen sensor and frequency valve. This system is used with a three-way catalytic converter. Oxygen sensor signals the ECU to have the frequency valve enrichen or lean mixture according to exhaust O$_2$ content

ing of 60, for instance, would be a frequency valve pulse rate of 60%. You can also use a sensitive dwell meter that reads to at least 70°F to measure duty cycle on the 4-cyl. scale. VWs using CIS with Lambda provide a test socket, so that a duty cycle tester can easily be hooked up.

The following is a general procedure for checking the duty cycle with a dwell meter.

1. Disconnect the thermo switch wiring. Shorting the switch will enrich the mixture to about 60% for a cold engine. The meter needle should stay steady, which indicates an "open loop". This means the system isn't being affected by the oxygen sensor. Reconnect the thermo switch.

2. Disconnect the oxygen sensor with a warm engine. The meter should register a 50% signal.

3. Reconnect the oxygen sensor. You should see a change from open to closed loop. The needle will stay steady in the middle at 50% for about a minute. When the oxygen sensor warms up, it should signal the frequency valve for closed loop operation. That will be shown by a swinging needle on the meter, when the system is working correctly.

Fuel Distributor

REMOVAL AND INSTALLATION

1. Release the pressure in the system by loosening the fuel line on the control pressure regulator (large connector). Have a rag ready to catch the fuel that escapes.

2. Mark the fuel lines in the top of the distributor so that you will be able to put them back in their correct positions.

NOTE: *Using different colored paints is usually a good marking device. When you mark each line, be sure to mark the spot where it connects to the distributor.*

3. Clean the fuel lines, then remove them from the distributor. Remove the little looped wire plug (the CO adjusting screw plug). Remove the two retaining screws in the top of the distributor.

NOTE: *When removing the fuel distributor be sure the control plunger does not fall out from underneath.*

4. If the control plunger has been removed, moisten it with gasoline before installing. The small shoulder on the plunger is inserted first.

NOTE: *Always use new gaskets and O-ring when removing and installing fuel distributor. Lock all retaining screws with Loctite® or its equivalent.*

CIS Thermostat

All Volkswagens with the Continuous Injection System (CIS) are equipped with air clean-

er thermostats which allow preheated air from the exhaust manifold to be directed into the intake manifold while the engine is cold in order to improve performance. The thermostat is located in the bottom of the air cleaner. To remove it, remove the hoses and attaching screws and pull the unit out. If you believe the thermostat is not functioning correctly, perform the following test.

1. Dip the thermostat in warm water that is below 68°F (20°C). The flap in the unit should stay open.

2. Next dip the unit in water heated above 93°F (34°C). The flap should close. If the flap does not perform as expected, replace the thermostat.

NOTE: *A manual lever is used on GTI models. Set the lever to warm position when tuning. Adjust to required temperature setting (warm or cold), depending on climate.*

DIESEL FUEL INJECTION SYSTEM

The diesel fuel system is an extremely complex and sensitive system. Very few repairs or adjustments are possible by the owner. Any service other than that listed here should be referred to an authorized VW dealer or diesel specialist. The injection pump itself is not repairable; it can only be replaced.

Any work done to the diesel fuel injection should be done with absolute cleanliness. Even

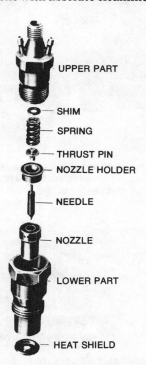

UPPER PART

SHIM

SPRING

THRUST PIN

NOZZLE HOLDER

NEEDLE

NOZZLE

LOWER PART

HEAT SHIELD

Diesel engine fuel injector (do not disassemble)

the smallest specks of dirt will have a disastrous effect on the injection system.

Do not attempt to remove the fuel injectors. They are very delicate and must be removed with a special tool to prevent damage. The fuel in the system is also under tremendous pressure (1,700–1,850 psi), so it's not wise to loosen any lines with the engine running. Exposing your skin to the spray from the injector at working pressure can cause fuel to penetrate the skin.

Adjustments

CHECKING INJECTION PUMP TIMING

Checking the injection pump timing also involves checking the valve timing. To alter the injection pump timing, the camshaft gear must be removed and repositioned. This also changes the valve timing. See the Timing Belt replacement section in Chapter 3.

ACCELERATOR CABLE ADJUSTMENT

The ball pin on the pump lever should be pointing up and be aligned with the mark in the slot. The accelerator cable should be attached

A manual shut-off valve is used on all 1983 diesels with automatic transmission. If the electric fuel shut-off solenoid malfunctions, the engine can be shut off manually

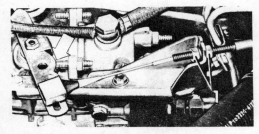

Accelerator cable adjustment

at the upper hole in the bracket. With the pedal in the full throttle position, adjust the cable so that the pump lever contacts the stop with no binding or strain.

COLD START CABLE ADJUSTMENT

When the cold start knob on the dash is pulled out, the fuel injection pump timing is advanced 2.5°. This improves cold starting and running until the engine warms up.

1. Insert the washer on the cable.
2. Insert the cable in the bracket with the rubber bushing. Install the cable in the pin.
3. Install the lockwasher.
4. Move the lever to the zero position (direction of arrow). Pull the inner cable tight and tighten the clamp screw.

Cold start cable adjustment

GLOW PLUG TESTING

See Chapter 3, under the "Engine Electrical" section for glow plug testing.

Turbocharging

A turbocharger is an exhaust-driven turbine which drives a centrifugal compressor wheel. The compressor is usually located between the air cleaner and the engine's intake manifold, while the turbine is located between the exhaust manifold and the muffler. Primarily, the turbocharger compresses the air entering the engine, forcing more air into the cylinders. This allows the engine to efficiently burn more fuel, thereby producing more horsepower.

All of the exhaust gases pass through the turbine housing. The expansion of these gases, acting on the turbine wheel, causes it to turn. After passing through the turbine the exhaust gases are routed to the atmosphere through the exhaust system.

The compressor and turbine are each en-

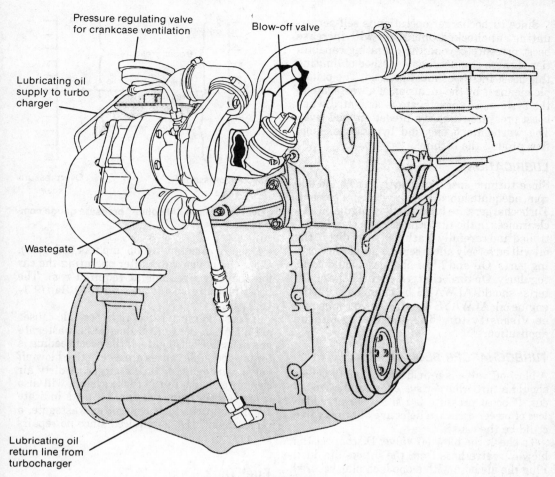

Pressure regulating valve
for crankcase ventilation

Blow-off valve

Lubricating oil
supply to turbo
charger

Wastegate

Lubricating oil
return line from
turbocharger

Turbocharger mounting

closed in their own housings and are directly connected by a shaft. The housings are constructed of light alloy and are designed for maximum heat dissipation. The only power loss from the turbine to the compressor is the slight friction of the shaft journal bearings. Air is drawn in through the filtered intake system, compressed by the compressor wheel and discharged into the intake manifold. The extra charge of air provided by the turbocharger allows more fuel to be burned, providing more power.

As engine speed increases, the length of time the intake valves are open decreases, giving the air less time to fill the cylinders. On an engine running at 2,500 rpm, the intake valves are open less than 0.017 second. The air drawn into a naturally aspirated engine's cylinder is less than atmospheric pressure. Turbochargers pack air into the cylinder at greater than atmospheric pressure at all speeds. The flow of exhaust gas from each cylinder occurs intermittantly as the exhaust valve opens.

This results in fluctuating gas pressures, also known as pulse energy, at the turbine inlet.

At high altitudes, a naturally aspirated engine drops 3% in horsepower per 1,000 feet elevation due to a 3% decrease in air density per 1,000 feet.With a turbocharged engine, an increase in altitude also increases the pressure drop across the turbine. Inlet turbine pressure remains the same, but the outlet pressure decreases as the altitude increases. Turbine speed also increases as the pressure difference increases. The compressor wheel turns faster, providing approximately the same inlet pressure as at sea level, even though the incoming air is less dense.

There are, however, limitations to the actual amount of compensation for altitude provided by the turbocharger. These limitations are primarily as a result of varying amounts of boost pressure and turbocharger-to-engine match. To make up for the difference in altitude compensation, an altitude compensator is added to the system.

Since turbocharger operation is self-perpetuating, unchecked operation will increase boost pressure beyond the operating capabilities of these engines. Some method of limiting this boost increases must be used. The principle means is by the inclusion of a wastegate in the system. The wastegate is activated when boost pressure reaches a predetermined level. The wastegate opens and bypasses exhaust flow around the turbine.

LUBRICATION

Since turbine speeds routinely reach 140,000 rpm, adequate lubrication is vitally important. Turbochargers are lubricated by engine oil. All clearances in the turbocharger are closely controlled and carefully machined. Any dirt in the oil will adversely affect service life of the working parts. Oil and filter changes should occur regularly. On turbocharged engines, the oil filter(s) should ALWAYS be changed with the engine oil. ALWAYS use oil of the recommended viscosity for that particular engine application.

TURBOCHARGER BLOW-OFF VALVE

A blow-off valve is provided as a safety device should a turbocharger system malfunction occur. If boost pressure is too low, or a sudden loss of power occurs, a defective blow-off valve could be the cause.

To check the blow-off valve: Disconnect the blow-off valve hose from the intake air duct. Plug the air hose with a one inch plug secured with a hose clamp. Perform a boost pressure test. If the boost pressure test is OK, replace the blow-off valve. If boost pressure test is still not OK, replace the turbocharger.

BOOST PRESSURE TEST

A special test gauge (VW1397) reading BAR and PSI is required. The VW gauge is an overpressure type gauge. Other test gauge manufacturer's produce absolute pressure gauges. On the overpressure gauge, a reading of 0.6 Bar is 23.52 psi. On an absolute pressure gauge, a reading on 1 Bar indicates normal atmospheric pressure. A reading of over 1 Bar indicates boost pressure. A reading below 1 bar on an absolute gauge indicates intake manifold pressure.

To install gauge: Connect gauge tee fitting to the boost pressure line at the injection pump. Route hose and gauge out of the corner of the hood and in through the passenger's window. Test drive the car with the engine at normal operating temperature. Open the valve to the pressure gauge. Accelerate in 3rd gear, or number 2 drive position, and hold the vehi-

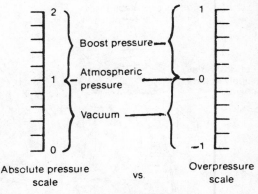

"Overboost" and "Absolute" pressure gauge comparison scales

cle speed constant at 35 mph (4,000 rpm). Close the gauge valve after operating the car for about two seconds at required rpm. The boost pressure should be 0.64–0.70 Bar (9.3–10.2 psi).

If boost pressure is too high, possible causes are a leak in the control line to the wastegate or a defective wastegate. If the boost reading is too low, possible causes are a defective blow-off valve, wastegate or turbocharger. A dirty air cleaner or leaks in the turbo system will also cause low pressure readings. If tests indicate problems in the turbocharger or wastegate, a replacement unit is required since no repairs are possible.

Fuel Tank

REMOVAL AND INSTALLATION

Rabbit (Except Pick-up), Golf, Scirocco, Jetta

1. Disconnect the battery.
2. Remove the drain plug and empty the tank. Disconnect the remove fuel pump on CIS models.
3. Disconnect the parking brake cables at the parking brake lever.
4. Disconnect and plug the rear brake lines.
5. Remove the rear axle mounting nuts and pull the rear axle down.
6. Disconnect the sending unit ground wire and gauge wire.
7. Loosen the clamps and pull off the fuel line(s).
   NOTE: *If more than one fuel line attaches to the sending unit, mark the lines to avoid confusion when assembly.*
8. Disconnect any other breather lines. Disconnect the filler pipe.
9. Remove the rubber exhaust hangers if they hinder removal of the fuel tank.
10. Remove the fuel tank straps and allow the tank to come down far enough to see if

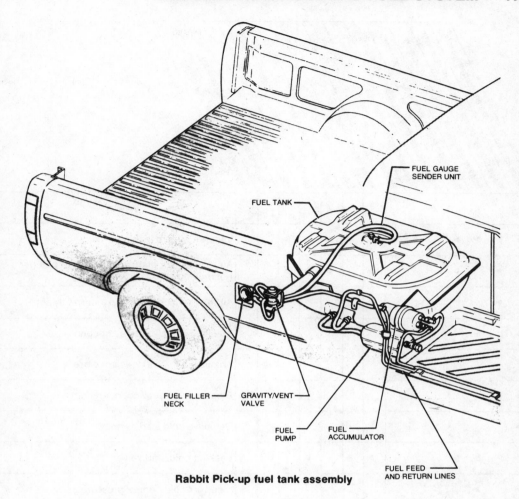

FUEL GAUGE
SENDER UNIT

FUEL TANK

FUEL FILLER
NECK

GRAVITY/VENT
VALVE

FUEL
PUMP

FUEL
ACCUMULATOR

FUEL FEED
AND RETURN LINES

Rabbit Pick-up fuel tank assembly

there are any other vent hoses to be disconnected.

11. After removing all vent hoses, remove the tank.

NOTE: *Many earlier models do not have these vent lines.*

12. Install the tank in the reverse order of removal.

13. Note the following:

a. Make sure that all breather and vent lines are not kinked

b. Use new clamps on all connections

c. Tighten the rear axle mounting nuts to 32 ft.lb.

d. Bleed the brakes

e. Adjust the parking brake.

Rabbit Pick-up Truck

The fuel tank is located to the rear of the cab.

1. Disconnect the battery.

2. Drain the fuel from the tank using a conventional siphon.

3. Remove and match mark all hoses from the tank, except for the breather hose in the sending unit.

4. Remove the wires from the sending unit.

5. Loosen the straps holding the tank and unhook them from their brackets.

6. Lower the tank and unhook the vent hose in the sending unit.

7. Remove the fuel tank.

8. Installation is the reverse of removal.

Dasher, Fox and Quantum

1. Remove the battery ground cable.

2. Remove the trunk floor mat.

3. Drain the fuel tank.

4. Disconnect the fuel line(s).

5. Disconnect the electrical plugs from the fuel tank gauge sending unit.

6. Detach the vent line from the tank.

7. Remove all the retaining bolts from the trunk floor.

8. Detach the filler tube from the tank filler.

9. Installation is the reverse of removal.

10. Reseal the edge of the lower trunk floor to prevent leaks.

Engine does not start or starts poorly when cold	Engine does not start or starts poorly when warm	Irregular idle (engine shakes) during warm-up	Irregular idle (engine shakes) with engine warm	Engine does not draw fuel smoothly with engine warm	Engine misfires under full load (backfires)	Insufficient power	Engine runs on (diesels)	Excessive fuel consumption	Flat spot during acceleration	Idle CO value too high	Idle CO value too low	Idle speed cannot be adjusted (too high)	Engine stalls immediately after starting	Cause(s)
►	►	►	►		►				►		►			Vacuum system leaking
►	►		►		►				►	►	►			Air flow sensor plate and/or control plunger not moving smoothly
	►					►								Air flow sensor plate stop incorrectly set
►		►												Auxiliary air valve does not open
												►		Auxiliary air valve does not close
►	►				►								►	Electric fuel pump not operating
►														Defective cold start system
		►	►			►		►		►				Leaking cold start valve
►		►												Incorrect cold control pressure
		►		►	►	►			►				►	Warm control pressure too high
			►	►	►			►	►	►			►	Warm control pressure too low
				►	►				►				►	Incorrect system pressure
►														Fuel system pressure leakage
►	►	►			►			►						Injection valve(s) leaking, opening pressure too low
			►	►		►			►					Unequal fuel delivery between cylinders
►	►	►	►						►	►	►	►	►	Basic idle and/or CO adjustment incorrect
						►								Throttle plate does not open completely

Chassis Electrical

5

UNDERSTANDING AND TROUBLESHOOTING ELECTRICAL SYSTEMS

For any electrical system to operate, it must make a complete circuit. This simply means that the power flow from the battery must make a complete circle. When an electrical component is operating, power flows from the battery to the component, passes through the component causing it to perform its function (lighting a light bulb, for example) and then returns to the battery through the ground of the circuit. This ground is usually (but not always) the metal part of the vehicle on which the electrical component is mounted.

Perhaps the easiest way to visualize this is to think of connecting a light bulb with two wires attached to it to your vehicle battery. The battery in your vehicle has two posts (negative and positive). If one of the two wires attached to the light bulb was attached to the negative post of the battery and the other wire was attached to the positive post of the battery, you would have a complete circuit. Current from the battery would flow out one post, through the wire attached to it and then to the light bulb, causing it to light. It would then leave the light bulb, travel through the other wire, and return to the other post of the battery.

The normal automotive circuit differs from this simple example in two ways. First, instead of having a return wire from the bulb to the battery, the light bulb returns the current to the battery through the chassis of the vehicle. Since the negative battery cable is attached to the chassis and the chassis is made of electrically conductive metal, the chassis of the vehicle can act as a ground wire to complete the circuit. Secondly, most automotive circuits contain switches to turn components on and off as required.

There are many types of switches, but the most common simply serves to prevent the passage of current when it is turned off. Since the switch is a part of the circle necessary for a complete circuit, it operates to leave an opening in the circuit, and thus an incomplete or open circuit, when it is turned off.

Some electrical components which require a large amount of current to operate also have a relay in their circuit. Since these circuits carry a large amount of current, the thickness of the wire (gauge size) in the circuit is also greater. If this large wire were connected from the component to the control switch on the instrument panel, and then back to the component, a voltage drop would occur in the circuit. To prevent this potential drop in voltage, an electromagnetic switch (relay) is used. The large wires in the circuit are connected from the vehicle battery to one side of the relay, and from the opposite side of the relay to the component. The relay is normally open, preventing current from passing through the circuit. An additional, smaller, wire is connected from the relay to the control switch to the circuit. When the control switch is turned on, it completes the circuit. This closes the relay and allows current to flow from the battery to the component. The horn, headlight, and starter circuits are three which use relays.

You have probably noticed how the vehicle's instrument panel lights get brighter the faster you rev the engine. This happens because you alternator (which supplies the battery) puts out more current at speeds above idle. This is normal. However, it is possible for larger surges of current to pass through the electrical system of your car. If this surge of current were to reach an electrical component, it could burn the component out. To prevent this from happening, fuses are connected into the current supply wires of most of the major electrical systems of your vehicle. The fuse serves to head off the surge at the pass. When an electrical current of excessive power passes through the component's fuse, the fuse blows out and breaks the circuit, saving it from destruction.

The fuse also protects the component from damage if the power supply wire to the component is grounded before the current reaches the component.

There is another important rule to the complete circle circuit. Every complete circuit from a power source must include a component which is using the power from the power source. If you were to disconnect the light bulb (from the previous example of a light bulb being connected to the battery by two wires together (take our word for it; don't try it) the result would literally be shocking. A similar thing happens (on a smaller scale) when the power supply wire to a component or the electrical component itself becomes grounded before the normal ground connection for the circuit. To prevent damage to the system, the fuse for the circuit blows to interrupt the circuit, protecting the components from damage. Because grounding a wire from a power source makes a complete circuit, less the required component to use the power, this phenomenon is called a short circuit. The most common causes of short circuits are: the rubber insulation on a wire breaking or rubbing through to expose the current carrying core of the wire to a metal part of the vehicle, or a short switch.

Some electrical systems on the vehicle are protected by a circuit breaker which is, basically, a self-repairing fuse. When either of the above described events takes place in a system which is protected by a circuit breaker, the circuit breaker opens the circuit the same way a fuse does. However, when either the short is removed from the circuit or the surge subsides, the circuit breaker resets itself and does not have to be replaced as a fuse does.

The final protective device in the chassis electrical system is a fuse link. A fuse link is a wire that acts as a fuse. It is connected between the starter relay and the main wiring harness for the car. This connection is under the hood, very near a similar fuse link which protects all the chassis electrical components. It is the probable cause of trouble when none of the electrical components function, unless the battery is disconnected or dead.

Electrical problems generally fall into one of three areas:

1. The component that is not functioning is not receiving current.
2. The component itself is not functioning.
3. The component is not properly grounded.

Problems that fall into the first category are by far the most complicated. It is the current supply system to the component which contains all the switches, relays, fuses, etc.

The electrical system can be checked with a test light and a jumper wire. A test light is a device that looks like a pointed screwdriver with a wire attached to it. It has a light bulb in its handle. A jumper wire is a piece of insulated wire with an alligator clip attached to each end.

If a light bulb is not working, you must follow a systematic plan to determine which of the three causes is the villain.

1. Turn on the switch that controls the inoperable bulb.
2. Disconnect the power supply wire from the bulb.
3. Attach the ground wire on the test light to a good metal ground.
4. Touch the probe end of the test light to the end of the power supply wire that was disconnected from the bulb. If the bulb is receiving current, the test light will go on.

NOTE: *If the bulb is one which works only when the ignition key is turned on (turn signal), make sure the key is turned on.*

If the test light does not go on, then the problem is in the circuit between the battery and the bulb. As mentioned before, this includes all the switches, fuses, and relays in the system. The problem is an open circuit between the battery and the bulb. If the fuse is blown and, when replaced, immediately blows again, there is a short circuit in the system which must be located and repaired. If there is a switch in the system, bypass it with a jumper wire. This is done by connecting one end of the jumper wire to the power supply wire into the switch, and the other end of the jumper wire to the wire coming out of the switch. If the test light lights with the jumper wire installed, the switch or whatever was bypassed is defective.

NOTE: *Never substitute the jumper wire for the bulb, as the bulb is the component required to use the power from the power source.*

5. If the bulb in the test light goes on, then the current is getting to the bulb that is not working in the vehicle. This eliminates the first of the three possible causes. Connect the power supply wire and connect a jumper wire from the bulb to a good metal ground. Do this with the switch which controls the bulb turned on, and also the ignition switch turned on if it is required for the light to work. If the bulb works with the jumper wire installed, then it has a bad ground. This is usually caused by the metal area on which the bulb mounts to the car being coated with some type of foreign matter or rust.

6. If neither test located the source of the

trouble, then the light bulb itself is defective.

The above test procedure can be applied to any of the components of the chassis electrical system by substituting the component that is not working for the light bulb. Remember that for any electrical system to work, all connections must be clean and tight.

HEATING AND AIR CONDITIONING SYSTEM

The heater core and blower on most models are contained in the heater box (fresh air housing) located in the center of the passenger compartment under the dashboard. On air conditioned Golfs, Foxs, Rabbits, Jettas, GTIs and Sciroccos, the evaporator is located in the heater box. On air conditioned Dashers and most Quantums the evaporator is located under the hood separate from the heater box.

The blower fan on non-air conditioned models before 1977 is open bladed, much like an airplane propeller. The blower fan on all air conditioned models and non-air conditioned models after 1977 is of the turbine type.

On some models, the fan and core can be removed without removing the heater box. The fan should be accessible from under the hood on these models, while the heater core is accessible from inside the passenger compartment.

CAUTION: *When working on air conditioning components, use extreme caution. The system is filled with refrigerant which is poisonous if mixed with an open flame, and can freeze your skin if allowed to contact it. Be careful!*

Heater Case

REMOVAL AND INSTALLATION

Without Center Console

1. Disconnect the battery ground cable.
2. Drain the cooling system.
3. Remove the windshield washer container from its mounts and remove the ignition coil only if they restrict your access to the heater components under the hood.
4. Disconnect the two hoses from the heater core connections at the firewall.
5. Unplug the blower fan electrical connections. Some models are equipped with an external series resistor mounted on the heater box. Do not try to remove the wires from the resistor.
6. Remove the heater control knobs on the dash.
7. Remove the two retaining screws and remove the controls from the dash complete with brackets.

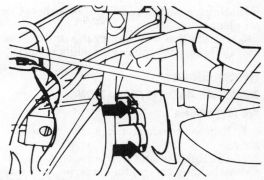

Heater hose connections at the firewall

8. Some models have a cable attached to a lever which is operated by a round knob on the dashboard. Remove the cable from the lever.
9. Remove either the clips or the screws holding the heater box in place and remove the heater box with the heater controls.
10. Installation is the reverse of removal. Be sure to refill the cooling system.

When installing the new type of housing in Rabbits and Sciroccos originally equipped with the older model heater box, proceed as follows:

Make a hole by cutting along the line (w). Clip the connections after installing the new air outlet pipe and seal the joint with a suitable adhesive.

With Center Console

1. Disconnect the negative battery cable.
2. Drain the engine coolant.
NOTE: *Save the coolant for reuse.*
3. Trace the heater hoses coming from the firewall and disconnect them. One leads to the back of the cylinder head and the other leads to the heater valve located above and behind the oil filter.
4. Detach the cable for the heater valve.
5. Remove the center console.
6. Remove the left and right covers below the instrument panel.
7. Pull off the fresh air/heater control knobs.
8. Pull off the trim plate.
9. Remove the screws for the controls.
10. Remove the center cover mounting screws and remove the cover.
11. Detach the right, left and center air ducts.
12. Remove the heater housing retaining spring.
13. Remove the cowl for the air plenum which is located under the hood and in front of the windshield.
14. Remove the heater housing mounting screws and remove the heater housing. The

mounting screws are under the hood where the air plenum was.

15. Installation is in the reverse order of removal. Be sure to replace all sealing material.

Heater Blower

REMOVAL AND INSTALLATION

Pre-1977 Models

1. Remove the heater box. See procedure above.

2. On Rabbits and Scirocco, remove the screws holding the heater cover in place and remove the heater cover. Remove the circular cutoff flap by unhooking it from its hinge. On Dashers, remove the heater cover by pulling out its pins.

3. On the Rabbit and Scirocco, the heater blower should pull right out of the asssembly.

4. On Dashers, remove the clips holding the heater box halves together and separate the halves. The fan should just pull out.

5. Installation is the reverse of removal.

NOTE: *On the Dasher, when installing the fan in the heater box halves, make sure the wiring connections on the fan face the wiring harness on the heater box. Also, when jointing the housing halves, make sure there is no side to side play in the blower motor.*

1977 and Later Models

1. Remove the heater unit from the vehicle. See above for procedures.

2. Remove the screws holding the cover on the heater box and remove the cover. Remove the blower motor cover, if so equipped.

3. Remove the electrical connections from the blower motor after matchmarking them to insure that you assemble them in the correct order.

4. Remove the clamp or screws holding the motor in place and remove the motor.

5. Installation is the reverse of removal.

Heater Core

REMOVAL AND INSTALLATION

NOTE: *On some 1977 and later models, it is possible to remove the heater core without removing the heater box. Proceed as follows:*

1. Remove the heater box from the vehicle.

2. If the unit has a core cover in its side, remove the screws or unclip the cover and remove it. The core should pull out.

3. On other models, remove the heater box clips that hold the two halves of the heater box together, separate the halves after removing any components that are in the way, and remove the heater core.

Cut hole along line (W)—Rabbit, Scirocco

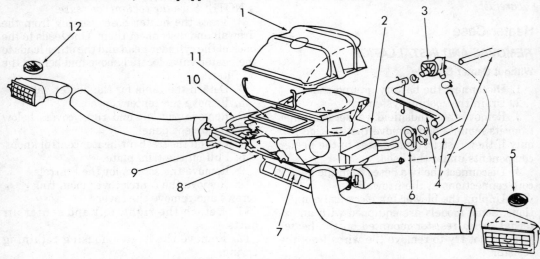

1. Heater cover	5. Vent for side windows	9. Heater controls
2. Main heater assembly	6. Double grommet	10. Cutoff flap cable
3. Heater valve	7. Control flap cable	11. Fresh air housing
4. Heater hoses	8. Heater valve cable	12. Vent for side windows

Dasher heater assembly

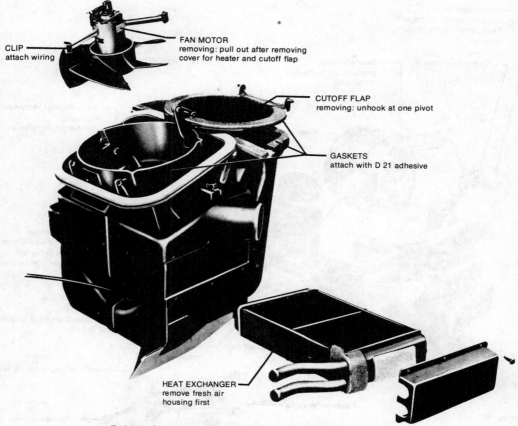

CLIP
attach wiring

FAN MOTOR
removing: pull out after removing
cover for heater and cutoff flap

CUTOFF FLAP
removing: unhook at one pivot

GASKETS
attach with D 21 adhesive

HEAT EXCHANGER
remove fresh air
housing first

Rabbit, Scirocco heat exchanger and fan motor—to 1977

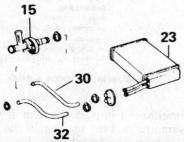

Rabbit, Scirocco and Jetta heater core (23), hoses (30 and 32), and heater control valve (15)

RADIO

NOTE: *Most radios are a dealer installed option.*

REMOVAL AND INSTALLATION

1. Remove the knobs from the radio.
2. Remove the nuts from the radio control shafts.
3. Detach the antenna lead from the jack on the radio case.

CAUTION: *Never operate the radio without a speaker; severe damage to the output transistor will result. If the speaker must be replaced, use a speaker of the correct impedance (ohms) or else the output transistors will be damaged and require replacement.*

4. Detach the power and speaker leads.
5. Remove the radio support nuts and bolts.
6. Withdraw the radio from beneath the dashboard.
7. Installation is performed in the reverse order of removal.

WINDSHIELD WIPERS

Wiper Refill
REPLACEMENT

1. Pull the wiper arms up off the windshield.
2. Using a pair of pliers, squeeze the two steel inserts at the open end of the blade.
3. Pull the insert of the rubber filler.
4. Remove the rubber filler.
5. Insert the new rubber filler making sure

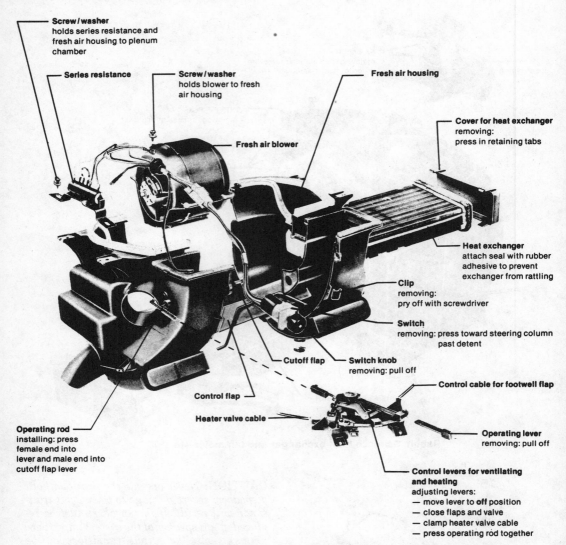

Screw/washer holds series resistance and fresh air housing to plenum chamber

Series resistance

Screw/washer holds blower to fresh air housing

Fresh air housing

Fresh air blower

Cover for heat exchanger removing: press in retaining tabs

Heat exchanger attach seal with rubber adhesive to prevent exchanger from rattling

Clip removing: pry off with screwdriver

Switch removing: press toward steering column past detent

Switch knob removing: pull off

Cutoff flap

Control flap

Control cable for footwell flap

Heater valve cable

Operating lever removing: pull off

Operating rod installing: press female end into lever and male end into cutoff flap lever

Control levers for ventilating and heating adjusting levers:
— move lever to **off** position
— close flaps and valve
— clamp heater valve cable
— press operating rod together

1977 and later Dasher heater assembly—1977 and later Rabbit, Jetta, Scirocco similar

that the retainers engage the recesses in the second grooves.

6. Slide the metal inserts into the upper grooves of the rubber blade so that the notch in the insert faces the rubber. Engage the projections in grooves on both sides.

Arms

REMOVAL AND INSTALLATION

NOTE: *There are two different styles of wiper arms. On the first, the arm pivot attaching nut is covered with a plastic cap that pulls off. On the second, the arm pivot is covered by a spring-loaded metal cap that slips back off the nut.*

1. Lift the blade and arm up off the windshield.

2. Simultaneously push the arm down and lift the smaller end cap up, or pull the plastic cap off, to expose the retaining nut.

3. Remove the retaining nut and lift the arm off the shaft.

4. Install the arm in the reverse order of removal. When properly installed, the blades should be as shown.

Front Motor

REMOVAL AND INSTALLATION

Dasher, Fox and Quantum

NOTE: *Do not remove the wiper drive crank from the wiper motor shaft. If it must be removed for any reason, matchmark the shaft, motor and crank for installation.*

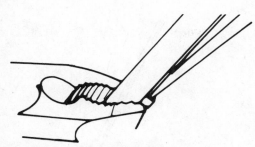

Squeezing the wiper blade insert

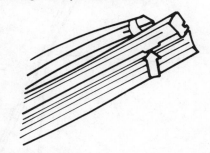

Notch in blade insert

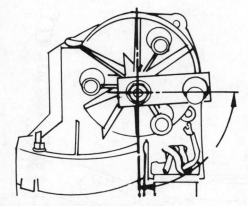

Dasher wiper motor-to-arm angle

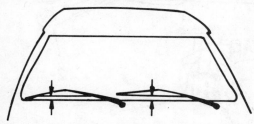

Blade-to-molding distance should be 1⅜ in. for both wipers on the Dasher and for the Rabbit's and Jetta's driver's side, and 1 in. on the Scirocco driver's side. Passenger's side should be 2½ in. on Rabbit, and Jetta, 1³/₁₆ in. on Scirocco. Single blade Scirocco is 2³/₁₆ in.

1. Unplug the multiconnector from the wiper motor.

2. Remove the motor-to-linkage bracket retaining screws.

3. Carefully pry the motor crank out of the two linkage arms.

4. Remove the motor from the car.

5. Install the motor in the reverse order of removal. The crank arm should be at a right angle to the motor.

Golf, Rabbit, Scirocco, Jetta and GTI

When removing the wiper motor, leave the mounting frame in place. On all models with two front wiper arms, do not remove the wiper drive crank from the motor shaft.

On Sciroccos with one front wiper arm, matchmark the drive crank and motor arm and then remove the arm.

NOTE: *If, for any reason you must remove the wiper drive crank from the motor shaft on two wiper arm models, matchmark both parts for reassembly.*

1. Access is with the hood open. Disconnect the battery ground cable.

2. Detach the connecting rods or motor crank arm from the motor.

3. Pull off the wiring plug.

4. Remove the four mounting bolts. You may have to energize the motor for access to the top bolt.

5. Remove the motor. Reverse the procedure for installation.

Rear Motor

There are 2 kinds of rear wiper motors used on Rabbits. Until 1976, a gear housing with a smooth cover plate was used; later models used a ribbed gear housing. Parts are different and cannot be combined between the two systems, except that the new style wiper motor bracket can be installed on earlier models. Sciroccos' motors are totally interchangeable, and their linkage remains unchanged.

Dasher Fox and Quantum station wagons are also equipped with rear windshield wipers (optional).

NOTE: *On all models, do not interchange the wires of terminal 53 and 53a on the rear wiper switch. Damage to the motor will result.*

INSTRUMENTS AND SWITCHES

Instrument Cluster

REMOVAL AND INSTALLATION

Dasher

THROUGH 1977

1. Disconnect the battery ground cable.

2. Unscrew the speedometer cable from the rear of the cluster.

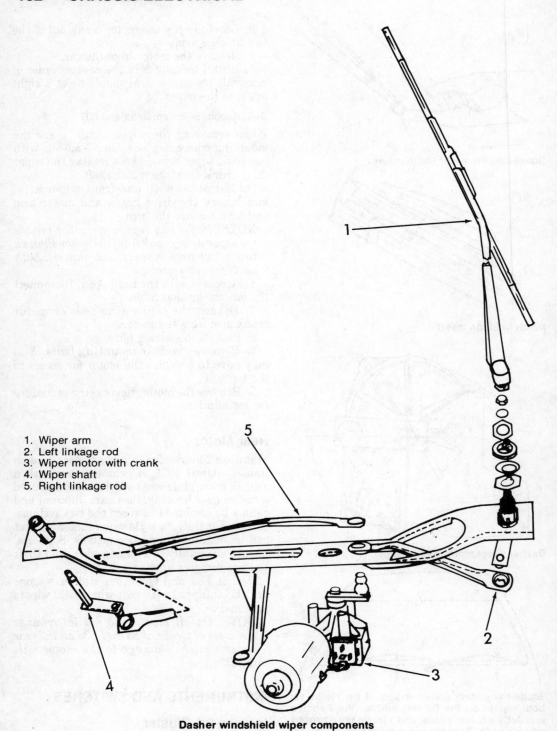

1. Wiper arm
2. Left linkage rod
3. Wiper motor with crank
4. Wiper shaft
5. Right linkage rod

Dasher windshield wiper components

3. Using needle nosed pliers, detach the retaining springs on either side of the clustesr.
4. Pivot the instrument cluster out of the dash.

5. Disconnect the multi-connector plug at the rear of the cluster.
6. Remove the cluster from the dash.
7. Installation is the reverse of removal.

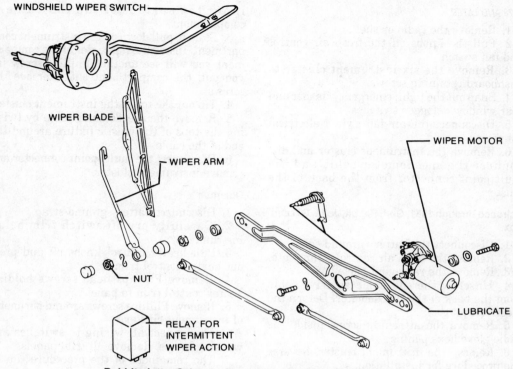

WINDSHIELD WIPER SWITCH

WIPER BLADE

WIPER ARM

NUT

WIPER MOTOR

LUBRICATE

RELAY FOR
INTERMITTENT
WIPER ACTION

Rabbit, Jetta, Scirocco front wiper motor and linkage

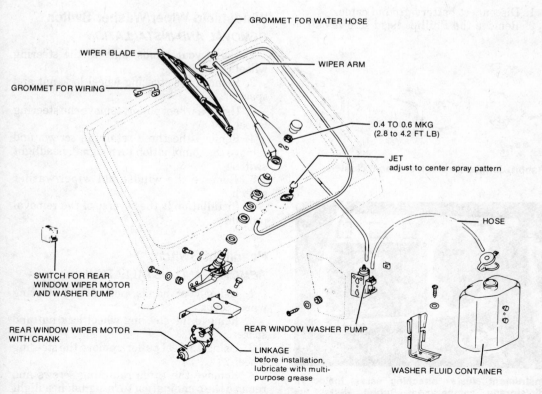

GROMMET FOR WATER HOSE

WIPER BLADE

WIPER ARM

GROMMET FOR WIRING

0.4 TO 0.6 MKG
(2.8 to 4.2 FT LB)

JET
adjust to center spray pattern

HOSE

SWITCH FOR REAR
WINDOW WIPER MOTOR
AND WASHER PUMP

REAR WINDOW WASHER PUMP

REAR WINDOW WIPER MOTOR
WITH CRANK

LINKAGE
before installation,
lubricate with multi-
purpose grease

WASHER FLUID CONTAINER

Rabbit, Scirocco rear wiper motor and linkage

1978 AND LATER

1. Remove the radio or shelf.
2. Pull the knobs off the fresh air control and fan switch.
3. Remove the six instrument cluster to dashboard retaining screws.
4. Snap out the light, emergency flasher and rear window defogger switches.
5. Disconnect the air fan switch electrical connector.
6. Remove the instrument cluster and disconnect the speedometer cable and the multipoint connector from the back of the cluster.

Scirocco through 1981, Golf, Rabbit, Jetta, GTI and Fox

1. Disconnect the battery ground cable.
2. Remove the fresh air controls trim plate.
3. Remove the radio and glove box.
4. Unscrew the speedometer drive cable from the back of the speedometer. Detach the electrical plug.
5. Remove the attaching screw inside the radio/glove box opening.
6. Remove the instrument cluster. Reverse the procedure for installation.

1982 and Later Scirocco

1. Disconnect battery ground cable.
2. Remove the Phillips head screws on the

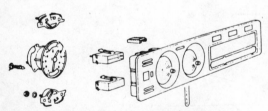

Rabbit, Jetta, Scirocco instrument cluster

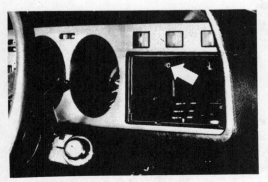

Instrument cluster attaching screw inside radio/storage compartment—Rabbit, Jetta, Scirocco

inner top surface of the instrument compartment.
3. Start to pull down on the instrument compartment. Inside the top center of the compartment you will see another Phillips screw (as you pull the compartment out). Remove the screws.
4. Tip out the top of the instrument cluster.
5. Remove the speedometer cable by twisting the tabs of the plastic fixture around the end of the cable.
6. Disconnect the multi-point connector and remove instrument cluster.

Quantum

1. Disconnect battery ground strap.
2. Carefully pry off switch trim below instruments.
3. Pull heater control knobs off and press out heater control trim.
4. Remove Phillips head screws holding heater control trim to panel.
5. Remove Phillips screws around perimeter of instrument cluster.
6. Disconnect all wiring to switches and warning lamps. Remove all trim panels.
7. The remainder of the procedure can be completed by following the Scirocco (from 1982) procedure beginning at Step 3.

Windshield Wiper/Washer Switch
REMOVAL AND INSTALLATION

1. Using your hands, pull off the steering wheel cover.
2. Remove the steering wheel lock nut and spacer.
3. Using a wheel puller, remove the steering wheel.
4. Remove the three retaining screws and remove the combination turn signal, headlight switch.
5. Remove the windshield wiper/washer switch.
6. Installation is the reverse of the removal procedure.

Headlight Switch
REMOVAL AND INSTALLATION

1. Using your hands, pull off the steering wheel cover.
2. Remove the steering wheel lock nut and spacer.
3. Using a wheel puller, remove the steering wheel.
4. Remove the three retaining screws and remove the combination turn signal, headlight switch.

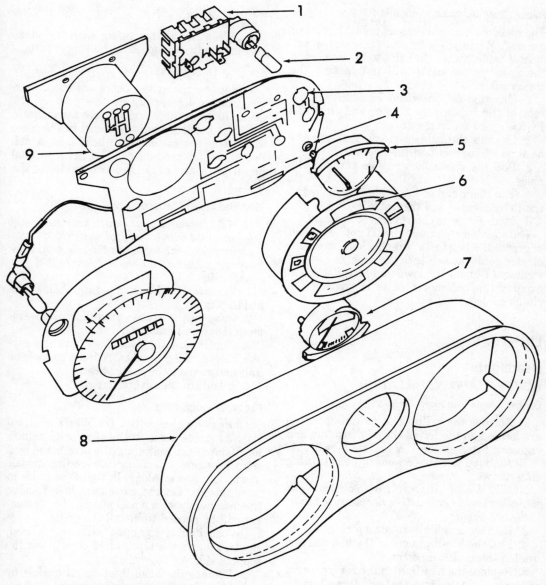

1. Voltage stabilizer
2. Bulb
3. Printed circuit board
4. Washer
5. Fuel gauge
6. Trim plate
7. Coolant temperature gauge
8. Instrument cluster
9. Cover

Dasher instrument cluster

5. Installation is the reverse of the removal procedure.

Speedometer Cable

REMOVAL AND INSTALLATION

Dasher, Fox and Quantum

1. Unscrew the speedometer cable from the rear of the instrument cluster.

2. Unsnap the rubber grommets from the dash panel support and the firewall.

3. Pull the speedometer cable through the holes from the engine compartment.

4. Use pliers to unscrew the cable from the transaxle.

NOTE: *Some models may have the EGR mileage counter box mounted between the speedometer and the transmission. In this case the speedometer cable is unscrewed from the EGR box*

5. Installation is the reverse of removal.

Rabbit, Golf, Scirocco, Jetta and GTI

The speedometer cable should not be kinked or greased. When installing the Scirocco speedometer cable, attach the cable to the bracket so the speedometer cable will not contact the clutch cable.

1. Unscrew the spesedometer cable from the rear of the instrument cluster and from the EGR elapsed mileage counter.

2. Unsnap the rubber grommets from the dash panel support and the firewall.

3. Pull the speedometer cable through the holes.

4. The other end of the cable is attached to the EGR counter and transaxle.

5. Installation is the reverse of removal.

The speedometer cable should not be kinked or greased. When installing the Scirocco speedometer cable, attach it to the bracket (see Instrument Cluster Removal and Installation) to avoid the speedometer cable contacting the clutch cable.

LIGHTING

Headlights

REMOVAL AND INSTALLATION

Dasher Single Headlight Models

1. Remove the grille. The retaining screws are located on the left of the VW insignia and one each between the VW and the headlight.

2. Remove the three headlight retaining ring screws.

NOTE: *Do not disturb the two headlight aiming screws or it will be necessary to reaim the headlights.*

3. Remove headlight retaining ring.

4. Pull the headlight out of the housing and unplug the multiconnector.

5. Replace the new bulb in the reverse order of removal. Make sure that the three lugs on the bulb engage the slots in the housing.

Dasher Dual Headlight Models

1. Remove the radiator grille. Pry up the two retaining clips, one located at each end of the top of the grille. Unsnap the four plastic tabs along the top of the grille and remove it.

2. Remove the three small screws and remove the retaining ring. Don't fiddle with the spring loaded adjusting screws or you will have to have the light reamed. Pull the light out and unhook it.

3. When installing new headlight, be aware that the outside lights have both high beam and low beam filaments while the inside lights have only high beam filaments. Be sure to

mention which one you need when buying replacement.

4. When installing, make sure the glass lugs on the light engage in the support ring.

Scirocco Through 1981

1. Remove the grille. There are about fourteen screws located inside the grids of the grille. Remove these and remove the grille.

2. The headlights are removed in the same manner as the Dasher dual headlight model. See above for procedures. The Scirocco dual headlights are arranged the same as the Dasher.

1982 and Later Scirocco

NOTE: *Depending on model, your car could be equipped with either Halogen sealed beam or incandescent sealed beam units. Always replace a burned out sealed beam with a new like unit.*

1. Remove the black moldings below the headlights.

2. Remove the screws retaining the headlamp mounting bracket.

3. Gently pull the headlamp from the support, unplug the connector from the back of the unit and remove the sealed beam.

4. Install in the reverse order.

Rabbit Through 1980

1. Remove the grille. On Westmoreland Rabbits (those made in the U.S., with square headlamps), the radiator grille is retained by 2 snap tabs and 4 fasteners on earlier models and by four screws along the top of the grille on later models. On the earlier models, remove the fasteners with a small punch. New fasteners will be needed to install the grille.

On the Rabbit equipped with round headlights, remove the screws and clips along the top and sides of the grille.

2. Remove the head light on all models by removing the retaining ring screws and removing the ring and the light. Unhook the electrical connector.

3. When installing new light, be sure to

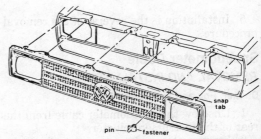

Grille and retaining pins used on Westmoreland Rabbits

Remove the grille retaining screws

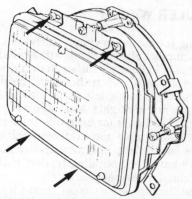

Remove the screws (arrows) holding the trim ring on Jetta and Westmoreland Rabbits. Do not disturb the headlight aiming screws (top and right side)

align the lugs in the light with their positions in the frame.

1981 and Later Rabbit and 1987 Fox

NOTE: *Depending on model, your vehicle could be equipped with either Halogen sealed beam or incandescent sealed beam units. Always replace a burned out sealed beam with a new like unit.*

ROUND SEALED BEAM

1. Remove the screws and clips along the top and side of the grille and remove the grille.
2. Remove the three retaining screws that hold the headlamp mounting bracket.
3. Gently pull the headlamp from the support, unplug the connector from the back of the unit and remove the sealbeam.
4. Install in the reverse order.

RECTANGULAR SEALED BEAM

1. Remove the four screws located around the headlamp trim cover and remove the cover.
2. Remove the four screws retaining the headlamp mounting bracket.
3. Gently pull the headlamp from the support, unplug the connector from the back of the unit and remove the sealed beam.
4. Install in the reverse order.

Jetta and GTI

Remove the grille by removing the two screws and the clip, swinging the side grille forward and lifting it out of the lower support holders. Remove the four screws in the face of the ring and remove the headlight after unhooking its electrical connector. When inserting new light, make sure the lugs in the light align with their supports in the ring.

Be aware when buying new headlights that the two inner lights have only high beam fila-

Screws at points (A) remove headlight. Screws at points (B) are used for aiming

ments while the outer two have both low and high beam filaments.

Quantum

NOTE: *Never substitute and incandescent sealed beam for one of the Halogen design.*

1. Open the hood. Loosen the lower parking/signal lamp retaining screws until the cover lens can be removed.
2. Remove the two lower and one upper screws that retain the headlamp trim housing.
3. Remove the four screws that mount the headlamp retaining bracket.
4. Gently pull the headlamp from the support, unplug the connector from the back of the sealed beam.
5. Install in the reverse order.

TRAILER WIRING

Wiring the car for towing is fairly easy. There are a number of good wiring kits available and these should be used, rather than trying to design your own. All trailers will need brake lights and turn signals as well as tail lights and side marker lights. Most states require extra marker lights for overwide trailers. Also, most states have recently required back-up lights for trailers, and most trailer manufacturers have been building trailers with back-up lights for several years.

Additionally, some Class I, most Class II and just about all Class III trailers will have electric brakes.

Add to this number an accessories wire, to operate trailer internal equipment or to charge the trailer's battery, and you can have as many as seven wires in the harness.

Determine the equipment on your trailer and buy the wiring kit necessary. The kit will contain all the wires needed, plus a plug adapter set which included the female plug, mounted on the bumper or hitch, and the male plug, wired into, or plugged into the trailer harness.

When installing the kit, follow the manufacturer's instructions. The color coding of the wires is standard throughout the industry.

One point to note: some domestic vehicles, and most imported vehicles, have separate turn signals. On most domestic vehicles, the brake lights and rear turn signals operate with the same bulb. For those vehicles with separate turn signals, you can purchase an isolation unit so that the brake lights won't blink whenever the turn signals are operated, or, you can go to your local electronics supply house and buy four diodes to wire in series with the brake and turn signal bulbs. Diodes will isolate the brake and turn signals. The choice is yours. The isolation units are simple and quick to install, but far more expensive than the diodes. The diodes, however, require more work to install properly, since they require the cutting of each bulb's wire and soldering in place of the diode.

One, final point, the best kits are those with a spring loaded cover on the vehicle mounted socket. This cover prevent dirt and moisture from corroding the terminals. Never let the vehicle socket hang loosely; always mount it securely to the bumper or hitch.

CIRCUIT PROTECTION

The 1975–87 Dasher and the 1987 Fox fuse/relay panel is located under the hood on the driver's side fender. The fuse/relay panel on all other models is located in the lower left side of the dashboard. Use VW ceramic fuses. VW recommends that relays be replaced by your dealer.

Fuses

Fuses are listed according to numbers on the fuse box cover.

WIRING DIAGRAMS

Wiring diagrams have been left out of this book. As cars have become more complex, and available with longer and longer option lists, wiring diagrams have grown in size and complexity also. It has become virtually impossible to provide a readable reproduction in a reasonable number of pages.

ts

ıtion

ıe

ılb

titution

Troubleshooting Basic Lighting Problems

Problem	Cause	Solution
Lights		
One or more lights don't work, but others do	• Defective bulb(s) • Blown fuse(s) • Dirty fuse clips or light sockets • Poor ground circuit	• Replace bulb(s) • Replace fuse(s) • Clean connections • Run ground wire from light socket housing to car frame
Lights burn out quickly	• Incorrect voltage regulator setting or defective regulator • Poor battery/alternator connections	• Replace voltage regulator • Check battery/alternator connections
Lights go dim	• Low/discharged battery • Alternator not charging • Corroded sockets or connections • Low voltage output	• Check battery • Check drive belt tension; repair or replace alternator • Clean bulb and socket contacts and connections • Replace voltage regulator
Lights flicker	• Loose connection • Poor ground • Circuit breaker operating (short circuit)	• Tighten all connections • Run ground wire from light housing to car frame • Check connections and look for bare wires
Lights "flare"—Some flare is normal on acceleration—if excessive, see "Lights Burn Out Quickly"	• High voltage setting	• Replace voltage regulator
Lights glare—approaching drivers are blinded	• Lights adjusted too high • Rear springs or shocks sagging • Rear tires soft	• Have headlights aimed • Check rear springs/shocks • Check/correct rear tire pressure
Turn Signals		
Turn signals don't work in either direction	• Blown fuse • Defective flasher • Loose connection	• Replace fuse • Replace flasher • Check/tighten all connections
Right (or left) turn signal only won't work	• Bulb burned out • Right (or left) indicator bulb burned out • Short circuit	• Replace bulb • Check/replace indicator bulb • Check/repair wiring
Flasher rate too slow or too fast	• Incorrect wattage bulb • Incorrect flasher	• Flasher bulb • Replace flasher (use a variable load flasher if you pull a trailer)
Indicator lights do not flash (burn steadily)	• Burned out bulb • Defective flasher	• Replace bulb • Replace flasher
Indicator lights do not light at all	• Burned out indicator bulb • Defective flasher	• Replace indicator bulb • Replace flasher

Troubleshooting Basic Dash Gauge Problems

Problem	Cause	Solution
Coolant Temperature Gauge		
Gauge reads erratically or not at all	• Loose or dirty connections • Defective sending unit	• Clean/tighten connections • Bi-metal gauge: remove the wire from the sending unit. Ground the wire for an instant. If the gauge registers, replace the sending unit.

Troubleshooting Basic Dash Gauge Problems (cont.)

Problem	Cause	Solution
Coolant Temperature Gauge (cont.)		
Gauge reads erratically or not at all (cont.)	• Defective gauge	• Magnetic gauge: disconnect the wire at the sending unit. With ignition ON gauge should register COLD. Ground the wire; gauge should register HOT.
Ammeter Gauge—Turn Headlights ON (do not start engine). Note reaction		
Ammeter shows charge	• Connections reversed on gauge	• Reinstall connections
Ammeter shows discharge	• Ammeter is OK	• Nothing
Ammeter does not move	• Loose connections or faulty wiring	• Check/correct wiring
	• Defective gauge	• Replace gauge
Oil Pressure Gauge		
Gauge does not register or is inaccurate	• On mechanical gauge, Bourdon tube may be bent or kinked	• Check tube for kinks or bends preventing oil from reaching the gauge
	• Low oil pressure	• Remove sending unit. Idle the engine briefly. If no oil flows from sending unit hole, problem is in engine.
	• Defective gauge	• Remove the wire from the sending unit and ground it for an instant with the ignition ON. A good gauge will go to the top of the scale.
	• Defective wiring	• Check the wiring to the gauge. If it's OK and the gauge doesn't register when grounded, replace the gauge.
	• Defective sending unit	• If the wiring is OK and the gauge functions when grounded, replace the sending unit
All Gauges		
All gauges do not operate	• Blown fuse	• Replace fuse
	• Defective instrument regulator	• Replace instrument voltage regulator
All gauges read low or erratically	• Defective or dirty instrument voltage regulator	• Clean contacts or replace
All gauges pegged	• Loss of ground between instrument voltage regulator and car	• Check ground
	• Defective instrument regulator	• Replace regulator
Warning Lights		
Light(s) do not come on when ignition is ON, but engine is not started	• Defective bulb	• Replace bulb
	• Defective wire	• Check wire from light to sending unit
	• Defective sending unit	• Disconnect the wire from the sending unit and ground it. Replace the sending unit if the light comes on with the ignition ON.
Light comes on with engine running	• Problem in individual system	• Check system
	• Defective sending unit	• Check sending unit (see above)

Troubleshooting the Turn Signal Switch (cont.)

Problem	Cause	Solution
Hazard signal lights will not flash—turn signal functions normally (cont.)	• Disconnect column to chassis connector. Connect new switch into system without removing old. Depress the hazard warning lights. If they now work normally, turn signal switch is defective.	• Replace turn signal switch
	• If lights do not flash, check wiring harness "K" lead for open between hazard flasher and connector. If open, fuse block is defective	• Repair or replace brown wire or connector as required

Drive Train

✚6

MANUAL TRANSAXLE

From 1974–1984 a four speed manual transaxle was standard on the Rabbit (except convertible), Dasher and Scirocco with a five speed transaxle available as an option. The Rabbit convertible and the Jetta come standard with the five speed transmission. In 1985 the five speed manual transaxle became standard equipment on all models except the 1987 Fox. A four speed manual transmission is standard equipment on this model. A three speed automatic is optional on all models except the Fox.

Transaxle describes a unit which combines the transmission gears and the drive axle gears in one housing. Volkswagen is a past master at this type of assembly, it being the design used in the VW Beetle for over thirty years. Besides being mounted in the front of the vehicle instead of the rear as in the Beetle, the Rabbit, Jetta and Scirocco transaxle is rather unconventional in that it is mounted side by side with the engine. The Dasher and Fox transaxle is mounted behind the engine, much like a conventional automobile engine/transmission layout, except that the differential is mounted ahead of the transmission.

Because of the complexity of the transaxle, no overhaul procedures are given in this book. However, transaxle removal, installation and adjustment, and halfshaft removal and installation are covered.

Adjustments

SHIFT LINKAGE

Dasher to Chassis No. 3–5 2 044 764

1. Shift into Neutral.
2. Remove the round floor cover.
3. Loosen the nuts and move the bearing housing so that the shift lever inclines approximately 5° to the rear.
4. Tighten the nuts.

5. Shift into second gear.
6. Loosen the stop plate bolts.
7. Adjust the plate so that the shift lever has ⅜–⅝″ lateral movement at the shift knob.
   NOTE: *Moving the plate to the right in-*

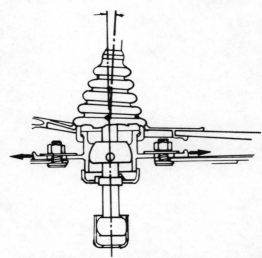

Neutral adjustment—Dasher to chassis no. 3-5 2 044 764

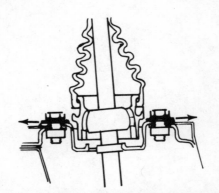

Second gear adjustment—Dasher to chassis 3-5 044 764

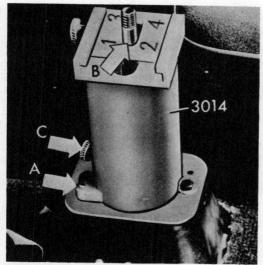

VW tool 3014 used to adjust shift linkage on later Dashers

creases play; moving the plate to the left decreases play.

8. Tighten the bolts. Check the shift pattern and make sure that reverse engages easily.

Dasher from Chassis No. 3–5 2 044 765 and Quantum

An adjusting tool, VW 3014, must be used on these models.

1. Place the lever in Neutral.

2. Working under the car, loosen the clamp nut.

3. Inside the car, remove the gear lever knob and the shift boot. It is not necessary to remove the console. Align the centering holes of the lever housing and the lever bearing housing.

4. Install the tool with the locating pin toward the front. Push the lever to the left side of the tool cutout. Tighten the lower knurled knob to secure the tool.

5. Move the top slide of the tool to the left stop and tighten the upper knurled knob.

6. Push the shift lever to the right side of the cutout. Align the shift rod and shift finger under the car, and tighten the clamp nut. Remove the tool.

7. Place the lever in first. Press the lever to the left side against the stop. Release the lever: it should spring back ¼–½". If not, move the lever housing slightly sideways to correct. Check that all gears can be engaged easily, particularly reverse.

Fox

1. Shift into Neutral.

2. Remove the gear shift lever knob and shift boot.

3. Loosen the clamp nuts and check that shift finger slides freely on the shift rod.

4. Move the gear shift lever to the right side, between third and fourth gear position. The gear shift lever should remain perpendicular to the ball housing.

5. With the inner shift lever in neutral and the gear shift lever between second and third gear, tighten the clamp nut.

6. Check the engagement of all gears, including reverse, and make sure that the gear shift lever moves freely.

Rabbit, Scirocco and Jetta
WITH ADJUSTABLE LINKAGE

1. Adjust the long rod over the left driveshaft coupling to a length of 6.42–6.50".

2. Adjust the short angle rod that attaches to the final drive housing to a length of 1.18–1.25".

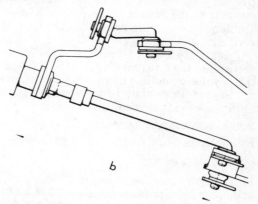

The long rod on the Rabbit and Scirocco shift linkage is to be adjusted to a length (b) of 6.42–6.50 in.

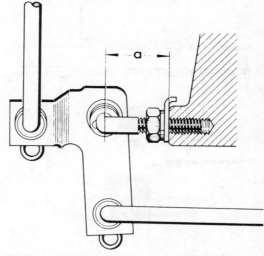

Adjust the relay lever (a) to 1.18–1.25 in. Rabbit and Scirocco with adjustable linkage

Adjusting gear shift lever, Rabbit and Scirocco with adjustable linkage

Adjusting the shift rod end: 1977 and later Rabbit, Jetta, Scirocco

3. Make the lower part of the floorshift lever vertical (in the side to side plane) in the first gear position by loosening the bearing plate that supports the end of the long shift rod that connects to the bottom of the floorshift lever. Tighten the mounting nuts when the lever is vertical.

4. Make the lower part of the floorshift lever vertical (in the fore and aft plane) in the Neutral position by pulling up the boot and loosening the two lever plate bolts. Move the plate until the lever is vertical.

MODELS WITH NONADJUSTABLE LINKAGE

Follow Steps 3 and 4 of the 1975 procedure.

1977 AND LATER MODELS

This category includes some late 1976 models, and is for Rabbits from chassis no. 176 3 000 001, Sciroccos from chassis no. 536 2 000 001 and all Jettas.

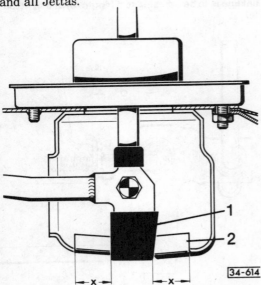

1977 and later Rabbit, Jetta and Scirocco—shift finger (1) must be in the center of the stopping gate (2)

1. Align the holes of the lever housing plate with the holes of the lever bearing plate. With the shifter in neutral.

2. Loosen the shift rod clamp so that the selector lever moves easily on the shift rod. On four speed transmissions, pull the boot off the lever housing under the car and push it out of the way. It may be necessary to loosen the screws in the coverplate to free the boot.

3. Check that the shift finger (the rubber covered protrusion at the bottom of the shifter) is in the center of the stopping plate.

4. Adjust the shift rod end so that (A) is $\frac{3}{4}$" ($\frac{9}{32}$" for 5-speed transmissions). Tighten the shift rod clamp and check the shifter operation.

SELECTOR SHAFT LOCKBOLT ADJUSTMENT

Rabbit, Scirocco, Jetta Only

These selector shaft lockbolt adjustments are for Rabbits, Sciroccos and Jettas only. The adjustments are the same for both four and five speed manual transmissions.

NOTE: *For five speed transmission fifth gear lockbolt adjustment, see the following section.*

Make this adjustment if, after completing the linkage adjustment, the linkage still feels spongy or jams. There are 2 kinds of lockbolts: those with plastic caps (1975) or those with lockrings (1976 and later). The lockbolt is located on the top of the transmission.

1975 Models

1. Remove the linkage from the selector shaft lever and put the transmission in Neutral.

2. Turn the slotted plunger until the plunger hits bottom. The nut will start to move out.

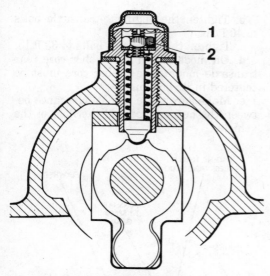

On 1975 Rabbit, Scirocco, turn the plunger (1) until the nut (2) starts to move

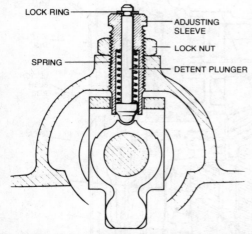

On 1976 and later Rabbit, Jetta, Scirocco, loosen the locknut and turn the adjusting sleeve

3. From here, turn the plunger back ¼ turn and install the plastic cap.

4. Reconnect the linkage.

1976 and Later Models

1. Disconnect the shift linkage and put the transmission in Neutral.

2. Loosen the locknut and turn the adjusting sleeve in until the lockring lifts off the sleeve.

3. Turn the adjusting sleeve back until the lockring just contacts the sleeve. Tighten the locknut.

4. Turn the shaft slightly. The lockring should lift as soon as the shaft is turned.

5. Reconnect the linkage.

FIFTH GEAR LOCKBOLT ADJUSTMENT

Rabbit, Scirocco, Jetta Only

This adjustment is made with the transmission in neutral. The fifth gear lockbolt is located on top of the transmission next to the selector shaft lockbolt. It has a large protective cap over it.

1. Remove the protective cap.

2. Loosen the locknut and tighten the adjusting sleeve until the detent plunger in the center of the sleeve just begins to move up.

3. Loosen the adjusting sleeve ⅓ of a turn and tighten the locknut. Make sure the transmission shifts in and out of fifth gear easily. Replace the protective cap.

BACK-UP LIGHT SWITCH

The Dasher and Quantum back-up light switch is screwed into the back of the gear shift housing above the shift lever for manual transaxles.

The Fox back-up light switch is screwed into the back of the transaxle housing.

The back-up light switch on the manual Rabbit and Scirocco is mounted in one of three positions: screwed into the front face of the transaxle beside the oil filler plug; screwed into the top of the transaxle case to the left of the shift linkage; mounted as a microswitch on top of the transaxle with a lever that is activated by the external shift linkage.

The manual transaxle Jetta back-up light switch is screwed into the top of the transaxle case to the left of the shift linkage.

The Rabbit and Scirocco microswitch can be adjusted by bending the bracket. No other back-up light switch can be adjusted.

Transaxle

REMOVAL AND INSTALLATION

Dasher And Fox

1. Disconnect the battery ground cable.

2. Disconnect the exhaust pipe from the manifold and its bracket on the transaxle.

3. Remove the square-headed bolt on the shift linkage. Later models have a hex head bolt.

4. Press the shift linkage coupling off.

5. Disconnect the clutch cable.

6. Disconnect the speedometer cable.

7. Detach the axle shafts from the transaxle.

8. Remove the starter.

9. Remove the inspection plate.

10. Remove the engine-to-transaxle bolts.

11. Remove the transaxle crossmember.

12. Support the transaxle with a jack.

13. Pry the transaxle out from the engine.

14. Lift the transaxle out of the car with an assistant.

15. Installation is the reverse of removal. Observe the following when installing the transaxle.

   a. When installing the transaxle crossmember, do not fully tighten the bolts until the transaxle is aligned and fully installed in the vehicle.

   b. Tighten the engine-to-transaxle bolts to 40 ft.lb.

   c. Tighten the axle shaft bolts to 33 ft.lb.

   d. On models with the rubber core rear transaxle mount, the rubber core must be centered in its housing.

   e. Make sure there is a ⅜″ clearance between the header pipe and the floor of the vehicle.

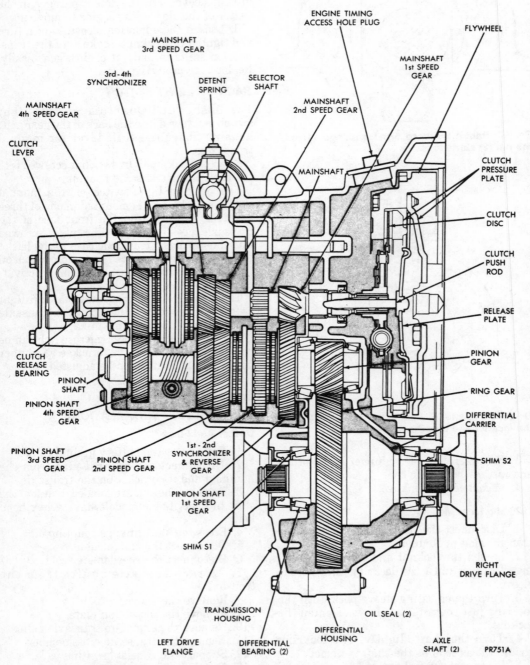

Rabbit, Scirocco, four speed manual transaxle—five speed similar

f. Adjust the clutch (see section in this chapter).

Quantum

1. Disconnect battery ground strap.
2. Disconnect exhaust pipe from the manifold and its bracket.
3. Unhook the clutch cable.
4. Detach speedometer cable.
5. Remove upper engine/transmission bolts.
6. Remove engine support bolts on both sides of engine block (front).
7. Remove front muffler and exhaust pipe.
8. Unbolt both driveshafts (halfshafts) at the transmission.
9. Disconnect back-up light wiring.
10. Remove the inspection plate on bottom of transmission case.
11. Remove starter bolt.
12. Remove shift rod coupling bolt. Pry off shift rod coupling ball with a prybar.
13. Pull off shift rod coupling from shift rod.
14. Place a jack under the transmission and lift slightly.
15. Remove transmission support bolts, and transmission rubber mounts.
16. Remove front transmission support bolts, lower transmission/engine support bolts.
17. Slowly pry transmission from engine.
18. Lower transmission out of the car.

When installing transmission in reverse order of removal, make sure mainshaft splines are clean and lubricated with a molybdenumdisulfide grease. Make sure inspection plate is properly seated, and that all engine/transmission mounting bolts are aligned and free of tension (holes lined up) before tightening everything. Readjust shift mechanism if necessary.

a. Tighten transmission-to-engine bolts to 40 ft.lb.

b. Tighten driveshaft-to-drive flange bolts to 33 ft.lb.

c. Front transmission support-to-transmission is tightened to 18 ft.lb.

d. Transmission-to-body bolts are tightened to 80 ft.lb.

Golf, Rabbit, Scirocco, Jetta, GTI

The engine and transaxle may be removed together as explained under Engine Removal and Installation or the transaxle may be removed alone, as explained here.

1. Disconnect the battery ground cable.
2. Support the left end of the engine at the lifting eye.
3. Remove the left transmission mount bolts (between the transmission and the firewall and ground strap.)
4. Turn the engine until the lug on the flywheel (to the left to the TDC mark) aligns with the flywheel timing pointer. The transmission/engine must be in this position to be separated.
5. Detach the speedometer drive cable, backup light wire, and clutch cable.
6. Remove the engine to transmission bolts.
7. Disconnect the shift linkage.
8. Detach the transmission ground strap.
9. Remove the starter.
10. Remove the engine mounting support near the starter.
11. Remove the rear transmission mount.
12. Unbolt and wire up the driveshafts.
13. From underneath, remove the bolts for the large cover plate, but don't remove it. Unbolt the small cover plate on the firewall side of the engine. Remove the engine to transmission nut immediately below the small plate.
14. Press the transmission off the dowels and remove it from below the car.

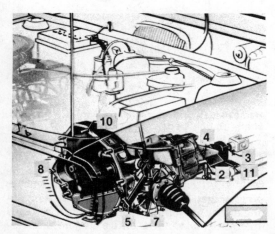

Removal points for Dasher manual transaxle

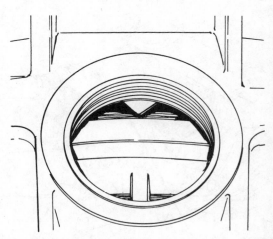

Align the lug on the flywheel with the timing pointer to remove Rabbit, Jetta, Scirocco transaxle

To install the transaxle:

15. The recess in the flywheel edge must be at 3:00 o'clock (facing the left end of the engine). Tighten the engine to transmission bolts to 47 ft.lb. Tighten the engine mounting support bolts to 47 ft.lb. Tighten the driveshaft bolts to 32 ft.lb.

16. Check the adjustment of the shift linkage.

Axle Shaft (Halfshaft)

REMOVAL AND INSTALLATION

Dasher, Fox and Quantum

NOTE: *When removing the right axle shaft, you must detach the exhaust pipe from the manifold and the transaxle bracket. Be sure to buy a new exhaust flange gasket.*

1. With the car on the ground, remove the front axle nut.

NOTE: *Use a longer breaker bar with an extension (length of pipe).*

2. Raise and support the front of the vehicle.

3. Remove the socket head bolts retaining the axle shaft to the transaxle.

NOTE: *When removing the left size axle shaft on automatic transmission models, matchmark the ball joint (left side) mounting position in relation to the lower control arm. Remove the two ball joint retaining nuts and remove the ball joint from the control arm to create room to remove the axle shaft.*

4. Pull the transaxle side of the driveshaft out and up and place it on the top of the transaxle.

5. Pull the axle shaft from the steering knuckle.

6. Installation is the reverse of removal. Tighten the transaxle bolts of 25–33 ft.lb. The

axle nut should be tightened to 145 ft.lb. (M18 nut), or 175 ft.lb. (M20 nut).

NOTE: *Be aware that the axle shafts are two different lengths on automatic transmission models with the left side axle shaft being slightly longer than the right. Manual transmission and automatic transmission axle shafts are of different lengths and should not be interchanged.*

Rabbit, Scirocco, Jetta

1. Complete steps 1 through 3 under Dasher in this section. Disregard the first NOTE.

2. Remove the bolt holding the ball joint to the steering knuckle and separate the knuckle from the ball joint.

3. Removing the ball joint from the knuckle should give enough clearance to remove the axle shaft. It pulls right out of the steering hub.

4. Installation is the reverse of removal. Tighten the axle shaft to transaxle bolts to 32 ft.lb., the ball joint bolt to 21 ft.lb. and the axle nut to 173 ft.lb. Be sure to check the alignment after work is completed.

NOTE: *The axle shafts on the Rabbit, Jetta and Scirocco differ in length from the left and right sides. The left side shaft is longer than the right side shaft. To insure that the shafts are in perfect balance with each other, the longer shaft is hollow, while the shorter shaft is solid, making both shafts weight exactly the same amount.*

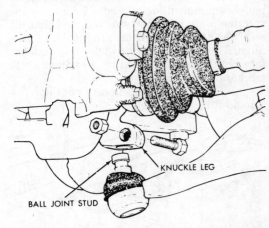

Remove ball joint from knuckle to remove axle shaft—Rabbit, Jetta, Scirocco

AXLE SHAFT REPAIR

The constant velocity joints (CV joints) of the axle shaft can be disassembled. However, Volkswagen states that the components making up the CV joint are machined to a matched tolerance and that the entire CV joint must be replaced as a set.

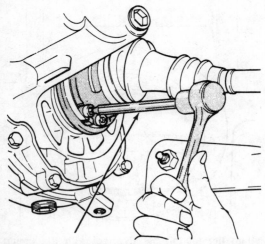

Remove the socket head bolts holding the axle shaft to the transaxle

CLUTCH

Adjustments

PEDAL FREE-PLAY ADJUSTMENT

Clutch pedal free-play should be ⅝″ for all Dashers and pre-1979 Rabbits and Sciroccos. 1979 and later models should have $^{27}/_{32}$–1″ free-play.

Clutch pedal free-play is the distance the pedal can be depressed before the linkage starts to act on the throwout bearing. Clutch free-play insures that the clutch plate is fully engaged and not slipping. Clutches with no or insufficient free-play often wear out quickly and give marginal power performance.

1. Adjust the clutch pedal free-play by loosening or tightening the two nuts (or locknut and threaded sleeve) on the cable near the oil filter on Fox, Dasher and Quantum: or on the Rabbit, Jetta, GTI and Scirocco, the left side (drivers) at the front of the transaxle.

NOTE: *Correct free-play cannot be measured correctly if floor covering interferes with clutch pedal travel. See following sec-*

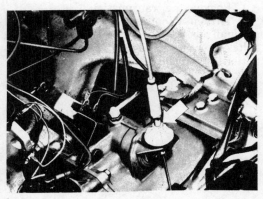

Rabbit, Jetta, Scirocco clutch pedal free-play adjustment

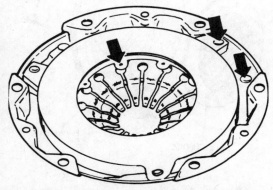

Check the Dasher pressure plate for surface wear. Make sure the cover straps are not cracked or the rivets loose

tion for instructions on late model adjustment.

2. Loosen the locknut and loosen or tighten the adjusting nut or sleeve until desired play is present. Depress the clutch pedal several times and recheck free-play. Readjust if necessary. Tighten locknut.

3. On late models, VW recommends that a special tool (US5043) be used to determine proper adjustment. The procedure for adjustment follows: depress the clutch pedal several times. Loosen the locknut and insert the tool. Adjust the sleeve until zero clearance between sleeve and tool is reached. Tighten locknut. Remove tool and depress clutch pedal at least five times. Check free-play at clutch pedal.

CHECKING TOTAL CLUTCH PEDAL TRAVEL

Prior to free-play adjustment, check total pedal travel as follows:

1. Hook a tape measure to the top of the clutch pedal. Measure distance between the top of the pedal and the centerline of the steering wheel.

2. Depress the pedal and measure the total distance again. If the difference between the measurements exceeds 4.68″, the floor covering may be interfering with pedal travel.

Clutch Cable

REMOVAL AND INSTALLATION

1. Loosen the adjustment.
2. Disengage the cable from the clutch arm.
3. Unhook the cable from the pedal. Remove the threaded eye from the end of the cable. Remove the adjustment nut(s).
4. Remove the C-clip which holds the outer cable at the adjustment point. Remove all the washers and bushings, first noting their locations.
5. Pull the cable out of the firewall toward the engine compartment side.
6. Install and connect the new cable. Adjust the pedal free-play.

Pressure Plate and Driven Disc

REMOVAL AND INSTALLATION

CAUTION: *The clutch driven disc contains asbestos, which has been determined to be a cancer causing agent. Never clean clutch surfaces with compressed air! Avoid inhaling any dust from any clutch surface! When cleaning clutch surfaces, use a commercially available brake cleaning fluid.*

Dasher, Fox and Quantum

1. Remove the transaxle.
2. Matchmark the flywheel and pressure

Rabbit, Jetta, Scirocco—a timing notch must be cut into new flywheels. A = ⅝ in. (7½° BTDC) and B = ³/₃₂ in. (3° ATDC)

plate if the pressure plate is being re-used.

3. Gradually loosen the pressure plate bolts one or two turns at a time in a criss-cross pattern to prevent distortion.

4. Remove the pressure plate and disc.

5. Check the clutch disc for uneven or excessive lining wear. The rivets in the plate should be tight and indented in the mating surface, not level with it.

6. Examine the pressure plate for cracking, scorching, or scoring. Replace any questionable components.

7. Install the clutch disc and pressure plate. Use a pilot shaft (available at most autoparts stores) or an old transaxle shaft to keep the disc centered.

NOTE: *The use of the proper pilot shaft is a necessity: if you can't obtain one, don't use dead reckoning to line up the clutch. You'll spend a long, sweaty time trying to force the*

transmission spline into the misaligned clutch.

8. Gradually tighten the pressure plate-to-flywheel bolts in a criss-cross pattern. Tighten the bolts to 18 ft.lb.

9. Install the throwout bearing, if removed.

10. Apply a light film of grease to the input spline on the transaxle to aid in inserting it into the clutch. Don't go overboard with the amount of grease.

11. Install the transaxle.

Rabbit, Scirocco, Jetta, GTI

NOTE: *Your'll need special tool VW 547 or equipment to center the clutch disc.*

These cars use a type of clutch more common to motorcycles than to cars. The pressure plate is bolted to the crankshaft and the flywheel bolted to the pressure plate; in other words, these two parts have switched places. The clutch release lever and bearing are in the left end of the transmission. The clutch is actuated by a release rod which passes through a hollow transmission shaft. The throwout bearing is in the transaxle and lubricated with transmission oil.

1. Remove the transmission.

2. Attach a toothed flywheel holder and gradually loosen the flywheel to pressure plate bolts one or two turns at a time in a crisscross pattern to prevent distortion.

3. Remove the flywheel and the clutch disc.

NOTE: *If replacing the flywheel, the new one has only a TDC mark. Additional timing marks must be cut into the flywheel as shown.*

4. Use a small pry bar to remove the release plate retaining ring. Remove the release plate.

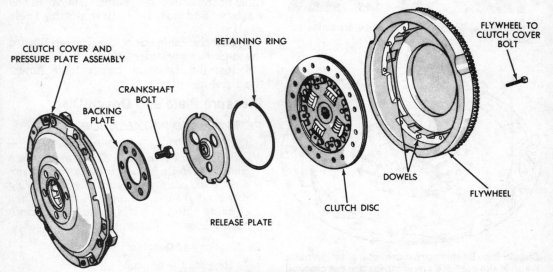

CLUTCH COVER AND PRESSURE PLATE ASSEMBLY

BACKING PLATE

CRANKSHAFT BOLT

RETAINING RING

RELEASE PLATE

CLUTCH DISC

DOWELS

FLYWHEEL TO CLUTCH COVER BOLT

FLYWHEEL

Rabbit, Jetta, Scirocco clutch assembly

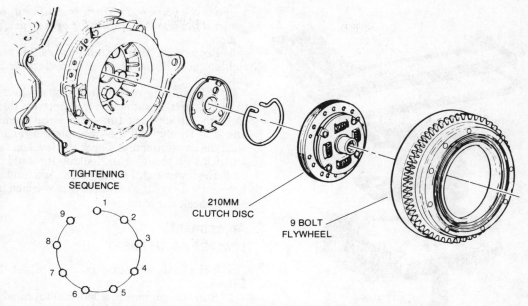

TIGHTENING
SEQUENCE

210MM
CLUTCH DISC

9 BOLT
FLYWHEEL

Late model, 210mm clutch assembly and flywheel tightening sequence

5. Lock the pressure plate in place and unbolt it from the crankshaft. Loosen the bolts one or two turns at a time in a crisscross pattern to prevent distortion.

6. On installation, use new bolts to attach the pressure plate to the crankshaft. Use a thread locking compound and torque the bolts in a diagonal pattern to 54 ft.lb.

7. Lubricate the clutch disc splines, release plate contact surface, and pushrod socket with multipurpose grease. Install the release plate, retaining ring, and clutch disc.

8. Use special tool VW 547 to center the clutch disc.

9. Install the flywheel, tightening the bolts one or two turns at a time in a crisscross pattern to prevent distortion. Torque the bolts to 14 ft.lb.

10. Replace the transmission. Adjust the clutch free-play.

AUTOMATIC TRANSAXLE

Normal maintenance such as fluid checking, adding and filter cleaning is discussed in Chapter 1. Halfshaft removal is described in the manual transaxle section in this chapter.

Transaxle Fluid Pan

REMOVAL AND INSTALLATION, STRAINER SERVICE

Dasher and Quantum

NOTE: *As of transmission no. 13 03 8, an additional oil strainer is installed between* the oil pump and the valve body inside the transmission (see illustration). When installing it, be sure it fits into the locating lug of the transfer plate.

1. Four (4) quarts of automatic transmission fluid (Dexron®II) and a pan gasket are required.

2. Slide a drain pan under the transmission. Jack up the front of the car and support it.

3. Remove the drain plug and allow all the fluid to drain.

NOTE: *Some models are not equipped with pan drain plugs. In this cases, empty the pan by loosening the pan bolts and allowing the fluid to drain out.*

4. Remove the pan retaining bolts and drop the pan.

5. Discard the old gasket and clean the pan with solvent.

6. Unscrew the strainer. If it is dirty, it should be replaced.

7. Install the strainer, but don't tighten the bolt too much specified torque is only 4 ft.lb.

8. Refill the transmission with about 2¾ qts. of fluid. Check the level with the dipstick. Run the car for a few minutes and check again. Add fluid as necessary.

Golf, Rabbit, Scirocco, Jetta, GTI

NOTE: *As of transmission No. 09096 a new, cleanable oil filter is used which requires a deeper oil pan. Also beginning with transmission number EQ-15 106, the drain plug was no longer installed in the oil pan.*

1. Remove the drain plug and let the fluid

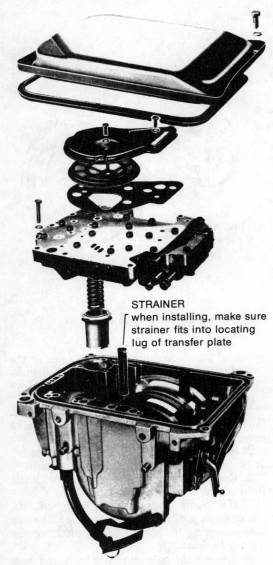

STRAINER
when installing, make sure
strainer fits into locating
lug of transfer plate

Beginning with transaxle 13 03 8, an additional strainer is used beneath the valve body. It cannot be installed on earlier models

drain into a pan. If the pan has no drain plug, loosen the pan bolts until a corner of the pan can be lowered to drain the fluid.

2. Remove the pan bolts and take off the pan.

3. Discard the old gasket and clean the pan out. Be very careful not to get any threads or lint from rags into the pan.

4. The manufacturer says that the filter needn't be replaced unless the fluid is very dirty and burnt smelling. When replacing the strainer be careful, the specified torque for the strainer screws is 2 ft.lb.

NOTE: *Beginning with Transmission number 13 03 8, there is an additional strainer*

under the valve body. When installing it, be sure it fits into the locating lug of the transfer plate.

5. Replace the pan with a new gasket and tighten the bolts, in a criss-cross pattern, to 14 ft.lb.

6. Using a long necked funnel, pour in 2½ qts. of Dexron®II automatic transmission fluid through the dipstick tube. Start the engine and shift through all the transmission ranges with the car stationary. Check the level on the dipstick with the lever in Neutral. It should be up to the lower end of the dipstick. Add fluid as necessary. Drive the car until it is warmed up and recheck the level.

Adjustments
LINKAGE ADJUSTMENT

Check the cable adjustments on all models as follows:

1. Run the engines at 1000–1200 rpm with the parking brake on and the wheels blocked.

2. Select REVERSE. A drop in engine speed should be noticed.

3. Select PARK. Engine speed should increase. Pull the shift lever against the stop in the direction of REVERSE. The engine speed should not drop (because reverse gear has not been engaged).

4. Move the shift lever to engage REVERSE. Engine speed should drop as the gear engages.

5. Move the shift lever into NEUTRAL. An increase in engine speed should be noticed.

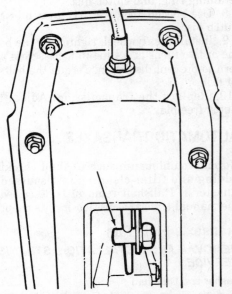

Dasher automatic transaxle linkage adjustment—before chassis no. 3-5 2 044 957

6. Shift into DRIVE. A noticeable drop in engine speed should result.

7. Shift into 1. The lever must engage without having to overcome any resistance.

8. To adjust the cable, shift into PARK. On Dashers, before chassis no. 3–5 2 044 957, remove the cover from the bottom of the shift lever case under the car and loosen the cable clamp. Using pliers, press the lever on the transmission to the rear (against spring tension) until it hits the stop and tighten the clamp.

On Dashers from chassis no. 3–5 2 044 957 and later, and Quantum the shift cable clamp is loosened from inside the passengers compartment. Have an assistant under the car press the transmission lever toward the Park position and tighten the clamp.

On the Rabbit, Golf, Jetta, GTI and Scirocco, shift into Park, loosen the cable clamp at the transmission end of the cable, press the transmission lever all the way to the left and tighten the cable clamp.

TRANSMISSION CABLE ADJUSTMENT

NOTE: *Early Dashers with the type 003 automatic transmission (identified by the modulator hose attached to the driver's side front of the transmission above the pan) have a kickdown switch rather than a throttle cable. See below for switch test.*

Make sure the throttle is closed, and the choke and fast idle cam are off (carbureted models).

1. Detach the cable end at the transmission.

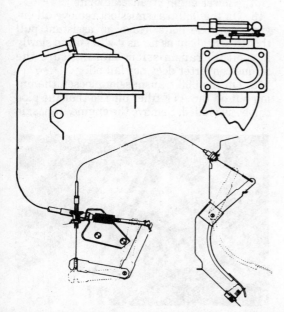

Rabbit, Jetta, Scirocco automatic transmission cable arrangement—fuel injected

2. Press the lever at the transmission into its closed throttle position.

3. You should be able to attach the cable end onto the transmission lever without moving the lever.

4. Adjust the cable length to the correct setting.

KICKDOWN SWITCH CHECK

Dasher

NOTE: *Early Dashers with the type 003 automatic transmission (identified by the modulator hose attached to the driver's side front of the transmission above the pan) are the only VWs equipped with kickdown switches. All other models have throttle cable kickdowns (see above).*

1. Turn the ignition switch ON.

2. Floor the accelerator. You should hear a click from the solenoid on the transmission.

3. Replace the solenoid if no sound is heard. The solenoid is housed in the valve body and is accessible only by removing this unit from the transmission: a job you should depend on a qualified mechanic to perform.

FIRST AND SECOND GEAR (FRONT AND REAR) BAND ADJUSTMENTS

Dasher w/Type 003 Transmission Only

The type 003 transmission is identified by the modulator hose attached to the driver's side front of the transmission above the pan.

NOTE: *The transmission must be horizontal when the band adjustments are performed.*

The adjustment screws are located at the top of the transmission housing with the first gear band being closest to the front of the unit on the passenger's side of the car. The second gear band adjustment screw is located toward the

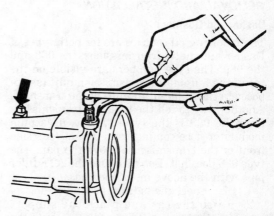

Dasher type 003 transaxle band adjustment —front band (first gear) being adjusted, arrow locates second gear band adjustment screw

rear of the unit on the driver's side of the vehicle.

1. To adjust the first gear band, loosen the locknut and tighten the adjusting screw to 7 ft.lb.

2. Loosen the screw and retighten it to 3.5 ft.lb.

3. Turn the screw out 3¼–3½ turns and then tighten the locknut.

4. To adjust the second gear band, repeat steps 1 and 2 on the second gear band adjusting screw, then turn the screw out exactly 2½ turns and tighten the locknut.

SECOND GEAR (REAR) BAND ADJUSTMENT

Dasher and Quantum w/Type 089 Transmission, Golf, Rabbit, Jetta, GTI, Scirocco

NOTE: *The transmission must be horizontal when band adjustments are performed.*

1. Loosen the locknut on the adjusting screw, which is located on the front of the Rabbit and Scirocco transmission and the driver's side on the Dasher and Quantum.

2. Tighten the adjusting screw to 7 ft.lb.

3. Loosen the screw and tighten it again to 4 ft.lb.

4. Turn the screw out exactly 2½ turns and then tighten the locknut.

NEUTRAL START/BACKUP LIGHT SWITCH

The combination neutral start and backup light switch is mounted inside the shifter housing. The starter should operate in Park or Neutral only. Adjust the switch by moving it on its mounts. The backup lights should only come on when the shift selector is in the Reverse position.

Transaxle
REMOVAL AND INSTALLATION

Dasher and Quantum

The following procedures are for both types of Dasher automatic transmissions, the 003 and the 089. The type numbers are visible on the top of the automatic transmission unit (as opposed to the differential unit) of the transaxle. Another way to tell the type 003 transmission from the 089 is the type 003 has a vacuum modulator hose coming from the driver's side front of the transmission above the pan. The type 089 does not. Don't confuse the ATF filler pipe with the above mentioned hose.

1. Disconnect the battery ground strap.

2. Raise the car and place the support stands so that you will have free access to the transaxle and axle shafts.

3. Disconnect the speedometer cable.

4. On the 089, remove the accelerator cable from the throttle valve housing.

5. Remove two of the upper engine/transaxle bolts. On the 089 transmission, support the engine with either special tool 10–222 or an appropriate jack.

6. Disconnect the exhaust pipe.

7. Remove the torque converter cover plate. On the 003 transmission, remove the vacuum modulator hose.

8. Remove the circlip holding the selector lever cable to the lever and remove the cable.

9. Remove the starter.

10. On the 003 disconnect the kickdown switch wires.

11. The torque converter is mounted to the flywheel by three bolts. The bolts are accessible through the starter hole. You'll have to turn the engine over by hand to remove all three.

12. Remove the axle shaft to transaxle socket head bolts.

13. Matchmark the position of the ball joint on the left control arm and remove the ball joint from the arm. Hold the wheel assembly out away from the arm to provide clearance between the axle shaft and the transmission.

14. Remove the exhaust pipe from the transaxle bracket.

15. Disconnect the remaining transmission controls. Those you cannot reach can be removed when the transaxle is lowered a little.

16. Unbolt the transaxle crossmember and remove it from the transaxle.

17. Support the transaxle on a jack and loosen the lower engine/transaxle bolts.

18. On the 089 transmission, remove all engine/transaxle bolts. Have an assistant pull the left wheel out as far as it will go and slowly lower the transmission, making sure the torque converter does not fall off.

19. On the 003 transmission, loosen the union nut on the ATF filler pipe so that the pipe can be swivelled. Remove the engine/transaxle

Dasher type 003 automatic transaxle has vacuum modulator hose (to left of arrow)

bolts and lower the unit. You may have to pull the left wheel out a little so that the axle shaft clears the transaxle case. Make sure the torque converter does not fall off.

20. Installation is the reverse of removal with the following notes.

On both transaxles, the torque converter nipple must be about $1^3/_{16}''$ from the bell housing face surface. If it sticks out further than this, the oil pump shaft has probably pulled out. You'll have to manipulate the converter and shaft until it goes in again.

Tighten the engine/transaxle bolts to 40 ft.lb. and the torque converter bolts to 20–23 ft.lb. New torque converter bolts should be used. Torque the axle shaft bolts to 33 ft.lb., and the ball joint to control arm bolts to 45 ft.lb.

Check the shift linkage adjustment.

Rabbit, Golf, Scirocco, Jetta, GTI

The engine and transaxle may be removed together as explained under Engine Removal and Installation or the transaxle may be removed along, as explained here.

1. Disconnect both battery cables.
2. Disconnect the speedometer cable at the transmission.
3. Support the left end of the engine at the lifting eye. Attach a hoist to the transaxle.
4. Unbolt the rear transmission carrier from the body then from the transaxle. Unbolt the left side carrier from the body.
5. Unbolt the driveshafts and wire them up.
6. Remove the starter.
7. Remove the three converter to drive plate bolts.
8. Shift into P and disconnect the floorshift linkage at the transmission.

9. Remove the accelerator and carburetor cable bracket at the transmission.
10. Unbolt the left side transmission carrier from the transmission.
11. Unbolt the front transmission mount from the transmission.
12. Unbolt the bottom of the engine from the transmission. Lift the transaxle slightly, swing the left driveshaft up, remove the rest of the bolts, pull the transmission off the mounting dowels, and lower the transaxle out of the car. Secure the converter so it doesn't fall out.

CAUTION: *Don't tilt the torque converter.*
To install the transaxle:

13. Push the transmission onto the mounting dowels and install two bolts. Be sure the torque converter is fully seated on the clutch support. The distance A should be $1^3/_{16}''$. Lift the unit until the left driveshaft can be installed and install the rest of the bolts. Torque them to 39 ft.lb. Align the transmission the left mount must be in the center of the body mount. Dimension X on both sides should be equal.
14. Tighten the front transmission mount bolts to 39 ft.lb. Install the left side transmission carrier to the transmission.
15. Connect the accelerator and carburetor cable bracket. Connect the floorshift linkage.
16. Tighten the torque converter to drive plate bolts to 22 ft.lb. Torque the driveshaft bolts to 32 ft.lb.
17. Connect the speedometer cable and battery cables.

Align the engine/transaxle mount on Rabbit, Jetta, Scirocco. Dimension X must be equal

Axle Shaft (Half Shaft)
REMOVAL AND INSTALLATION
Dasher and Quantum

NOTE: *When removing the right axle shaft, you must detach the exhaust pipe from the manifold and the transaxle bracket. Be sure to buy a new exhaust flange gasket.*

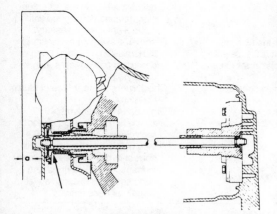

Rabbit, Dasher, Jetta, Scirocco—When attaching transmission to engine, be sure torque converter is seated on the one-way clutch support (arrow). When converter is properly seated, A = $1^3/_{16}$ in.

1. With the car on the ground, remove the front axle nut.

NOTE: *Use a longer breaker bar with an extension (length of pipe).*

2. Raise and support the front of the vehicle.

3. Remove the socket head bolts retaining the axle shaft to the transaxle.

NOTE: *When removing the left side axle shaft on automatic transmission models, matchmark the ball joint (left side) mounting position in relation to the lower control arm. Remove the two ball joint retaining nuts and remove the ball joint from the control arm to create room to remove the axle shaft.*

4. Pull the transaxle side of the driveshaft out and up and place it on the top of the transaxle.

5. Pull the axle shaft from the steering knuckle.

6. Installation is the reverse of removal. Tighten the transaxle bolts of 25–33 ft.lb. The axle nut should be tightened to 145 ft.lb. (M18 nut), or 175 ft.lb. (M20 nut).

NOTE: *Be aware that the axle shafts are two different lengths on automatic transmission models with the left side axle shaft being slightly longer than the right. Manual transmission and automatic transmission axle shafts are of different lengths and should not be interchanged.*

Rabbit, Scirocco, Golf, Jetta, GTI

1. Complete steps 1 through 3 under Dasher in this section. Disregard the first NOTE.

2. Remove the bolt holding the ball joint to the steering knuckle and separate the knuckle from the ball joint.

3. Removing the ball joint from the knuckle should give enough clearance to remove the axle shaft. It pulls right out of the steering hub.

4. Installation is the reverse of removal. Tighten the axle shaft to transaxle bolts to 32 ft.lb., the ball joint bolt to 21 ft.lb. and the axle nut to 173 ft.lb. Be sure to check the alignment after work is completed.

NOTE: *The axle shafts on the Rabbit, Jetta and Scirocco differ in length from the left and right sides. The left side shaft is longer than the right side shaft. To insure that the shafts are in perfect balance with each other, the longer shaft is hollow, while the shorter shaft is solid, making both shafts weight exactly the same amount.*

AXLE SHAFT REPAIR

The constant velocity joints (CV joints) of the axle shaft can be disassembled. However, Volkswagen states that the components making up the CV joint are machined to a matched tolerance and that the entire CV joint must be replaced as a set.

Troubleshooting the Manual Transmission and Transfer Case

Problem	Cause	Solution
Transmission shifts hard	• Clutch adjustment incorrect • Clutch linkage or cable binding • Shift rail binding	• Adjust clutch • Lubricate or repair as necessary • Check for mispositioned selector arm roll pin, loose cover bolts, worn shift rail bores, worn shift rail, distorted oil seal, or extension housing not aligned with case. Repair as necessary.
	• Internal bind in transmission caused by shift forks, selector plates, or synchronizer assemblies • Clutch housing misalignment • Incorrect lubricant • Block rings and/or cone seats worn	• Remove, dissemble and inspect transmission. Replace worn or damaged components as necessary. • Check runout at rear face of clutch housing • Drain and refill transmission • Blocking ring to gear clutch tooth face clearance must be 0.030 inch or greater. If clearance is correct it may still be necessary to inspect blocking rings and cone seats for excessive wear. Repair as necessary.
Gear clash when shifting from one gear to another	• Clutch adjustment incorrect • Clutch linkage or cable binding • Clutch housing misalignment	• Adjust clutch • Lubricate or repair as necessary • Check runout at rear of clutch housing

Troubleshooting the Manual Transmission and Transfer Case (cont.)

Problem	Cause	Solution
Gear clash when shifting from one gear to another (cont.)	• Lubricant level low or incorrect lubricant	• Drain and refill transmission and check for lubricant leaks if level was low. Repair as necessary.
	• Gearshift components, or synchronizer assemblies worn or damaged	• Remove, disassemble and inspect transmission. Replace worn or damaged components as necessary.
Transmission noisy	• Lubricant level low or incorrect lubricant	• Drain and refill transmission. If lubricant level was low, check for leaks and repair as necessary.
	• Clutch housing-to-engine, or transmission-to-clutch housing bolts loose	• Check and correct bolt torque as necessary
	• Dirt, chips, foreign material in transmission	• Drain, flush, and refill transmission
	• Gearshift mechanism, transmission gears, or bearing components worn or damaged	• Remove, disassemble and inspect transmission. Replace worn or damaged components as necessary.
	• Clutch housing misalignment	• Check runout at rear face of clutch housing
Jumps out of gear	• Clutch housing misalignment	• Check runout at rear face of clutch housing
	• Gearshift lever loose	• Check lever for worn fork. Tighten loose attaching bolts.
	• Offset lever nylon insert worn or lever attaching nut loose	• Remove gearshift lever and check for loose offset lever nut or worn insert. Repair or replace as necessary.
	• Gearshift mechanism, shift forks, selector plates, interlock plate, selector arm, shift rail, detent plugs, springs or shift cover worn or damaged	• Remove, disassemble and inspect transmission cover assembly. Replace worn or damaged components as necessary.
	• Clutch shaft or roller bearings worn or damaged	• Replace clutch shaft or roller bearings as necessary
	• Gear teeth worn or tapered, synchronizer assemblies worn or damaged, excessive end play caused by worn thrust washers or output shaft gears	• Remove, disassemble, and inspect transmission. Replace worn or damaged components as necessary.
	• Pilot bushing worn	• Replace pilot bushing
Will not shift into one gear	• Gearshift selector plates, interlock plate, or selector arm, worn, damaged, or incorrectly assembled	• Remove, disassemble, and inspect transmission cover assembly. Repair or replace components as necessary.
	• Shift rail detent plunger worn, spring broken, or plug loose	• Tighten plug or replace worn or damaged components as necessary
	• Gearshift lever worn or damaged	• Replace gearshift lever
	• Synchronizer sleeves or hubs, damaged or worn	• Remove, disassemble and inspect transmission. Replace worn or damaged components.
Locked in one gear—cannot be shifted out	• Shift rail(s) worn or broken, shifter fork bent, setscrew loose, center detent plug missing or worn	• Inspect and replace worn or damaged parts
	• Broken gear teeth on countershaft gear, clutch shaft, or reverse idler gear	• Inspect and replace damaged part
	Gearshift lever broken or worn, shift mechanism in cover incorrectly assembled or broken, worn damaged gear train components	• Disassemble transmission. Replace damaged parts or assemble correctly.

Troubleshooting the Manual Transmission and Transfer Case (cont.)

Problem	Cause	Solution
Transfer case difficult to shift or will not shift into desired range	• Vehicle speed too great to permit shifting	• Stop vehicle and shift into desired range. Or reduce speed to 3–4 km/h (2–3 mph) before attempting to shift.
	• If vehicle was operated for extended period in 4H mode on dry paved surface, driveline torque load may cause difficult shifting	• Stop vehicle, shift transmission to neutral, shift transfer case to 2H mode and operate vehicle in 2H on dry paved surfaces
	• Transfer case external shift linkage binding	• Lubricate or repair or replace linkage, or tighten loose components as necessary
	• Insufficient or incorrect lubricant	• Drain and refill to edge of fill hole with SAE 85W-90 gear lubricant only
	• Internal components binding, worn, or damaged	• Disassemble unit and replace worn or damaged components as necessary
Transfer case noisy in all drive modes	• Insufficient or incorrect lubricant	• Drain and refill to edge of fill hole with SAE 85W-90 gear lubricant only. Check for leaks and repair if necessary. Note: If unit is still noisy after drain and refill, disassembly and inspection may be required to locate source of noise.
Noisy in—or jumps out of four wheel drive low range	• Transfer case not completely engaged in 4L position	• Stop vehicle, shift transfer case in Neutral, then shift back into 4L position
	• Shift linkage loose or binding	• Tighten, lubricate, or repair linkage as necessary
	• Shift fork cracked, inserts worn, or fork is binding on shift rail	• Disassemble unit and repair as necessary
Lubricant leaking from output shaft seals or from vent	• Transfer case overfilled	• Drain to correct level
	• Vent closed or restricted	• Clear or replace vent if necessary
	• Output shaft seals damaged or installed incorrectly	• Replace seals. Be sure seal lip faces interior of case when installed. Also be sure yoke seal surfaces are not scored or nicked. Remove scores, nicks with fine sandpaper or replace yoke(s) if necessary.
Abnormal tire wear	• Extended operation on dry hard surface (paved) roads in 4H range	• Operate in 2H on hard surface (paved) roads

Troubleshooting Basic Clutch Problems

Problem	Cause
Excessive clutch noise	Throwout bearing noises are more audible at the lower end of pedal travel. The usual causes are: • Riding the clutch • Too little pedal free-play • Lack of bearing lubrication A bad clutch shaft pilot bearing will make a high pitched squeal, when the clutch is disengaged and the transmission is in gear or within the first 2″ of pedal travel. The bearing must be replaced. Noise from the clutch linkage is a clicking or snapping that can be heard or felt as the pedal is moved completely up or down. This usually requires lubrication.

Troubleshooting Basic Clutch Problems (cont.)

Problem	Cause
Excessive clutch noise (cont.)	Transmitted engine noises are amplified by the clutch housing and heard in the passenger compartment. They are usually the result of insufficient pedal free-play and can be changed by manipulating the clutch pedal.
Clutch slips (the car does not move as it should when the clutch is engaged)	This is usually most noticeable when pulling away from a standing start. A severe test is to start the engine, apply the brakes, shift into high gear and SLOWLY release the clutch pedal. A healthy clutch will stall the engine. If it slips it may be due to: • A worn pressure plate or clutch plate • Oil soaked clutch plate • Insufficient pedal free-play
Clutch drags or fails to release	The clutch disc and some transmission gears spin briefly after clutch disengagement. Under normal conditions in average temperatures, 3 seconds is maximum spin-time. Failure to release properly can be caused by: • Too light transmission lubricant or low lubricant level • Improperly adjusted clutch linkage
Low clutch life	Low clutch life is usually a result of poor driving habits or heavy duty use. Riding the clutch, pulling heavy loads, holding the car on a grade with the clutch instead of the brakes and rapid clutch engagement all contribute to low clutch life.

Troubleshooting Basic Automatic Transmission Problems

Problem	Cause	Solution
Fluid leakage	• Defective pan gasket • Loose filler tube • Loose extension housing to transmission case • Converter housing area leakage	• Replace gasket or tighten pan bolts • Tighten tube nut • Tighten bolts • Have transmission checked professionally
Fluid flows out the oil filler tube	• High fluid level • Breather vent clogged • Clogged oil filter or screen • Internal fluid leakage	• Check and correct fluid level • Open breather vent • Replace filter or clean screen (change fluid also) • Have transmission checked professionally
Transmission overheats (this is usually accompanied by a strong burned odor to the fluid)	• Low fluid level • Fluid cooler lines clogged • Heavy pulling or hauling with insufficient cooling • Faulty oil pump, internal slippage	• Check and correct fluid level • Drain and refill transmission. If this doesn't cure the problem, have cooler lines cleared or replaced. • Install a transmission oil cooler • Have transmission checked professionally
Buzzing or whining noise	• Low fluid level • Defective torque converter, scored gears	• Check and correct fluid level • Have transmission checked professionally
No forward or reverse gears or slippage in one or more gears	• Low fluid level • Defective vacuum or linkage controls, internal clutch or band failure	• Check and correct fluid level • Have unit checked professionally
Delayed or erratic shift	• Low fluid level • Broken vacuum lines • Internal malfunction	• Check and correct fluid level • Repair or replace lines • Have transmission checked professionally

Lockup Torque Converter Service Diagnosis

Problem	Cause	Solution

No lockup	• Faulty oil pump
	• Sticking governor valve
	• Valve body malfunction
	  (a) Stuck switch valve
	  (b) Stuck lockup valve
	  (c) Stuck fail-safe valve
	• Failed locking clutch
	• Leaking turbine hub seal
	• Faulty input shaft or seal ring
		• Replace oil pump
		• Repair or replace as necessary
		• Repair or replace valve body or its internal components as necessary
		
		• Replace torque converter
		• Replace torque converter
		• Repair or replace as necessary

Will not unlock	• Sticking governor valve
	• Valve body malfunction
	  (a) Stuck switch valve
	  (b) Stuck lockup valve
	  (c) Stuck fail-safe valve
		• Repair or replace as necessary
		• Repair or replace valve body or its internal components as necessary

Stays locked up at too low a speed in direct	• Sticking governor valve
	• Valve body malfunction
	  (a) Stuck switch valve
	  (b) Stuck lockup valve
	  (c) Stuck fail-safe valve
		• Repair or replace as necessary
		• Repair or replace valve body or its internal components as necessary

Locks up or drags in low or second	• Faulty oil pump
	• Valve body malfunction
	  (a) Stuck switch valve
	  (b) Stuck fail-safe valve
		• Replace oil pump
		• Repair or replace valve body or its internal components as necessary

Sluggish or stalls in reverse	• Faulty oil pump
	• Plugged cooler, cooler lines or fittings
	• Valve body malfunction
	  (a) Stuck switch valve
	  (b) Faulty input shaft or seal ring
		• Replace oil pump as necessary
		• Flush or replace cooler and flush lines and fittings
		• Repair or replace valve body or its internal components as necessary

Loud chatter during lockup engagement (cold)	• Faulty torque converter • Failed locking clutch • Leaking turbine hub seal	• Replace torque converter • Replace torque converter • Replace torque converter
Vibration or shudder during lockup engagement	• Faulty oil pump • Valve body malfunction • Faulty torque converter • Engine needs tune-up	• Repair or replace oil pump as necessary • Repair or replace valve body or its internal components as necessary • Replace torque converter • Tune engine
Vibration after lockup engagement	• Faulty torque converter • Exhaust system strikes underbody • Engine needs tune-up • Throttle linkage misadjusted	• Replace torque converter • Align exhaust system • Tune engine • Adjust throttle linkage
Vibration when revved in neutral Overheating: oil blows out of dip stick tube or pump seal	• Torque converter out of balance • Plugged cooler, cooler lines or fittings • Stuck switch valve	• Replace torque converter • Flush or replace cooler and flush lines and fittings • Repair switch valve in valve body or replace valve body
Shudder after lockup engagement	• Faulty oil pump • Plugged cooler, cooler lines or fittings • Valve body malfunction • Faulty torque converter • Fail locking clutch • Exhaust system strikes underbody • Engine needs tune-up • Throttle linkage misadjusted	• Replace oil pump • Flush or replace cooler and flush lines and fittings • Repair or replace valve body or its internal components as necessary • Replace torque converter • Replace torque converter • Align exhaust system • Tune engine • Adjust throttle linkage

FRONT SUSPENSION

Strut

REMOVAL AND INSTALLATION

Dasher, Fox and Quantum

1. With the car on the ground, remove the front axle nut. Loosen the wheel bolts.

2. Raise and support the front of the car. Use support stands. Remove the wheels.

3. Remove the brake caliper from the strut and hang it with wire. Detach the brake line clips from the strut.

4. At the tie rod end, remove the cotter pin, back off the castellated nut, and pull the tie rod end from the strut with a puller.

5. Loosen the stabilizer bar bushings and detach the end from the strut being removed.

6. Remove the ball joint from the strut.

7. Pull the axle driveshaft from the strut.

8. Remove the upper strut-to-fender retaining nuts located under the engine hood.

9. Pull the strut assembly down and out of the car.

10. Installation is the reverse of removal. The axle nut is tightened to 145 ft.lb. (M18 nut) or 175 ft.lb. (M20 nut). Tighten the ball joint-to-strut nut to 25 ft.lb. (M8 nut) or 36 ft.lb. (M10 nut), the caliper-to-strut bolts to 44 ft.lb. and the stabilizer-to-control arm bolts to 7 ft.lb.

Golf, Rabbit, Scirocco, Jetta, GTI

1. Jack up the front of the vehicle and support it on stands.

2. Remove the wheel.

3. Remove the brake hose from the strut clip.

4. Mark the position of the camber adjustment bolts before removing them from the hub (wheel bearing housing).

5. Remove the upper mounting nuts and remove the strut from the vehicle.

6. Installation is the reverse of removal. The upper nuts are tightened to 14 ft.lb., and the adjusting bolt (upper) to hub to 58 ft.lb. Tighten the lower adjusting bolt-to-hub to 43 ft.lb. Use new washers on the lower bolts. If the shock absorber was replaced, camber will have to be adjusted. See procedures in this chapter.

STRUT OVERHAUL

(Includes Coil Spring and Shock Absorber Removal)

NOTE: *You must obtain a spring compressor, either the Volkswagen type (VW 340/5 and VW 340) or a comparable consumer type.*

1. Remove the strut from the vehicle. See above for procedures.

2. Anchor the strut in a vise so it cannot move and attach the spring compressor. Be sure to follow the compressor instructions to the letter. The coil spring is under considerable pressure and has the potential to seriously harm you.

3. Compress the spring and loosen the center nut at the top of the strut assembly. To aid in removing the nut, fit an allen wrench in the top of the shock absorber rod and loosen the nut with a closed end wrench.

4. Remove the collar parts from the top of the spring and arrange the parts in the order of removal to aid you in reassembly.

5. Slowly release the pressure on the spring and remove the spring from the strut.

NOTE: *The springs are color coded. When replacing, make sure both replacement springs have the same color code.*

Dashers after chassis no. 3–5 2 117 398 and all Golfs, Rabbits, Jettas, GTIs and Sciroccos have nonremovable shock absorbers in the struts. If the shock absorbers on these models wear out, you must replace the entire strut assembly (except for the coil spring and its attaching parts).

To replace the removable shock absorber

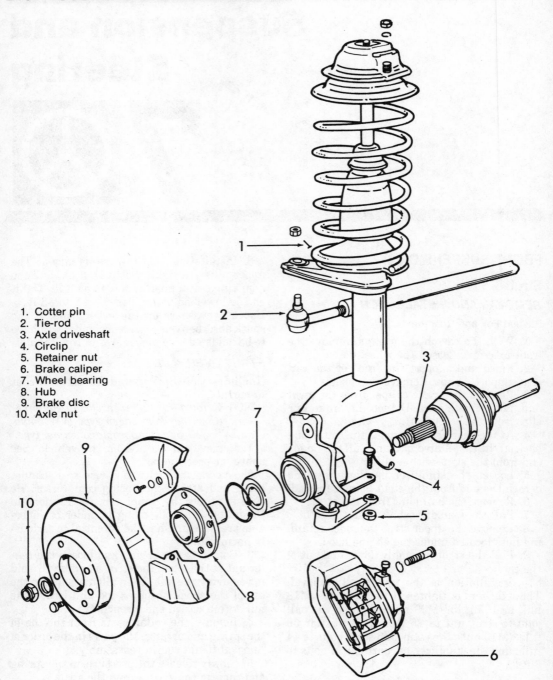

1. Cotter pin
2. Tie-rod
3. Axle driveshaft
4. Circlip
5. Retainer nut
6. Brake caliper
7. Wheel bearing
8. Hub
9. Brake disc
10. Axle nut

Dasher front suspension components

cartridge in Dashers before chassis no. 3–5 2 117 398, and 1987 and later Foxs, proceed as follows:

6. Remove the rubber cap and collar on the shock tube and remove the round, threaded retaining cap. There is a special VW tool (40–201) for this job, but you should be able to loosen the cap with a pipe wrench. Be careful not to bend or dent the cap when removing.

7. Pull the shock absorber cartridge out of the strut. You may have to put the nut back on the shock absorber rod and use it as a stop-point to tap the cartridge out of the strut. When installing, the threaded retaining cap should be tightened to 108 ft.lb.

8. Installation of the coil spring is the reverse of removal. Tighten the coil spring retaining nut to 44 ft.lb. on the Dasher, Fox and

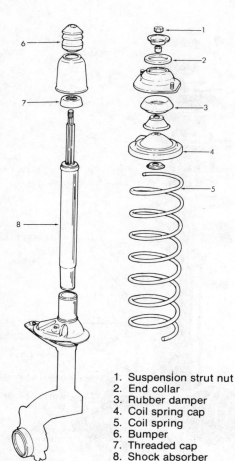

1. Suspension strut nut
2. End collar
3. Rubber damper
4. Coil spring cap
5. Coil spring
6. Bumper
7. Threaded cap
8. Shock absorber

Dasher suspension strut—before chassis no. 3-5 2 117 398

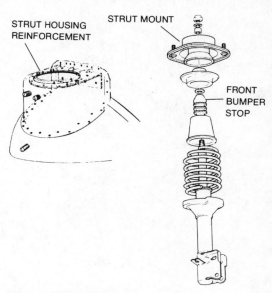

GTI strut installation

Quantum, 58 ft.lb. on the Rabbit, Golf, Jetta, GTI and Scirocco.

Make sure the coil spring fits into its grooves in the strut. If the strut has been replaced, the camber must be adjusted. See the section in this chapter.

Shock Absorbers
TESTING

The function of a shock absorber is to dampen harsh spring movement and provide a means of dissipating the motion of the wheels so that the roughness encountered by the wheels is not totally transmitted to the body and, therefore, to you and your passengers. As the wheel moves up and down, the shock absorber shortens and lengthens, thereby imposing a restraint on movement by its hydraulic action.

A simple way to see if your shock absorbers are functioning correctly is to push one corner of the car down a few times. This will compress the spring on that side of the car as well as the shock absorber. If the shock absorber is func-

tioning properly, it will control the spring's tendency to remain in motion. Thus the car will level itself almost instantly when you release the downward pressure. If the car continues to bounce up and down several times, the shock absorber is worn out and should be replaced. Examine the strut body for heavy oil streaking, which would indicate shock leakage. Replace a leaky shock absorber.

REMOVAL AND INSTALLATION

Shock absorber removal and installation is contained in the strut overhaul section, above. Be aware, however, that on all models except Dashers up to chassis no. 3–5 2 117 398, and 1987 and later Foxs, replacing the shock absorber means replacing the strut itself (except for the coil spring and its attaching parts).

Coil Spring
REMOVAL AND INSTALLATION

Coil spring removal and installation procedures are contained in the strut overhaul section, above. The coil springs are color coded and must be matched with other springs of the same color code.

Ball Joints
INSPECTION

Visually check the ball joint rubber dust cap for cracks and rips. Make sure the ball joint is mounted securely on the lower control arm, and check the up and down play (as opposed to side to side movement) of the joint itself. If the

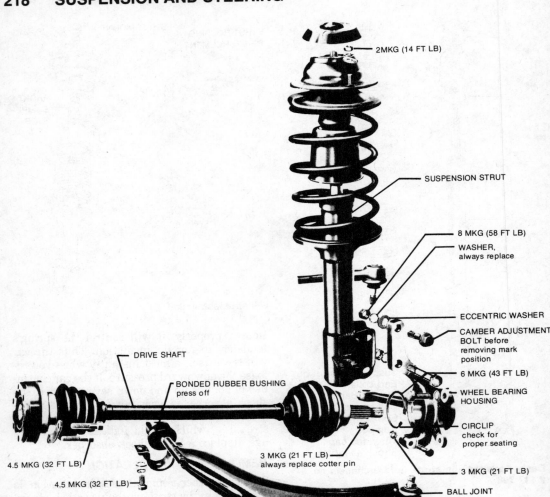

2MKG (14 FT LB)

SUSPENSION STRUT

8 MKG (58 FT LB)

WASHER, always replace

ECCENTRIC WASHER

CAMBER ADJUSTMENT BOLT before removing mark position

6 MKG (43 FT LB)

WHEEL BEARING HOUSING

CIRCLIP check for proper seating

3 MKG (21 FT LB)

BALL JOINT

WISHBONE

DRIVE SHAFT

BONDED RUBBER BUSHING press off

4.5 MKG (32 FT LB)

4.5 MKG (32 FT LB)

3 MKG (21 FT LB) always replace cotter pin

BONDED RUBBER BUSHING

6 MKG (43 FT LB)

Rabbit, Jetta, Scirocco front suspension—typical

up and down play is more than 0.10″, replace the ball joint.

REMOVAL AND INSTALLATION

1. Jack up the front of the vehicle and support it on jackstands.
2. Matchmark the ball joint-to-control arm position on the Dasher, Fox and Quantum.
3. Remove the retaining bolt and nut from the hub (wheel bearing housing).
4. Pry the lower control arm and ball joint down and out of the strut.
5. Remove the two ball joint-to-lower control arm retaining nuts and bolts on the Dasher, Fox or Quantum. Drill out the rivets on the

Rabbit, Jetta, GTI and Scirocco; enlarge the holes to $\frac{9}{32}$″.
6. Remove the ball joint assembly.
7. Install the Dasher, Fox or Quantum ball joint in the reverse order of removal. If no parts were installed other than the ball joint, align the match marks made in Step 2. No camber adjustment is necessary if this is done. Pull the ball joint into alignment with pliers. Tighten the two control arm-to-ball joint bolts to 47 ft.lb., and the strut-to-ball joint bolt to 25 ft.lb. (M8 bolt) or 36 ft.lb. (M10 bolt).
8. On the Golf, Rabbit, Jetta, GTI and Scirocco, bolt the new ball joint in place (bolts are provided with the replacement ball joint), and

WISHBONE — BOLT

SPRING
WASHER
2.5 mkg.
(18 ft lb)

BALL JOINT

Rabbit, Jetta, Scirocco ball joint assembly

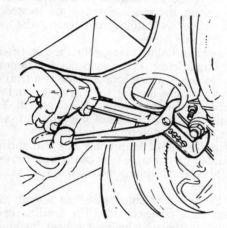

Aligning ball joint—Dasher and Quantum

tighten them to 18 ft.lb. Tighten the retaining bolt holding the ball joint to the hub to 21 ft.lb.

Axle Shaft

REMOVAL AND INSTALLATION

Axle shaft removal and installation procedures are covered in Chapter 6 Clutch and Transaxle.

Lower Control Arm (Wishbone)

REMOVAL AND INSTALLATION

Volkswagen refers to the lower control arm as the wishbone.

NOTE: *When removing the left side (driver's side) control arm on the Rabbit, Jetta, GTI and Scirocco equipped with an automatic transmission, remove the front left engine mounting, remove the nut for the rear mounting, remove the engine mounting support and raises the engine to expose the front control arm bolt.*

1. Raise the vehicle and support it on jack stands. Remove the road wheel.

2. Remove the nut and bolt attaching the ball joint to the hub (wheel bearing housing) and pry the joint down and out of the hub.

3. Unfasten the stabilizer bar on the Dasher, Fox or Quantum.

4. Unbolt and remove the control arm-to-subframe (crossmember) mounting bolts on the Dasher or Quantum. On the Golf, Rabbit, Jetta, GTI and Scirocco remove the control arm mounting bolts from the frame.

5. Remove the control arm. See procedures above for ball joint removal and installation.

6. Installation is the reverse of removal. Tighten the Dasher, Fox or Quantum control arm-to-subframe bolts to 50 ft.lb., and the Rabbit, Jetta, GTI and Scirocco control arm-to-frame front bolt to 43 ft.lb., rear bolts to 32 ft.lb. Tighten the ball joint to hub bolt to 21 ft.lb. on the Rabbit, Jetta, GTI and Scirocco, and to 25 ft.lb. (M8 nut) or 36 ft.lb. (M10 nut).

Front Wheel Bearings

The front wheel bearings are non-adjustable on all models and are sealed, so they should be maintenance free. Removing the front wheel bearings requires a stand press and a myriad of special Volkswagen tools, so the procedure is not given here.

Front End Alignment

NOTE: *When checking wheel alignment, the car must be empty, tire pressure correct and on a level surface.*

CAMBER ADJUSTMENT

Camber angle is the number of degrees which the centerline of the wheel is inclined from the vertical. Camber reduces loading of the outer wheel bearing and improves tire contact while cornering.

Dasher, Fox and Quantum

Camber is adjusted by loosening the two ball joint-to-lower control arm bolts, and moving the ball joint in or out as necessary.

Golf, Rabbit, Scirocco, Jetta, GTI

Camber is adjusted by loosening the nuts of the two bolts holding the top of the wheel bearing housing to the bottom of the strut, and turning the top eccentric bolt. The range of adjustment is 2°.

CASTER

Caster angle is the number of degrees in which a line drawn through the steering knuckle pivots is inclined from the vertical, toward the front or rear of the car. Positive caster improves direction stability and decreases susceptibility to cross winds or road surface deviations. Other than the replacement of damaged suspension components, caster is not adjustable.

TOE-IN

Dasher and Quantum

Toe-in is checked with the wheels straight ahead. The left tie rod is adjustable. Loosen the nuts and clamps and adjust the length of the tie rod for correct toe-out. If the steering wheel is crooked, remove and align it.

Fox

NOTE: *Steering gear tool 3075 must be used to adjust toe on vehicles with twp adjustable tie rods.*

1. Turn the steering gear to the center position.
2. Remove front bolt A from the steering gear cover.
3. Attach centering tool 3075 with bracket B over mounting nut on the left tie rod.
4. Remove the bolt from the spacer on the chain of the centering tool.
5. Put the spacer under the hole marked with an L and insert a bolt through this hole and the hole in the spacer, then tighten to the steering gear.
6. Measure and divide the total toe in half.
7. Loosen the clamps and outer lock nut on both sides.
8. Turn both tie rods until the specified setting for Toe is reached.
9. Tighten the clamps and lock nuts on the tie rods.
10. Check and reposition steering wheel in center position if necessary.
11. Remove the centering tool and tighten bolt A to 15 ft.lb. (20 Nm).
12. If the steering wheel is crooked after the

Top eccentric bolt provides camber adjustment on Rabbit, Scirocco, Jetta

toe adjustment has been made, remove, straighten and reinstall the wheel.

Golf, Rabbit, Scirocco, Jetta, GTI

Toe-in is checked with the wheels straight ahead. Only the right tie rod is adjustable, but replacement left tie rods are adjustable. Replacement left tie rods should be set to the same length as the original. Toe-in should be adjusted only with the right tie rod. If the steering wheel is crooked, remove and align it.

REAR SUSPENSION

The Dasher rear suspinsion has a rear axle beam tube on each side. The trailing arms mount to the unit body in rubber bushings. A coil spring and shock absorber are located at each wheel. A Panhard rod locates the axle against side forces.

The Golf, Rabbit (except the Pick-up truck), Jetta and Scirocco rear suspension includes a torsion beam which connects the two trailing arms. On these models, the coil spring and the shock absorber are combined into a strut. The Quantum rear axle assembly is similar to this type, but uses different axle bushings.

The Rabbit Pick-up truck has leaf springs mounted on a simple axle beam with conventional shock absorbers mounted at each side of the beam.

The Fox rear suspinsion has a rear axle beam tube on each side. The trailing arms mount to the unit body in rubber bushings. The coil spring and the shock absorber are combined into a strut.

Coil Spring

REMOVAL AND INSTALLATION

Dasher Only

NOTE: *This operation requires the use of either special tool VW 655/3 or a suitable spring compressor.*

1. Raise the car and support it on jack stands. Do not place the jack stands under the axle beam.
2. Remove the road wheel.
3. Attach special tool VW 655/3 between the axle beam and a prefabricated hook hung on the body frame above the beam. Use the special tool or spring compressor to compress the spring.
4. Unbolt the shock absorber from the axle beam. If you used a spring compressor, you should be able to remove the spring now. Do not allow the axle to hang by its body mounts. If you used special tool VW 655/3, lower the axle beam enough to remove the spring.

5. Installation is the reverse of removal.
NOTE: *It is not necessary to replace both springs if only one is damaged.*

Shock Absorber
REMOVAL AND INSTALLATION
Dasher Only

NOTE: *Only remove one shock absorber at a time. Do not allow the rear axle to hang by its body mounts only, as it may damage the brake lines.*

This operation requires the use of either special tool VW 655/3 or a suitable spring compressor and floor jack.

1. Raise the car and support it on jack stands. Do not place the jack stands under the axle beam.
2. Remove the wheel.
3. Attach special tool VW 655/3 between the axle beam and a prefabricated hook hung on the body frame above the beam. Jack the tool until you can see the shock absorber compressing. If you are using a spring compressor and a floor jack, compress the springs little and, placing the floor jack under the beam below the spring, jack it up until you see the shock absorber compress.
4. Unbolt and remove the shock absorber.
5. Installation is the reverse of removal. Tighten the shock absorber bolts to 43 ft.lb.
NOTE: *There are two types of shock absorbers for the Dasher and they have different mounts. Make sure you get the correct type for your vehicle.*

Strut Assembly
REMOVAL AND INSTALLATION
Fox, Rabbit (Except Pick-Up), Scirocco, Jetta, Golf, GTI

1. Raise the car on a lift or jack it up and support it on stands. Support the axle with a floor jack, but do not put any pressure on the springs.
2. Remove the rubber guard from inside the car.
3. Remove the nut, washer and mounting disc.
4. Unbolt the strut assembly from the rear axle and remove it.
5. Installation is the reverse of removal. Tighten the top mount bolt to 23 ft.lb. and the bottom bolt to 32 ft.lb.

Quantum

1. Remove shock strut cover inside car.
2. Unscrew strut from body.
3. Slowly lift vehicle until wheels are slightly off ground.

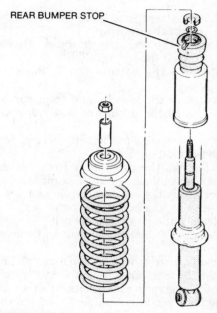

REAR BUMPER STOP

GTI rear strut installation

4. Unscrew strut from axle.
5. Take strut out of lower mounting. Press wheel down slightly when removing strut.
CAUTION: *Do not remove both suspension struts at the same time as this will overload the axle beam bushings.*
6. Guide strut out carefully between wheel and wheel housing. Do not damage paint on spring and wheel housing.
7. Installation is the reverse of removal.

STRUT OVERHAUL (COIL SPRING AND SHOCK ABSORBER)

A spring compressor is necessary for this operation. Also, do not exchange a Rabbit/Jetta, Scirocco coil spring, since they are different in size and/or hardness.

1. Clamp the strut in a vise.
2. Attach the spring compressor and compress the spring.
3. Remove the slotted nut at the top of the strut and remove the collar and the spring.
4. Installation is the reverse of removal. Tighten the slotted nut to 14 ft.lb.

Leaf Spring
REMOVAL AND INSTALLATION
Rabbit Pick-Up

CAUTION: *The springs are under considerable tension, so be careful.*
1. Jack up the rear of the truck and support it with jackstands placed under the frame. Remove the wheel.

2. Remove the parking brake cable from the spring and cut the tie-wrap.

3. Support the rear axle on a jack. Do not put pressure on the spring.

4. Remove the bottom shock absorber mount bolt.

5. Removes the U-bolts and their spring plates. Loosen the upper and lower shackle bolts.

6. When removing the left side spring, perform these additional steps:

   a. Remove the three bolts from the exhaust system flange on the flex pipe.

   b. Unhook the exhaust system hangers.

   c. Remove the exhaust system.

7. Remove the lower shackle bolt.

8. Remove the front spring bolt and remove the spring.

9. Installation is the reverse of removal. The weight of the truck must be on the rear wheels before the leaf spring and shock absorber attaching bolts are fully tightened. Tighten the rear shackle bolts to 45 ft.lb., and the front bolt to 68 ft.lb. Tighten the U-bolt nuts and the lower shock absorber bolt to 29 ft.lb.

Shock Absorber
REMOVAL AND INSTALLATION
Rabbit Pick-Up

1. Jack up the rear of the truck and support the axle on jack stands.

2. Unbolt and remove the shock absorber, taking care to notice the direction of mounting bolts for installation.

3. Installation is the reverse of removal. Tighten the mounting bolts to 29 ft.lb.

Stub Axle
REMOVAL AND INSTALLATION
All Models

1. Remove the grease cap.

2. Remove the cotter pin, nutlock, adjusting nut, spacer, wheel bearing and brake drum.

3. Detach the brake line and plug it.

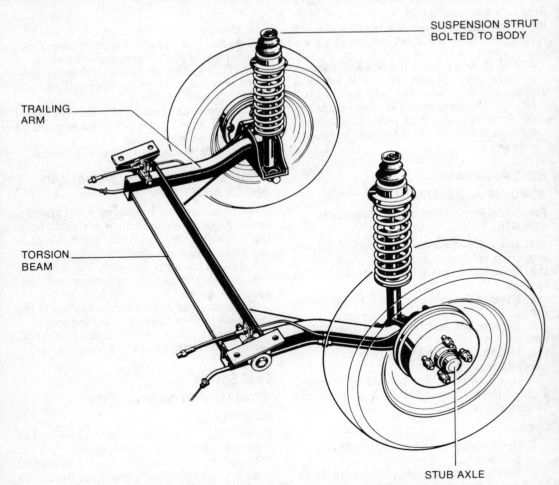

SUSPENSION STRUT BOLTED TO BODY

TRAILING ARM

TORSION BEAM

STUB AXLE

Rabbit, Jetta, Scirocco rear suspension. Jettas also have stabilizers

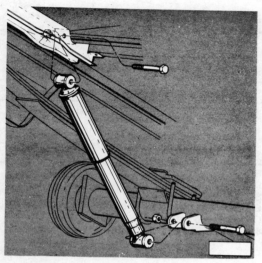

Rabbit Pick-up shock absorber

4. Remove the brake backing plate complete with brake assembly.

5. Unbolt and remove the stub axle.

6. Installation is the reverse of removal. Always replace the spring washer with a new one and bleed the brakes. Pack the bearings and adjust the bearing end-play.

Rear Wheel Bearing Adjustment

Before attempting to adjust the wheel bearings, tighten the adjustment nut while turning the wheel to seat the bearings. Wheel bearing clearance is correctly adjusted when the thrust washer under the adjusting nut can be moved slightly with a screwdriver. Do not twist or pry with the screwdriver. Install a new cotter pin.

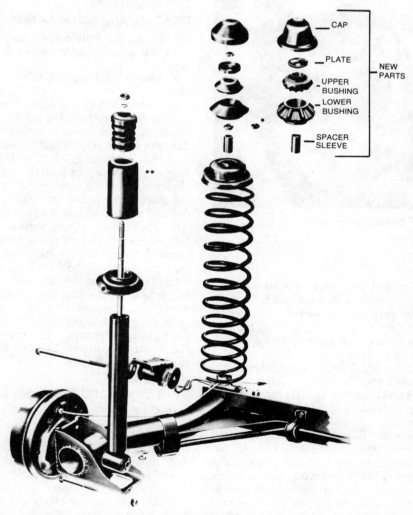

Rabbit, Jetta, Scirocco rear suspension—except Rabbit Pick-up. Note new parts used beginning 1978

Wheel Alignment

Year	Model	Caster ①		Camber ②		Toe-in ③ (in.)	Steering Axis Inclination ① (deg)
		Range (deg)	Pref Setting (deg)	Range (deg)	Pref Setting (deg)		
All	Dasher	0°–1°	0°30′	0–1°	0°30′	0.08	10°30′
All	Rabbit, Fox Scirocco Jetta	+ 1°20′–2°20′	+ 1°50′	– 10°– + 50′	+ 20′	0.08	10°30′
'82–'87	Quantum	+ 30′ ± 30′	+ 30′	– 40′ ± 30′	– 40′	N.A.	N.A.

① Not adjustable;
② Rear wheel camber (not adjustable)
  Rabbit (to Ch. No. 176 3 241 690)—1°N ± 30′
  Rabbit (from Ch. No. 176 3 261 691)—1¼°N ± 30′
  Scirocco (all)—1°N ± 30′
  Dasher (all)—½°N ± 30′
  Quantum 1982—1°40′ ± 20′
  Jetta—1¼°N ± 30′

③ Rear wheel toe-in (not adjustable)
  Rabbit—0° ± 15′
  Scirocco (to Ch. No. 536 2 031 722)—10°P ± 30′
  Scirocco (from Ch. No. 536 2 031 723)—20′P ± 30′
  Quantum + 25′ ± 15′
  Jetta—0° ± 15′

Rear wheel bearing adjustment

STEERING

The Dasher and Fox uses rack and pinion steering gear with center mounted tie rods. This allows very little toe-in change during suspension travel. A steering damper reduces road shock transmittal to the steering wheel. No maintenance is required.

The Golf, Rabbit, Jetta, GTI and Scirocco are equipped with rack and pinion steering. The tie rods are end mounted. One tie rod is adjustable. No maintenance is required on the rack and pinion.

The Quantum is equipped with standard power steering (rack and pinion). The only periodic maintenance required is a check of the power steering fluid reservoir, and a check when underneath the car (oil change time is convenient) for steering system leaks. Replace fluid reservoir filter when changing fluid or when replacing steering system components.

Steering Wheel
REMOVAL AND INSTALLATION

1. Grasp the center cover pad and pull it from the wheel. (Cover varies depending on model).
2. Loosen and remove the steering shaft nut.
3. Matchmark the steering wheel position in relation to the steering shaft so that when you install it, the wheel is perfectly level when the road wheels are straight ahead.
4. Pull the steering wheel off the shaft. You may need a puller to perform this operation. Under no circumstances should you bang on the shaft to try to free the wheel, or you may damage the collapsible steering column.
5. Disconnect the horn wire.
6. Replace the wheel in the reverse order of removal. On the Rabbit, Jetta and Scirocco, install the steering wheel with the road wheels straight ahead and the cancelling lug pointing to the left. On the Fox, Dasher and Quantum with the road wheels straight ahead, the cancelling lug on the steering wheel must point to the right and the turn signal lever must be in the neutral position. Tighten the steering shaft nut to 36 ft.lb.

Turn Signal and Headlight Dimmer Switch
REMOVAL AND INSTALLATION

1. Disconnect the battery ground cable.
2. Remove the steering wheel.
3. Remove the switch retaining screws.
4. Pry the switch housing off the column.
5. Disconnect the electrical plugs at the back of the switch.
6. Remove the switch housing.

7. Replace in the reverse order of removal.
NOTE: *On the Rabbit, Jetta and Scirocco, tap spacer sleeve into column (carefully) until there is 0.080–0.16" clearance between the wheel and the hub.*

Ignition Switch
REMOVAL AND INSTALLATION

The ignition switch is located at the bottom of the ignition key cylinder body. To remove the ignition switch, remove the steering lock body, see below for procedures. On all models except Dashers made before 1978, remove the switch by removing the screw at the bottom of the switch and pulling the switch out. On Dashers made before 1978, the screw is located in the side of the cylinder body. Installation is the reverse of removal.

Steering Lock
REMOVAL AND INSTALLATION

On some models, the hole in the lock body for removing the steering lock cylinder was not drilled by Volkswagen. To make the hole, use the following measurements in conjunction with the illustrations. Drill the hole where "a" and "b" intersect on the lock body. The hole should be drilled ⅛" deep.
- 1974–77 Dasher
  a = 11.5mm (0.453")
  b = 8.0mm (0.315")
- 1975–76 Rabbit, Scirocco
  a = 11mm (⁷⁄₁₆")
  b = 11mm (⁷⁄₁₆")
- 1977–87 Rabbit, Jetta, Scirocco, 1978–87 Dasher, Quantum, Fox
  a = 12mm (0.472")
  b = 10mm (0.393")

NOTE: *Measurements are given in metric form first because this unit of measurement will be easier to make.*

Remove the lock cylinder by pushing a small drill bit or piece of wire into the hole and pulling the cylinder out. It might be easier to insert the ignition key, turn it to the right a little and pull on it.
NOTE: *On 1976 Rabbits and Sciroccos, the lock cylinder can also be removed by removing the steering and windshield wiper components and removing the locking plate holding the cylinder with a pair of pliers. When installing the plate, peen it slightly to hold it in place.*
To remove the lock body, proceed as follows:
1. Remove the steering wheel and turn signal switch. See above for procedures. Remove the steering column shaft covers.

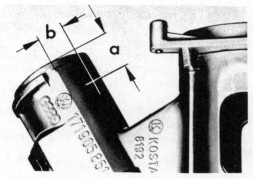

Lock cylinder removal, all Rabbit, Jetta, Scirocco, 1978 and later Dasher

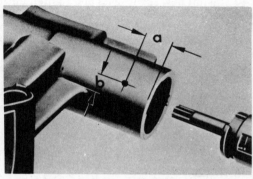

Lock cylinder removal, 1977 and earlier Dasher

2. The lock is clamped to the steering column with special bolts whose heads shear off on installation. These must be drilled out in order to remove the switch.
3. On replacement, make sure that the lock tang is aligned with the slot in the steering column.

Steering Column
REMOVAL AND INSTALLATION

1. Disconnect the negative battery cable.
2. Working from the inside of the vehicle, remove the steering wheel as previously discribed.
3. Remove the turn signal/headlight and wiper/washer switches.
4. Remove the ignition switch and the ignition lock housing.
5. Remove the upper and lower column covers. Pry off the bearing support ring.
6. Remove the shear bolt cover and drill out the shear bolt(s). Then remove the steering shaft support bolts and lower the steering column.
7. Working from under the hood of the car, lower the dust boot and remove the bolt which secures the steering column to the universal joint shaft.

NOTE: *On the 1987 Fox the steering column is connected to a flange tube. Remove the retainer which holds the steering shaft to the flange tube and remove the column. During installation, hold the flange tube and the steering column together with water pump pliers and install the retainer.*

8. Working fron inside the vehicle, remove the steering column.

9. Installation is the reverse of the removal procedures.

10. Torque the universal shaft bolt to 22 ft.lb. (30 Nm).

11. Torque the steering shaft support bolt to 14 ft.lb. (20 Nm).

12. Install new shear bolts and tighten until the heads shear off.

NOTE: *Do not push the steering column into the universal joint using more than 100–200 lbs of force.*

13. Install the remaining components in the reverse of their removal.

14. Make sure that the road wheels are straight ahead when the steering wheel is installed.

15. Torque the steering wheel retaining bolt to 36 ft.lb. (50 Nm).

Tie Rods

REMOVAL AND INSTALLATION

Dasher Fox and Quantum

Because of the demand for optional wheel rims which require more clearance at the tie rod, several different length adjustable and non-adjustable tie rods are available. Which tie rod is right for your car depends on the transmission used (manual or automatic), and the year of production. Consult your dealer for this information.

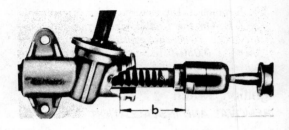

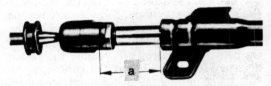

Rabbit, Jetta, Scirocco steering rack adjustment

1. Raise the car and remove the front wheels.

2. Disconnect the outer end of the steering tie rod from the steering knuckle by removing the cotter pin and nut and pressing out the tie rod end. A small puller or press is required to free the tie rod end.

3. Under the hood, pry off the lock plate and remove the mounting bolts from both tie rod inner ends. Pry the tie rod out of the mounting pivot and remove.

4. Installation is the reverse of removal. If you are replacing an adjustable tie rod, adjust the new tie rod to the same length. If replacing a new, non-adjustable shorter tie rod, the other side tie rod will have to be adjusted. Tighten the tie rod to steering knuckle nut to 22 ft.lb., and the inner pivot bolt to 40 ft.lb. Check the toe.

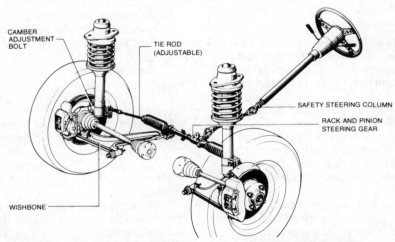

Rabbit, Jetta, Scirocco steering and front suspension components

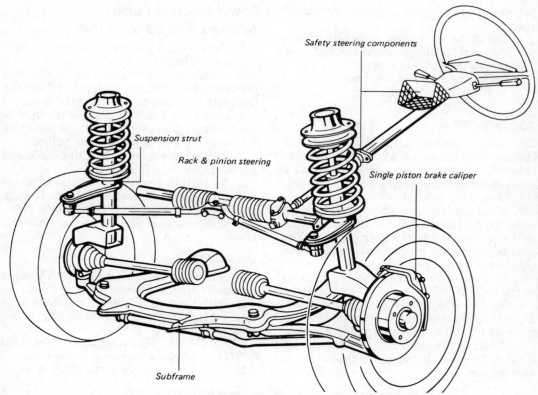

Safety steering components

Suspension strut

Rack & pinion steering

Single piston brake caliper

Subframe

Dasher front suspension and steering components

Golf, Rabbit, Jetta, GTI, Scirocco

1. Center the steering wheel.
2. Remove the cotter pin and nut from the tie rod end.
3. Disconnect the tie rod from the steering rack after removing the rubber boot from the end of the rack. The left side tie rod end cannot be removed from the tie rod, therefore the entire tie rod must be replaced if the ball joint goes bad. Loosen the lock ring and unscrew the tie rod. See steps 5 and 6 of the Rabbit and Scirocco Steering Gear Removal and Installation. Adjust the left tie rod for Toe. Tighten the tie rod end nuts to 21 ft.lb., and install new cotter pins.

Steering Gear
REMOVAL AND INSTALLATION
Dasher, Fox and Quantum

1. Pry off the lock plate and remove both tie rod mounting bolts from the steering rack, inside the engine compartment. Pry the tie rods out of the mounting pivot.
2. Remove the lower instrument panel trim.
3. Remove the shaft clamp bolt, pry off the clip, and drive the shaft toward the inside of the car with a brass drift.
4. Disconnect power steering hoses (if equipped). Remove the steering gear mounting bolts.
5. Turn the wheels all the way to the right and remove the steering gear through the opening in the right wheelhousing.
6. For installation, temporarily install the tie rod mounting pivot to the rack with both mounting bolts. Remove one bolt, install the tie rod, and replace the bolt. Do the same on the other tie rod. Make sure to install a new lock plate. Torque the tie rod bolts to 39 ft.lb., the mounting pivot bolt to 15 ft.lb., and the steering gear to body mounting bolts to 15 ft.lb.

Golf, Rabbit, Scirocco GTI and Jetta

1. Disconnect the steering shaft universal joint and wire up out of the way.
2. Disconnect the tie rods at the steering rack and wire up and out of the way. Disconnect power steering hoses (if equipped).
3. Remove the steering rack and drive.
4. Install the steering rack and drive and torque the attaching hardware to 14 ft.lb.
5. Set the steering rack with equal distances

between the housing on the right side and left side.

6. Install the tie rods and screw both sides in until an equal distance is reached on both rods.

7. Install the steering shaft.

8. Check the front end alignment.

ADJUSTMENT

The steering gear on all models, except the Dasher before chassis no. 4 2 186 215, is adjustable. The adjustment is made at the junction where the steering wheel shaft meets the rack.

1. Loosen the locknut.

2. Hand tighten the adjusting screw in the center of the locknut until it just touches the thrust washer inside the gear housing. You can't see the thrust washer, but you should be able to tell by the feel of the screw.

3. Hold the screw in this position and tighten the locknut.

4. Road test the car. If the steering is stiff or does not center itself after a turn, the screw is probably too tight. If the steering still rattles, the adjustment is too loose, or other components of the steering system (tie rods, etc.) are wearing out.

Power Steering Pump

REMOVAL AND INSTALLATION

1. Place a catch pan under the power steering pump to catch the fluid.

2. Remove the suction hose and the prewssure line from the pump, then drain the fluid into the catch pan (discard the fluid).

3. Loosen the tensioning bolt at the front of the tensioning bracket and remove the drive belt from the fronmt of the drive pulley.

4. Remove the pumps mounting bolts and lift the pump from the vehicle.

5. To install, reverse the removal procedures. Torque the mounting bolts to 15 ft.lb. (20 Nm). Tension the drive belt. Fill the reservoir with approved power steering fluid and bleed the system.

BLEEDING

1. Fill the reservoir to the MAX level markwith approved power steering fluid.

2. With the engine idling, turn the wheels from the right to the left side as far as possible, several times.

NOTE:Continue bleeding the system until NO air bubbles are present in the fluid.

3. Refill the reservoir to the MAX level.

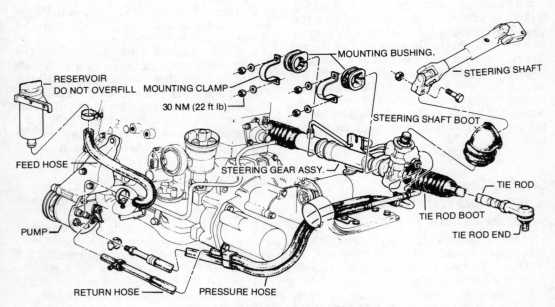

Typical rack and pinion power steering

Troubleshooting Basic Driveshaft and Rear Axle Problems

When abnormal vibrations or noises are detected in the driveshaft area, this chart can be used to help diagnose possible causes. Remember that other components such as wheels, tires, rear axle and suspension can also produce similar conditions.

BASIC DRIVESHAFT PROBLEMS

Problem	Cause	Solution
Shudder as car accelerates from stop or low speed	• Loose U-joint • Defective center bearing	• Replace U-joint • Replace center bearing
Loud clunk in driveshaft when shifting gears	• Worn U-joints	• Replace U-joints
Roughness or vibration at any speed	• Out-of-balance, bent or dented driveshaft • Worn U-joints • U-joint clamp bolts loose	• Balance or replace driveshaft • Replace U-joints • Tighten U-joint clamp bolts
Squeaking noise at low speeds	• Lack of U-joint lubrication	• Lubricate U-joint; if problem persists, replace U-joint
Knock or clicking noise	• U-joint or driveshaft hitting frame tunnel • Worn CV joint	• Correct overloaded condition • Replace CV joint

BASIC REAR AXLE PROBLEMS

First, determine when the noise is most noticeable.

Drive Noise: Produced under vehicle acceleration.

Coast Noise: Produced while the car coasts with a closed throttle.

Float Noise: Occurs while maintaining constant car speed (just enough to keep speed constant) on a level road.

Road Noise

Brick or rough surfaced concrete roads produce noises that seem to come from the rear axle. Road noise is usually identical in Drive or Coast and driving on a different type of road will tell whether the road is the problem.

Tire Noise

Tire noises are often mistaken for rear axle problems. Snow treads or unevenly worn tires produce vibrations seeming to originate elsewhere. **Temporarily** inflating the tires to 40 lbs will significantly alter tire noise, but will have no effect on rear axle noises (which normally cease below about 30 mph).

Engine/Transmission Noise

Determine at what speed the noise is most pronounced, then stop the car in a quiet place. With the transmission in Neutral, run the engine through speeds corresponding to road speeds where the noise was noticed. Noises produced with the car standing still are coming from the engine or transmission.

Front Wheel Bearings

While holding the car speed steady, lightly apply the foot-brake; this will often decease bearing noise, as some of the load is taken from the bearing.

Rear Axle Noises

Eliminating other possible sources can narrow the cause to the rear axle, which normally produces noise from worn gears or bearings. Gear noises tend to peak in a narrow speed range, while bearing noises will usually vary in pitch with engine speeds.

NOISE DIAGNOSIS

The Noise Is	Most Probably Produced By
• Identical under Drive or Coast	• Road surface, tires or front wheel bearings
• Different depending on road surface	• Road surface or tires
• Lower as the car speed is lowered	• Tires
• Similar with car standing or moving	• Engine or transmission
• A vibration	• Unbalanced tires, rear wheel bearing, unbalanced driveshaft or worn U-joint
• A knock or click about every 2 tire revolutions	• Rear wheel bearing
• Most pronounced on turns	• Damaged differential gears
• A steady low-pitched whirring or scraping, starting at low speeds	• Damaged or worn pinion bearing
• A chattering vibration on turns	• Wrong differential lubricant or worn clutch plates (limited slip rear axle)
• Noticed only in Drive, Coast or Float conditions	• Worn ring gear and/or pinion gear

Troubleshooting Basic Steering and Suspension Problems

Problem	Cause	Solution
Hard steering (steering wheel is hard to turn)	• Low or uneven tire pressure	• Inflate tires to correct pressure
	• Loose power steering pump drive belt	• Adjust belt
	• Low or incorrect power steering fluid	• Add fluid as necessary
	• Incorrect front end alignment	• Have front end alignment checked/adjusted
	• Defective power steering pump	• Check pump
	• Bent or poorly lubricated front end parts	• Lubricate and/or replace defective parts
Loose steering (too much play in the steering wheel)	• Loose wheel bearings	• Adjust wheel bearings
	• Loose or worn steering linkage	• Replace worn parts
	• Faulty shocks	• Replace shocks
	• Worn ball joints	• Replace ball joints
Car veers or wanders (car pulls to one side with hands off the steering wheel)	• Incorrect tire pressure	• Inflate tires to correct pressure
	• Improper front end alignment	• Have front end alignment checked/adjusted
	• Loose wheel bearings	• Adjust wheel bearings
	• Loose or bent front end components	• Replace worn components
	• Faulty shocks	• Replace shocks
Wheel oscillation or vibration transmitted through steering wheel	• Improper tire pressures	• Inflate tires to correct pressure
	• Tires out of balance	• Have tires balanced
	• Loose wheel bearings	• Adjust wheel bearings
	• Improper front end alignment	• Have front end alignment checked/adjusted
	• Worn or bent front end components	• Replace worn parts
Uneven tire wear	• Incorrect tire pressure	• Inflate tires to correct pressure
	• Front end out of alignment	• Have front end alignment checked/adjusted
	• Tires out of balance	• Have tires balanced

Troubleshooting the Steering Column

Problem	Cause	Solution
Will not lock	· Lockbolt spring broken or defective	· Replace lock bolt spring
High effort (required to turn ignition key and lock cylinder)	· Lock cylinder defective · Ignition switch defective · Rack preload spring broken or deformed · Burr on lock sector, lock rack, housing, support or remote rod coupling · Bent sector shaft · Defective lock rack · Remote rod bent, deformed · Ignition switch mounting bracket bent · Distorted coupling slot in lock rack (tilt column)	· Replace lock cylinder · Replace ignition switch · Replace preload spring · Remove burr · Replace shaft · Replace lock rack · Replace rod · Straighten or replace · Replace lock rack
Will stick in "start"	· Remote rod deformed · Ignition switch mounting bracket bent	· Straighten or replace · Straighten or replace
Key cannot be removed in "off-lock"	· Ignition switch is not adjusted correctly · Defective lock cylinder	· Adjust switch · Replace lock cylinder
Lock cylinder can be removed without depressing retainer	· Lock cylinder with defective retainer · Burr over retainer slot in housing cover or on cylinder retainer	· Replace lock cylinder · Remove burr
High effort on lock cylinder between "off" and "off-lock"	· Distorted lock rack · Burr on tang of shift gate (automatic column) · Gearshift linkage not adjusted	· Replace lock rack · Remove burr · Adjust linkage
Noise in column	· One click when in "off-lock" position and the steering wheel is moved (all except automatic column) · Coupling bolts not tightened · Lack of grease on bearings or bearing surfaces · Upper shaft bearing worn or broken · Lower shaft bearing worn or broken · Column not correctly aligned · Coupling pulled apart · Broken coupling lower joint · Steering shaft snap ring not seated · Shroud loose on shift bowl. Housing loose on jacket—will be noticed with ignition in "off-lock" and when torque is applied to steering wheel.	· Normal—lock bolt is seating · Tighten pinch bolts · Lubricate with chassis grease · Replace bearing assembly · Replace bearing. Check shaft and replace if scored. · Align column · Replace coupling · Repair or replace joint and align column · Replace ring. Check for proper seating in groove. · Position shroud over lugs on shift bowl. Tighten mounting screws.
High steering shaft effort	· Column misaligned · Defective upper or lower bearing · Tight steering shaft universal joint · Flash on I.D. of shift tube at plastic joint (tilt column only) · Upper or lower bearing seized	· Align column · Replace as required · Repair or replace · Replace shift tube · Replace bearings
Lash in mounted column assembly	· Column mounting bracket bolts loose · Broken weld nuts on column jacket · Column capsule bracket sheared	· Tighten bolts · Replace column jacket · Replace bracket assembly

Troubleshooting the Steering Column (cont.)

Problem	Cause	Solution
Lash in mounted column assembly (cont.)	• Column bracket to column jacket mounting bolts loose	• Tighten to specified torque
	• Loose lock shoes in housing (tilt column only)	• Replace shoes
	• Loose pivot pins (tilt column only)	• Replace pivot pins and support
	• Loose lock shoe pin (tilt column only)	• Replace pin and housing
	• Loose support screws (tilt column only)	• Tighten screws
Housing loose (tilt column only)	• Excessive clearance between holes in support or housing and pivot pin diameters	• Replace pivot pins and support
	• Housing support-screws loose	• Tighten screws
Steering wheel loose—every other tilt position (tilt column only)	• Loose fit between lock shoe and lock shoe pivot pin	• Replace lock shoes and pivot pin
Steering column not locking in any tilt position (tilt column only)	• Lock shoe seized on pivot pin	• Replace lock shoes and pin
	• Lock shoe grooves have burrs or are filled with foreign material	• Clean or replace lock shoes
	• Lock shoe springs weak or broken	• Replace springs
Noise when tilting column (tilt column only)	• Upper tilt bumpers worn	• Replace tilt bumper
	• Tilt spring rubbing in housing	• Lubricate with chassis grease
One click when in "off-lock" position and the steering wheel is moved	• Seating of lock bolt	• None. Click is normal characteristic sound produced by lock bolt as it seats.
High shift effort (automatic and tilt column only)	• Column not correctly aligned	• Align column
	• Lower bearing not aligned correctly	• Assemble correctly
	• Lack of grease on seal or lower bearing areas	• Lubricate with chassis grease
Improper transmission shifting—automatic and tilt column only	• Sheared shift tube joint	• Replace shift tube
	• Improper transmission gearshift linkage adjustment	• Adjust linkage
	• Loose lower shift lever	• Replace shift tube

Troubleshooting the Manual Steering Gear

Problem	Cause	Solution
Hard or erratic steering	• Incorrect tire pressure	• Inflate tires to recommended pressures
	• Insufficient or incorrect lubrication	• Lubricate as required (refer to Maintenance Section)
	• Suspension, or steering linkage parts damaged or misaligned	• Repair or replace parts as necessary
	• Improper front wheel alignment	• Adjust incorrect wheel alignment angles
	• Incorrect steering gear adjustment	• Adjust steering gear
	• Sagging springs	• Replace springs
Play or looseness in steering	• Steering wheel loose	• Inspect shaft spines and repair as necessary. Tighten attaching nut and stake in place.
	• Steering linkage or attaching parts loose or worn	• Tighten, adjust, or replace faulty components
	• Pitman arm loose	• Inspect shaft splines and repair as necessary. Tighten attaching nut and stake in place
	• Steering gear attaching bolts loose	• Tighten bolts
	• Loose or worn wheel bearings	• Adjust or replace bearings
	• Steering gear adjustment incorrect or parts badly worn	• Adjust gear or replace defective parts

Troubleshooting the Manual Steering Gear (cont.)

Problem	Cause	Solution
Wheel shimmy or tramp	• Improper tire pressure	• Inflate tires to recommended pressures
	• Wheels, tires, or brake rotors out-of-balance or out-of-round	• Inspect and replace or balance parts
	• Inoperative, worn, or loose shock absorbers or mounting parts	• Repair or replace shocks or mountings
	• Loose or worn steering or suspension parts	• Tighten or replace as necessary
	• Loose or worn wheel bearings	• Adjust or replace bearings
	• Incorrect steering gear adjustments	• Adjust steering gear
	• Incorrect front wheel alignment	• Correct front wheel alignment
Tire wear	• Improper tire pressure	• Inflate tires to recommended pressures
	• Failure to rotate tires	• Rotate tires
	• Brakes grabbing	• Adjust or repair brakes
	• Incorrect front wheel alignment	• Align incorrect angles
	• Broken or damaged steering and suspension parts	• Repair or replace defective parts
	• Wheel runout	• Replace faulty wheel
	• Excessive speed on turns	• Make driver aware of conditions
Vehicle leads to one side	• Improper tire pressures	• Inflate tires to recommended pressures
	• Front tires with uneven tread depth, wear pattern, or different cord design (i.e., one bias ply and one belted or radial tire on front wheels)	• Install tires of same cord construction and reasonably even tread depth, design, and wear pattern
	• Incorrect front wheel alignment	• Align incorrect angles
	• Brakes dragging	• Adjust or repair brakes
	• Pulling due to uneven tire construction	• Replace faulty tire

Troubleshooting the Power Steering Gear

Problem	Cause	Solution
Hissing noise in steering gear	• There is some noise in all power steering systems. One of the most common is a hissing sound most evident at standstill parking. There is no relationship between this noise and performance of the steering. Hiss may be expected when steering wheel is at end of travel or when slowly turning at standstill.	• Slight hiss is normal and in no way affects steering. Do not replace valve unless hiss is extremely objectionable. A replacement valve will also exhibit slight noise and is not always a cure. Investigate clearance around flexible coupling rivets. Be sure steering shaft and gear are aligned so flexible coupling rotates in a flat plane and is not distorted as shaft rotates. Any metal-to-metal contacts through flexible coupling will transmit valve hiss into passenger compartment through the steering column.
Rattle or chuckle noise in steering gear	• Gear loose on frame	• Check gear-to-frame mounting screws. Tighten screws to 88 N·m (65 foot pounds) torque.
	• Steering linkage looseness	• Check linkage pivot points for wear. Replace if necessary.
	• Pressure hose touching other parts of car	• Adjust hose position. Do not bend tubing by hand.
	• Loose pitman shaft over center adjustment	• Adjust to specifications

Troubleshooting the Power Steering Gear (cont.)

Problem	Cause	Solution
Rattle or chuckle noise in steering gear (cont.)	**NOTE:** A slight rattle may occur on turns because of increased clearance off the "high point." This is normal and clearance must not be reduced below specified limits to eliminate this slight rattle. • Loose pitman arm	• Tighten pitman arm nut to specifications
Squawk noise in steering gear when turning or recovering from a turn	• Damper O-ring on valve spool cut	• Replace damper O-ring
Poor return of steering wheel to center	• Tires not properly inflated • Lack of lubrication in linkage and ball joints • Lower coupling flange rubbing against steering gear adjuster plug • Steering gear to column misalignment • Improper front wheel alignment • Steering linkage binding • Ball joints binding • Steering wheel rubbing against housing • Tight or frozen steering shaft bearings • Sticking or plugged valve spool • Steering gear adjustments over specifications • Kink in return hose	• Inflate to specified pressure • Lube linkage and ball joints • Loosen pinch bolt and assemble properly • Align steering column • Check and adjust as necessary • Replace pivots • Replace ball joints • Align housing • Replace bearings • Remove and clean or replace valve • Check adjustment with gear out of car. Adjust as required. • Replace hose
Car leads to one side or the other (keep in mind road condition and wind. Test car in both directions on flat road)	• Front end misaligned • Unbalanced steering gear valve **NOTE:** If this is cause, steering effort will be very light in direction of lead and normal or heavier in opposite direction	• Adjust to specifications • Replace valve
Momentary increase in effort when turning wheel fast to right or left	• Low oil level • Pump belt slipping • High internal leakage	• Add power steering fluid as required • Tighten or replace belt • Check pump pressure. (See pressure test)
Steering wheel surges or jerks when turning with engine running especially during parking	• Low oil level • Loose pump belt • Steering linkage hitting engine oil pan at full turn • Insufficient pump pressure • Pump flow control valve sticking	• Fill as required • Adjust tension to specification • Correct clearance • Check pump pressure. (See pressure test). Replace relief valve if defective. • Inspect for varnish or damage, replace if necessary
Excessive wheel kickback or loose steering	• Air in system • Steering gear loose on frame • Steering linkage joints worn enough to be loose • Worn poppet valve • Loose thrust bearing preload adjustment	• Add oil to pump reservoir and bleed by operating steering. Check hose connectors for proper torque and adjust as required. • Tighten attaching screws to specified torque • Replace loose pivots • Replace poppet valve • Adjust to specification with gear out of vehicle

Troubleshooting the Power Steering Gear (cont.)

Problem	Cause	Solution
Excessive wheel kickback or loose steering (cont.)	• Excessive overcenter lash	• Adjust to specification with gear out of car
Hard steering or lack of assist	• Loose pump belt • Low oil level **NOTE:** Low oil level will also result in excessive pump noise • Steering gear to column misalignment • Lower coupling flange rubbing against steering gear adjuster plug • Tires not properly inflated	• Adjust belt tension to specification • Fill to proper level. If excessively low, check all lines and joints for evidence of external leakage. Tighten loose connectors. • Align steering column • Loosen pinch bolt and assemble properly • Inflate to recommended pressure
Foamy milky power steering fluid, low fluid level and possible low pressure	• Air in the fluid, and loss of fluid due to internal pump leakage causing overflow	• Check for leak and correct. Bleed system. Extremely cold temperatures will cause system aeration should the oil level be low. If oil level is correct and pump still foams, remove pump from vehicle and separate reservoir from housing. Check welsh plug and housing for cracks. If plug is loose or housing is cracked, replace housing.
Low pressure due to steering pump	• Flow control valve stuck or inoperative • Pressure plate not flat against cam ring	• Remove burrs or dirt or replace. Flush system. • Correct
Low pressure due to steering gear	• Pressure loss in cylinder due to worn piston ring or badly worn housing bore • Leakage at valve rings, valve body-to-worm seal	• Remove gear from car for disassembly and inspection of ring and housing bore • Remove gear from car for disassembly and replace seals

Troubleshooting the Power Steering Pump

Problem	Cause	Solution
Chirp noise in steering pump	• Loose belt	• Adjust belt tension to specification
Belt squeal (particularly noticeable at full wheel travel and stand still parking)	• Loose belt	• Adjust belt tension to specification
Growl noise in steering pump	• Excessive back pressure in hoses or steering gear caused by restriction	• Locate restriction and correct. Replace part if necessary.
Growl noise in steering pump (particularly noticeable at stand still parking)	• Scored pressure plates, thrust plate or rotor • Extreme wear of cam ring	• Replace parts and flush system • Replace parts
Groan noise in steering pump	• Low oil level • Air in the oil. Poor pressure hose connection.	• Fill reservoir to proper level • Tighten connector to specified torque. Bleed system by operating steering from right to left—full turn.
Rattle noise in steering pump	• Vanes not installed properly • Vanes sticking in rotor slots	• Install properly • Free up by removing burrs, varnish, or dirt
Swish noise in steering pump	• Defective flow control valve	• Replace part

Troubleshooting the Power Steering Pump (cont.)

Problem	Cause	Solution
Whine noise in steering pump	• Pump shaft bearing scored	• Replace housing and shaft. Flush system.
Hard steering or lack of assist	• Loose pump belt • Low oil level in reservoir **NOTE:** Low oil level will also result in excessive pump noise • Steering gear to column misalignment • Lower coupling flange rubbing against steering gear adjuster plug • Tires not properly inflated	• Adjust belt tension to specification • Fill to proper level. If excessively low, check all lines and joints for evidence of external leakage. Tighten loose connectors. • Align steering column • Loosen pinch bolt and assemble properly • Inflate to recommended pressure
Foaming milky power steering fluid, low fluid level and possible low pressure	• Air in the fluid, and loss of fluid due to internal pump leakage causing overflow	• Check for leaks and correct. Bleed system. Extremely cold temperatures will cause system aeriation should the oil level be low. If oil level is correct and pump still foams, remove pump from vehicle and separate reservoir from body. Check welsh plug and body for cracks. If plug is loose or body is cracked, replace body.
Low pump pressure	• Flow control valve stuck or inoperative • Pressure plate not flat against cam ring	• Remove burrs or dirt or replace. Flush system. • Correct
Momentary increase in effort when turning wheel fast to right or left	• Low oil level in pump • Pump belt slipping • High internal leakage	• Add power steering fluid as required • Tighten or replace belt • Check pump pressure. (See pressure test)
Steering wheel surges or jerks when turning with engine running especially during parking	• Low oil level • Loose pump belt • Steering linkage hitting engine oil pan at full turn • Insufficient pump pressure • Sticking flow control valve	• Fill as required • Adjust tension to specification • Correct clearance • Check pump pressure. (See pressure test). Replace flow control valve if defective. • Inspect for varnish or damage, replace if necessary
Excessive wheel kickback or loose steering	• Air in system	• Add oil to pump reservoir and bleed by operating steering. Check hose connectors for proper torque and adjust as required.
Low pump pressure	• Extreme wear of cam ring • Scored pressure plate, thrust plate, or rotor • Vanes not installed properly • Vanes sticking in rotor slots • Cracked or broken thrust or pressure plate	• Replace parts. Flush system. • Replace parts. Flush system. • Install properly • Freeup by removing burrs, varnish, or dirt • Replace part

8

BRAKE SYSTEM

The base model 1976–78 Rabbit is equipped with front and rear drum brakes. The optional 1976–78 Rabbit, and most 1979 and later Rabbits, and all Quantums, Dashers, Jettas, Fox and Sciroccos are equipped with front disc brakes and rear drum brakes. The Golf and GTI are equipped with front and rear disk brakes.

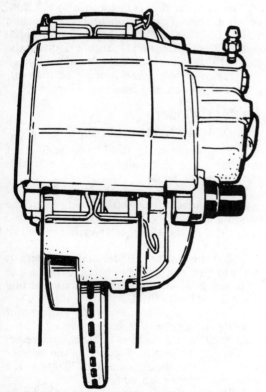

The Rabbit GTI is equipped with a vented brake disc rotor. Brake pads, on these models, should be replaced when minimum thickness (including backing) reaches 3/8 in.

The hydraulic system is a dual circuit type that has the advantage of retaining 50% braking effectiveness in the event of failure in one system. The circuits are arranged so that you always have one front and one rear brake for a more controlled emergency stop. The right front and left rear are in one circuit; the left front and right rear are in the second circuit.

There is also a brake failure switch and a proportioning valve. The brake failure unit is a hydraulic valve/electrical switch which warns of brake problems by the warning light on the instrument panel. A piston inside the switch is kept centered by one brake system pressure on one side and the other system pressure on the opposite side. Should a failure occur in one system, the piston would go to the failed side and complete an electrical circuit to the warning lamp. This switch also functions as a parking brake reminder light and will go out when the parking brake is released. The proportioning valve, actually two separate valves on manual transmission Dasher sedans, provides balances front-to-rear braking during hard stops.

Extreme brake line pressure will overcome the spring pressure on the piston within the valve causing it to proportionately restrict pressure to the rear brakes. In this manner, the rear brakes are kept from locking. The proportioner doesn't operate under normal braking conditions.

Adjustment

The front disc brakes require no adjustment, as disc brakes automatically adjust themselves to compensate for pad wear. The drum brakes on some models must be adjusted whenever free-play is 1/3 or more of the total pedal travel. All 1979 and later Dashers and Quantums, and some 1979 and later Rabbits and Sciroccos are equipped with self-adjusting rear drum brakes. The only way to tell if the brakes are self-adjusting without removing the drum is the absence of the adjusting holes in the brake backing plate. All Golfs, Foxs, Rabbit Pick-ups and Jettas have self-adjusting rear brakes.

FRONT DRUM BRAKES

Rabbit Only

1. Raise and support the front of the car. Block the rear wheels.
2. Remove the rubber plugs covering the adjusters.
3. Insert a screwdriver through the hole and turn the adjuster clockwise until the brake locks.
4. Back off the adjuster until the wheel can be turned. The shoes should drag lightly.
5. Back off the adjuster two notches. The wheel should spin without brake drag. Replace the rubber plugs.

REAR DRUM BRAKES

All Models

NOTE: *On most models except manual transmission Dasher sedans, it is necessary to push the brake pressure regulator lever toward the rear axle to relieve the pressure in the right rear brake line.*

1. Raise the rear of the car and support on stands. Refer to Jacking in chapter 1.
2. Block the front wheels and release the parking brake. Step on the brake pedal hard to center the linings.
3. Remove the rubber plug from the rear of the backing plate on each wheel.
4. Insert a brake adjusting tool or wide-bladed screwdriver and turn the adjuster wheel clockwise until the brakes drag as you turn the wheel in the forward direction.
5. Turn the adjuster in the opposite direction until you just pass the point of drag.

Typical drum brake adjustment

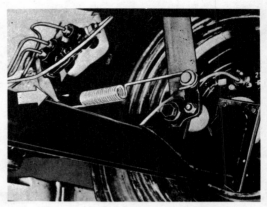

Relieving pressure at the brake pressure regulator valve—Dasher shown. Push lever in direction of arrow

6. Repeat on the other wheel.
7. Lower the car and road test. Readjust, if necessary.

Wheel Bearings

There is no front wheel bearing adjustment. The bearing is pressed into the steering knuckle. The axle nut should be torqued to 174 ft.lb. on all Rabbits, Foxs, Jettas and Sciroccos and either 145 ft.lb. (M18 nut) or 175 ft.lb. (M20 nut) on the Dasher and Quantum. Tighten the nut with the wheels on the ground.

NOTE: *For rear wheel bearing adjustment, see Suspension and Steering, Chapter 7.*

Master Cylinder

REMOVAL AND INSTALLATION

1. To prevent brake fluid from spilling out and damaging this paint, place a protective cover over the fender.
2. Disconnect and plug the brake lines.
3. Disconnect the electrical plug from the sending unit for the brake failure switch.
4. Remove the two master cylinder mounting nuts.
5. Lift the master cylinder and reservoir out of the engine compartment being careful not to spill any fluid on the fender. Empty out and discard the brake fluid.

CAUTION: *Do not depress the brake pedal while the master cylinder is removed.*

6. Position the master cylinder and reservoir assembly onto the studs for the booster and install the washers and nuts. Tighten the nuts to no more than 10 ft.lb.
7. Remove the plugs and connect the brake lines.
8. Bleed the entire brake system as explained further on in this chapter.

snapring (circlip); remove it, using snapring pliers.

6. Shake out the secondary piston assembly. If the primary piston remains lodged in the bore, it can be forced by applying compressed air to the open brake line fitting.

7. Disassemble the secondary piston. The secondary ring(s) will be replaced with those in the rebuilding kit. Save the washers and spacers.

8. Carefully clamp the secondary piston, slightly compress the spring and screw out the stroke limiting bolt.

9. Remove the secondary piston stop sleeve bolt, spring, spring seat, and support washer.

10. Replace all parts with those supplied in the overhaul kit.

11. Clean all metal parts in denatured alcohol and dry them with compressed air.

12. Check every part you are reusing. Pay close attention to the cylinder bores. If there is any scoring or rust, have the master cylinder honed or replace it.

13. Lightly coat the bores and cups with brake fluid. Assemble the cylinder components in the exact sequence shown in the illustration.

14. Install the primary piston assembly, notice that the primary spring is conically shaped. Be sure that you aren't using the secondary spring.

NOTE: *Models with either Teves or ATE master cylinders (the cylinder body should be marked with the brand name), the primary cup and the secondary cup(s) of the secondary (inner) piston have small grooves on their lips. Use the illustrations to tell the cups apart.*

15. Using a plastic rod or other nonmetallic tool, push the primary piston assembly into the housing until the stop bolt (with a new seal) can be screwed in and tightened.

16. Assemble the secondary piston. Fasten the spring, spring seat, primary cup, and stop sleeve to the piston with the stroke limiting bolt.

17. Assemble the remaining master cylinder components in the reverse order of disassembly. Ensure that the snapring is fully seated and that the piston caps are properly positioned. Install the secondary piston with master cylinder opening face down.

18. Install and tighten the brake failure warning sending unit.

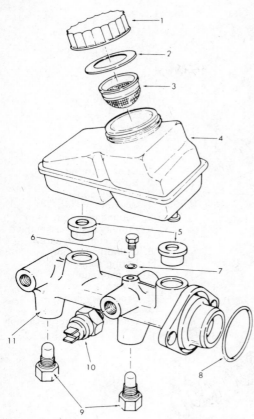

1. Reservoir cap
2. Washer
3. Filter screen
4. Reservoir
5. Master cylinder plugs
6. Stop screw
7. Stop screw seal
8. Master cylinder seal
9. Residual pressure valves
10. Warning light sender unit
11. Brake master cylinder housing

Typical master cylinder body and reservoir

OVERHAUL

Purchase a genuine VW overhaul kit and sufficient brake fluid before starting this procedure.

1. Remove the master cylinder from the booster.

2. Firmly mount the master cylinder in a vise. Use clean rags to protect the cylinder from the vise jaws.

3. Grasp the plastic reservoir and pull it out of the rubber plugs. Remove the plugs.

4. Remove the stop-screw from the center of the cylinder. Discard the stop screw seal, a new one is in the kit.

5. At the end of the master cylinder is a

Bleeding

NOTE: *Use only new, unused and approved brake fluid (DOT3 or DOT4).*

Anytime a brake line has been disconnected

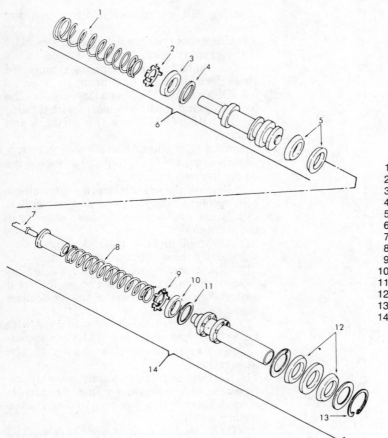

1. Conical spring
2. Spring seat
3. Primary cup
4. Washer
5. Secondary cups
6. Primary piston assembly
7. Stroke limiting screw
8. Cylindrical spring
9. Spring seat
10. Primary cup
11. Washer
12. Secondary cups
13. Circlip
14. Secondary piston assembly

Exploded view of master cylinder components (vehicles with brake booster)

the hydraulic system should be bled. The brakes should also be bled when the pedal travel becomes unusually long (soft pedal) or the car pulls to one side during braking. The proper bleeding sequence is: right rear wheel, left rear wheel, right front caliper, and left front caliper. You'll need a helper to pump the brake pedal while you open the bleeder valves.

NOTE: *If the system has been drained, first*

refill it with fresh brake fluid. Following the above sequence, open each bleeder valve by ½–¾ of a turn and pump the brake pedal until fluid runs out of the valve. Proceed with the bleeding as outlined below.

1. Remove the bleeder valve dust cover and install a rubber bleeder hose.

2. Insert the other end of the hose into a container about ⅓ full of brake fluid.

3. Have an assistant pump the brake pedal several times until the pedal pressure increases.

4. Hold the pedal under pressure and then start to open the bleeder valve about ½–¾ of a turn. At this point, have your assistant depress the pedal all the way and then quickly close the valve. The helper should allow the pedal to return slowly.

NOTE: *Keep a close check on the brake fluid in the reservoir and top it up as necessary throughout the bleeding process.*

5. Keep repeating this procedure until no more air bubbles can be seen coming from the hose in the brake fluid.

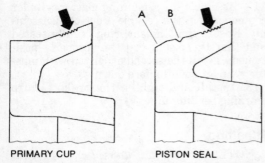

PRIMARY CUP   PISTON SEAL

The primary cup and the piston seal have identifying marks

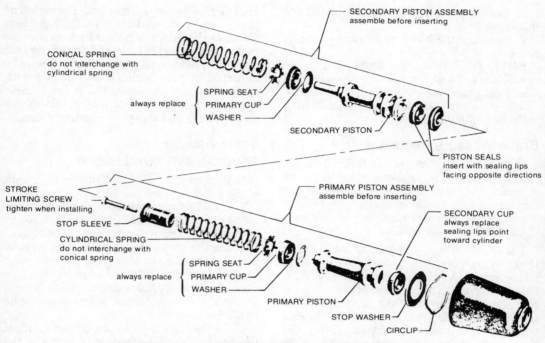

CONICAL SPRING
do not interchange with
cylindrical spring

SECONDARY PISTON ASSEMBLY
assemble before inserting

always replace

SPRING SEAT
PRIMARY CUP
WASHER

SECONDARY PISTON

PISTON SEALS
insert with sealing lips
facing opposite directions

STROKE
LIMITING SCREW
tighten when installing

STOP SLEEVE

CYLINDRICAL SPRING
do not interchange with
conical spring

always replace

SPRING SEAT
PRIMARY CUP
WASHER

PRIMARY PISTON ASSEMBLY
assemble before inserting

SECONDARY CUP
always replace
sealing lips point
toward cylinder

PRIMARY PISTON

STOP WASHER

CIRCLIP

Exploded view of master cylinder without brake booster

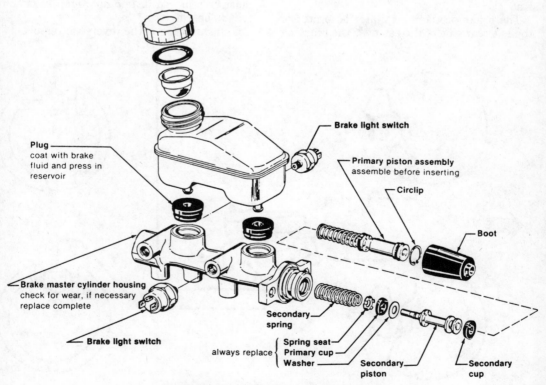

Plug
coat with brake
fluid and press in
reservoir

Brake light switch

Primary piston assembly
assemble before inserting

Circlip

Boot

Brake master cylinder housing
check for wear, if necessary
replace complete

Brake light switch

Secondary
spring

always replace

Spring seat
Primary cup
Washer

Secondary
piston

Secondary
cup

Exploded view of Bendix master cylinder

6. Remove the bleeder hose and install the dust cover.

7. Continue the bleeding at each wheel in sequence.

NOTE: *Don't splash any brake fluid on the paintwork. Brake fluid is very corrosive and will eat paint away. Any fluid accidentally spilled on the body should be immediately flushed off with water.*

Brake Pressure Regulator

NOTE: *The Dasher has two different kinds of brake pressure regulators: two pressure sensitive regulators mounted at the master cylinder and one load sensitive regulator mounted at the rear axle. Other models have only load sensitive regulators.*

The Brake Pressure Regulator insures that the front and rear brakes evenly distribute the stopping load in order of their efficiency. With only the driver in the car, most of the weight of the vehicle is hung over the front wheels (in the form of the engine and transaxle.) In this situation, the front disc brakes receive the lion's share of the stopping responsibility. As the rear compartment of the vehicle is loaded and the body sits lower on the rear springs, a lever on the brake pressure regulator attached to the rear axle by a spring is pulled, allowing the rear brakes to take on more of the stopping load.

The brake pressure regulator is located on the left rear side of the car near the rear axle (except the Rabbit Pickup and Dasher). The Dasher and Fox regulator is on the right rear side near the axle. The Rabbit Pick-up is at the center rear of the vehicle in front of the rear axle. The pressure ratio of the regulator can be adjusted by your Volkswagen dealer with special pressure gauges and alignment tools.

NOTE: *Not all Rabbits and Sciroccos are equipped with brake proportioning valves.*

Brake Booster

REMOVAL AND INSTALLATION

1. Remove the master cylinder from in front of the booster.

2. In the driver's compartment, remove the clevis pin on the end of the booster pushrod by unclipping it and pulling it out of the clevis.

3. On the gasoline engine models, remove the vacuum line running from the booster to intake manifold. On diesel engines, the line connects to a special vacuum pump located where the distributor on a gasoline engine would be. Remove the line.

4. On the Rabbit, Jetta and Scirocco, unbolt the booster bracket where it connects to the firewall. On the Dasher, Fox and Quantum remove the two nuts from inside the driver's compartment, or the four nuts holding the booster to its bracket. Remove the booster.

5. The brake booster cannot be repaired and must be replaced if its diaphragm leaks or it fails to operate.

6. Installation is the reverse of removal.

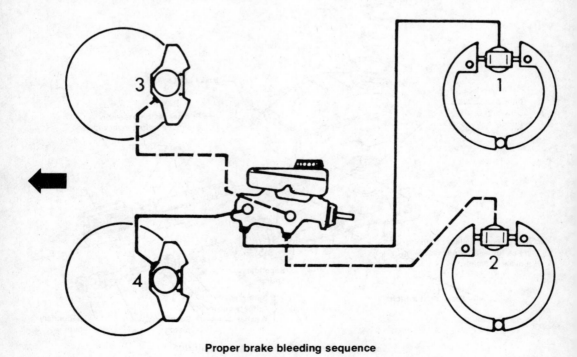

Proper brake bleeding sequence

Diesel engine brake booster vacuum pump

NOTE: *On 1977 and earlier Dashers, the clevis and booster push have been shortened. When replacing the brake booster on these models, you'll have to enlarge the clevis pin hole in the brake pedal to ⅓". Also, the booster used in 1978 and later Dashers is an inch wider in diameter (9") than the old model (8").*

7. Bleed the brakes after installing the master cylinder. See above for procedures.

8. After the system is installed, check to make sure that the rear brake lights work. If not, you have misaligned the light switch at the brake pedal.

Vacuum Pump

REMOVAL AND INSTALLATION

Diesel Engines with Power Brakes Only

One line of the vacuum pump runs to the power brake booster and the other line runs to the engine. Unclamp and remove both lines. Unbolt and remove the pump. The diaphragm inside the pump is replaceable. Remove the screws holding the vacuum hose inlet cover to the pump body and remove the cover. Unscrew the retaining nut and remove the diaphragm. Install the new diaphragm with the molded

center toward the top. Don't overtighten the retaining nut.

FRONT DISC BRAKES

There are four types of disc brake calipers used on these Volkswagens. Refer to the illustrations to identify the type used on your car.

NOTE: *The 1985 Golf and Jetta use a new style MARK II front brake caliper. The wheel bearing housing is designed to form an integral part of the brake assembly. Thus making rewmoval and replacement of the brake pads simpler. Removal and installation of the new Mark II style caliper and the brake pads are similar to the procedure for the Kelsey-Hayes floating type caliper.*

Brake Pads

REMOVAL AND INSTALLATION

Kelsey-Hayes Floating Caliper

This unit is a single piston, one piece caliper which floats on two guide pins screwed into the adapter (anchor plate). The adaptor, in turn, is held to the steering knuckle with two bolts. As the brake pads wear, the caliper floats along the adapter and guide pins during braking.

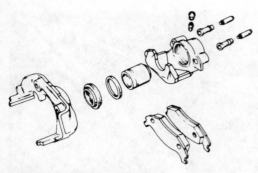

Kelsey-Hayes floating caliper

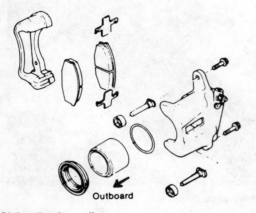

Outboard

Girling floating caliper

1. Raise the front of the vehicle and support it with jackstands. Remove the wheel.

2. Siphon some brake fluid from the master cylinder reservoir to prevent its overflowing when the piston is retracted into the cylinder bore.

3. Disconnect the brake pad warning indicator if so equipped.

4. Using a pair of needlenose pliers or the like, remove the anti-rattle springs.

5. Using an Allen wrench, back out the two guide pins that attach the caliper to the anchor plate.

NOTE: *When replacing pads only, it is not necessary to remove the guide pins completely from the rubber bushings, as they may be difficult to reinstall.*

6. Lift off the caliper and position it out of the way with some wire. You need not remove the brake lines.

CAUTION: *Never allow the caliper to hang by its brake lines.*

7. Slide the outer pad out of the anchor plate and then remove the inner pad. Check the rotor as detailed in the appropriate section. Check the caliper for fluid leaks or cracked boots. If any damage is found, the caliper will require overhauling or replacement.

8. Carefully clean the anchor plate with a wire brush or some other abrasive material. Install the new brake pads into position on the anchor plate. The inner pad usually has chamfered edges.

NOTE: *When replacing brake pads, always replace both pads on both sides of the vehicle. Mixed pads will cause uneven braking.*

9. Slowly and carefully push the piston into its bore until it's bottomed and then position the caliper onto the anchor plate. Install the guide pins and tighten them to 25–30 ft.lb.

NOTE: *The upper guide pin is usually longer than the lower one.*

CAUTION: *Use extreme care so as not to cross-thread the guide pins when tightening.*

10. Install the anti-rattle springs between the anchor plate and brake pads ears. The loops on the springs should be positioned inboard.

11. Fill the reservoir with brake fluid and pump the brake pedal several times to set the piston. It should not be necessary to bleed the system; however, if a firm pedal cannot be obtained, the system must be bled (see Bleeding the Brakes in this section).

12. Install the wheel and lower the vehicle.

Girling Floating Caliper

Although similar in many respects to a sliding caliper, this single piston unit floats on guide pins and bushings which are threaded into a mounting bracket. The mounting bracket is bolted to the steering knuckle.

Variations in pad retainers, shims, anti-rattle and retaining springs will be encountered but the service procedures are all basically the same. Note the position of all springs, clips or shims when removing the pads. Work on one side at a time and use the other for reference.

1. Raise and support the front of the vehicle on jackstands. Remove the wheel.

2. Siphon a sufficient quantity of brake fluid from the master cylinder reservoir to prevent the brake fluid from overflowing the master cylinder when removing or installing new pads. This is necessary as the piston must be forced into the cylinder bore to provide sufficient clearance to remove the pads.

3. Grasp the caliper from behind and pull it toward you. This will push the piston back into the cylinder bore.

4. Disconnect the brake pad lining wear indicator if so equipped. Remove any anti-rattle springs or clips if so equipped.

NOTE: *Depending on the model and year of the particular caliper, you may not have to remove it entirely to get at the brake pads. If the caliper is the swing type, remove the lower guide bolt, pivot the caliper on the upper bolt and swing it upward exposing the brake pads. If this method is employed, skip to Step 7.*

5. Remove the caliper guide pins.

6. Remove the caliper from the rotor by slowly sliding it out and away from the rotor. Position the caliper out of the way and support it with wire so that it doesn't hang by the brake line.

7. Slide the outboard pad out of the adapter.

8. Remove the inboard pad. Remove any shims or shields behind the pads and note their positions.

9. Install the anti-rattle hardware and then the pads (in their proper positions!).

10. Install any pad shims or heat shields.

11. Reposition the caliper and install the guide pins.

NOTE: *If the caliper is the "swing" type, you need only pivot it back into position and install the lower guide pin.*

12. Refill the master cylinder with fresh brake fluid.

13. Install the tire and wheel assembly and then pump the brake pedal several times to bring the pads into adjustment. Road test the vehicle.

NOTE: *If a firm pedal cannot be obtained, bleed the system as detailed in Bleeding the Brakes.*

Sliding Yoke Caliper

This unit is a single piston, two piece caliper. It has a fixed mounting frame which is bolted to the steering knuckle. The pads are retained in the fixed frame. A floating frame, or yoke, slides on the fixed frame. The cylinder attaches to this yoke, creating a caliper. Braking pressure forces the piston against the inner pad. The reaction causes the yoke to move in the opposite direction, applying pressure to the outer pad.

1. Raise the front of the vehicle and support it with jackstands. Remove the wheel.

2. Siphon a sufficient quantity of brake fluid from the master cylinder reservoir to prevent the brake fluid from overflowing the master cylinder when removing or installing new pads. This is necessary as the position must be forced into the cylinder bore to provide sufficient clearance to remove the pads.

3. Disconnect the wire connector leading to the brake pad wear indicator.

4. Remove the brake pad retaining clips on the inside of the caliper and then drive out the retaining pins. Don't lose the pad positioner (spreader) that is held down by the pins.

5. Pull out the inner brake pad.

6. The outer pads are secured by a notch at the top of the pad. Grasp the caliper assembly from the inside and pull it toward yourself. Re-

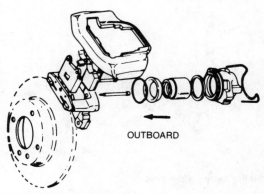

OUTBOARD

Sliding yoke caliper

move the pad and detach the wear indicator.

7. Check the brake disc (rotor) as detailed in the appropriate section.

8. Inspect the caliper and piston assembly for breaks, cracks or other damage. Overhaul or replace the caliper as necessary.

9. Use a C-clamp and press the piston back into the cylinder bore.

10. Install the wear indicator on the outer pad and then install both pads.

11. Installation of the remaining components is the reverse order of removal.

12. Top off the master cylinder with fresh brake fluid.

13. Pump the brake pedal several times to bring the pads into adjustment. Road test the vehicle. If a firm pedal cannot be obtained, bleed the brakes as detailed in Bleeding the Brakes.

Girling Sliding Yoke Caliper

This unit is a double piston, one piece caliper. The cylinder body contains two pistons, back-to-back, in a through-bore. The cylinder body is bolted to the steering knuckle, with both pistons inboard of the rotor. A yoke, which slides on the cylinder body, is installed over the rotor and the caliper.

When the brakes are applied, hydraulic pressure forces the pistons apart in the double ended bore. The piston closest to the rotor applies force directly to the inboard pad. The other piston applies force to the yoke, which transmits the force to the outer pad, creating a friction force on each side of the rotor.

One variation has a yoke that floats on guide pins screwed into the cylinder body.

Some designs incorporate parking brake mechanisms which are actuated by a lever and cam working between the piston and the yoke. The yokes do not have to be removed to replace the brake pads.

1. Raise and support the front of the vehicle on jackstands. Remove the wheel.

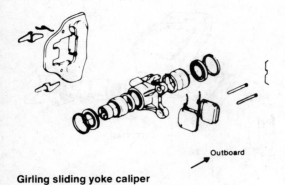

Girling sliding yoke caliper

2. Siphon a sufficient quantity of brake fluid from the master cylinder reservoir to prevent the brake fluid from overflowing the master cylinder when removing or installing new pads. This is necessary as the piston must be forced into the cylinder bore to provide sufficient clearance to remove the pads.

3. Disconnect the brake pad lining wear indicator if so equipped.

4. Remove the dust cover and/or anti-rattle (damper) clip if so equipped.

5. Lift off the wire clip(s) which hold the guide pins or retaining pin in place.

6. Remove the upper guide pin and the two hanger springs. Carefully tap out the lower guide pin.

CAUTION: *The lower guide pin usually contains an anti-rattle coil spring. Be careful not to lose this spring. If a retaining pin is used, pull the pin out and remove the two hanger springs.*

7. Slide the yoke outward and remove the outer brake pad and the anti-noise shim (if so equipped).

8. Slide the yoke inward and repeat Step 7.

9. Check the rotor as detailed in the appropriate section.

10. Inspect the caliper and piston assembly for breaks, cracks or other damage. Overhaul or replace the caliper as necessary.

11. Push the piston next to the rotor back into the cylinder bore until the end of the piston is flush with the boot retaining ring.

CAUTION: *If the piston is pushed further than this, the seal will be damaged and the caliper assembly will have to be overhauled.*

12. Retract the piston farthest from the rotor by pulling the yoke toward the outside of the vehicle.

13. Install the outboard pad. Anti-noise shims (if so equipped) must be located on the plate side of the pad with the triangular cutout pointing toward the top of the caliper.

14. Install the inboard pad with the shims (if so equipped) in the correct position.

15. Replace the lower guide pin and the anti-rattle coil spring.

16. Hook the hanger springs under the pin and over the brake pads.

17. Install the upper guide pin over the ends of the hanger springs.

NOTE: *If a single two sided retaining pin is used, install the pin and then install the hanger springs as in Steps 16–17.*

18. Insert the wire clip locks into the holes in the guide pins or retaining pin.

19. Refill the master cylinder with fresh brake fluid.

20. Install the tire and wheel assembly. Pump the brake pedal several times to bring the pads into adjustment. Road test the vehicle. If a firm pedal cannot be obtained, refer to "Bleeding the Brakes".

REAR DISC BRAKES

Rear disc brake removal and installation is very similar to the procedure for Kelsey-Hayes floating caliper front disc brakes removal and installation.

Calipers

NOTE: *The 1985 Golf and Jetta use a new style Mark II front brake caliper. The wheel bearing housing is designed to form an integral part of the brake assembly. This makes brake pad removal and replacement simpler.*

REMOVAL AND INSTALLATION

1. Jack up the front of the car and support it on stands.

2. Remove the brake pads as outlined above if caliper mounted. If support mounted, the pads may be allowed to remain in place.

3. If you are removing the caliper for overhaul, disconnect and plug the brake line at the caliper. If not, do not remove the hose, hang it by a wire.

4. Remove the two caliper-to-strut retaining bolts and remove the caliper.

5. Installation is the reverse of removal. Tighten the two retaining bolts to 43 ft.lb. for the Dasher, 36 ft.lb. for other models.

6. Bleed the brakes.

OVERHAUL

NOTE: *Purchase an overhaul kit and sufficient brake fluid before starting.*

1. Remove the caliper as outlined above.

NOTE: *Remove and overhaul one caliper at a time. In this way you can use the other caliper as a reference.*

2. Mount the caliper in a soft jawed vise or place rags over the jaws to protect the caliper.

3. Depending on type, pry the fixed mounting frame off the floating frame.

4. Or, drive the caliper cylinder off the floating frame with a brass drift. Do not damage the piston(s).

5. On all models, remove the dust boot(s) and retaining ring(s) from the piston(s) either by hand or using a screwdriver. Some models do not have a retaining ring.

6. Remove the piston(s) from the cylinder. If the piston(s) is stubborn, remove the bleeder screw and use compressed air to force it out.

CAUTION: *Hold the piston(s) between blocks of wood when doing this, as they will fly out with considerable force.*

7. When the piston pops out of the caliper, remove the rubber seal with a wood or plastic pin to avoid damaging the seal groove.

8. Clean all metal parts in denatured alcohol. Never use a mineral based solvent such as gasoline, kerosene, acetone or the like; these solvents deteriorate rubber parts. Inspect the pistons and their bores. They must be free of scoring and pitting. Replace the cylinder if there is any damage.

9. Discard all rubber parts. The caliper rebuilding kit includes new boots and seals which should be used as the caliper is reassembled.

10. Lightly coat the cylinder bore, piston and seal with brake assembly paste or fresh brake fluid.

11. Install the piston into the cylinder. Fit the dust cover.

12. Installation is the reverse of removal. Be sure to install the guide or mounting springs in the correct position.

13. Install the pads and caliper and bleed the brakes.

Brake Disc

INSPECTION AND CHECKING

Brake discs may be checked for lateral runout while installed on the car. This check will require a dial indicator gauge and stand to mount it on the caliper. VW has a special tool for this purpose which mounts the dial indicator to the caliper, but it can also be mounted on the shaft of a C-clamp attached to the outside of the caliper.

1. Remove the wheel and reinstall the wheel bolts (tightened to 65 ft.lb.) to retain the disc to the hub.

2. Mount the dial indicator securely to the caliper. The feeler should touch the disc about ½" below the outer edge.

3. Rotate the disc and observe the gauge. Radial runout (wobble) must not exceed 0.004" (0.1mm). A disc which exceeds this specification must be replaced or refinished.

4. Brake discs which have excessive radial runout, sharp ridges, or scoring can be refinished. First grinding must be done on both sides of the disc to prevent squeaking and vibrating. Discs which have only light grooves and are otherwise acceptable can be used without refinishing.

The standard disc is 0.47" (12mm) thick. It should not be ground to less than 0.41" (10.5mm).

REMOVAL AND INSTALLATION

1. Loosen the wheel bolts. Remove the hub cap.

2. Jack up the front of the car and place it on stands. Remove the wheel(s).

3. Remove the caliper as outlined above.

4. Remove the disc-to-hub retaining screw.

5. Grip the disc with both hands and give it a sharp pull to remove it. A stubborn disc should be removed with a puller. Never strike the disc with a hammer.

6. The disc is installed in the reverse order of removal. Don't forget to install the retaining screw. Install the caliper and bleed the brakes.

7. Install the wheel and lower the car. Tighten the wheel bolts diagonally to 65 ft.lb. This is doubly important because the bolts not only retain the wheels, but attach the disc to the hub.

DRUM BRAKES

NOTE: *The following information applies to both front and rear brakes.*

Brake Drums

REMOVAL AND INSTALLATION

1. On all but rear self adjusting brakes, jack up vehicle and remove the wheels. On self adjusting models, jack up vehicle, remove one lug bolt, position and using a screw driver through the lug hole push the adjusting wedge upward.

2. On the Rabbit with front drum brakes, pull off the brake drum after removing the securing screw in the drum face. On all rear drum brakes, pry off the hub (dust) cap.

3. Remove and discard the cotter pin.

4. Remove the castellated nut, hex nut and washers.

5. Work the inner race of the wheel bearing out.

NOTE: *On models with self adjusting rear brakes, leave the road wheel attached to the brake drum when removing.*

6. Pull off the brake drum. Be careful not to lose the inner race of the outer bearing.

NOTE: *If the brake drum is stubborn, remove the rubber cover at the backing plate and back off the brake adjuster with an adjusting tool or wide bladed screwdriver. If this doesn't work, use a puller. Never heat the drum or beat on it with a hammer.*

7. Check the brake drum for any cracks, scores, grooves, or an out-of-round condition. Replace a drum which slows cracking. Smooth light scoring with fine emery cloth. If scoring is extensive have the drum turned. Never have a drum turned more than 0.03″.

8. The stub axle bearings in the brake drum must be pressed out for replacement. Take the drum(s) to a competent machinist to have them removed. Always use new seals on reassembly.

9. After greasing the bearings and installing them in the drum with new seals, place the drum onto the sub axle.

10. Install the washer and the hex nut. Tighten the nut and then loosen it. Retighten the nut slightly so that the washer between the nut and the bearing can just be moved with a screwdriver (refer to the illustration). Correct bearing play is 0.0012–0.0027″ (0.03–0.03mm).

11. Install the drum on Rabbit front drum brakes and install the retaining screw. On rear drum brakes, install the castellated nut and insert a new cotter pin. Fill the hub cap with grease and install it.

12. Install the wheel and lower the car.

Brake Shoes
REMOVAL AND INSTALLATION
Rabbit Front Brake Shoes

NOTE: *Only do one side at a time. This way, you will always have one side intact as a reference.*

1. Remove the wheel and the brake drum. The brake drum is held by a screw located between the wheel lugs.

2. Using pliers, unhook the lower return springs.

3. Unhook the two spring clips holding the shoes to the backing plate.

4. Pull the lower part of the brake shoe over the wheel hub and unhook the upper retaining springs. Remove the adjuster with the retaining spring.

5. Installation is the reverse of removal.

Adjustable Rear Brake Shoes

NOTE: *Only do one side at a time. This way, you will always have one side intact as a reference.*

1. Remove the brake drum. See above for procedures.

2. On the Rabbit and the Scirocco, remove the horseshoe shaped spring with a pair of pliers. Be careful, the spring is under pressure.

3. Remove the lower springs. Remove the spring clips holding the shoes to backing plate.

4. Detach the parking brake cable by pressing back the spring with a pair of needle nose pliers and then disconnecting the cable at the lever.

5. On the Rabbit and Scirocco, remove the brake shoes with the adjusting mechanism. On the Dasher, raise up the brake shoes from the bottom and remove the adjusting mechanism. Lift up the brake shoes and remove the upper springs. Remove the brake shoes.

6. Clean and inspect all brake parts. Spray solvents are available for brake cleaning which do not affect linings. Do not spray rubber parts with solvent.

7. Check the wheel cylinders for boot condition and leaking.

8. Installation is the reverse of removal. When completed, install the drum and make an initial adjustment by turning the adapter wheel until a slight drag is felt between the shoes and drum, and back off about ¼ turn. Complete adjustment as described earlier in this chapter.

Self Adjusting Rear Brake Shoes

NOTE: *Only do one side at a time. This way, you will always have one side intact as a reference.*

1. Remove the brake drum. See above for procedures.

2. Remove the spring retainers which hold the shoes to the brake backing plate by pressing in against the springs and turning the little cap until its slot lines up with the pin head.

3. Pull the bottom of the brake shoes free of their stop and allow them to come together close enough to remove the bottom spring.

4. Unhook the parking brake cable from its lever by pulling the spring on the cable back with a pair of needle nose pliers and then unhooking the cable.

5. Unhook the three springs at the top of the shoes (except the adjustment rod spring) and remove the shoes.

6. Place the adjustment rod in a vise and unhook the tension spring.

7. To install new brake shoes, with the adjustment rod in the vise, hook the tension spring on the rod and brake shoe. Insert the adjusting wedge with the lug on the wedge facing the backing plate.

8. Attach the other brake shoe with the lever to the adjusting rod.

CHILTON'S
AUTO BODY
REPAIR TIPS

Tools and Materials • Step-by-Step Illustrated Procedures
How To Repair Dents, Scratches and Rust Holes
Spray Painting and Refinishing Tips

With a little practice, basic body repair procedures can be mastered by any do-it-yourself mechanic. The step-by-step repairs shown here can be applied to almost any type of auto body repair.

TOOLS & MATERIALS

You may already have basic tools, such as hammers and electric drills. Other tools unique to body repair — body hammers, grinding attachments, sanding blocks, dent puller, half-round plastic file and plastic spreaders — are relatively inexpensive and can be obtained wherever auto parts or auto body repair parts are sold. Portable air compressors and paint spray guns can be purchased or rented.

Auto Body Repair Kits

The best and most often used products are available to the do-it-yourselfer in kit form, from major manufacturers of auto body repair products. The same manufacturers also merchandise the individual products for use by pros.

Kits are available to make a wide variety of repairs, including holes, dents and scratches and fiberglass, and offer the advantage of buying the materials you'll need for the job. There is little waste or chance of materials going bad from not being used. Many kits may also contain basic body-working tools such as body files, sanding blocks and spreaders. Check the contents of the kit before buying your tools.

BODY REPAIR TIPS

Safety

Many of the products associated with auto body repair and refinishing contain toxic chemicals. Read all labels before opening containers and store them in a safe place and manner.

• Wear eye protection (safety goggles) when using power tools or when performing any operation that involves the removal of any type of material.

• Wear lung protection (disposable mask or respirator) when grinding, sanding or painting.

Sanding

1 Sand off paint before using a dent puller. When using a non-adhesive sanding disc, cover the back of the disc with an overlapping layer or two of masking tape and trim the edges. The disc will last considerably longer.

2 Use the circular motion of the sanding disc to grind *into* the edge of the repair. Grinding or sanding away from the jagged edge will only tear the sandpaper.

3 Use the palm of your hand flat on the panel to detect high and low spots. Do not use your fingertips. Slide your hand slowly back and forth.

WORKING WITH BODY FILLER

Mixing The Filler

Cleanliness and proper mixing and application are extremely important. Use a clean piece of plastic or glass or a disposable artist's palette to mix body filler.

1 Allow plenty of time and follow directions. No useful purpose will be served by adding more hardener to make it cure (set-up) faster. Less hardener means more curing time, but the mixture dries harder; more hardener means less curing time but a softer mixture.

2 Both the hardener and the filler should be thoroughly kneaded or stirred before mixing. Hardener should be a solid paste and dispense like thin toothpaste. Body filler should be smooth, and free of lumps or thick spots.

Getting the proper amount of hardener in the filler is the trickiest part of preparing the filler. Use the same amount of hardener in cold or warm weather. For contour filler (thick coats), a bead of hardener twice the diameter of the filler is about right. There's about a 15% margin on either side, but, if in doubt use less hardener.

3 Mix the body filler and hardener by wiping across the mixing surface, picking the mixture up and wiping it again. Colder weather requires longer mixing times. Do not mix in a circular motion; this will trap air bubbles which will become holes in the cured filler.

Applying The Filler

1 For best results, filler should not be applied over 1/4" thick.

Apply the filler in several coats. Build it up to above the level of the repair surface so that it can be sanded or grated down.

The first coat of filler must be pressed on with a firm wiping motion.

Apply the filler in one direction only. Working the filler back and forth will either pull it off the metal or trap air bubbles.

REPAIRING DENTS

Before you start, take a few minutes to study the damaged area. Try to visualize the shape of the panel before it was damaged. If the damage is on the left fender, look at the right fender and use it as a guide. If there is access to the panel from behind, you can reshape it with a body hammer. If not, you'll have to use a dent puller. Go slowly and work the metal a little at a time. Get the panel as straight as possible before applying filler.

1 This dent is typical of one that can be pulled out or hammered out from behind. Remove the headlight cover, headlight assembly and turn signal housing.

2 Drill a series of holes ½ the size of the end of the dent puller along the stress line. Make some trial pulls and assess the results. If necessary, drill more holes and try again. Do not hurry.

3 If possible, use a body hammer and block to shape the metal back to its original contours. Get the metal back as close to its original shape as possible. Don't depend on body filler to fill dents.

4 Using an 80-grit grinding disc on an electric drill, grind the paint from the surrounding area down to bare metal. Use a new grinding pad to prevent heat buildup that will warp metal.

5 The area should look like this when you're finished grinding. Knock the drill holes in and tape over small openings to keep plastic filler out.

6 Mix the body filler (see Body Repair Tips). Spread the body filler evenly over the entire area (see Body Repair Tips). Be sure to cover the area completely.

7 Let the body filler dry until the surface can just be scratched with your fingernail. Knock the high spots from the body filler with a body file ("Cheesegrater"). Check frequently with the palm of your hand for high and low spots.

8 Check to be sure that trim pieces that will be installed later will fit exactly. Sand the area with 40-grit paper.

9 If you wind up with low spots, you may have to apply another layer of filler.

10 Knock the high spots off with 40-grit paper. When you are satisfied with the contours of the repair, apply a thin coat of filler to cover pin holes and scratches.

11 Block sand the area with 40-grit paper to a smooth finish. Pay particular attention to body lines and ridges that must be well-defined.

12 Sand the area with 400 paper and then finish with a scuff pad. The finished repair is ready for priming and painting (see Painting Tips).

Materials and photos courtesy of Ritt Jones Auto Body, Prospect Park, PA.

REPAIRING RUST HOLES

There are many ways to repair rust holes. The fiberglass cloth kit shown here is one of the most cost efficient for the owner because it provides a strong repair that resists cracking and moisture and is relatively easy to use. It can be used on large and small holes (with or without backing) and can be applied over contoured areas. Remember, however, that short of replacing an entire panel, no repair is a guarantee that the rust will not return.

1 Remove any trim that will be in the way. Clean away all loose debris. Cut away all the rusted metal. But be sure to leave enough metal to retain the contour or body shape.

2 Grind away all traces of rust with a 24-grit grinding disc. Be sure to grind back 3-4 inches from the edge of the hole down to bare metal and be sure all traces of paint, primer and rust are removed.

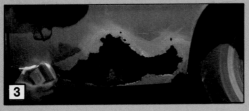

3 Block sand the area with 80 or 100 grit sandpaper to get a clear, shiny surface and feathered paint edge. Tap the edges of the hole inward with a ball peen hammer.

4 If you are going to use release film, cut a piece about 2-3" larger than the area you have sanded. Place the film over the repair and mark the sanded area on the film. Avoid any unnecessary wrinkling of the film.

5 Cut 2 pieces of fiberglass matte to match the shape of the repair. One piece should be about 1" smaller than the sanded area and the second piece should be 1" smaller than the first. Mix enough filler and hardener to saturate the fiberglass material (see Body Repair Tips).

6 Lay the release sheet on a flat surface and spread an even layer of filler, large enough to cover the repair. Lay the smaller piece of fiberglass cloth in the center of the sheet and spread another layer of filler over the fiberglass cloth. Repeat the operation for the larger piece of cloth.

7 Place the repair material over the repair area, with the release film facing outward. Use a spreader and work from the center outward to smooth the material, following the body contours. Be sure to remove all air bubbles.

8 Wait until the repair has dried tack-free and peel off the release sheet. The ideal working temperature is 60°-90° F. Cooler or warmer temperatures or high humidity may require additional curing time. Wait longer, if in doubt.

9 Sand and feather-edge the entire area. The initial sanding can be done with a sanding disc on an electric drill if care is used. Finish the sanding with a block sander. Low spots can be filled with body filler; this may require several applications.

10 When the filler can just be scratched with a fingernail, knock the high spots down with a body file and smooth the entire area with 80-grit. Feather the filled areas into the surrounding areas.

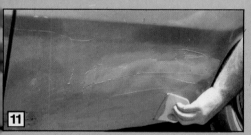

11 When the area is sanded smooth, mix some topcoat and hardener and apply it directly with a spreader. This will give a smooth finish and prevent the glass matte from showing through the paint.

12 Block sand the topcoat smooth with finishing sandpaper (200 grit), and 400 grit. The repair is ready for masking, priming and painting (see Painting Tips).

Materials and photos courtesy Marson Corporation, Chelsea, Massachusetts

PAINTING TIPS

Preparation

1 SANDING — Use a 400 or 600 grit wet or dry sandpaper. Wet-sand the area with a ¼ sheet of sandpaper soaked in clean water. Keep the paper wet while sanding. Sand the area until the repaired area tapers into the original finish.

2 CLEANING — Wash the area to be painted thoroughly with water and a clean rag. Rinse it thoroughly and wipe the surface dry until you're sure it's completely free of dirt, dust, fingerprints, wax, detergent or other foreign matter.

3 MASKING — Protect any areas you don't want to overspray by covering them with masking tape and newspaper. Be careful not get fingerprints on the area to be painted.

4 PRIMING — All exposed metal should be primed before painting. Primer protects the metal and provides an excellent surface for paint adhesion. When the primer is dry, wet-sand the area again with 600 grit wet-sandpaper. Clean the area again after sanding.

Painting Techniques

Paint applied from either a spray gun or a spray can (for small areas) will provide good results. Experiment on an old piece of metal to get the right combination before you begin painting.

SPRAYING VISCOSITY (SPRAY GUN ONLY) — Paint should be thinned to spraying viscosity according to the directions on the can. Use only the recommended thinner or reducer and the same amount of reduction regardless of temperature.

AIR PRESSURE (SPRAY GUN ONLY) — This is extremely important. Be sure you are using the proper recommended pressure.

TEMPERATURE — The surface to be painted should be approximately the same temperature as the surrounding air. Applying warm paint to a cold surface, or vice versa, will completely upset the paint characteristics.

THICKNESS — Spray with smooth strokes. In general, the thicker the coat of paint, the longer the drying time. Apply several thin coats about 30 seconds apart. The paint should remain wet long enough to flow out and no longer; heavier coats will only produce sags or wrinkles. Spray a light (fog) coat, followed by heavier color coats.

DISTANCE — The ideal spraying distance is 8"-12" from the gun or can to the surface. Shorter distances will produce ripples, while greater distances will result in orange peel, dry film and poor color match and loss of material due to overspray.

OVERLAPPING — The gun or can should be kept at right angles to the surface at all times. Work to a wet edge at an even speed, using a 50% overlap and direct the center of the spray at the lower or nearest edge of the previous stroke.

RUBBING OUT (BLENDING) FRESH PAINT — Let the paint dry thoroughly. Runs or imperfections can be sanded out, primed and repainted.

Don't be in too big a hurry to remove the masking. This only produces paint ridges. When the finish has dried for at least a week, apply a small amount of fine grade rubbing compound with a clean, wet cloth. Use lots of water and blend the new paint with the surrounding area.

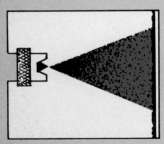

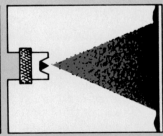

WRONG	CORRECT	WRONG
Thin coat. Stroke too fast, not enough overlap, gun too far away.	*Medium coat. Proper distance, good stroke, proper overlap.*	*Heavy coat. Stroke too slow, too much overlap, gun too close.*

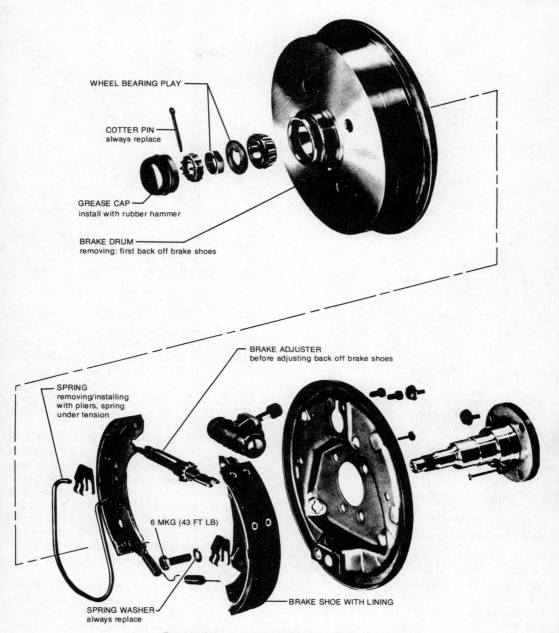

WHEEL BEARING PLAY

COTTER PIN
always replace

GREASE CAP
install with rubber hammer

BRAKE DRUM
removing: first back off brake shoes

BRAKE ADJUSTER
before adjusting back off brake shoes

SPRING
removing/installing
with pliers, spring
under tension

6 MKG (43 FT LB)

SPRING WASHER
always replace

BRAKE SHOE WITH LINING

Rabbit, Scirocco adjustable rear drum brakes

9. Install the upper return spring.

10. Place parking brake lever into its cable.

11. Fit the shoes on the brake cylinder pistons. Hook the lower return spring into the brake shoe.

12. Remaining installation is the reverse of removal. See section in this chapter for wheel bearing adjustment.

Wheel Cylinders

REMOVAL AND INSTALLATION

1. Remove the brake shoes.

2. Loosen the brake line on the rear of the cylinder, but do not pull the line away from the cylinder or it may bend.

3. Remove the bolts and lockwashers that

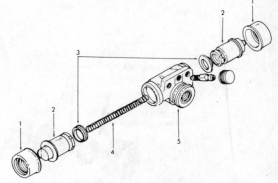

1. Wheel cylinder boot
2. Piston
3. Cup
4. Wheel cylinder spring
5. Wheel cylinder housing

Exploded view of brake cylinder

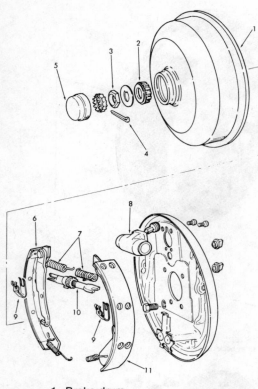

1. Brake drum
2. Wheel bearing
3. Retaining nut
4. Cotter pin
5. Grease cap
6. Brake shoe with parking brake lever
7. Return spring
8. Wheel cylinder
9. Hold-down spring
10. Adjuster
11. Brake shoe

Dasher adjustable drum brake components

attach the wheel cylinder to the backing plate and remove the cylinder.

4. Position the new wheel cylinder on the backing plate and install the cylinder attaching bolts and lockwashers.

5. Attach the metal brake line or rubber hose by reversing the procedure given in step two or three.

6. Install the brakes and bleed the brake system.

OVERHAUL

1. Remove the brakes.

2. Place a bucket or some old newspapers under the brake backing plate to catch the brake fluid that will run out of the wheel cylinder.

3. Remove the boots from the ends of the wheel cylinders.

4. Push one piston toward the center of the cylinder to force the opposite piston and cup out the other end of the cylinder. Reach in the open end of the cylinder and push the spring, cup, and piston out of the cylinder.

5. Remove the bleeder screw from the rear of the cylinder, on the back of the backing plate.

6. Inspect the inside of the wheel cylinder. If it is scored in any way, the cylinder must be honed with a wheel cylinder hone or fine emery paper, and finished with crocus cloth if emery paper is used. If the inside of the cylinder is excessively worn, the cylinder will have to be replaced, as only 0.003″ of material can be removed from the cylinder walls. Whenever honing or cleaning wheel cylinders, keep a small amount of brake fluid in the cylinder to serve as a lubricant.

7. Clean any foreign matter from the pistons. The sides of the pistons must be smooth for the wheel cylinders to operate properly.

8. Clean the cylinder bore with alcohol and a lint-free rag. Pull the rag through the bore several times to remove all foreign matter and dry the cylinder.

9. Install the bleeder screw and the return spring in the cylinder.

10. Coat new cylinder cups with new brake fluid and install them in the cylinder. Make sure that they are square in the bore or they will leak.

11. Install the pistons in the cylinder after coating them with new brake fluid.

12. Coat the insides of the boots with new brake fluid and install them on the cylinder. Install and bleed the brakes.

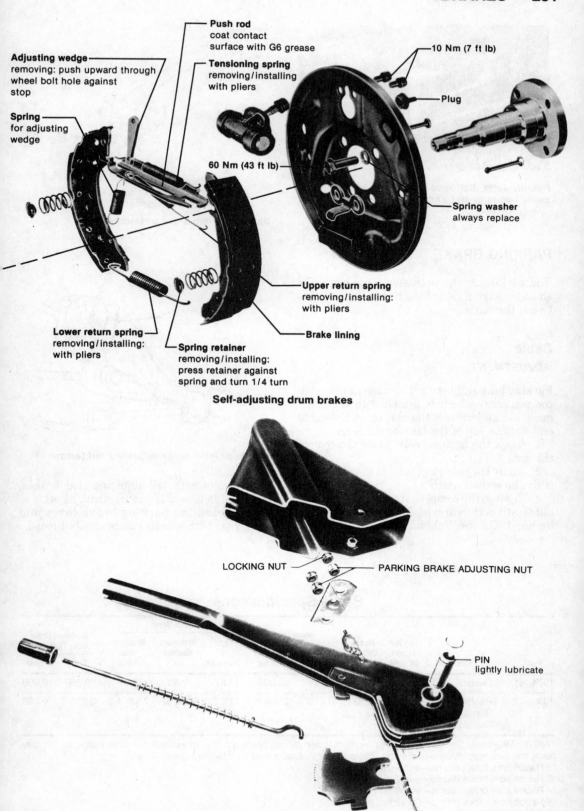

Push rod
coat contact
surface with G6 grease

Adjusting wedge
removing: push upward through
wheel bolt hole against
stop

Tensioning spring
removing/installing
with pliers

10 Nm (7 ft lb)

Spring
for adjusting
wedge

Plug

60 Nm (43 ft lb)

Spring washer
always replace

Upper return spring
removing/installing:
with pliers

Lower return spring
removing/installing:
with pliers

Spring retainer
removing/installing:
press retainer against
spring and turn 1/4 turn

Brake lining

Self-adjusting drum brakes

LOCKING NUT

PARKING BRAKE ADJUSTING NUT

PIN
lightly lubricate

Rabbit, Jetta, Scirocco parking brake handle assembly

Rabbit, Jetta, Scirocco—adjust parking brake at cable locknuts on handle

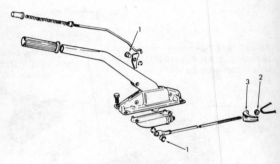

1. Retaining pin
2. Parking brake adjusting nut
3. Cable compensator

Dasher parking brake assembly

PARKING BRAKE

The parking brake activates the rear brake shoes through a cable attached to the lever between the seats.

Cable

ADJUSTMENT

Parking brake adjustment is made at the cable compensator, which is attached to the lever push rod underneath the car, or at the cable end nuts on top of the handbrake lever.

1. Block the front wheels. Raise the rear of the car.

2. Apply the parking brake so that the lever is on the second notch.

3. Tighten the compensator nut or adjusting nuts until both rear wheels can just be turned by hand. On the Rabbit, Jetta and Scirocco,

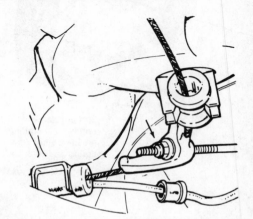

Dasher parking brake adjusting nut (arrow)

and Dashers with self adjusting rear brakes, you shouldn't be able to turn them at all.

4. Release the parking brake lever and check that both wheels can be easily turned.

Brake Specifications

Year	Model	Lug Nut Torque (ft. lbs.)	Master Cylinder Bore	Brake Disc		Brake Drum			Minimum Brake Lining Thickness *	
				Minimum Thickness	Maximum Run-out	Diameter	Maximum Machine a/s	Maximum Wear Limit	Front	Rear
1974–81	Dasher	65	0.82	0.41	0.004	7.87	7.90	7.97	0.250	0.098
1975–87	Rabbit, Jetta, Scirocco, Fox Quantum	65	0.82	0.41 ⑥	0.004 ⑥	7.08 ①	7.10 ②	7.12 ③⑤	0.250 ④	0.098

*NOTE: *Minimum lining thickness is as recommended by manufacturer. Due to variations in state inspection regulations, the minumum thickness may be different than that recommended by the manufacturer.*
① Rabbit front brake drums—9.05–9.06 in.
② Rabbit front brake drums—9.087 in.
③ Rabbit front brake drums—9.106 in.
④ Rabbit front brake drums—0.039 in.
⑤ 7.91 on Quantum
⑥ GTI with finned rotors: thickness—.728; run-out—.002

Troubleshooting the Brake System

Problem	Cause	Solution
Low brake pedal (excessive pedal travel required for braking action.)	• Excessive clearance between rear linings and drums caused by inoperative automatic adjusters	• Make 10 to 15 alternate forward and reverse brake stops to adjust brakes. If brake pedal does not come up, repair or replace adjuster parts as necessary.
	• Worn rear brakelining	• Inspect and replace lining if worn beyond minimum thickness specification
	• Bent, distorted brakeshoes, front or rear	• Replace brakeshoes in axle sets
	• Air in hydraulic system	• Remove air from system. Refer to Brake Bleeding.
Low brake pedal (pedal may go to floor with steady pressure applied.)	• Fluid leak in hydraulic system	• Fill master cylinder to fill line; have helper apply brakes and check calipers, wheel cylinders, differential valve tubes, hoses and fittings for leaks. Repair or replace as necessary.
	• Air in hydraulic system	• Remove air from system. Refer to Brake Bleeding.
	• Incorrect or non-recommended brake fluid (fluid evaporates at below normal temp).	• Flush hydraulic system with clean brake fluid. Refill with correct-type fluid.
	• Master cylinder piston seals worn, or master cylinder bore is scored, worn or corroded	• Repair or replace master cylinder
Low brake pedal (pedal goes to floor on first application—o.k. on subsequent applications.)	• Disc brake pads sticking on abutment surfaces of anchor plate. Caused by a build-up of dirt, rust, or corrosion on abutment surfaces	• Clean abutment surfaces
Fading brake pedal (pedal height decreases with steady pressure applied.)	• Fluid leak in hydraulic system	• Fill master cylinder reservoirs to fill mark, have helper apply brakes, check calipers, wheel cylinders, differential valve, tubes, hoses, and fittings for fluid leaks. Repair or replace parts as necessary.
	• Master cylinder piston seals worn, or master cylinder bore is scored, worn or corroded	• Repair or replace master cylinder
Decreasing brake pedal travel (pedal travel required for braking action decreases and may be accompanied by a hard pedal.)	• Caliper or wheel cylinder pistons sticking or seized	• Repair or replace the calipers, or wheel cylinders
	• Master cylinder compensator ports blocked (preventing fluid return to reservoirs) or pistons sticking or seized in master cylinder bore	• Repair or replace the master cylinder
	• Power brake unit binding internally	• Test unit according to the following procedure: (a) Shift transmission into neutral and start engine (b) Increase engine speed to 1500 rpm, close throttle and fully depress brake pedal (c) Slow release brake pedal and stop engine (d) Have helper remove vacuum check valve and hose from power unit. Observe for backward movement of brake pedal. (e) If the pedal moves backward, the power unit has an internal bind—replace power unit

Troubleshooting the Brake System (cont.)

Problem	Cause	Solution
Spongy brake pedal (pedal has abnormally soft, springy, spongy feel when depressed.)	• Air in hydraulic system	• Remove air from system. Refer to Brake Bleeding.
	• Brakeshoes bent or distorted	• Replace brakeshoes
	• Brakelining not yet seated with drums and rotors	• Burnish brakes
	• Rear drum brakes not properly adjusted	• Adjust brakes
Hard brake pedal (excessive pedal pressure required to stop vehicle. May be accompanied by brake fade.)	• Loose or leaking power brake unit vacuum hose	• Tighten connections or replace leaking hose
	• Incorrect or poor quality brakelining	• Replace with lining in axle sets
	• Bent, broken, distorted brakeshoes	• Replace brakeshoes
	• Calipers binding or dragging on mounting pins. Rear brakeshoes dragging on support plate.	• Replace mounting pins and bushings. Clean rust or burrs from rear brake support plate ledges and lubricate ledges with molydisulfide grease. **NOTE:** If ledges are deeply grooved or scored, do not attempt to sand or grind them smooth—replace support plate.
	• Caliper, wheel cylinder, or master cylinder pistons sticking or seized	• Repair or replace parts as necessary
	• Power brake unit vacuum check valve malfunction	• Test valve according to the following procedure: (a) Start engine, increase engine speed to 1500 rpm, close throttle and immediately stop engine (b) Wait at least 90 seconds then depress brake pedal (c) If brakes are not vacuum assisted for 2 or more applications, check valve is faulty
	• Power brake unit has internal bind	• Test unit according to the following procedure: (a) With engine stopped, apply brakes several times to exhaust all vacuum in system (b) Shift transmission into neutral, depress brake pedal and start engine (c) If pedal height decreases with foot pressure and less pressure is required to hold pedal in applied position, power unit vacuum system is operating normally. Test power unit. If power unit exhibits a bind condition, replace the power unit.
	• Master cylinder compensator ports (at bottom of reservoirs) blocked by dirt, scale, rust, or have small burrs (blocked ports prevent fluid return to reservoirs).	• Repair or replace master cylinder **CAUTION:** Do not attempt to clean blocked ports with wire, pencils, or similar implements. Use compressed air only.
	• Brake hoses, tubes, fittings clogged or restricted	• Use compressed air to check or unclog parts. Replace any damaged parts.
	• Brake fluid contaminated with improper fluids (motor oil, transmission fluid, causing rubber components to swell and stick in bores	• Replace all rubber components, combination valve and hoses. Flush entire brake system with DOT 3 brake fluid or equivalent.
	• Low engine vacuum	• Adjust or repair engine

Troubleshooting the Brake System (cont.)

Problem	Cause	Solution
Grabbing brakes (severe reaction to brake pedal pressure.)	• Brakelining(s) contaminated by grease or brake fluid	• Determine and correct cause of contamination and replace brakeshoes in axle sets
	• Parking brake cables incorrectly adjusted or seized	• Adjust cables. Replace seized cables.
	• Incorrect brakelining or lining loose on brakeshoes	• Replace brakeshoes in axle sets
	• Caliper anchor plate bolts loose	• Tighten bolts
	• Rear brakeshoes binding on support plate ledges	• Clean and lubricate ledges. Replace support plate(s) if ledges are deeply grooved. Do not attempt to smooth ledges by grinding.
	• Incorrect or missing power brake reaction disc	• Install correct disc
	• Rear brake support plates loose	• Tighten mounting bolts
Dragging brakes (slow or incomplete release of brakes)	• Brake pedal binding at pivot	• Loosen and lubricate
	• Power brake unit has internal bind	• Inspect for internal bind. Replace unit if internal bind exists.
	• Parking brake cables incorrrectly adjusted or seized	• Adjust cables. Replace seized cables.
	• Rear brakeshoe return springs weak or broken	• Replace return springs. Replace brakeshoe if necessary in axle sets.
	• Automatic adjusters malfunctioning	• Repair or replace adjuster parts as required
	• Caliper, wheel cylinder or master cylinder pistons sticking or seized	• Repair or replace parts as necessary
	• Master cylinder compensating ports blocked (fluid does not return to reservoirs).	• Use compressed air to clear ports. Do not use wire, pencils, or similar objects to open blocked ports.
Vehicle moves to one side when brakes are applied	• Incorrect front tire pressure	• Inflate to recommended cold (reduced load) inflation pressure
	• Worn or damaged wheel bearings	• Replace worn or damaged bearings
	• Brakelining on one side contaminated	• Determine and correct cause of contamination and replace brakelining in axle sets
	• Brakeshoes on one side bent, distorted, or lining loose on shoe	• Replace brakeshoes in axle sets
	• Support plate bent or loose on one side	• Tighten or replace support plate
	• Brakelining not yet seated with drums or rotors	• Burnish brakelining
	• Caliper anchor plate loose on one side	• Tighten anchor plate bolts
	• Caliper piston sticking or seized	• Repair or replace caliper
	• Brakelinings water soaked	• Drive vehicle with brakes lightly applied to dry linings
	• Loose suspension component attaching or mounting bolts	• Tighten suspension bolts. Replace worn suspension components.
	• Brake combination valve failure	• Replace combination valve
Chatter or shudder when brakes are applied (pedal pulsation and roughness may also occur.)	• Brakeshoes distorted, bent, contaminated, or worn	• Replace brakeshoes in axle sets
	• Caliper anchor plate or support plate loose	• Tighten mounting bolts
	• Excessive thickness variation of rotor(s)	• Refinish or replace rotors in axle sets
Noisy brakes (squealing, clicking, scraping sound when brakes are applied.)	• Bent, broken, distorted brakeshoes	• Replace brakeshoes in axle sets
	• Excessive rust on outer edge of rotor braking surface	• Remove rust

Troubleshooting the Brake System (cont.)

Problem	Cause	Solution
Noisy brakes (squealing, clicking, scraping sound when brakes are applied.) (cont.)	• Brakelining worn out—shoes contacting drum of rotor	• Replace brakeshoes and lining in axle sets. Refinish or replace drums or rotors.
	• Broken or loose holdown or return springs	• Replace parts as necessary
	• Rough or dry drum brake support plate ledges	• Lubricate support plate ledges
	• Cracked, grooved, or scored rotor(s) or drum(s)	• Replace rotor(s) or drum(s). Replace brakeshoes and lining in axle sets if necessary.
	• Incorrect brakelining and/or shoes (front or rear).	• Install specified shoe and lining assemblies
Pulsating brake pedal	• Out of round drums or excessive lateral runout in disc brake rotor(s)	• Refinish or replace drums, re-index rotors or replace

EXTERIOR

Doors

REMOVAL AND INSTALLATION

1. Open the door and support it securely. Remove the door check strap sleeve and remove the door check strap.
2. Have an assistant hold the door, and remove the door hinge bolts.
3. Remove the door from the vehicle.
4. Position the door to the door hinges.
5. Make sure to install new door hinge bolts and tighten the bolts securely.
6. Install the check strap and sleeve, and check the operation of the door.

Door Locks

REMOVAL AND INSTALLATION

1. Lock the door lock with either the locking knob or the key.
2. Remove both of the door lock retaining screws, and pull the lock approximately 3/8"–1/2" (10–12mm) away from the door.

3. Insert a screwdriver into the access hole at the bottom of the lock mechanism and hold the remote control lever in the pulled out position.
4. Detach the remote control lever from the pull rod.
5. Pull the locking lever, at the top of the mechanism, out of the sleeve.
6. Remove the lock from the door.
7. Close the rotary latch and lock it with the locking lever.
8. Insert a screw driver into the access hole at the bottom of the lock mechanism and hold the remote control lever in the pulled out position.
9. Insert the locking lever into the sleeve and attach the remote control lever to the pull rod.
10. Pull the screwdriver out of the access hole.
11. Mount the door lock to the door, insert the retainer screws and tighten securely.

A. Remote control lever
B. Rotary latch
C. Locking lever 1
D. Locking lever 2   detach lever A from pull rod G
E. Access hole   pull locking lever C out of sleeve H

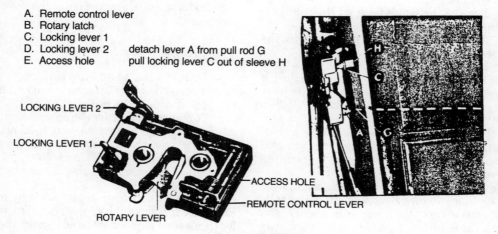

LOCKING LEVER 2

LOCKING LEVER 1

ROTARY LEVER

ACCESS HOLE

REMOTE CONTROL LEVER

Door lock installation

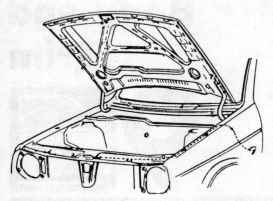

Hood removal

Hood

REMOVAL AND INSTALLATION

1. Raise the hood and support it securely.
2. While an assistant holds the hood, remove the hinge-to-hood retaining bolts.
3. Remove the hood from the vehicle.
4. Reverse the procedure to install the hood.

ALIGNMENT

Loosen the hinge to hood attaching bolts and move the hood from side to side until there is an equal amount of clearance on both sides of the hood and fender. Tighten the hood attaching bolts.

Trunk Lid

REMOVAL AND INSTALLATION

1. Open and support the trunk lid securely.
2. Mark the position of the trunk lid hinge in relation to the trunk lid.
3. Remove the two bolts attaching the hinge to the trunk lid.
4. Remove the trunk lid from the vehicle.
To Install:
1. Align the marks on the trunk lid with the hinges.
2. Install the hinge-to-trunk lid bolts.
3. Tighten the trunk lid bolts and adjust if necessary.

ADJUSTMENT

To make the to-and-fro or side-to-side adjustment, loosen the trunk lid attaching bolts and move the trunk lid as necessary. Tighten the trunk lid attaching bolts.

To make the up-and-down adjustment, loosen the hinge-to-hinge support attaching bolts and raise or lower the hinge as necessary. The trunk lid is at the correct height when it is flush with the trunk deck.

Trunk Lid Lock

ADJUSTMENT

To adjust the trunk lid lock, loosen the striker attaching bolts, and move the striker as required, then tighten the attaching bolts.

Hatch or Rear Door

REMOVAL AND INSTALLATION

1. Open the rear door fully and disconnect the negative battery cable.
2. Carefully remove the trim fasteners with a flat screwdriver and and remove the door trim.
3. Disconnect the wiring couplings and the ground wire.
4. Pull out the wiring harness from the rear door.
5. Disconnect the washer hose at the nozzle located on the back door and pull it out of the rear door (if equipped).
6. Support the rear door with a suitable bar. Then remove the ball studs from both the upper and lower ends of the stay dampers. Remove the stay dampers.
CAUTION: *Never disassemble the stay damper as gas is filled in the cylinder. Do not apply an oil or paint onto the piston rod. Be careful not to damage the piston rod. Do not turn the piston rod and the cylinder when the piston rod is extended. When discarding the stay damper, drill a 0.08–0.12" (2–3mm) hole in the bottom of the damper to release the gas. Make sure to protect yourself against any metal particles that may be thrown into the air by the compressed gas during drilling.*
7. Remove the rear door-to-hinge attaching bolts and remove the rear door.
8. Installation is the reverse of the removal procedure.

ALIGNMENT

1. To align the to-and-fro position of the door, loosen the hinge attaching bolts on both the back door and the body.
2. To adjust the door for the up and down position, loosen the hinge attaching bolts on the back door side, the door lock attaching bolts, and the door striker attaching bolts.
3. Adjust the rear for closing, by moving the door lock and striker.
4. Make all necessary adjustments by moving the rear door in the appropriate directions for the desired adjustments and tighten the attaching bolts.

Hatch and Rear Door Lock
REMOVAL AND INSTALLATION

1. Using a flat screwdriver, gently remove the trim fasteners and remove the door trim.
2. Disconnect the rod for the push button release.
3. Remove the push button securing clip and remove the push button.
4. Remove the door lock attaching bolts and remove the door lock.
5. Installation is the reverse of the removal procedure.
6. Adjust the door as described above.

Windshield

NOTE: *Bonded windshields require special tools and procedures. For this reason we recommend that all removal, installation and repair work be referred to a qualified technician.*

REMOVAL AND INSTALLATION

Special tool set (431 898 099A) is required to perform this procedure. You will also need VW glass cutting tool 1351, double suction pad holders, for holding the glass, and a caulking gun for applying the bonding and sealing compound.
1. Remove the rear view mirror, sun visors, front pillar trim, and front header trim.
2. Remove the wiper arms and cowl grille.
3. Remove the front window molding.
4. Remove the glass by separating the glass from the sealant using a commercial power or manually operated remover tool, or use the following procedure.
   a. Use an awl to make a hole in the sealant.
   b. Pass a piece of piano wire, about 1/8" (3mm) in diameter, through the hole, and attach wood bars to both ends.
   c. Two people should hold the bars, one inside and one outside the vehicle, and then "saw" the sealant from around the glass, cutting along the border between the glass and the sealant.
   d. Then, with the help of an assistant, remove the glass from the vehicle. Make sure that no spacers or clips are lost during windshield removal.
To Install:
1. Use a knife to smoothly trim the sealant on the body. Leave a layer about 0.04–0.08" (1–2mm) thick.
   NOTE: *If there are small gaps or flakes in the sealant use new sealant to patch it.*
2. Carefully clean and remove any dirt or grease from a 1.97" (50mm) wide area around

the circumference of the glass and the remaining bond of the body.
3. Bond a dam along the circumference of the glass 0.20" (5mm) from the edge.
   NOTE: *Securely bond the dam and allow it to dry before proceeding to the next step.*
4. Apply primer with a brush to the circumference of the glass and the body, and allow it to naturally dry for 20 to 30 minutes.
   CAUTION: *Be sure not to allow dirt, water, oil, etc. to come in contact with the coated surfaces and do not touch it with your hand.*
5. Install the spacers in the positions shown in the figure. Replace any clips with flaws.
6. When the primer has dried, apply an 0.43" (11mm) thick bead of repair seal, 0.20" (7mm) from the frame of the glass using a sealant gun. Cut the nozzle of the sealant gun to the angle shown in the figure. If necessary, smooth the repair seal to correct any irregularities.
7. Place the windshield into the frame. Fully lower the side windows to prevent any pressure from being exerted on the windshield should the doors be closed suddenly. Keep the door glass open until the repair seal dries to some degree.
8. Remove any access, or add repair seal where necessary.
9. Check the windshield for water leaks. If a leak is found, wipe off the water and add repair seal.
10. After checking for water leakage, mount the pillar garnish, cowl panel, cowl grill, wipers, etc.
11. Attach the front header trim, sun visor, interior mirror, etc.

Rear Window Glass
REMOVAL AND INSTALLATION

The procedure for removing and installing the rear window glass is the same as the front windshield removal and installation procedures.

Hatchback Window Glass
REMOVAL AND INSTALLATION

1. Remove the wiper arm, wiper motor, back door trim and defogger connector.
2. Remove the rear window molding.
4. Use an awl to make a hole in the sealant.
5. Pass a piece of piano wire, about 1/8" (3mm) in diameter, through the hole, and attach wood bars to both ends.
6. Two people should hold the bars, one inside and one outside the vehicle, and then "saw" the sealant from around the glass, cutting along the border between the glass and the sealant.

7. Then, with the help of an assistant, remove the glass from the vehicle. Make sure that no spacers or clips are lost during windshield removal.

To Install:

1. Use a knife to smoothly trim the sealant on the body. Leave a layer about 0.04–0.08″ (1–2mm) thick.

NOTE: *If there are small gaps or flakes in the sealant use new sealant to patch it.*

2. Carefully clean and remove any dirt or grease from a 1.97″ (50mm) wide area around the circumference of the glass and the remaining bond of the body.

3. Bond a dam along the circumference of the glass 0.31″ (8mm) from the edge.

NOTE: *Securely bond the dam and allow it to dry before proceeding to the next step.*

4. Apply primer with a brush to the circumference of the glass and the body, and allow it to naturally dry for 20 to 30 minutes.

CAUTION: *Be sure not to allow dirt, water, oil, etc. to come in contact with the coated surfaces and do not touch it with your hand.*

5. Install the spacers in the positions shown in the figure. Replace any clips with flaws.

6. When the primer has dried, apply an 0.43″ (11mm) thick bead of repair seal, 0.20″ (7mm) from the frame of the glass using a sealant gun. Cut the nozzle of the sealant gun to the angle shown in the figure. If necessary, smooth the repair seal to correct any irregularities.

7. Attach the back door glass to the body. Fully lower the side windows to prevent any pressure from being exerted on the back door glass should the doors be closed suddenly. Keep the side windows open until the repair seal dries to some degree.

Refer to the seal hardening chart in the front windshield removal and installation section.

8. Remove any access, or add repair seal where necessary.

9. Check the back door glass for water leaks. If a leak is found, wipe off the water and add repair seal.

10. After checking for water leaks, install the molding.

11. Install the wiper arm, wiper motor door trim and defogger connector.

Side Quarter Glass

REMOVAL AND INSTALLATION

1. Pry the cover from the door handle using a flat screwdriver, remove the screws and detach the door handle.

2. Wind down the rear window and remove the window regulator handle.

3. Remove the door trim panel from the door

and remove the bolts and oversize spring washers.

4. Remove the screw at the top of the door and the two bolts on the inside of the door, that secure the window guide channel.

5. Remove the window guide channel and the rear quarter window.

6. Lubricate the seal on the rear quarter window.

7. Installation is the reverse of the removal procedure.

INTERIOR

Door Panels

REMOVAL AND INSTALLATION

1. Remove the window regulator handle.
2. Remove the arm rest.
3. Remove the door lock knob.
4. Remove the inner door handle cover.
5. Using a flat screwdriver, gently separate the door trim panel clips from the door.
6. Remove the door trim panel.

To Install:

1. Place the door trim panel into position on the door.

2. Apply pressure to the trim panel in the areas where the trim panel clips attach to the door.

3. Install the inner door handle cover, door lock knob and the arm rest.

Door Glass and Regulator

REMOVAL AND INSTALLATION

1. Lower the window glass and remove the inner handle cover, door lock knob (if necessary), the window regulator handle and the door trim panel.

NOTE: *On vehicles with power windows, disconnect the wiring coupling.*

2. Carefully peel off the door screen so that it can be reused.

3. On convertible models remove the seven screws attaching the window regulator to the door and one screw from the winder.

4. On all other models replace the window regulator handle and position the door glass so that the door glass installation bolts can be removed from the service hole.

5. Remove the door glass installation bolts.

6. On convertible models, remove the door glass and take out the window regulator through the large access hole.

7. On all other models, remove the door glass. Disconnect the retainer clips from the window winder, then remove the winder through the service access hole.

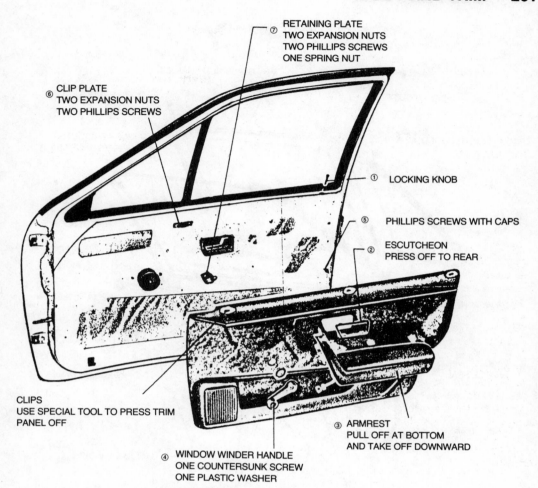

RETAINING PLATE
⑦ TWO EXPANSION NUTS
TWO PHILLIPS SCREWS
ONE SPRING NUT

⑥ CLIP PLATE
TWO EXPANSION NUTS
TWO PHILLIPS SCREWS

① LOCKING KNOB

⑤ PHILLIPS SCREWS WITH CAPS

② ESCUTCHEON
PRESS OFF TO REAR

CLIPS
USE SPECIAL TOOL TO PRESS TRIM
PANEL OFF

③ ARMREST
PULL OFF AT BOTTOM
AND TAKE OFF DOWNWARD

④ WINDOW WINDER HANDLE
ONE COUNTERSUNK SCREW
ONE PLASTIC WASHER

Exploded view, door panel assembly

8. Installation is the reverse of the removal procedure.

Electric Window Motor

REMOVAL AND INSTALLATION

1. Lower the window glass and remove the inner handle cover, door lock knob (if necessary), the window regulator handle and the door trim panel.

2. Disconnect the wiring coupling. Carefully peel off the door screen so that it can be reused.

3. Pull the glass run channel out of the window guide. Remove the retaining screws that secure the front and rear window guides and remove the window guides. Then remove the front quarter window glass from the vehicle.

4. On the convertible models remove the six bolts attaching the window regulator to the door.

5. On all other models replace the window

regulator handle and position the door glass so that the door glass installation bolts can be removed from the service hole.

6. Remove the door glass installation bolts.

7. On the convertible models, remove the door glass and take out the window regulator through the large access hole.

8. On all other models, remove the door glass. Remove the winder cable installation clips, and then remove the window winder through the service access hole.

9. Remove the window motor mounting bolts, then remove the motor from the regulator/winder cable.

10. Lubricate the front quarter window glass gasket.

11. Installation is the reverse of the removal procedure.

Headliner

REMOVAL AND INSTALLATION

1. Remove the rear view mirror, sun visors, sunvisor holders and the assist grip.

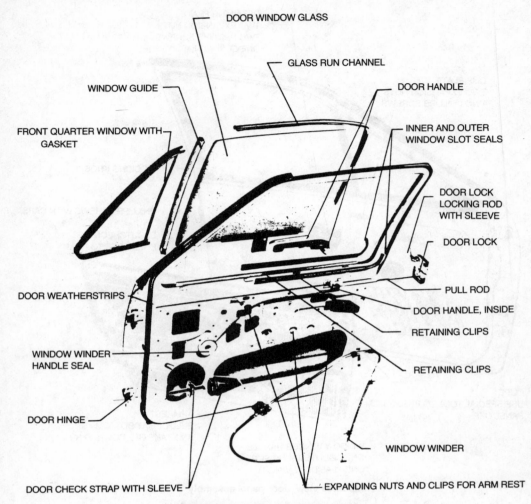

DOOR WINDOW GLASS

GLASS RUN CHANNEL

DOOR HANDLE

WINDOW GUIDE

INNER AND OUTER
WINDOW SLOT SEALS

FRONT QUARTER WINDOW WITH
GASKET

DOOR LOCK
LOCKING ROD
WITH SLEEVE

DOOR LOCK

PULL ROD

DOOR WEATHERSTRIPS

DOOR HANDLE, INSIDE

RETAINING CLIPS

WINDOW WINDER
HANDLE SEAL

RETAINING CLIPS

DOOR HINGE

WINDOW WINDER

DOOR CHECK STRAP WITH SLEEVE

EXPANDING NUTS AND CLIPS FOR ARM REST

Exploded view, door glass assembly

2. Remove the lens of the interior light and remove the screws.

3. Disconnect the interior lamp harness coupler.

4. Remove the weatherstrip.

6. Remove the seaming welt.

7. Remove the front door trim by prying with a flat screwdriver.

8. Remove the center pillar trim.

9. Remove the weatherstrip, fasteners, and then remove the rear pillar trim.

10. Remove the fasteners from the roof lining.

11. Remove the floor lining rear end plate. NOTE: *On the sedan, remove the plate while pushing the weatherstrip away from the end plate.*

12. Remove the rear of the roof lining by pulling it free from the corners.

13. Move the roof lining brace rearward and remove the front part of the roof lining.

14. Installation is done in the reverse of the removal procedure.

Headliner

REMOVAL AND INSTALLATION

Vehicle With Sunroof

1. Remove the overhead console, rear view mirror, sun visors, sunvisor holders and the assist grip.

2. Remove the lens of the interior light and remove the screws.

3. Disconnect the interior lamp harness coupler and remove the interior lamp.

4. Remove the seaming welt from the sunroof opening.

5. Remove the front of the door opening seaming welts.

6. Remove the front pillar trims.

7. Remove the roof lining front lace.

8. Remove the rear of the door opening seaming welts.

9. Remove the rear pillar trim.

10. Remove the roof lining rear lace.

11. Remove the side pillar trim.

12. Remove the attaching screws of the roof lining side lace and remove the side lace.

13. Remove the fasteners at the side of the roof lining and remove the roof lining.

14. Installation is the reverse of the removal procedure.

Mechanic's Data

General Conversion Table

Multiply By	To Convert	To	
	LENGTH		
2.54	Inches	Centimeters	.3937
25.4	Inches	Millimeters	.03937
30.48	Feet	Centimeters	.0328
.304	Feet	Meters	3.28
.914	Yards	Meters	1.094
1.609	Miles	Kilometers	.621
	VOLUME		
.473	Pints	Liters	2.11
.946	Quarts	Liters	1.06
3.785	Gallons	Liters	.264
.016	Cubic inches	Liters	61.02
16.39	Cubic inches	Cubic cms.	.061
28.3	Cubic feet	Liters	.0353
	MASS (Weight)		
28.35	Ounces	Grams	.035
.4536	Pounds	Kilograms	2.20
—	To obtain	From	Multiply by

Multiply By	To Convert	To	
	AREA		
.645	Square inches	Square cms.	.155
.836	Square yds.	Square meters	1.196
	FORCE		
4.448	Pounds	Newtons	.225
.138	Ft./lbs.	Kilogram/meters	7.23
1.36	Ft./lbs.	Newton-meters	.737
.112	In./lbs.	Newton-meters	8.844
	PRESSURE		
.068	Psi	Atmospheres	14.7
6.89	Psi	Kilopascals	.145
	OTHER		
1.104	Horsepower (DIN)	Horsepower (SAE)	.9861
.746	Horsepower (SAE)	Kilowatts (KW)	1.34
1.60	Mph	Km/h	.625
.425	Mpg	Km/1	2.35
—	To obtain	From	Multiply by

Tap Drill Sizes

National Coarse or U.S.S.

Screw & Tap Size	Threads Per Inch	Use Drill Number
No. 5	40	39
No. 6	32	36
No. 8	32	29
No. 10	24	25
No. 12	24	17
1/4	20	8
5/16	18	F
3/8	16	5/16
7/16	14	U
1/2	13	27/64
9/16	12	31/64
5/8	11	17/32
3/4	10	21/32
7/8	9	49/64

National Coarse or U.S.S.

Screw & Tap Size	Threads Per Inch	Use Drill Number
1	8	7/8
1 1/8	7	63/64
1 1/4	7	1 7/64
1 1/2	6	1 11/32

National Fine or S.A.E.

Screw & Tap Size	Threads Per Inch	Use Drill Number
No. 5	44	37
No. 6	40	33
No. 8	36	29
No. 10	32	21

National Fine or S.A.E.

Screw & Tap Size	Threads Per Inch	Use Drill Number
No. 12	28	15
1/4	28	3
5/16	24	1
3/8	24	Q
7/16	20	W
1/2	20	29/64
9/16	18	33/64
5/8	18	37/64
3/4	16	11/16
7/8	14	13/16
1 1/8	12	1 3/64
1 1/4	12	1 11/64
1 1/2	12	1 27/64

Drill Sizes In Decimal Equivalents

Inch	Decimal	Wire	mm	Inch	Decimal	Wire	mm	Inch	Decimal	Wire & Letter	mm	Inch	Decimal	Letter	mm	Inch	Decimal	mm
1/64	.0156		.39		.0730	49			.1614		4.1		.2717		6.9		.4331	11.0
	.0157		.4		.0748		1.9		.1654		4.2		.2720	I		7/16	.4375	11.11
	.0160	78			.0760	48			.1660	19			.2756		7.0		.4528	11.5
	.0165		.42		.0768		1.95		.1673		4.25		.2770	J		29/64	.4531	11.51
	.0173		.44	5/64	.0781		1.98		.1693		4.3		.2795		7.1	15/32	.4688	11.90
	.0177		.45		.0785	47			.1695	18			.2810	K			.4724	12.0
	.0180	77			.0787		2.0	11/64	.1719		4.36	9/32	.2812		7.14	31/64	.4844	12.30
	.0181		.46		.0807		2.05		.1730	17			.2835		7.2		.4921	12.5
	.0189		.48		.0810	46			.1732		4.4		.2854		7.25	1/2	.5000	12.70
	.0197		.5		.0820	45			.1770	16			.2874		7.3		.5118	13.0
	.0200	76			.0827		2.1		.1772		4.5		.2900	L		33/64	.5156	13.09
	.0210	75			.0846		2.15		.1800	15			.2913		7.4	17/32	.5312	13.49
	.0217		.55		.0860	44			.1811		4.6		.2950	M			.5315	13.5
	.0225	74			.0866		2.2		.1820	14			.2953		7.5	35/64	.5469	13.89
	.0236		.6		.0886		2.25		.1850	13		19/64	.2969		7.54		.5512	14.0
	.0240	73			.0890	43			.1850		4.7		.2992		7.6	9/16	.5625	14.28
	.0250	72			.0906		2.3		.1870		4.75		.3020	N			.5709	14.5
	.0256		.65		.0925		2.35	3/16	.1875		4.76		.3031		7.7	37/64	.5781	14.68
	.0260	71			.0935	42			.1890		4.8		.3051		7.75		.5906	15.0
	.0276		.7	3/32	.0938		2.38		.1890	12			.3071		7.8	19/32	.5938	15.08
	.0280	70			.0945		2.4		.1910	11			.3110		7.9	39/64	.6094	15.47
	.0292	69			.0960	41			.1929		4.9	5/16	.3125		7.93		.6102	15.5
	.0295		.75		.0965		2.45		.1935	10			.3150		8.0	5/8	.6250	15.87
	.0310	68			.0980	40			.1960	9			.3160	O			.6299	16.0
1/32	.0312		.79		.0981		2.5		.1969		5.0		.3189		8.1	41/64	.6406	16.27
	.0315		.8		.0995	39			.1990	8			.3228		8.2		.6496	16.5
	.0320	67			.1015	38			.2008		5.1		.3230	P		21/32	.6562	16.66
	.0330	66			.1024		2.6		.2010	7			.3248		8.25		.6693	17.0
	.0335		.85		.1040	37		13/64	.2031		5.16	21/64	.3268		8.3	43/64	.6719	17.06
	.0350	65			.1063		2.7		.2040	6			.3281		8.33	11/16	.6875	17.46
	.0354		.9		.1065	36			.2047		5.2		.3307		8.4		.6890	17.5
	.0360	64			.1083		2.75		.2055	5			.3320	Q		45/64	.7031	17.85
	.0370	63		7/64	.1094		2.77		.2067		5.25		.3346		8.5		.7087	18.0
	.0374		.95		.1100	35			.2087		5.3		.3386		8.6	23/32	.7188	18.25
	.0380	62			.1102		2.8		.2090	4			.3390	R			.7283	18.5
	.0390	61			.1110	34			.2126		5.4		.3425		8.7	47/64	.7344	18.65
	.0394		1.0		.1130	33			.2130	3		11/32	.3438		8.73		.7480	19.0
	.0400	60			.1142		2.9		.2165		5.5		.3445		8.75	3/4	.7500	19.05
	.0410	59			.1160	32		7/32	2188		5.55		.3465		8.8	49/64	.7656	19.44
	.0413		1.05		.1181		3.0		.2205		5.6		.3480	S			.7677	19.5
	.0420	58			.1200	31			.2210	2			.3504		8.9	25/32	.7812	19.84
	.0430	57			.1220		3.1		.2244		5.7		.3543		9.0		.7874	20.0
	.0433		1.1	1/8	.1250		3.17		.2264		5.75		.3580	T		51/64	.7969	20.24
	.0453		1.15		.1260		3.2		.2280	1			.3583		9.1		.8071	20.5
3/64	.0465	56			.1280		3.25		.2283		5.8	23/64	.3594		9.12	13/16	.8125	20.63
	.0469		1.19		.1285	30			.2323		5.9		.3622		9.2		.8268	21.0
	.0472		1.2		.1299		3.3		.2340	A			.3642		9.25	53/64	.8281	21.03
	.0492		1.25		.1339		3.4	15/64	.2344		5.95		.3661		9.3	27/32	.8438	21.43
	.0512		1.3		.1360	29			.2362		6.0		.3680	U			.8465	21.5
	.0520	55			.1378		3.5		.2380	B			.3701		9.4	55/64	.8594	21.82
	.0531		1.35		.1405	28			.2402		6.1		.3740		9.5		.8661	22.0
	.0550	54		9/64	.1406		3.57		.2420	C		3/8	.3750		9.52	7/8	.8750	22.22
	.0551		1.4		.1417		3.6		.2441		6.2		.3770	V			.8858	22.5
	.0571		1.45		.1440	27			.2460	D			.3780		9.6	57/64	.8906	22.62
	.0591		1.5		.1457		3.7		.2461		6.25		.3819		9.7		.9055	23.0
	.0595	53			.1470	26			.2480		6.3		.3839		9.75	29/32	.9062	23.01
	.0610		1.55		.1476		3.75	1/4	.2500	E	6.35		.3858		9.8	59/64	.9219	23.41
1/16	.0625		1.59		.1495	25			.2520		6.		.3860	W			.9252	23.5
	.0630		1.6		.1496		3.8		.2559		6.5		.3898		9.9	15/16	.9375	23.81
	.0635	52			.1520	24			.2570	F		25/64	.3906		9.92		.9449	24.0
	.0650		1.65		.1535		3.9		.2598		6.6		.3937		10.0	61/64	.9531	24.2
	.0669		1.7		.1540	23			.2610	G			.3970	X			.9646	24.5
	.0670	51		5/32	.1562		3.96		.2638		6.7		.4040	Y		31/32	.9688	24.6
	.0689		1.75		.1570	22		17/64	.2656		6.74	13/32	.4062		10.31		.9843	25.0
	.0700	50			.1575		4.0		.2657		6.75		.4130	Z		63/64	.9844	25.0
	.0709		1.8		.1590	21			.2660	H			.4134		10.5	1	1.0000	25.4
	.0728		1.85		.1610	20			.2677		6.8	27/64	.4219		10.71			

AIR/FUEL RATIO: The ratio of air to gasoline by weight in the fuel mixture drawn into the engine.

AIR INJECTION: One method of reducing harmful exhaust emissions by injecting air into each of the exhaust ports of an engine. The fresh air entering the hot exhaust manifold causes any remaining fuel to be burned before it can exit the tailpipe.

ALTERNATOR: A device used for converting mechanical energy into electrical energy.

AMMETER: An instrument, calibrated in amperes, used to measure the flow of an electrical current in a circuit. Ammeters are always connected in series with the circuit being tested.

AMPERE: The rate of flow of electrical current present when one volt of electrical pressure is applied against one ohm of electrical resistance.

ANALOG COMPUTER: Any microprocessor that uses similar (analogous) electrical signals to make its calculations.

ARMATURE: A laminated, soft iron core wrapped by a wire that converts electrical energy to mechanical energy as in a motor or relay. When rotated in a magnetic field, it changes mechanical energy into electrical energy as in a generator.

ATMOSPHERIC PRESSURE: The pressure on the Earth's surface caused by the weight of the air in the atmosphere. At sea level, this pressure is 14.7 psi at 32°F (101 kPa at 0°C).

ATOMIZATION: The breaking down of a liquid into a fine mist that can be suspended in air.

AXIAL PLAY: Movement parallel to a shaft or bearing bore.

BACKFIRE: The sudden combustion of gases in the intake or exhaust system that results in a loud explosion.

BACKLASH: The clearance or play between two parts, such as meshed gears.

BACKPRESSURE: Restrictions in the exhaust system that slow the exit of exhaust gases from the combustion chamber.

BAKELITE: A heat resistant, plastic insulator material commonly used in printed circuit boards and transistorized components.

BALL BEARING: A bearing made up of hardened inner and outer races between which hardened steel ball roll.

BALLAST RESISTOR: A resistor in the primary ignition circuit that lowers voltage after the engine is started to reduce wear on ignition components.

BEARING: A friction reducing, supportive device usually located between a stationary part and a moving part.

BIMETAL TEMPERATURE SENSOR: Any sensor or switch made of two dissimilar types of metal that bend when heated or cooled due to the different expansion rates of the alloys. These types of sensors usually function as an on/off switch.

BLOWBY: Combustion gases, composed of water vapor and unburned fuel, that leak past the piston rings into the crankcase during normal engine operation. These gases are removed by the PCV system to prevent the build-up of harmful acids in the crankcase.

BRAKE PAD: A brake shoe and lining assembly used with disc brakes.

BRAKE SHOE: The backing for the brake lining. The term is, however, usually applied to the assembly of the brake backing and lining.

BUSHING: A liner, usually removable, for a bearing; an anti-friction liner used in place of a bearing.

BYPASS: System used to bypass ballast resistor during engine cranking to increase voltage supplied to the coil.

CALIPER: A hydraulically activated device in a disc brake system, which is mounted straddling the brake rotor (disc). The caliper contains at least one piston and two brake pads. Hydraulic pressure on the piston(s) forces the pads against the rotor.

CAMSHAFT: A shaft in the engine on which are the lobes (cams) which operate the valves. The camshaft is driven by the crankshaft, via a belt, chain or gears, at one half the crankshaft speed.

CAPACITOR: A device which stores an electrical charge.

CARBON MONOXIDE (CO): a colorless, odorless gas given off as a normal byproduct of combustion. It is poisonous and extremely dangerous in confined areas, building up slowly to toxic levels without warning if adequate ventilation is not available.

CARBURETOR: A device, usually mounted on the intake manifold of an engine, which mixes the air and fuel in the proper proportion to allow even combustion.

CATALYTIC CONVERTER: A device installed in the exhaust system, like a muffler, that converts harmful byproducts of combustion into carbon dioxide and water vapor by means of a heat-producing chemical reaction.

CENTRIFUGAL ADVANCE: A mechanical method of advancing the spark timing by using flyweights in the distributor that react to centrifugal force generated by the distributor shaft rotation.

CHECK VALVE: Any one-way valve installed to permit the flow of air, fuel or vacuum in one direction only.

CHOKE: A device, usually a moveable valve, placed in the intake path of a carburetor to restrict the flow of air.

CIRCUIT: Any unbroken path through which an electrical current can flow. Also used to describe fuel flow in some instances.

CIRCUIT BREAKER: A switch which protects an electrical circuit from overload by opening the circuit when the current flow exceeds a predetermined level. Some circuit breakers must be reset manually, while other reset automatically

COIL (IGNITION): A transformer in the ignition circuit which steps of the voltage provided to the spark plugs.

COMBINATION MANIFOLD: An assembly which includes both the intake and exhaust manifolds in one casting.

COMBINATION VALVE: A device used in some fuel systems that routes fuel vapors to a charcoal storage canister instead of venting them into the atmosphere. The valve relieves fuel tank pressure and allows fresh air into the tank as fuel level drops to prevent a vapor lock situation.

COMPRESSION RATIO: The comparison of the total volume of the cylinder and combustion chamber with the piston at BDC and the piston at TDC.

CONDENSER: 1. An electrical device which acts to store an electrical charge, preventing voltage surges.
2. A radiator-like device in the air conditioning system in which refrigerant gas condenses into a liquid, giving off heat.

CONDUCTOR: Any material through which an electrical current can be transmitted easily.

CONTINUITY: Continuous or complete circuit. Can be checked with an ohmmeter.

COUNTERSHAFT: An intermediate shaft which is rotated by a mainshaft and transmits, in turn, that rotation to a working part.

CRANKCASE: The lower part of an engine in which the crankshaft and related parts operate.

CRANKSHAFT: The main driving shaft of an engine which receives reciprocating motion from the pistons and converts it to rotary motion.

CYLINDER: In an engine, the round hole in the engine block in which the piston(s) ride.

CYLINDER BLOCK: The main structural member of an engine in which is found the cylinders, crankshaft and other principal parts.

CYLINDER HEAD: The detachable portion of the engine, fastened, usually, to the top of the cylinder block, containing all or most of the combustion chambers. On overhead valve engines, it contains the valves and their operating parts. On overhead cam engines, it contains the camshaft as well.

DEAD CENTER: The extreme top or bottom of the piston stroke.

DETONATION: An unwanted explosion of the air fuel mixture in the combustion chamber caused by excess heat and compression, advanced timing, or an overly lean mixture. Also referred to as "ping".

DIAPHRAGM: A thin, flexible wall separating two cavities, such as in a vacuum advance unit.

DIESELING: A condition in which hot spots in the combustion chamber cause the engine to run on after the key is turned off.

DIFFERENTIAL: A geared assembly which allows the transmission of motion between drive axles, giving one axle the ability to turn faster than the other.

DIODE: An electrical device that will allow current to flow in one direction only.

DISC BRAKE: A hydraulic braking assembly consisting of a brake disc, or rotor, mounted on an axle, and a caliper assembly containing, usually two brake pads which are activated by hydraulic pressure. The pads are forced against the sides of the disc, creating friction which slows the vehicle.

DISTRIBUTOR: A mechanically driven device on an engine which is responsible for electrically firing the spark plug at a predetermined point of the piston stroke.

DOWEL PIN: A pin, inserted in mating holes in two different parts allowing those parts to maintain a fixed relationship.

DRUM BRAKE: A braking system which consists of two brake shoes and one or two wheel cylinders, mounted on a fixed backing plate, and a brake drum, mounted on an axle, which revolves around the assembly. Hydraulic action applied to the wheel cylinders forces the shoes outward against the drum, creating friction and slowing the vehicle.

DWELL: The rate, measured in degrees of shaft rotation, at which an electrical circuit cycles on and off.

ELECTRONIC CONTROL UNIT (ECU): Ignition module, module, amplifier or igniter. See Module for definition.

ELECTRONIC IGNITION: A system in which the timing and firing of the spark plugs is controlled by an electronic control unit, usually called a module. These systems have not points or condenser.

ENDPLAY: The measured amount of axial movement in a shaft.

ENGINE: A device that converts heat into mechanical energy.

EXHAUST MANIFOLD: A set of cast passages or pipes which conduct exhaust gases from the engine.

FEELER GAUGE: A blade, usually metal, of precisely predetermined thickness, used to measure the clearance between two parts. These blades usually are available in sets of assorted thicknesses.

F-Head: An engine configuration in which the intake valves are in the cylinder head, while the camshaft and exhaust valves are located in the cylinder block. The camshaft operates the intake valves via lifters and pushrods, while it operates the exhaust valves directly.

FIRING ORDER: The order in which combustion occurs in the cylinders of an engine. Also the order in which spark is distributed to the plugs by the distributor.

FLATHEAD: An engine configuration in which the camshaft and all the valves are located in the cylinder block.

FLOODING: The presence of too much fuel in the intake manifold and combustion chamber which prevents the air/fuel mixture from firing, thereby causing a no-start situation.

FLYWHEEL: A disc shaped part bolted to the rear end of the crankshaft. Around the outer perimeter is affixed the ring gear. The starter drive engages the ring gear, turning the flywheel, which rotates the crankshaft, imparting the initial starting motion to the engine.

FOOT POUND (ft.lb. or sometimes, ft. lbs.): The amount of energy or work needed to raise an item weighing one pound, a distance of one foot.

FUSE: A protective device in a circuit which prevents circuit overload by breaking the circuit when a specific amperage is present. The device is constructed around a strip or wire of a lower amperage rating than the circuit it is designed to protect. When an amperage higher than that stamped on the fuse is present in the circuit, the strip or wire melts, opening the circuit.

GEAR RATIO: The ratio between the number of teeth on meshing gears.

GENERATOR: A device which converts mechanical energy into electrical energy.

HEAT RANGE: The measure of a spark plug's ability to dissipate heat from its firing end. The higher the heat range, the hotter the plug fires.

HUB: The center part of a wheel or gear.

HYDROCARBON (HC): Any chemical compound made up of hydrogen and carbon. A major pollutant formed by the engine as a byproduct of combustion.

HYDROMETER: An instrument used to measure the specific gravity of a solution.

INCH POUND (in.lb. or sometimes, in. lbs.): One twelfth of a foot pound.

INDUCTION: A means of transferring electrical energy in the form of a magnetic field. Principle used in the ignition coil to increase voltage.

INJECTION PUMP: A device, usually mechanically operated, which meters and delivers fuel under pressure to the fuel injector.

INJECTOR: A device which receives metered fuel under relatively low pressure and is activated to inject the fuel into the engine under relatively high pressure at a predetermined time.

INPUT SHAFT: The shaft to which torque is applied, usually carrying the driving gear or gears.

INTAKE MANIFOLD: A casting of passages or pipes used to conduct air or a fuel/air mixture to the cylinders.

JOURNAL: The bearing surface within which a shaft operates.

KEY: A small block usually fitted in a notch between a shaft and a hub to prevent slippage of the two parts.

MANIFOLD: A casting of passages or set of pipes which connect the cylinders to an inlet or outlet source.

MANIFOLD VACUUM: Low pressure in an engine intake manifold formed just below the throttle plates. Manifold vacuum is highest at idle and drops under acceleration.

MASTER CYLINDER: The primary fluid pressurizing device in a hydraulic system. In automotive use, it is found in brake and hydraulic clutch systems and is pedal activated, either directly or, in a power brake system, through the power booster.

MODULE: Electronic control unit, amplifier or igniter of solid state or integrated design which controls the current flow in the ignition primary circuit based on input from the pickup coil. When the module opens the primary circuit, the high secondary voltage is induced in the coil.

NEEDLE BEARING: A bearing which consists of a number (usually a large number) of long, thin rollers.

OHM: (Ω) The unit used to measure the resistance of conductor to electrical flow. One ohm is the amount of resistance that limits current flow to one ampere in a circuit with one volt of pressure.

OHMMETER: An instrument used for measuring the resistance, in ohms, in an electrical circuit.

OUTPUT SHAFT: The shaft which transmits torque from a device, such as a transmission.

OVERDRIVE: A gear assembly which produces more shaft revolutions than that transmitted to it.

OVERHEAD CAMSHAFT (OHC): An engine configuration in which the camshaft is mounted on top of the cylinder head and operates the valve either directly or by means of rocker arms.

OVERHEAD VALVE (OHV): An engine configuration in which all of the valves are located in the cylinder head and the camshaft is located in the cylinder block. The camshaft operates the valves via lifters and pushrods.

OXIDES OF NITROGEN (NOx): Chemical compounds of nitrogen produced as a byproduct of combustion. They combine with hydrocarbons to produce smog.

OXYGEN SENSOR: Used with the feedback system to sense the presence of oxygen in the exhaust gas and signal the computer which can reference the voltage signal to an air/fuel ratio.

PINION: The smaller of two meshing gears.

PISTON RING: An open ended ring which fits into a groove on the outer diameter of the piston. Its chief function is to form a seal between the piston and cylinder wall. Most automotive pistons have three rings: two for compression sealing; one for oil sealing.

PRELOAD: A predetermined load placed on a bearing during assembly or by adjustment.

PRIMARY CIRCUIT: Is the low voltage side of the ignition system which consists of the ignition switch, ballast resistor or resistance wire, bypass, coil, electronic control unit and pick-up coil as well as the connecting wires and harnesses.

PRESS FIT: The mating of two parts under pressure, due to the inner diameter of one being smaller than the outer diameter of the other, or vice versa; an interference fit.

RACE: The surface on the inner or outer ring of a bearing on which the balls, needles or rollers move.

REGULATOR: A device which maintains the amperage and/or voltage levels of a circuit at predetermined values.

RELAY: A switch which automatically opens and/or closes a circuit.

RESISTANCE: The opposition to the flow of current through a circuit or electrical device, and is measured in ohms. Resistance is equal to the voltage divided by the amperage.

RESISTOR: A device, usually made of wire, which offers a preset amount of resistance in an electrical circuit.

RING GEAR: The name given to a ring-shaped gear attached to a differential case, or affixed to a flywheel or as part a planetary gear set.

ROLLER BEARING: A bearing made up of hardened inner and outer races between which hardened steel rollers move.

ROTOR: 1. The disc-shaped part of a disc brake assembly, upon which the brake pads bear; also called brake disc.
2. The device mounted atop the distributor shaft, which passes current to the distributor cap tower contacts.

SECONDARY CIRCUIT: The high voltage side of the ignition system, usually above 20,000 volts. The secondary includes the ignition coil, coil wire, distributor cap and rotor, spark plug wires and spark plugs.

SENDING UNIT: A mechanical, electrical, hydraulic or electromagnetic device which transmits information to a gauge.

SENSOR: Any device designed to measure engine operating conditions or ambient pressures and temperatures. Usually electronic in nature and designed to send a voltage signal to an on-board computer, some sensors may operate as a simple on/off switch or they may provide a variable voltage signal (like a potentiometer) as conditions or measured parameters change.

SHIM: Spacers of precise, predetermined thickness used between parts to establish a proper working relationship.

SLAVE CYLINDER: In automotive use, a device in the hydraulic clutch system which is activated by hydraulic force, disengaging the clutch.

SOLENOID: A coil used to produce a magnetic field, the effect of which is produce work.

SPARK PLUG: A device screwed into the combustion chamber of a spark ignition engine. The basic construction is a conductive core inside of a ceramic insulator, mounted in an outer conductive base. An electrical charge from the spark plug wire travels along the conductive core and jumps a preset air gap to a grounding point or points at the end of the conductive base. The resultant spark ignites the fuel/air mixture in the combustion chamber.

SPLINES: Ridges machined or cast onto the outer diameter of a shaft or inner diameter of a bore to enable parts to mate without rotation.

TACHOMETER: A device used to measure the rotary speed of an engine, shaft, gear, etc., usually in rotations per minute.

THERMOSTAT: A valve, located in the cooling system of an engine, which is closed when cold and opens gradually in response to engine heating, controlling the temperature of the coolant and rate of coolant flow.

TOP DEAD CENTER (TDC): The point at which the piston reaches the top of its travel on the compression stroke.

TORQUE: The twisting force applied to an object.

TORQUE CONVERTER: A turbine used to transmit power from a driving member to a driven member via hydraulic action, providing changes in drive ratio and torque. In automotive use, it links the driveplate at the rear of the engine to the automatic transmission.

TRANSDUCER: A device used to change a force into an electrical signal.

TRANSISTOR: A semi-conductor component which can be actuated by a small voltage to perform an electrical switching function.

TUNE-UP: A regular maintenance function, usually associated with the replacement and adjustment of parts and components in the electrical and fuel systems of a vehicle for the purpose of attaining optimum performance.

TURBOCHARGER: An exhaust driven pump which compresses intake air and forces it into the combustion chambers at higher than atmospheric pressures. The increased air pressure allows more fuel to be burned and results in increased horsepower being produced.

VACUUM ADVANCE: A device which advances the ignition timing in response to increased engine vacuum.

VACUUM GAUGE: An instrument used to measure the presence of vacuum in a chamber.

VALVE: A device which control the pressure, direction of flow or rate of flow of a liquid or gas.

VALVE CLEARANCE: The measured gap between the end of the valve stem and the rocker arm, cam lobe or follower that activates the valve.

VISCOSITY: The rating of a liquid's internal resistance to flow.

VOLTMETER: An instrument used for measuring electrical force in units called volts. Voltmeters are always connected parallel with the circuit being tested.

WHEEL CYLINDER: Found in the automotive drum brake assembly, it is a device, actuated by hydraulic pressure, which, through internal pistons, pushes the brake shoes outward against the drums.

ABBREVIATIONS AND SYMBOLS

A: Ampere

AC: Alternating current

A/C: Air conditioning

A-h: Ampere hour

AT: Automatic transmission

ATDC: After top dead center

μA: Microampere

bbl: Barrel

BDC: Bottom dead center

bhp: Brake horsepower

BTDC: Before top dead center

BTU: British thermal unit

C: Celsius (Centigrade)

CCA: Cold cranking amps

cd: Candela

cm^2: Square centimeter

cm^3, cc: Cubic centimeter

CO: Carbon monoxide

CO_2: Carbon dioxide

cu.in., in^3: Cubic inch

CV: Constant velocity

Cyl.: Cylinder

DC: Direct current

ECM: Electronic control module

EFE: Early fuel evaporation

EFI: Electronic fuel injection

EGR: Exhaust gas recirculation

Exh.: Exhaust

F: Fahrenheit

F: Farad

pF: Picofarad

μF: Microfarad

FI: Fuel injection

ft.lb., ft. lb., ft. lbs.: foot pound(s)

gal: Gallon

g: Gram

HC: Hydrocarbon

HEI: High energy ignition

HO: High output

hp: Horsepower

Hyd.: Hydraulic

Hz: Hertz

ID: Inside diameter

in.lb.; in. lb.; in. lbs: inch pound(s)

Int.: Intake

K: Kelvin

kg: Kilogram

kHz: Kilohertz

km: Kilometer

km/h: Kilometers per hour

$k\Omega$: Kilohm

kPa: Kilopascal

kV: Kilovolt

kW: Kilowatt

l: Liter

l/s: Liters per second

m: Meter

mA: Milliampere

mg: Milligram

mHz: Megahertz

mm: Millimeter

mm^2: Square millimeter

m^3: Cubic meter

MΩ: Megohm

m/s: Meters per second

MT: Manual transmission

mV: Millivolt

μm: Micrometer

N: Newton

N-m: Newton meter

NOx: Nitrous oxide

OD: Outside diameter

OHC: Over head camshaft

OHV: Over head valve

Ω: Ohm

PCV: Positive crankcase ventilation

psi: Pounds per square inch

pts: Pints

qts: Quarts

rpm: Rotations per minute

rps: Rotations per second

R-12: A refrigerant gas (Freon)

SAE: Society of Automotive Engineers

SO$_2$: Sulfur dioxide

T: Ton

t: Megagram

TBI: Throttle Body Injection

TPS: Throttle Position Sensor

V: 1. Volt; 2. Venturi

μV: Microvolt

W: Watt

∝: Infinity

‹: Less than

›: Greater than

Index

Chilton's Repair & Tune-Up Guides

The Complete line covers domestic cars, imports, trucks, vans, RV's and 4-wheel drive vehicles.

RTUG Title	Part No.
AMC 1975-82	7199
Covers all U.S. and Canadian models	
Aspen/Volare 1976-80	6637
Covers all U.S. and Canadian models	
Audi 1970-73	5902
Covers all U.S. and Canadian models.	
Audi 4000/5000 1978-81	7028
Covers all U.S. and Canadian models including turbocharged and diesel engines	
Barracuda/Challenger 1965-72	5807
Covers all U.S. and Canadian models	
Blazer/Jimmy 1969-82	6931
Covers all U.S. and Canadian 2- and 4-wheel drive models, including diesel engines	
BMW 1970-82	6844
Covers U.S. and Canadian models	
Buick/Olds/Pontiac 1975-85	7308
Covers all U.S. and Canadian full size rear wheel drive models	
Cadillac 1967-84	7462
Covers all U.S. and Canadian rear wheel drive models	
Camaro 1967-81	6735
Covers all U.S. and Canadian models	
Camaro 1982-85	7317
Covers all U.S. and Canadian models	
Capri 1970-77	6695
Covers all U.S. and Canadian models	
Caravan/Voyager 1984-85	7482
Covers all U.S. and Canadian models	
Century/Regal 1975-85	7307
Covers all U.S. and Canadian rear wheel drive models, including turbocharged engines	
Champ/Arrow/Sapporo 1978-83	7041
Covers all U.S. and Canadian models	
Chevette/1000 1976-86	6836
Covers all U.S. and Canadian models	
Chevrolet 1968-85	7135
Covers all U.S. and Canadian models	
Chevrolet 1968-79 Spanish	7082
Chevrolet/GMC Pick-Ups 1970-82 Spanish	7468
Chevrolet/GMC Pick-Ups and Suburban 1970-86	6936
Covers all U.S. and Canadian 1/2, 3/4 and 1 ton models, including 4-wheel drive and diesel engines	
Chevrolet LUV 1972-81	6815
Covers all U.S. and Canadian models	
Chevrolet Mid-Size 1964-86	6840
Covers all U.S. and Canadian models of 1964-77 Chevelle, Malibu and Malibu SS; 1974-77 Laguna; 1978-85 Malibu; 1970-86 Monte Carlo; 1964-84 El Camino, including diesel engines	
Chevrolet Nova 1986	7658
Covers all U.S. and Canadian models	
Chevy/GMC Vans 1967-84	6930
Covers all U.S. and Canadian models of 1/2, 3/4, and 1 ton vans, cutaways, and motor home chassis, including diesel engines	
Chevy S-10 Blazer/GMC S-15 Jimmy 1982-85	7383
Covers all U.S. and Canadian models	
Chevy S-10/GMC S-15 Pick-Ups 1982-85	7310
Chevy II/Nova 1962-79	6841
Covers all U.S. and Canadian models	
Chrysler K- and E-Car 1981-85	7163
Covers all U.S. and Canadian front wheel drive models	
Colt/Challenger/Vista/Conquest 1971-85	7037
Covers all U.S. and Canadian models	
Corolla/Carina/Tercel/Starlet 1970-85	7036
Corona/Cressida/Crown/Mk.II/Camry/Van 1970-84	7044
Covers all U.S. and Canadian models	

RTUG Title	Part No.
Corvair 1960-69	6691
Covers all U.S. and Canadian models	
Corvette 1953-62	6576
Covers all U.S. and Canadian models	
Corvette 1963-84	6843
Covers all U.S. and Canadian models	
Cutlass 1970-85	6933
Covers all U.S. and Canadian models	
Dart/Demon 1968-76	6324
Covers all U.S. and Canadian models	
Datsun 1961-72	5790
Covers all U.S. and Canadian models of Nissan Patrol; 1500, 1600 and 2000 sports cars; Pick-Ups; 410, 411, 510, 1200 and 240Z	
Datsun 1973-80 Spanish	7083
Datsun/Nissan F-10, 310, Stanza, Pulsar 1977-86	7196
Covers all U.S. and Canadian models	
Datsun/Nissan Pick-Ups 1970-84	6816
Covers all U.S and Canadian models	
Datsun/Nissan Z & ZX 1970-86	6932
Covers all U.S. and Canadian models	
Datsun/Nissan 1200, 210, Sentra 1973-86	7197
Covers all U.S. and Canadian models	
Datsun/Nissan 200SX, 510, 610, 710, 810, Maxima 1973-84	7170
Covers all U.S. and Canadian models	
Dodge 1968-77	6554
Covers all U.S. and Canadian models	
Dodge Charger 1967-70	6486
Covers all U.S. and Canadian models	
Dodge/Plymouth Trucks 1967-84	7459
Covers all 1/2, 3/4, and 1 ton 2- and 4-wheel drive U.S. and Canadian models, including diesel engines	
Dodge/Plymouth Vans 1967-84	6934
Covers all 1/2, 3/4, and 1 ton U.S. and Canadian models of vans, cutaways and motor home chassis	
D-50/Arrow Pick-Up 1979-81	7032
Covers all U.S. and Canadian models	
Fairlane/Torino 1962-75	6320
Covers all U.S. and Canadian models	
Fairmont/Zephyr 1978-83	6965
Covers all U.S. and Canadian models	
Fiat 1969-81	7042
Covers all U.S. and Canadian models	
Fiesta 1978-80	6846
Covers all U.S. and Canadian models	
Firebird 1967-81	5996
Covers all U.S. and Canadian models	
Firebird 1982-85	7345
Covers all U.S. and Canadian models	
Ford 1968-79 Spanish	7084
Ford Bronco 1966-83	7140
Covers all U.S. and Canadian models	
Ford Bronco II 1984	7408
Covers all U.S. and Canadian models	
Ford Courier 1972-82	6983
Covers all U.S. and Canadian models	
Ford/Mercury Front Wheel Drive 1981-85	7055
Covers all U.S. and Canadian models Escort, EXP, Tempo, Lynx, LN-7 and Topaz	
Ford/Mercury/Lincoln 1968-85	6842
Covers all U.S. and Canadian models of FORD Country Sedan, Country Squire, Crown Victoria, Custom, Custom 500, Galaxie 500, LTD through 1982, Ranch Wagon, and XL; MERCURY Colony Park, Commuter, Marquis through 1982, Gran Marquis, Monterey and Park Lane; LINCOLN Continental and Towne Car	
Ford/Mercury/Lincoln Mid-Size 1971-85	6696
Covers all U.S. and Canadian models of FORD Elite, 1983-85 LTD, 1977-79 LTD II, Ranchero, Torino, Gran Torino, 1977-85 Thunderbird; MERCURY 1972-85 Cougar,	

continued on next page

RTUG Title	Part No.	RTUG Title	Part No.
1983-85 Marquis, Montego, 1980-85 XR-7; LINCOLN 1982-85 Continental, 1984-85 Mark VII, 1978-80 Versailles		**Mercedes-Benz 1974-84** Covers all U.S. and Canadian models	6809
Ford Pick-Ups 1965-86 Covers all ½, ¾ and 1 ton, 2- and 4-wheel drive U.S. and Canadian pick-up, chassis cab and camper models, including diesel engines	6913	**Mitsubishi, Cordia, Tredia, Starion, Galant 1983-85** Covers all U.S. and Canadian models	7583
		MG 1961-81 Covers all U.S. and Canadian models	6780
Ford Pick-Ups 1965-82 Spanish	7469	**Mustang/Capri/Merkur 1979-85** Covers all U.S. and Canadian models	6963
Ford Ranger 1983-84 Covers all U.S. and Canadian models	7338	**Mustang/Cougar 1965-73** Covers all U.S. and Canadian models	6542
Ford Vans 1961-86 Covers all U.S. and Canadian ½, ¾ and 1 ton van and cutaway chassis models, including diesel engines	6849	**Mustang II 1974-78** Covers all U.S. and Canadian models	6812
		Omni/Horizon/Rampage 1978-84 Covers all U.S. and Canadian models of DODGE omni, Miser, 024, Charger 2.2; PLYMOUTH Horizon, Miser, TC3, TC3 Tourismo; Rampage	6845
GM A-Body 1982-85 Covers all front wheel drive U.S. and Canadian models of BUICK Century, CHEVROLET Celebrity, OLDSMOBILE Cutlass Ciera and PONTIAC 6000	7309	**Opel 1971-75** Covers all U.S. and Canadian models	6575
		Peugeot 1970-74 Covers all U.S. and Canadian models	5982
GM C-Body 1985 Covers all front wheel drive U.S. and Canadian models of BUICK Electra Park Avenue and Electra T-Type, CADILLAC Fleetwood and deVille, OLDSMOBILE 98 Regency and Regency Brougham	7587	**Pinto/Bobcat 1971-80** Covers all U.S. and Canadian models	7027
		Plymouth 1968-76 Covers all U.S. and Canadian models	6552
		Pontiac Fiero 1984-85 Covers all U.S. and Canadian models	7571
GM J-Car 1982-85 Covers all U.S. and Canadian models of BUICK Skyhawk, CHEVROLET Cavalier, CADILLAC Cimarron, OLDSMOBILE Firenza and PONTIAC 2000 and Sunbird	7059	**Pontiac Mid-Size 1974-83** Covers all U.S. and Canadian models of Ventura, Grand Am, LeMans, Grand LeMans, GTO, Phoenix, and Grand Prix	7346
		Porsche 924/928 1976-81 Covers all U.S. and Canadian models	7048
GM N-Body 1985-86 Covers all U.S. and Canadian models of front wheel drive BUICK Somerset and Skylark, OLDSMOBILE Calais, and PONTIAC Grand Am	7657	**Renault 1975-85** Covers all U.S. and Canadian models	7165
		Roadrunner/Satellite/Belvedere/GTX 1968-73 Covers all U.S. and Canadian models	5821
GM X-Body 1980-85 Covers all U.S. and Canadian models of BUICK Skylark, CHEVROLET Citation, OLDSMOBILE Omega and PONTIAC Phoenix	7049	**RX-7 1979-81** Covers all U.S. and Canadian models	7031
		SAAB 99 1969-75 Covers all U.S. and Canadian models	5988
GM Subcompact 1971-80 Covers all U.S. and Canadian models of BUICK Skyhawk (1975-80), CHEVROLET Vega and Monza, OLDSMOBILE Starfire, and PONTIAC Astre and 1975-80 Sunbird	6935	**SAAB 900 1979-85** Covers all U.S. and Canadian models	7572
		Snowmobiles 1976-80 Covers Arctic Cat, John Deere, Kawasaki, Polaris, Ski-Doo and Yamaha	6978
Granada/Monarch 1975-82 Covers all U.S. and Canadian models	6937	**Subaru 1970-84** Covers all U.S. and Canadian models	6982
Honda 1973-84 Covers all U.S. and Canadian models	6980	**Tempest/GTO/LeMans 1968-73** Covers all U.S. and Canadian models	5905
International Scout 1967-73 Covers all U.S. and Canadian models	5912	**Toyota 1966-70** Covers all U.S. and Canadian models of Corona, MkII, Corolla, Crown, Land Cruiser, Stout and Hi-Lux	5795
Jeep 1945-87 Covers all U.S. and Canadian CJ-2A, CJ-3A, CJ-3B, CJ-5, CJ-6, CJ-7, Scrambler and Wrangler models	6817	
		Toyota 1970-79 Spanish	7467
Jeep Wagoneer, Commando, Cherokee, Truck 1957-86 Covers all U.S. and Canadian models of Wagoneer, Cherokee, Grand Wagoneer, Jeepster, Jeepster Commando, J-100, J-200, J-300, J-10, J20, FC-150 and FC-170	6739	**Toyota Celica/Supra 1971-85** Covers all U.S. and Canadian models	7043
		Toyota Trucks 1970-85 Covers all U.S. and Canadian models of pick-ups, Land Cruiser and 4Runner	7035
		Valiant/Duster 1968-76 Covers all U.S. and Canadian models	6326
Laser/Daytona 1984-85 Covers all U.S. and Canadian models	7563	**Volvo 1956-69** Covers all U.S. and Canadian models	6529
Maverick/Comet 1970-77 Covers all U.S. and Canadian models	6634	**Volvo 1970-83** Covers all U.S. and Canadian models	7040
Mazda 1971-84 Covers all U.S. and Canadian models of RX-2, RX-3, RX-4, 808, 1300, 160C, Cosmo, GLC and 626	6981	**VW Front Wheel Drive 1974-85** Covers all U.S. and Canadian models	6962
		VW 1949-71 Covers all U.S. and Canadian models	5796
Mazda Pick-Ups 1972-86 Covers all U.S. and Canadian models	7659	**VW 1970-79 Spanish**	7081
Mercedes-Benz 1959-70 Covers all U.S. and Canadian models	6065	**VW 1970-81** Covers all U.S. and Canadian Beetles, Karmann Ghia, Fastback, Squareback, Vans, 411 and 412	6837
Mereceds-Benz 1968-73 Covers all U.S. and Canadian models	5907	

Chilton's Repair & Tune-Up Guides are available at your local retailer or by mailing a check or money order for **$13.95** plus **$3.25** to cover postage and handling to:

Chilton Book Company
Dept. DM
Radnor, PA 19089

NOTE: When ordering be sure to include your name & address, book part No. & title.